Otto Pfleiderer

The Development of Theology in Germany Since Kant

and its progress in Great Britain since 1825

Otto Pfleiderer

The Development of Theology in Germany Since Kant
and its progress in Great Britain since 1825

ISBN/EAN: 9783337735067

Printed in Europe, USA, Canada, Australia, Japan

Cover: Foto ©Lupo / pixelio.de

More available books at **www.hansebooks.com**

THE

DEVELOPMENT OF THEOLOGY

IN GERMANY SINCE KANT,

AND ITS

PROGRESS IN GREAT BRITAIN SINCE 1825.

BY

OTTO PFLEIDERER, D.D.,

Professor of Theology in the University of Berlin.

TRANSLATED UNDER THE AUTHOR'S SUPERVISION BY

J. FREDERICK SMITH.

LONDON:
SWAN SONNENSCHEIN & CO.,
NEW YORK: MACMILLAN & CO.
1890.

BUTLER & TANNER,
THE SELWOOD PRINTING WORKS,
FROME, AND LONDON.

PREFACE.

Two years ago I was asked by the Editor of the Library of Philosophy to write the volume tracing the Development of Theology since Kant. According to the more precise statement of its scope, the work was to deal principally with the History of Modern Theology in Germany, but it was desired that it should include an account of the Protestant Theology of this century in other countries, particularly in Great Britain. Although I did not shut my eyes to the difficulties of the task, I resolved to undertake it, with the hope that I might thereby contribute a little towards a better mutual understanding between the German and English nations, especially towards the removal of numerous prejudices that still prevail in Great Britain with regard to the tendencies of the German mind and make it difficult for Englishmen to form a just view of our national character and aims.

But no sooner was the work actually taken in hand than the necessity appeared of a reduction of its scope within narrower limits in several respects. An account of theology outside Germany which should be at all satisfactory seemed to me impossible without a study of it on the spot in the respective countries. On this account I was compelled to leave entirely out of my survey the Theology of Holland[1] and America, and to confine myself to that of Great Britain. With British Theology I had for years kept myself so far in touch that a sojourn of some weeks in England and Scotland was sufficient, with the kind assistance of

---

[1] I have made an exception in the case of the critical labours of Dr. Kuenen, of Leyden, which have had a decided influence on the progress of German Theology. This scientific annexation of the distinguished Theologian of the Netherlands will, I hope, be considered excusable.

friendly theologians there, to supply the gaps in my knowledge and enable me to make a survey of the development of the Philosophy of Religion and Theology in Britain during the present century; though notwithstanding all the pains I have bestowed upon the survey, I must fall back upon the kind consideration of my British readers.

But even when the range of the work had been thus reduced, the extent of the matters to be dealt with exceeded the limits of a volume of this series, so that I was obliged to lay down definite lines in the selection of what really belongs to my subject. As this is the development of theological *thought*, everything that belongs to the department of practical church life, such as ecclesiastico-political events and party conflicts, or philanthropic movements of church societies, could at once be excluded. It was more difficult to draw the line with reference to non-theological science, particularly philosophy. Philosophy has in various ways had so much influence on the Theology of our century, that it is impossible quite to ignore it in a history of the latter. I have therefore brought it within the limits of my account so far, and only so far, as it has exerted a direct influence on the development of Theology. From the nature of the case, the line drawn cannot be so hard and fast that the concurrence of all readers in the selection made is to be expected. And those readers who may perhaps look for a more detailed treatment of the Philosophy of Religion in Germany, may be referred to my *History of the Philosophy of Religion from Spinoza to the Present Time*, of which there is an English translation.

As regards the treatment of the materials, I have throughout abstained from giving a complete, statistical enumeration of all the writers and titles of books holding a place in the theological literature of this century. Such a catalogue would have served but little the purpose of this book. I have regarded it as far more appropriate to deal somewhat more fully with the characteristic and important men and movements, rather than by a mass of unimportant details to render the survey of the course of development difficult. Further, I dislike above all things that method of writing history which presents nothing but the writer's subjective judgment of people, without so much as allowing them to say what their own opinions and views are. To take all men as what they show themselves to be, is the only way in which we can pay due regard to historical justice.

I have found but very few books to help me in my work. For the period under review Dorner's *History of Protestant Theology* is much too meagre. The books of Carl Schwarz and Landerer on Recent Theology, unlike as they are as regards style, the first being as brilliant as the second is dry, are very much alike in this, that both have much more to say of men than they allow men to say for themselves. In the survey of English Theology, Dr. Tulloch's *Movements of Religious Thought* has supplied me with useful points of observation, at all events for some parts of my sketch.

OTTO PFLEIDERER.

GROSS LICHTERFELDE, NEAR BERLIN.

EDITOR'S NOTE.

Dr. Pfleiderer's work is not a translation in the ordinary sense. It has been written for the Library of Philosophy, and appears first in English. This involves the disadvantage that the reader will not have (as usually in translations) the original to which to refer in case of doubt. For this reason special care has been taken to secure a clear and accurate rendering. The Author's MS. has been translated into English by Mr. J. Frederick Smith, whose work has been revised in proof by Dr. Pfleiderer, by the translator, and by myself.

GENERAL EDITOR.

CONTENTS.

Book I.
THE BASIS OF MODERN THEOLOGY IN GERMAN IDEALISTIC PHILOSOPHY.

		PAGE
Chapter I.	Kant	3
„ II.	Herder	21
„ III.	Schleiermacher	44
„ IV.	Fichte	57
„ V.	Schelling	62
„ VI.	Hegel	68

Book II.
THE DEVELOPMENT OF DOGMATIC THEOLOGY UNDER THE INFLUENCE OF IDEALISTIC PHILOSOPHY.

Chapter I.	The Theology of the School of Kant	85
„ II.	The Theology of the School of Schleiermacher	103
„ III.	Speculative Theology	131
„ IV.	Eclectic Theologians	154

Book III.
BIBLICAL AND HISTORICAL THEOLOGY.

Chapter I.	New Testament Criticism and Exegesis	209
„ II.	Old Testament Criticism and Exegesis	252
„ III.	History of the Church and of Dogma	277

Book IV.
A SURVEY OF THE PROGRESS OF THEOLOGY IN GREAT BRITAIN SINCE 1825.

Chapter I.	The Schools of Philosophy in their relation to Theology	303
„ II.	Parties and Movements in Theology	355

Index		402

BOOK I.

THE BASIS OF MODERN THEOLOGY IN GERMAN IDEALISTIC PHILOSOPHY.

CHAPTER I.

KANT.

IN the year 1784 Kant wrote an essay upon the question, *What is Aufklärung?*[1] In it he reviews the tendencies of his age, and at the same time indicates in what sense he considers them justifiable and is willing to further them. This essay may be regarded as the programme of the task to which German philosophy in Kant and his successors has devoted itself.

"Free Thought," says Kant, "is the advance of man beyond the state of voluntary immaturity. By immaturity is meant, inability to use his own understanding except under the guidance of another. The immaturity is voluntary when the cause of it is not want of intelligence, but of resolution and courage to use it without another's guidance. *Sapere aude!* Dare to use thy *own* understanding! is therefore the motto of Free Thought. If the question be asked, 'Do we live in a free-thinking age?' the answer is, 'No; but we live in an age of free-thought.' As things are at present, men as a whole are very far from possessing, or even from being able to acquire, the power of making a sure and right use of their own understandings in religious matters without the guidance of others. On the other hand, we have clear indications that the field now lies nevertheless open before them, to which they can freely make their way, and that the hindrances to general Freedom of Thought, or the abandonment of the state of voluntary immaturity, are gradually becoming less. In this sense the present age is the age of Free Thought, or the century of Frederick the Great."

---

[1] *Aufklärung.* Any translation of this *terminus technicus* may mislead. From Kant's authoritative definition of the thing, it appears that our English "*Free-thinking*" substantially represents it.—Tr.

It is only by slow degrees that the people generally can reach Freedom of Thought. It is not by means of a revolution, which can never effect a real reform in habits of thought; a revolution only exchanges old prejudices for new, which then, as much as the old ones, serve as leading-strings to the unthinking crowd. The one proper method is the free use of reason as a public right, whereby the wise are put in a position to diffuse their superior intelligence and render it the common property of all. To check the free public employment of reason, in the interests of any existing social institutions or laws, would, in Kant's view, be "a sin against the nature of man, the primary purpose of which consists in just this advance in Free Thinking." Moreover, this public use of reason by the learned, Kant argues, involves no danger, inasmuch as it does not seek by any means to put an end to the performance of civil duties or of the obligations imposed on each man by his calling; it was precisely under the veil of severe civil discipline, as it existed in the State of Frederick, that freedom of mind had more room to spread than is usually the case where there is greater civil liberty. When once however by freedom of *thought* the mental habits of a nation have been so educated that it is rendered more capable of freedom in *action*, this education finally reacts upon the maxims of the government in such a way that it treats men no longer as machines but in a manner suited to their true dignity.

We see from this essay that Kant participated to the full in the movement of his age towards *Aufklärung*, but that he gauged its meaning otherwise and more profoundly than did his contemporaries. He is no less opposed to the complacent vanity of the German popular philosophers, who thought that they already possessed *Aufklärung*—the truth in religion and morals,—than he is to the radicalism of the French party of progress, who imagined that they could reach the goal by means of revolution, by abjuring in theory and practice all existing beliefs and institutions. Of course, according to Kant, mankind is bound to be rationally free and enlightened, but they are *not* so as yet; and will not become so by merely discarding old prejudices, but only by a "true reform in habits of thought," whereby they will be enabled to "make a sure and right use" of their own understandings. To educate mankind for this true employment of the understanding is the vocation of men of letters, and more especially of philosophers, a task which was made possible in Frederick's State.

It is therefore not enough for men to learn to use their *own* understanding; they must also learn to use it *rightly;* to help them to do this is the primary and essential vocation of philosophy as Kant understood it. But if we wish to ensure the true use of the understanding by a method which is universally valid, we must first critically examine the *laws* which are involved in the very nature of the understanding itself. For the knowledge of a truth which is valid for every one is possible only when based on laws which are involved in the nature of the human mind as such, and have not been imported into it from without through facts of experience which must always be accidental and conditional. Kant is convinced of the existence of such primary laws, involved in the very constitution of the human mind. He looks upon them as laws which do not arise from experience, but which are rather prior to all experience, and, as determining its form, lie at the root of all theoretical, practical, and æsthetic judgments out of which the world of consciousness is built up. He has thrown this conviction into a scientific shape in the three critiques, namely of the Pure and of the Practical Reason, and of the Faculty of Judgment. On the one hand, Empirical Philosophy had held that all knowledge arises purely from without, from experienced perceptions, but had not been able to explain the fact that experience always conforms to law. Rationalistic Philosophy, again, had sought to derive all knowledge from the constitution of the mind itself, from its innate ideas, but had left out of consideration its dependence upon experience, and had confounded the empty creations of thought with reality. Once more, both the rival schools of Empirical and Rationalistic philosophers had agreed at least in regarding all knowledge as something given—whether from without or from within—and the knowing mind as only its passive recipient. Kant, on the contrary, taught that all cognition rests upon the union of the mind's activity and receptivity; inasmuch as the material is given us in the multiformity of our perceptions, sensations, and sense-affections; but the formation of this material into a system of knowledge is the work of our own activity, this activity, in accordance with its own laws, giving to the material the form of rationality, which constitutes the truth of our cognition. In opposition, therefore, to

Rationalistic philosophy, Kant taught the dependence of the act of cognition on the material supplied in experience in space and time, and the impossibility of knowing the reality (*das Ding an sich*) lying behind these facts of experience. In opposition to Empirical philosophy, he taught that it is the subject which, by means of its characteristic perception of things under the forms of space and time and of the categories, converts this chaotic material into the regular orderly world called "experience"; and that in this respect the understanding itself is to be regarded as imposing laws on nature.

It was this latter conception, viz., of reason, both in theoretical knowledge and in practical judgments, imposing laws upon itself, which was the essence of Kant's thought and the opening of a new era of philosophy. Of this there can be no doubt in the mind of any one who recognises the connexion between the different parts of the system, and its relation to the theories which preceded and followed it. It has, however, been widely supposed for some time, and particularly in theological circles, that the main point in Kant's philosophy is the limitation of human knowledge to phenomena, and the proof that we cannot know anything of the region lying beyond them. Nor can it be denied that Kant himself laid great emphasis upon this side of his teaching, inasmuch as this limitation of the speculative reason seemed to him the preliminary basis of the unconditional character of the practical reason. Nevertheless this view is obviously erroneous; were it true, it would be impossible to say what claim to originality Kant's philosophy possessed, and how it could lay down the lines for future development. For a glance at English philosophy prior to Kant shows that Locke, Berkeley, and especially Hume, had limited our knowledge to the phenomena of consciousness, and had pronounced the reference of these phenomena to a trans-subjective reality a supposition incapable of proof, and likewise valueless, on account of the incognisability of the problematical external object. In the case of Hume this was the necessary consequence of his sceptical dissolution of the idea of causation, in which he saw only the expression of the customary transition of imagination from one idea to another, a subjective fiction which could not possibly carry us from the phenomena of consciousness to trans-subjective reality. If, therefore, this negative side of Kant's philosophy—the limitation of our knowledge to experience—were the important part of it, it would have been a repetition of that of his predecessor, Hume. Indeed, we should be compelled to allow that, in point of consistency, Kant was inferior to Hume, since he admittedly broke through this limitation in several respects: he made things-in-themselves the causes of sensations or experience; the freedom of man's intelligible character the cause of actions in time; God the cause of the existence of the highest good, or of the unity of the natural and moral worlds. He thus indisputably extended the category of causation to transcendental objects, in spite of its presupposed limitation to the world of experience. Such inconsistency would be quite incomprehensible if, as is ordinarily supposed, this sceptical doctrine were the gist and real object of Kant's theory of knowledge. The real state of the case is as follows: Kant had been impressed by the imposing character of Hume's sceptical philosophy, and had adopted its doctrine of the incognisability of things-in-themselves; this principle he had accepted prior to his own critical inquiry into the forms of cognition inherent in the human mind, but afterwards regarded as the result of this inquiry, though, if he had undertaken the inquiry independently of this preconceived opinion, he would have come to the opposite conclusion. This timidity, which hesitated to leap, with the aid of the idea of causality, the confines of the phenomena of consciousness, and to lay hold of things-in-themselves, was a legacy from the scepticism of Hume, from which Kant was unable completely to free himself, even when, in opposition to Hume, he reasserted for the idea of causation its rightful position as one of the fundamental *à priori* forms of judgment. It was, therefore, not the desertion of Kant's philosophy, but simply the true and necessary carrying out of its speculative principle and most characteristic position, when his successors rejected this sceptical limitation of our knowledge, and credited thought with the power of theoretically conceiving Being, as well as of practically moulding it ; when, in other words, they put an end to the Kantian dualism of the Theoretical Reason, limited to the world of phenomena, and the Practical Reason, dwelling in the world of the intelligible.

The Practical Philosophy of Kant is partly the complement, partly the antithesis of his theoretical philosophy. In his theory of knowledge he had aimed at proving that cognition is governed by the *à priori* forms existing in the understanding,

independently of experience, but for that very reason limited
the action of the mind in cognition to merely the formal working-up of given conceptions. Similarly, in order that the law of moral action may possess unconditional and universal validity, it must, in Kant's view, be independent of experience, and belong to the reason *à priori*, *i.e.*, must be *autonomous*; it is as much the province of Reason as Practical to lay down laws for action, as of the Speculative Reason to do this for cognition ; but at the same time, if this practical law is to be *à priori*, it must be limited to the *form* of action merely, and must not include any object of desire since the will can be influenced by an object of desire, only by the expectation of pleasure, a motive which acts differently in different individuals, and belongs to the lower sense-faculty of desire and hence can never claim universal or unconditional validity. All material principles, whatever their contents, are, according to Kant, equally eudæmonistic; they depend upon self-love, or the lower faculty of desire, and have only a subjective and empirically conditioned validity ; they are therefore merely prudential maxims, not pure laws of reason. The autonomous law, characteristic of reason, must accordingly relate solely to the general form of action, without the slightest admixture of material motives, which would only sully its purity ; its command as the "Categorical Imperative" is : Act so that the rule governing thy will may also always serve as the principle of a universal legislation.

Thus far Kant's doctrine of the legislation of the practical reason seems to form a complete parallel to that of the speculative reason; but as soon as we look more closely at the relation of form and contents, an essential distinction becomes apparent. In the sphere of knowledge, form and contents, in spite of their different origin, are in no way really opposed, but only exist for, and with each other ; we are *compelled* to bring every object of sense-experience under the *à priori* forms of intuition and of thought, and our sense-perceptions, instead of being antagonistic to these forms, can only be apprehended by their means. It is quite otherwise in the sphere of action. The moral law is indeed the form of *à priori* validity, which we can and ought to apply as a criterion to every object of sense-desire—*i.e.*, to our empirical inclinations and actions ; but we are by no means compelled to do this ; we are able to follow the natural inclinations produced by the contents of our sense-experience, which so little submit without resistance to this *à priori* form, that, in Kant's view, they are invariably opposed to the law of reason, and so produce a never-ending struggle between duty and inclination. Hence the moral law is the form which, on the one hand, has need of the contents supplied by the empirical desires, since without them it would not reach action at all, and so the law find no application; but, on the other hand, this form is also represented as involved in a ceaseless opposition and conflict with their contents. This conception is plainly unrealisable; we cannot see how a moral law without contents, and simply opposed to all empirical inclinations could ever become a motive of action, or how definite obligatory actions could be deduced from it. It is, no doubt, true that there is often a conflict between duty and inclination, and that in this conflict the claims of duty are the higher, and the only absolute ones; it is the great merit of Kant's moral philosophy to have brought out this truth with all possible emphasis. But it is equally certain that the letter of his theory is untenable. His mistake lay in thinking that the law of reason must be made purely formal to have unconditional validity, and in attributing all actual motives of action, all inclinations, to sense-desire, thus representing them as hostile to reason. In this way his moral system acquired a harsh, ascetic character, exceeding in rigour even that of the Stoics. The ground of this was essentially the same in both cases: the absolute dualism between reason and sensation, between man as an "intelligible" being, endowed with freedom and reason, and man as a being of sense endowed with natural desire. If the two are so completely disjoined as abstract anti-natural Idealism, which still influenced Kant, maintained, we cannot understand how the commands of reason could ever coincide with man's actual wishes and actions. In order that anything may be a motive, it must be a possible object of desire; the moral law accordingly can be a higher motive than single accidental inclinations only by including a higher object, which, as unconditionally valuable, is superior to all merely conditional ends. If, however, the moral law includes a concrete end, it is no longer purely formal; it is no longer opposed to *all* inclinations, but can itself become the object of reasonable inclination; in that case there is no longer the absolute dualism, asserted by Kant, between man as desiring and man as thinking, and finally, there is from the first an inner connection between the sense-world of experience and the "intelligible world," which warrants the hope of the synthesis of both in human action and cognition.

In Kant himself we find several hints of this correction of the purely formal and dualistic character of his moral philosophy; and these hints only need working out in order to render the rational principle of this philosophy supreme in the sphere of ethics. Kant was at bottom really held back here only by the same want of courage in working out his speculative principle as is traceable in his theory of knowledge; the hindrance there was the influence of the scepticism of Hume, here it was the dread of sullying the purity of idealistic ethical principles, by a compromise with empirical principles. His demand of a purely formal ethical principle was violated by Kant himself even in the definition of moral philosophy as the science of the ends of pure reason, and by the deduction of the supreme, unconditionally desirable end from the dignity of man as a rational being; whence he derived the formula of his *First Principles of the Metaphysics of Ethics:* "Act so as to use humanity, both in thine own person and in the person of every other man, always as an end, never solely as a means." To treat humanity in each individual as an end in itself, clearly means the recognition of a general end of humanity, and making its realisation in each man our object. Thus the moral law acquires as its contents a definite material end, from which the particular moral ends also may be deduced. This deduction can, however, only be made by means of empirical observation, both of the capacities and faculties involved in the natures of man, and of their employment and development as gathered from history. From the admission of this empirical observation Kant was deterred for the reasons given above, and was thus prevented from utilising in science this pregnant formula. In his theory of virtue he did, indeed, try to deduce the necessity of our own personal perfection and of the happiness of others as the two main divisions of the virtues. But it is clear that he could not do this consistently with his own premises. If, as he is elsewhere never tired of insisting, any appeal to empirical motives derived from the desire for happiness is a pollution of morality, it is difficult to see how to seek the happiness of others can be reasonably made a duty;

for if happiness is in no respect a desirable moral end, the happiness of others can no more than our own be such an end; while, conversely, if the happiness of others is to be sought, it is not easy to see why our own should not be so also, more especially in view of the Kantian principle of the universal applicability of the moral rule—"what is right for the one must also be fair for the other." When we add that Kant, in the explanatory justification of his principle, has already emphasised the evil effects which every one would feel if his selfish conduct were made into a universal principle, we can hardly dissent from those who consider that in working out his moral system he did not remain true to the rigour of his primary principle, but fell back into that utilitarianism which he so greatly abhors. This inconsistency was only the natural result of the excessive rigour with which he insisted on his *à priori* principle, until it became a system of forms without contents, the defects of which necessitated a recourse to alien points of view.

Kant exhibits, however, surprising points of agreement, not only with the strictly philosophical, but also with the theological utilitarianism of his time. In the *Critique of Pure Reason* he had shown that the ideas of Freedom, Immortality (soul), and God could not be objects of theoretical knowledge, inasmuch as insoluble contradictions arise whenever a proof of them is attempted. But what is denied to the speculative, can, he maintains, be grasped by the practical reason. Though to the former the world of noumena lying behind phenomena is closed, to the latter it is directly revealed in the moral law, which makes man a citizen of the "intelligible world" of freedom. From this position the above ideas may be established as "Postulates," *i.e.*, as presuppositions which we feel compelled to make, not in order to enlarge our knowledge, but in order to render possible the realisation of the moral law. In the first place, we thus gain the postulate of freedom as the basis of the reality of moral law, just as this law is the basis of the cognisability of freedom; for, inasmuch as we *ought* to do the good, it follows that we *can* do it. Nevertheless the moral law is perpetually obstructed by the motives of sense-desire. These obstructions it is able and bound to overcome more and more; but can never do this so completely that the law will be fully realised in finite time; hence its realisation demands the infinite duration of the individual, or immortality. Finally, reason as a legislative faculty demands the realisation of an absolute end or supreme good, which must embrace both perfect virtue and a corresponding state of happiness, and happiness not included in virtue, but dependent upon natural conditions beyond our control. Hence arises the demand for a supreme Cause, capable of bringing nature into harmony with the moral law of rational beings, or of connecting happiness with the virtue that deserves it; in other words, the supreme good proposed by reason demands the existence of God as the condition of its possibility. Thus the transcendental ideas are the objects of a "moral faith" rooted in reason. It is true that by this faith the speculative reason receives no addition to its knowledge, but by its critical precautions it can render at least the negative service of keeping these ideas free from anthropomorphic impurities and superstitious abuse. It has indeed always been with good reason maintained that this mode of establishing belief in the existence of God can with difficulty be harmonized with the main principle of Kant's ethics. If the moral law is throughout to have nothing to do with sense-desire or happiness, it is hard to see how, on the other hand, happiness can be pronounced an integral part of the supreme good aimed at by reason and a divine cause be demanded to produce it. The affinity of this train of thought to theological utilitarianism is so obvious, that many have not unreasonably seen in it a retrogression on the part of Kant to the eudæmonistic point of view of the popular philosophy,[1] and that Kant's philosophical successors preferred to work out his speculative principle to its logical results without his theological postulates.

Still, fully justified as these objections to the literal form of Kant's postulate undoubtedly are, we cannot deny that underneath it lay a true idea, which appears in a purer form in the *Critique of Judgment*. Kant here tries to find some connecting link between the intelligible and sensible worlds, between freedom and nature, in the idea of a teleology common to both. In order to explain nature we find our-

---

[1] Jacobi, Fichte, Herder, Schleiermacher, unanimously rejected Kant's line of argument, sometimes in very strong terms. Of more recent authors, compare the criticisms of Dilthey (*Leben Schleiermachers*, I. 127, seq.), Biedermann (*Deutschland im 18 Jahrh.*, II. 902), Wundt (*Ethik*, 319, seq.).

selves compelled to combine the principle of teleology with the mechanical principle or causality; for in organic nature we see that the parts are determined by their relation to the whole, are means to the inner end of the organism. To the question, how the teleological explanation can be harmonised with that of causality, Kant's answer is, in the first instance, that the conception of ends in nature is not of such value as to add to our knowledge of facts, but is only a regulative principle for our reflective judgment; it is primarily owing to the structure of our subjective understanding merely that we cannot help regarding nature as governed by final causes. But Kant cannot rest in this sceptical subjectivity; he teaches that if the two principles are to be harmonised, they must be combined under one supreme common principle, viz., in a super-sensible substratum, or actual cause of nature; of this cause we must form a corresponding intellectual intuition, that is to say, we conceive it as not merely causal, but as at the same time the primal intellect, whose thought is not like ours discursive, but necessarily intuitive (thinking the whole simultaneously with its parts). It is true he does, at the same time, again sceptically confess that objectively we can neither assert nor deny the proposition that a Being, acting with a view to ends, as the cause of the universe, is behind what we rightly call the ends of nature; but he considers it is certain that, if we are to form judgments according to the conditions of our reason, we are absolutely compelled to regard a rational Being as the condition of the possibility of ends in nature. But the observation of nature's ends is not sufficient to enable us to further define this intelligent First Cause; we must under the guidance of teleology go beyond Nature. Nature presents not only individual products adapted to ends, but forms a system of ends which point to a supreme or final end. This final end can only be man, who alone acts with conscious purpose and uses all creatures as means to his ends. But man is not a final end, for in so far as man is a part of Nature, his sensuous, pleasure-seeking ends, are again dependent upon natural conditions, and are in no way the object of Nature's special regard. On the contrary, man is a final end only as a moral subject, as proposing to himself unconditional ends by his supersensible freedom of volition. His existence involves the supreme end, to which all Nature is subordinate as means. It is from this conception of man's moral nature, as constituting the supreme end of creation, that the study of Nature's ends must be supplemented, whereby the greater validity and definiteness of the argument for a supreme First Cause are secured, inasmuch as we must now think of this supreme Cause not only as Intelligence, and as a legislator for Nature, but also as the supreme Law-giver of a moral kingdom of ends. It is evident that this inductive method of arriving at the idea of God contrasts favourably with that given above; whilst by the first, God was postulated only for the dubious object of adding happiness to our autonomous morality, by the latter, His existence is inferred from a comprehensive survey of external and internal experience as the necessary condition of a teleological system of things, uniting the natural and moral worlds as means and end. This is a clear speculative conception, which, shadowed forth by Leibnitz, in various forms runs like a golden thread through the whole of Post-Kantian philosophy. A corollary of this thought is, that man, not only as a natural, but also as a moral being, is dependent upon the Divine Cause of the universe, and that his autonomy must therefore at the same time be an actual (not merely subjectively conceived) theonomy. But of this inference, affecting the very foundations of his philosophy, Kant would know nothing; however obviously it is suggested by the above line of induction, he refused to recognise it, through fear of impairing his idea of freedom; and instead of it he finally gave to his ethico-theological proof the form in which we find it in the *Critique of the Practical Reason* (viz., that God is necessary for the attainment of happiness, or in order to supplement our inadequate power over sensible nature), and which is open to the most serious objections. Here again we are expressly reminded that God is the object only of a moral faith, which must not be confounded with theoretical knowledge, nor made the basis of morality upon which it really rests.

Morality becomes religion when what it shows to be the end of man is conceived as also the end of the supreme Law-giver and Creator, or God. Religion is thus the recognition of all our duties as divine commands. The distinction between revealed and natural religion is stated by Kant to be, that in the former, I must know a thing to be a divine command before I can recognise it as my duty; in the latter, I must know it as my duty before I can consider it a command of God. If a man holds revealed religion to be necessary, he is a Supernaturalist; if unnecessary, a Rationalist; if impossible, a Naturalist. As a fourth possibility, a religion might conceivably be objectively natural and yet subjectively revealed; this would be the case if it were such that man might have arrived at it by the unaided use of reason, but at a later period; hence revelation might be useful, or even necessary for certain times and places, without being a permanent guarantee for the truth of the religion. The last is Kant's supposition with regard to Christianity, as it had been that of Lessing. But whence comes this, if only relative, necessity for revelation? And how are its contents to be understood as in unison with reason? These questions were discussed by Kant in the works, *Religion innerhalb der Grenzen der blossen Vernunft* (1793), and *Ueber den Streit der Fakultäten* (1798), in a style, whatever our opinion may be in other respects, which is at all events far superior in depth to the *Aufklärung* of the popular philosophy.

What made Kant capable of a truer appreciation of the doctrines of Christianity, was his deep moral earnestness. The self-complacent optimism of the philosophy of the *Aufklärung* had lacked the recognition of evil as a serious power in human life, while Kant made it the starting-point of his religious philosophy. He considered it as incontestably a fact of experience, that in our race there is inherent a "radical evil," or an original tendency to evil, viz., the preponderance of self-love over pure reverence for law. This wrong bias cannot be the result of inheritance from our first parents, since moral qualities cannot be thus transmitted, but are inseparable from the person. The source of this radical evil, according to Kant, is rather to be sought in an "intelligible act of freedom," which is not to be further explained. The question, then, is, how this evil disposition can be changed into a good one. Kant answers, Not by a gradual reformation, but by a fundamental revolution of the man's whole habit of thought, by a new birth. The problem is, to awaken in the mind the idea of the moral perfection for which we are from the first made. For this purpose, nothing is more effectual than the contemplation of this idea in an historical example of it of such surpassing moral grandeur as can be beheld in Jesus. For this reason, we may look upon him as if the ideal of goodness had been presented in him in flesh and blood, though we have not on that account any reason to regard him as other than a man born in the course of nature. The question, too, whether his historical personality altogether corresponded to the eternal ideal, is one which we neither can nor need answer; for, in any case, the real object of our religious faith is not this historic man, but the ideal of a humanity well-pleasing to God; and since this ideal is not our own creation, but given us in our supersensible nature, it may be conceived as the Son of God come down from heaven. Whoever believes in this ideal Son of God, to whom Jesus holds the relation of the representative example—that is, whoever receives into his heart the moral idea of a humanity pleasing to God, and lets it govern his life—may believe that he is justified in the eyes of the Searcher of Hearts, since the fundamental rightness of his disposition covers the imperfection of the details of his life. Nor need he have any anxiety with regard to the guilt of the past; for although the conception of the vicarious suffering of Christ as a satisfaction for sinners is, if taken literally, untrue, inasmuch as such a substitution cannot take place in the sphere of morality, still the conception may be regarded as the symbolical expression of the true idea, that in the daily pain of self-discipline, obedience, and patience, the new man in us suffers as it were vicariously for the old. Kant thus interprets the Church's doctrine of the Atonement, as once for all made by Christ, on the lines of Protestant mysticism, treating it as a continual ethical process in the heart of the religious man—an interpretation, the germs of which may be traced to the Apostle Paul. But while the Christian doctrine of salvation thus becomes an inward subjective experience of the heart, it is by no means Kant's intention to depreciate, from an abstract subjective point of view, the importance of the community. He sees very clearly that the supremacy of the good principle in the individual can only be assured when it is maintained in the community around him. But this can be accomplished only by the establishment and spread of a society having the laws of virtue both as its basis and its end. Such an ethical community, or "Kingdom of God," is distinguished from all civil States, by being founded, not upon the laws of civil justice, but upon the laws of personal virtue, and by having for its sovereign, not a human potentate, but the Searcher of Hearts;

and again by not being limited to a definite nation or country, but embracing in principle the whole of mankind. Moreover, this ideal ethical community is by no means identical with historic ecclesiastical communities, for while it can be based upon the faith of the reason alone, which is open to all alike, the ecclesiastical societies are founded upon positive creeds, which everywhere take different forms.

Having thus stated his view of religion, as it may be ascertained within the limits of reason, Kant proceeds to the critical investigation of the historical, or "statutory" forms of religion. He here shows that he fully shared the unhistorical way of looking at things characteristic of the age of the *Aufklärung*. The only explanation of the rise of the positive religions he can give is the false notion of mankind, that God demands special acts of ceremonial worship in addition to the worship of a morally good life. This was the origin of statutory religious regulations, which may for a time, in proportion to their association with moral ideas, be useful and even necessary as the means of inaugurating purely moral religious teaching, but in the end become hindrances to progress, and are therefore destined gradually to give place to the pure religion of reason. In Kant's view, the abolition of this servile belief, with the establishment of the sole authority of moral faith, was inaugurated by Jesus; but the real purpose of Jesus was often misunderstood in the Church, and what he originally intended to be simply preparatory means, was in later times made fundamental; whence arose much bigotry and fanaticism. It was not until his own time, Kant thinks, that the light at length fully shone forth after centuries of darkness; and he interprets the Christian hope of a final consummation, when God shall be all in all, of this development, then actually begun, of the true faith of reason out of the wrappings of the historic faith. It is the duty of religious teachers, Kant declared, to help on this development by means of the interpretation of the Bible and a fresh interpretation of the dogmas of the Church. At the end, he turns to the criticism of special points, in which he thought the danger of fanatical religious error and false worship especially serious. The notion of divine "operations of grace" he classes among those incomprehensible ideas of which reason disputes neither the possibility, nor the reality, nor even the necessity, but of which it can make no use either in speculation, owing to the impossibility of determining their characteristics, or in practice, since we can do nothing to produce them. Elsewhere, however, he indicates in what sense he is willing to accept the idea of divine grace, viz., if it is understood to mean the supersensible principle of good existing in our moral nature, which may be regarded as a divinely imparted impulse towards the good, the capacity for which has not been produced by our own effort, and which can be thought of as grace. Similarly he distinguishes in the means of grace between the true moral kernel and the ruder husk. Prayer, regarded as a formal act of worship and the statement of our wishes to a Being who needs no such statement, he considers a vain superstition and fetishism; but as the expression of our heart's desire to be well-pleasing to God, it is a valuable means of quickening good dispositions, and especially as public prayer is an effective ethical observance, calculated to awaken moral impulses in the members of a community. In the same way, Baptism and the Lord's Supper may be looked upon as ethical observances for the public confession and quickening of the feelings of duty and brotherly love in a community; but to regard them as means of grace in the sense that by these ceremonies the divine favour might be flattered and won, would be a heathenish superstition, and could only lead to contempt for virtue and the greater influence of the priesthood as the dispensers of grace.

In these utterances we cannot but recognise the lofty moral earnestness which was the soul of the Kantian philosophy and the main cause of its great and salutary effect upon its time. But the same defects are here observable as mark his moral philosophy: the onesidedness and inflexibility of his speculative principle prevented him from being just to those sides of man's nature which, while different from the intellect, are not wholly irrational, and must on no account be simply assigned to the lower sense-nature. I refer to the emotions and the imagination. The religious life originates and specially manifests itself in these very faculties of the soul as its domain; and we can therefore readily understand why Kant could not take an impartial view of its natural and characteristic phenomena. He was still held back by the abstract intellectualism which was a universal failing of the *Aufklärung*. To correct this error and supply what was lacking was the work of that party which had already protested, on the lines of Rousseau, against this worship of the intellect, and had proclaimed the rights of nature, of the heart, of the unfettered imagination, and of passionate enthusiasm. The party consisted of those allies in the "Storm and Stress" movement whose youthful excesses of enthusiasm were so modified and transformed in Herder and Goethe as to become a new and richer ideal of humanity.

Moreover, Kant's religious philosophy was unsatisfactory on account of the indefiniteness and uncertainty of its attitude towards the decisive question of man's relation to God. If religion consists, as it teaches, in regarding our duties as divine commands, the question at once arises, whether this is a purely subjective conception, or whether it is based upon an objective truth. In the former case, we have the anthropological theory of religion, since developed by Feuerbach and recent Positivism and Agnosticism; in the latter, there arises the further question, How can we arrive at a knowledge of the divine will? Now, the idea of revelation remains in Kant a *non liquet;* he concedes its possibility, perhaps even its necessity, and yet really leaves no room for it. If it is admitted, in the sense of an external announcement on the part of God, as the theological Kantians wished, the fate of Kant's fundamental principle of the autonomy of reason is at once sealed. If, on the other hand, the divine revelation is conceived as taking place within the human spirit, as in post-Kantian speculation, it cannot reasonably be limited to the practical and denied to the theoretical reason; the human spirit must then be conceived as standing generally as such in so close a relation to the divine that the eternal nature of the divine Reason must express and reveal itself in the regular course of the mind's own activity. But this carries us not only beyond the dualism of Kant's theory of knowledge, but also beyond the moral abstraction of his merely rational faith, and we are brought to an evolutionary idealism, as conceived by Herder and Hegel, in which the manifold moral and religious ideals of mankind take their place as integral members in the process of the development of divine revelation.

Thus, in the Kantian philosophy there lay side by side the germs of various tendencies of thought, which afterwards took widely different directions. And it was precisely this wealth of suggestions, which might be developed into totally distinct lines of thought, which constituted the vast importance of his philosophy for his age, at the same time rendering the preservation of its original form impossible. While no thinker of the time remained uninfluenced by it, not one adopted it in its entirety; and it was precisely its most distinguished disciples who advanced the furthest beyond it, and by developing its principles and correcting its imperfections gained fruitful points of view very helpful to a profounder understanding of religion.

CHAPTER II.

HERDER.

In the year 1784 appeared the beginning of Herder's *Ideas on the Philosophy of History*, which, together with Kant's *Critique of Pure Reason*, gives utterance, as Julian Schmidt justly considers, to the most important intellectual drift of the century. In this book meet, as in a focus, the combined results of Herder's various philosophical labours, labours which opened up new and magnificent points of view especially in those branches of study which were depreciated by Kant, viz., the emotional side of the life of the human soul and the development of mankind under the combined action of natural and spiritual forces in history. In England Shaftesbury's philosophy of the moral sense had been the counterpart of Hume's intellectual scepticism, and in France Rousseau's Gospel of Nature, that of Voltaire's Enlightenment; in the same way in Germany Kant's analyzing thought was supplemented by the synthetic intuitions of Herder, and subjective idealism, with its limitation to the analysis of the consciousness of the subject, by historical realism, with its eager attention to the laws of human nature in the whole course of history. Each of these modes of thought is evidently the complement of the other; and the right combination and fusion of the two was the problem bequeathed by the 18th century, then closing, to the philosophy of the 19th, a problem the solution of which is still far from completed. In order to understand what is really new in the thought of the 19th century, we must look at it as the synthesis of these two contrary tendencies, which occupied the second half of the 18th century.

A concise account of Herder's position it is not easy to give, for two reasons; firstly, because his style has more of the poetical, emotional, and rhetorical element than the clearness and precision of science; and secondly, because his views, especially on religious questions, underwent repeated modifications in the course of his literary labours. One unvarying drift does indeed pervade all these variations—a protest against the arrogance and poverty of the popular *Aufklärung*, which would let nothing pass but what was amenable to the calculations of the common understanding, and, without any sense for appreciating the productive forces and manifold phenomena of human history, sought to force all truth into the meagre moulds of its abstract intellectual conception. As a true disciple of Hamann and Rousseau, Herder abhorred this arid, levelling rationalism; he sought to understand the unity of all the powers of man's soul and the special nature of his habits of feeling; hence what interested him in poetry and religion was not the abstract rule, the artificial form of the schools, the doctrines of the Church, but the living feelings as they found natural expression in the songs of the people and the poetical picture-language of the oldest religious records. As in poetry he preferred the primitive strength and beauty of the songs of the people to the classicality of the schools, so in religion he set the strength and beauty of the Bible above the dogmatism of the Churches; for this very reason it was to him insufferable to see the Rationalists trying to thrust their rigid intellectuality into the Bible, and by their artificial interpretations dilute and dissipate both its religious strength and its poetic charm. Herder throughout remained perfectly true to himself in rejecting the Rationalists' arbitrary and unnatural treatment of the language of the Bible, and in demanding of the reader a loving sympathy with the special characteristics of the Biblical writers, so as to catch their enthusiasm and reproduce their poetical picture-language. He thereby rendered lasting service, striking the most decisive blow at the subjective arbitrariness of the Rationalistic methods of interpretation, and preparing the way for the really scientific, objective, and historical methods of Biblical study followed in our own time.

On the other hand, it cannot be denied that within the boundary lines of this position Herder wavered. During the earlier and later periods of his life (in Riga and Weimar respectively), his appreciation of the æsthetic beauty and ideal truth of the Bible never kept him from criticising it in the same fashion as the poetical literature and religious legends of other nations, or from explaining it in accordance with the psychological and historical conditions of its origin; so that he was compelled not to regard these legends, the rise of which could be historically traced, as direct revelations of God with objective truth. In one of his earliest works, the fragment, *Von Entstehung und Fortpflanzung der ersten Religionsbegriffe*, he adopts Hume's view, that fear was the mother of religion, and that the earliest religion consisted in the superstitious worship of harmful and beneficent deities, to appease the wrath and win the favour of whom, men felt bound to offer prayers, sacrifices, and ceremonies. When, however, mankind had provided for their most pressing needs, they began to speculate about the origin of things, and to embody their ideas in cosmogonies and genealogies; thus the first rude religion, the name of which is in almost all languages derived from fear, was followed by a kind of historico-physical philosophy. The question of the origin of the world received a mystical answer; these primitive legends took a completely national and local form; they were clothed in the rich figurative language of the senses; they became mythological poems. It is the work of the science of religion to study the spirit of these mythological poems as characteristic products of the individual nations. As a contribution to this object, Herder wrote his *Archäologie der Hebräer*, which combined in a common view his researches in the earliest history of poetry and in the origins of religion. He nowhere speaks in this work of a supernatural revelation; in the first chapters of Genesis he sees a national religious poem, which must be understood, like Homer, in accordance with its original spirit and meaning without any dogmatic bias. We must transplant ourselves into Eastern habits of thought in order to understand this poetical philosophy of nature; but light is also thrown upon it by similar imagery in modern poetry, in Ossian, Shakespeare, and Klopstock. To treat this Oriental national poetry as dogma, is contrary to all canons of taste and reason; it involves a violation of the natural difference in the various mental faculties, mutilates the intuitive emotions no less than the reason, and confounds together all classes of philosophy and knowledge. God gives us no revelation concerning natural science or metaphysics, except by means of the power bestowed by Him upon the human mind, of penetrating by its own force ever deeper into the nature of His creation.

While these views are identical with those of Herder's

most mature works, written while in Weimar, they differ appreciably from the position he held during the middle period of his life (while in Bückeburg). From being the æsthetic archæologist of literature he then became more and more the apologist of the supernatural. In his essay on *Die älteste Urkunde des Menschengeschlechts*, which belongs to this period, he still regards the account of the creation in Genesis as a poem, but now it is a divine, and not a human poem; it is no longer an Oriental myth, but a divine revelation. He does indeed still lay great stress upon the sense-intuition of nature, that is, the sight of the dawning day, which was in the prophet's mind; but in order that this everyday image might be interpreted as the type of the creation of the world, the prophet must also have heard the voice of a teacher, which could only have been that of God himself. Thus positive teaching of God is found at the beginning of all human history, and remains the supernatural spring from which all human wisdom and poetry take their rise. Even language, the natural origin of which Herder had himself expounded with much penetration, is now attributed to direct divine revelation, to definite instruction given by God. This original revelation is, in his view, the fundamental fact, the antithesis, as he vehemently proclaims, of all the artificial ideas and hypothesis of philosophy; he himself forgetting, however, that this so-called fundamental fact is itself only an hypothesis, and is mainly distinguished from others by boldly leaving the paths of sober empirical investigation to take refuge in the region of miracle, where imagination usurps the place of thought. With this essay on Genesis we may compare a work which appeared soon after: *Erläuterungen zum neuen Testament aus einer neueröffneten morgenländischen Quelle*, in which the New Testament is interpreted by the Zendavesta, Christ and his Apostles, as Herder assumes, being versed in the wisdom of the Chaldees. This work, like the last, contains a defence of the supernatural element in the Bible on the lines of Lavater; it maintains that all the miracles, from the miraculous birth of Jesus to his ascension, were facts, though in such a way that everywhere prominence is given to the spiritual truth of the narrative. Herder did not reflect that this truth would not be affected if the narrative were not actual history, but poetry and legend; the spiritual truth and beauty of a story was to him a direct guarantee of its historical reality, or rather appeared indistinguishable from it to his poetical imagination, which was then at all events without the checks of the critical intellect. As his biographer, Haym, aptly remarks: "He rightly insists that we ought to read the New Testament in the spirit of the New Testament itself, with a feeling and sense of the greatness of its contents. But the greatness, the deep religious and moral power of these writings, is too much for him; it carries him away and overpowers him. He loses in consequence all the freedom in regard to these writings which he had allowed himself in regard to poetical works. Here, as in the old Testament, he has failed to grasp the critical conception intermediate between poetry and faith— the conception of the myth."

That in giving the rein absolutely to the anti-rationalistic or mystical side of his nature, Herder could go so far as to renounce his earlier scientific and critical views, can be easily explained by his peculiar temperament and the influence of friends, both male and female, while he was at Bückeburg; and it would be quite wrong to think, with Hettner, of any conscious compromise from impure motives. We may, in fact, say with Haym, that only by this "mystical and enthusiastic method of interpretation," was it possible to regain the lost appreciation of religion as such, of the profoundly inward force of the chief truths of Christianity, and of the original meaning of the ancient words of our faith. Nevertheless, we shall also do well to call to mind, with Julian Schmidt, the old truth that all trifling with words must be avenged. This mysticism of Herder's, in which æsthetic taste combined with the noblest feeling and ideal pathos to drown the calm voice of critical reason, was indubitably the beginning of that irrational movement which was carried farther by Romanticism and blossomed forth luxuriantly in the reactionary theology of our century. But it is all the more interesting to observe how Herder again rescued himself from this sandbank upon which so many suffered shipwreck, and regained the right track marked out for him by his true genius. It was under the leadership of Lessing and Spinoza that he accomplished this, though the altered surroundings of his position in Weimar materially assisted the change. Herder had been engaged in a friendly correspondence with Lessing for nearly two years; and when, in February 1781, the news of Lessing's death came upon him as a painful shock, he paid a tribute to the memory of his friend, in which in enthusiastic terms he eulogised him as "a noble truth-seeker, truth-finder, and truth-champion," to whose nature no vice was so foreign as cringing hypocrisy, false courtesy, or, above all, that wearisome, sleepy rest in half the truth, which from the first eats like rust and canker into men's minds, in all branches of knowledge and inquiry. This was Herder's formal renunciation of theological fanaticism of every kind, not excepting that which had disfigured his own writings of the Bückeburg period. To the same date belongs the renewal of friendly relations between Herder and Goethe, with its productive mutual stimulus, as well as their study in common of the philosophy of Spinoza.

Jacobi had hoped to gain Herder as an ally in the campaign against Spinozism, having previously made a like attempt with Lessing; but the disappointment of his hopes was even more decisive in Herder's case than it had been in Lessing's. Herder confessed to him, that since he had busied himself with philosophy he had become more and more convinced of the truth of Lessing's saying, that as a matter of fact no other philosophy than Spinoza's was quite consistent with itself. Not that he could in everything agree with Spinoza, whose ideas were always undeveloped whenever his relations with Descartes were unduly close. But Spinoza did not deserve the traditional prejudice against him, which rested upon a misunderstanding of his philosophy. The first mistake of the opponents of Spinoza, is to suppose he looks on God as a nonentity, an abstract conception. On the contrary, Spinoza's God is the most real and most active unity, who alone says to himself, "I am that I am, and shall be in all the changes of my manifestations what I shall be." "What you people mean by 'existence outside the world' I do not understand. If God does not exist in the world, everywhere without measure, wholly and individually, he exists nowhere. Outside the world there is no space; space is an abstraction from experience, and arises when a world arises for us. Limited personality is not less inapplicable to an infinite Being, personality being to our minds inseparable from limitation. In God this illusion disappears; he is the highest, most truly living, and most active One. God is not the world, and the world is not God; of this there can be no doubt.

But nothing can be gained, it seems to me, from your *extra* and *supra*. When we speak of God, we must forget all our idola of space and time, else our best efforts will be fruitless." The sense in which he himself wished Spinoza's philosophy to be understood, and in which he could make it his own, was expounded by Herder in a little treatise entitled, *Gott: Einige Gespräche über Spinoza's System* (1787). He admits, in the first place, that the ideas inherited from Cartesius, of Substance, Attributes, and Modes are unsatisfactory, and that the mathematical method of proof is a mistake. These ideas must have life put into them by Leibnitz's idea of Force. God must therefore be conceived as "the underived, original, and universal force, underlying and including all forces, most active Being"; attributes, as organic forces in which the Deity manifests himself; and all things, as the modifications or active expressions, of the divine force. God, as the eternal original Force, possesses not only infinite force of thought, but also of operation; in him, therefore, existence, operation, and thought, or power, wisdom, and goodness, are indivisibly one. He is therefore as far removed from blind necessity as from any inoperative "deliberation and consultation, caprice, and velleity." Anthropomorphic conceptions of this kind were, with Leibnitz, merely the popular garb of his Theodicy, but his successors made them of prime importance, and the basis of all those physico-theological systems which resulted therefrom, which sought to reduce everything to the arbitrary will of God, and to break the golden chain of nature, in order to separate a few phenomena from the rest, and see, at this or that point, an electric flash of arbitrary divine purpose. All these delusions, in relation to which the holy name of God ought not to be misused, are escaped by the modest student of nature, who, though he does not divulge to us particular measures decided on in the council-chambers of the divine Will, observes instead the composition of actual things and the laws implanted in their nature. While apparently forgetting the purposes of God, he seeks and finds God in his totality, in every object and point of creation, *i.e.*, in everything an essential truth, harmony, and beauty, without which it would not and could not exist. Whoever could show men the laws of nature, how what we see of the so-called animate and inanimate creation works, lives, and acts according to an inner necessity, the result of the interaction of forces in definite organs, would promote the noblest admiration, love, and reverence for God, far more than the man who, as knowing the counsels of God, preached that we have feet in order to walk, and eyes in order to see, etc. Every true law of nature discovered would thus be also a discovered rule of the eternal divine Intelligence, whose thought alone can be truth, and whose activity reality.

We thus see that Herder's conception of God is a combination of Spinoza's monism with Leibnitz's theism; Spinoza's substance becomes operative thinking force; his modes of substance become living forces, resembling Leibnitz's monads, but operative as well as perceptive, whose harmony is therefore no longer, as in Leibnitz, pre-established, but is inherent in the actual interaction of the forces. With Spinoza, Herder rejects the external teleology of particular arbitrary purposes, but with Leibnitz he recognises in necessity according to law the internal adaptation of things to ends, in the laws of nature the thoughts of God, in the golden chain of nature the divine wisdom and goodness. Thus, Spinoza's naturalistic mechanical system is transformed into a theistic optimism, on the lines of Leibnitz and Shaftesbury. These two thinkers are also followed in Herder's ethical demand—"the attainment of the law of noble and beautiful necessity," and the performance of duty as if it were not duty but nature, happiness thus being included in virtue. Finally, Herder's doctrine of God comprehends also his doctrine of immortality and his philosophy of history, becoming a completely optimistic system. If all life is force, death must everywhere be only apparent death, merely the destruction of some appearance; in ceaseless motion and eternal palingenesia, force and the interaction of forces carry on their work; but the persistence of force is inconceivable without progress. In the kingdom of God there is no standing still, still less any going back; it is a necessary law, that chaos should become order, and latent capacities forces in operation.

In these thoughts, which Herder gathered from the three philosophers, Spinoza, Leibnitz, and Shaftesbury, as the quintessence of their systems, he found a conception of the world in which he could rest; and he was strengthened in his belief by the complete and unconditional assent of Goethe. From the standpoint of these views, shared and continually discussed by the two friends, Herder's principal work, the

Ideen zur Philosophie der Geschichte (1784–1791), was written. The leading thought of the work is, that man is the connecting link of two worlds. On the one hand, he is the child of earth, the highest of its organic products; on the other, a citizen of the spiritual world of freedom. The book begins, therefore, with a description of the earth, of its position in the universe, and of the stages of the operations of its organic forces—from the plant to the animal, from the lower to the higher animals, and finally to man. With all the great differences in these single organisms, nature seems "to have formed them all after one chief type of organization; and man seems to be, as it were, the central figure of the animal world, *i.e.*, the most fully developed form in which the essential characteristics of all the species around him are exquisitely combined." His upright carriage is man's most distinctive characteristic, upon which depend the dexterity of his hands, his power of language, and also his rationality; for his reason is not inborn like our instincts, but the acquired due proportion between his powers, senses, and instincts. But if man is the highest member of a progressive series of organic forces, which have constructed the body as their organ, his development cannot end with his appearance upon the earth; for the *humanity* to which we are destined is incompletely realised upon earth, the end for which we exist points to higher forms of development beyond our earthly life under other cosmical conditions, for which we are to prepare ourselves by cultivating the spiritual part of our nature, by striving after truth, goodness, and godlike beauty. From this glance at man's future development, Herder returns to the description of his historical development on earth; and the stress which he lays on its dependence upon natural conditions is so marked as to seem, if taken by itself, almost pure naturalism, to which, on the other hand, completely supernaturalistic declarations form a strange contrast. Man stands in a double relation of dependence, on the one hand to nature, and on the other to the culture and traditions of society. But whence came the first germs of the latter? Herder cannot find in the natural development of man's rationality a satisfactory answer to this question, but has recourse to an education by higher superhuman influences; the Elohim were the instructors of man, and from them he received language, the germ of all culture. This transition from a natural to a supernatural explanation shows the insufficiency of that one-sided empiricism, which will not, like Kant, regard reason as originating action, but only as a passive power of receptivity; hence it can only explain the first possession and employment of reason by deriving it from foreign mystical sources.

Herder proceeds to depict the life of the nations in history, and shows how each nation strove to fulfil the common destiny of man by attaining to humanity and happiness in the special way determined by its natural character and geographical position. As to the details we need only draw attention to the strangely unfavourable judgment passed upon the Jewish nation, whose religious superiority to other nations is outweighed by its want of political culture and of any real sense of honour and freedom. In the description of the Greeks, on the contrary, prominence is given to the bright points—their services to art and science and all human culture. So, too, in describing Christianity, Herder does indeed pay a tribute of the warmest admiration to the person of Jesus as the prophet of the truest humanity; but on the other hand he lays such great emphasis upon the human errors, abuses, and corruptions incorporated with the Christian religion ever since its first diffusion, he so decisively condemns the ecclesiastical system of dogmas and state Christianity, and in particular takes so adverse a view of the middle ages, as a time of the darkest barbarism and inhumanity, that he almost seems to have adopted in this connection the standpoint of the *Aufklärung*, which he had before so passionately denounced. The extent to which he still differed from it we shall see later on, when we come to the final account of his religious views; but it is in any case undeniable that the point of view of the *Ideen* is not the same as that of his earlier writings. This may be corroborated by a glance at the general principles of his philosophy of history.

Herder wishes us to look at the history of mankind as "simply the natural history of man's powers, actions, and impulses in relation to their time and place." Supernatural forces and arbitrary fictitious purposes may no more be introduced into the study of history than into that of natural science; in both alike all phenomena must be explained by their causes, not by any hypothetical ends. "The God whom I seek in history, must be the same as the God in nature; for man is only a small part of the universe, and his history, like that of the grub, is closely interwoven with the cell in which he lives. In this history therefore all the laws of nature involved in the nature of the case, must have validity; and so far from setting them aside, God, having established them, reveals himself *in them* in their mighty power with a beauty unchanging, wise, and beneficent." That things take place from the necessity of natural law involves instead of excluding an inner teleology. The most general law of nature, which holds good also in history, is that out of confusion order should arise, the conservative forces outweighing the destructive ones. All life aims at producing a maximum and a proportion of the forces that mutually limit each other, this being the condition of the perfection and happiness of individuals, nations, and the race. All disturbances of this effort to find a condition of stable equilibrium are always in the end counteracted; for in the struggle amongst the individual forces and impulses, reason and fairness only last and are established by the force of their own gravity. Hence we may hope "that wherever men dwell, there will one day dwell rational and happy men, happy not only by their own reason, but also by the common rationality of all their brethren." According to these views, the end of man's development, to be gained by conflict and struggle, is a maximum and a rational harmony of all his forces, together with the resulting happiness; but we also find other statements which seem to make the object of nature to consist in that happiness which is found everywhere in every living thing, viz., simple consciousness of its own existence. "If happiness is to be found upon earth, it is in *every* sentient being. Nature has exhausted all possible human forms upon the earth, in order that she might have for each of them, in its time and place, some pleasure with which to allure mortals through life. It is wrong to hold up *one* ideal to mankind, as if all earlier generations before they reached the ideal were to be branded with the stigma of imperfection. Nature everywhere contrives that with the need there shall arise the possibility of its satisfaction. Those nations to whom we think nature was but a cruel step-mother, were perhaps the best-loved children; cheerfulness, often combined with thoughtlessness, a lively feeling of their own well-being, constituted their happiness, destiny, and enjoyment of life. Neither our head nor our heart was made for an infinite variety of thoughts and feelings. How much too small would be the plan of creation, if every individual had been created for what we call culture."

It cannot be denied that these sentences represent a naturalism like that of Rousseau, the logical result of which would be to deprive culture of all value in comparison with nature, and history of any divine purpose. But they do not represent Herder's whole position; they only contain a reaction, carried to extremes, against the contrary one-sided view of Kant. Kant had met Herder's *Ideen* with his own *Ideen zu einer allgemeinen Geschichte in weltbürgerlicher Absicht* (1784), according to which, the end of history consists in an ideal condition of single States and cosmopolitan society, to be attained by means of the conflicts and sacrifices of the generations; he had himself felt it to be a difficulty in this view that the older generations seem to perform their weary labour only for the sake of those coming after them, the latest only enjoying the good fortune of dwelling in the building at which so long a line of their ancestors had worked with no object in view. What accentuates the harshness of this view is, that, according to Kant himself, the ideal goal is never to be attained, reason being able to control but never to destroy the tendency to evil in the race. We must acknowledge the justice of Herder's dissatisfaction with this view of Kant's; the doom of men to the lot of Tantalus in this form, to be ever striving after the unattainable with eternally fruitless toil, would, Herder contends, be unworthy both of man,—who, as Kant also insists, ought never to be merely a means but always at the same time an end in himself,—and of the Creator, who could not deceive us by holding out a mere dream of purpose. On the other hand, Kant was indisputably right in asserting (as against Rousseau and Herder) that the final end of mankind can only be an ideal of moral culture, not the physical happiness of a state of nature, which would not essentially differ from the condition of animals. Kant was right in conceiving the end of humanity as consisting in an ideal of society demanded by reason and to be realised by means of freedom; but his view of this ideal was too much an abstraction, the mere *form* of social life, and the mere *Thou shalt* to which no reality ever corresponds. Herder rightly perceived that the ends of humanity cannot be external to it, but must be realised in its *existence as a whole*, so that no part can ever be *merely* a means to an end outside it; but he thus incurred the danger of taking too low a view of the end and allowing the ideal of reason to sink to a *life according to nature*. The solution of this antinomy can only be found in the perception of the truth, that reason attains its absolute ends in an infinite series of relative ideals, which are each realised in the proper place and produce corresponding relative forms of happiness, while their imperfections act as incentives to the attainment of ever loftier ideals. By this conception of a development of reason itself in the course of human history, Hegel effected the synthesis of these conflicting views, a synthesis which Herder doubtless himself had vaguely caught sight of. We see from this instructive example how much critical idealism and historical realism (or the theory of evolution) mutually need each other to supply their defects.

The antagonism between Herder and Kant, which first appears in the department of the philosophy of history, Herder carried into all the chief points of the Kantian philosophy in his later writings ("*Metakritik*"; "*Kalligone*"; "*Von Religion, Lehrmeinungen und Gebräuchen*"). It is worth while to look at this a little more closely, as characteristically illustrating the two sides of modern thought. Herder wishes to substitute for Kant's critique of the reason a physiology of the cognitive faculties, which would explain the evolution of the higher from the lower faculties. He rejects the distinction between a purely receptive sensibility and a purely spontaneous understanding, as also that between the simple matter of experience and the *à priori* forms of perception—space and time. These last, in Herder's view the result of actual experience, being an abstraction from its contents; in themselves they are the objective forms in which forces work and manifest themselves to us. Our sense-perceptions are not given us as a chaotic multiplicity which our spontaneity only afterwards and arbitrarily unifies without reference to the object; on the contrary, our senses, by virtue of their own organic structure, give us a multiplicity reduced to an ordered unity inherent in the object itself, recognised, not created by us. Hence the understanding is not so specifically different from the sense-organism as Kant maintained, but operates as judgment and classification in all sense-perceptions and in memory, not excepting even the lowest sensation; it is the same primary force of nature, showing itself here less clearly, there more distinctly and actively, now in separate, then in a connected series of operations. So too in the distinction between phenomena and noumena, Herder can only see a delusion of the imagination, since the true noumena must not be conceived as outside and behind the phenomena, but as within and of them, viz., as the organising forces in organic processes; to look for "the thing-in-itself" behind the phenomenal world, is to look for the wood behind the trees. Again, Herder is equally unable to follow Kant in assigning freedom and necessity to the intelligible and phenomenal worlds respectively; on the contrary, the two are the inseparable elements of the very nature of all living force. In so far as forces act according to their own nature, they are free; in so far as they are limited by other similarly free acting forces, there arise higher equations, which we call laws of nature; these do not destroy freely acting forces, but presuppose them. Thus human freedom also is only the highest force of our nature, which is free in so far as by virtue of its self-determination it obeys our nature's laws. On the other hand, it would be mere confusion of thought to imagine a causality outside causality and a nature outside nature. Specially emphatic is Herder's condemnation of the way in which Kant, in the dialectic of pure reason, represents the idea of God as an illusion, which is afterwards required again by the practical reason; as if besides *the* reason which proscribed this fiction there were a second reason which could command its return from banishment in the realm of the fabulous. This, says Herder, is juggling with reason, and can neither lead to real conviction nor to pure morality; for a God thus postulated is no God at all, but only a last resource for a destitute moral system, while his existence is as problematical to the speculative reason as the man in the moon. But to reason not divided against itself God is certainly no problematical distant Being, whose existence must first be artificially inferred, or, failing this, be made a moral postulate. "On the contrary, he is the primal Being, recognised by the reason as given in all being, the primal force in all forces, the supreme reason of the world. If there is a reason which is, and knows that it is, its own cause, there is also a supreme reason which is and knows that it is the cause of the unity of all things."

This is the same line of thought as we found in Herder's

essay on Spinoza. It does not essentially differ from Kant's suggestion, in his *Critique of Judgment*, as to the divine basis of the reign of law and purpose in the natural and moral worlds. A reconciliation of the two points of view would, therefore, seem not impossible, especially when we remember Herder's statement elsewhere, that natural science only leads to the conception of nature as the totality of order and form, not directly to that God whom the religious mind desires to find in creation, because he would satisfy its longing for life and well-being. This involves the admission that the religious ideal of God and the metaphysical idea of a first cause answer to the needs of two different sides of our mind, which must not be directly identified. This was the truth contained in Kant's distinction between the ideal of the practical reason and the speculative idea of the unconditioned; Kant's error, against which Herder with good reason protested, lay in representing this valid distinction as a deep and apparently impassable gulf. This is characteristic generally of the whole antagonism between the two men; the whole truth is nowhere wholly on one side, each is strong just where the other is weak. Kant's critical and analytical method was met by Herder's bold, synthetical intuitions. In order to ensure to the mind its active share in all cognition, Kant had banished its object to the dim, incognisable distance of *das Dingansich*. Herder replied to this subjective theory by maintaining that all cognition is only the recognition of what is necessarily presupposed as given. Kant had separated the various functions of the mind in cognition; Herder emphasised their unbroken connection as members in the evolution of one and the same force. But Herder's theory of cognition never ceased to vacillate in an ill-defined way between a *naïve* realism and a rational idealism. He slurred over the antitheses, which Kant had laboured scientifically to solve, by the help of an indefinite intermediate idea. Herder's attempted correction of Kant could be accomplished only by starting from his critical philosophy and using its resources. This was, and still is, the task of post-Kantian philosophy.

Having thus reviewed Herder's philosophical position in its maturest stage, we come next to consider the form assumed by his theory of religion in accordance with it. He expounded his theory in a series of works, dealing partly with the Bible, partly with dogmatic theology, between the years 1793 and 1797. Their basal idea is much more nearly related to Kant's philosophy of religion than Herder, in the heat of his polemic, was able to see. The real difference is, that Kant's rationalism was softened by Herder's rich humanism, and brought by the help of history nearer to ecclesiastical Christianity. *Christianity is the ideal religion, and religion is ideal humanity.* This is the ruling idea in these theological writings of the last period of Herder's life. But in order to effect this equalisation of religion and humanity, he does not, like Kant, work from above downwards; he does not construct a religion "within the limits of reason," but he works upwards by the method of historical study. It had always been one of his fundamental convictions that Christianity is a history, an actual fact, an object of experience, and that it can therefore be only rightly understood by the aid of its historical documents—through the Bible. Hence the study of the Bible is the Alpha and Omega of all theological studies. This view he had expressed with eager enthusiastic warmth in his early *Notes on the New Testament* and his *Letters on the Study of Theology*. But now, while still remaining quite true to it, and as before giving an æsthetic interpretation of the Gospels which halts mid-way between rationalism and supernaturalism, an unmistakable change has taken place in his method of exegesis. His interest in the Gospel narratives had formerly been that of the religious apologist; but he is now at the same time the critical historian, investigating the origin of the Gospels and their relation to each other. Herder thus followed Semler, Lessing, and Eichhorn in that scientific examination of the documents of early Christianity which was fraught with such important consequences to the theology of our century; and though he was still prejudiced in favour of the traditional authors of the Gospels, he is nevertheless rich in subtle observations, especially with regard to the chronological order of the Gospels. His keen eye discovered in the Gospel of Mark the oldest written form of the apostolic tradition; next in order he placed the Gospel of the Hebrews. Both of these were used as authorities by the Hellenist Luke in writing his history; and only subsequently appeared the Greek Gospel of Matthew, consisting of a free translation and amplification of the Gospel of the Hebrews. Last of all came the Gospel of John, as "the echo of the older Gospels in a higher key." In it the

Apostle John wished not only to expound, but also to purify the Palestine gospel-tradition; hence he narrated only a few miracles, and even these only as symbols of the permanent miracle of the person of Christ. Whilst the earlier Gospels had still represented Christ as the Son of God in the narrower sense, John sought to teach the higher conception of the Son of God and Saviour of the world, and for this purpose made his whole Gospel systematically the Gospel of the Spirit.

This is really a just description of the Fourth Gospel. But a Gospel written with a dogmatic purpose, and standing in so close a connection with the speculative movements of its time, as Herder shows to be the case with this, cannot be an historical authority for the life of Jesus. Obvious as this inference is, it was drawn neither by Herder nor by Schleiermacher after him; and it may be added that the latter was inferior to his predecessor in insight into the peculiar character of this Gospel. The inability to draw this conclusion was due in both cases to sympathy, as idealistic theologians, with the spiritual Gospel which converts history into ideas and ideas into history, and thus, in a sense, furnishes the modern theologian with a pattern for his semi-allegorical, semi-apologetical interpretation of the Gospel narratives as "symbolic facts." For this reason Herder, like Schleiermacher, entertained a pronounced preference for John's Gospel, because,—assuming its apostolic authorship,—he thought he found in it the justification of his own procedure in interpreting the gospel history in harmony with his free idealising feeling, and in attributing everything repugnant to it to the national and temporal limitations of the narrators. Herder does not, it is true, carry this principle out so consistently as Schleiermacher. In relation to the gospel miracles, he is still unable to get beyond a strange vacillation between their symbolical interpretation and adherence to their real historical character. He quite agrees with Lessing, that the truth of a doctrine cannot be dependent upon miracle. "Was it necessary for fire to fall from heaven 2000 years ago in order that we may now see the bright sun? Must the laws of nature have been then suspended, if we are now to be convinced of the internal necessity, truth, and beauty of the moral and spiritual kingdom?" Nevertheless, Herder still regards at all events the three miracles of the Baptism, Transfiguration, and Resurrection of Christ "as the three bright spots in the celestial authentication of the consecrated one;" for, he characteristically continues, "they have a secret advocate in the human heart." Since the stories of the miraculous appealed to his feelings and æsthetic taste, he suppressed the doubts of his intellect, which had embraced, as we have seen above, a philosophical view of the world in which there was no place for miracles. It is not allowable, therefore, to explain this surprising hesitancy and want of clearness in Herder's treatment of the Biblical miracles simply on the principle of accommodation, or from his fear of the destructive tendencies of the time; but the reason of it must be found in his whole mode of thought. It was always such an essential peculiarity of his nature to look at ideas and actual facts in closest conjunction, that he was unable in the case of Biblical traditions to critically separate ideal contents from historical realities; in fact, he could scarcely understand that this was required by science. Instead of explaining the repugnant points in the miraculous narratives and dogmatic conceptions of the Biblical writers by reference to their psychological origin in the religious and poetical motives of the narrators or the community, Herder had recourse to a time-honoured substitute for scientific criticism; involuntarily and unconsciously he recast the language of the Bible in the mould of his own, he *allegorised*. The result of this procedure was essentially the same as the "moral interpretation of the Bible" demanded by Kant. Herder's fierce opposition to this latter only proves that he did not see the divergence of his rationalistic interpretation from the original sense of the text. The Christs of the Synoptists, and of John, and of Paul, freed respectively from the outer coverings of Nationality, of Alexandrian speculation, and of Pharisaic dogmatism, were all made together to teach *his* Christianity of humanity, because he was under the honest impression that he was thereby only translating the meaning of the Biblical writers into the language of our own time. This self-deception, though fatal to the scientific value of his Biblical labours, was really useful, and perhaps necessary to the practical success of his attempted reconciliation of ecclesiastical traditions and modern culture. Moreover, with all this, Herder was the immediate precursor and kindred spirit of Schleiermacher, whose influence in the reconstruction of dogma was also closely connected with the weakness of his historical criticism.

Like Lessing, Herder drew a distinction between Christ's

religion and the religion of which Christ is the object. Christ's religion is the rule of salvation, supplied by the teaching and life of Jesus in the perfect and universally valid form, viz., "The knowledge of God as the Father, of man as his instrument, of man's weakness as an object of grace and help, of the divine in man, of the strength, purity, and nobility, which must be roused and nourished. Love, therefore,—prevenient, pure, uniting, active,—is the only way of deliverance from all evils that oppress man, the only motive power capable of establishing a kingdom of God among men." Precisely this, according to Herder, was the ruling idea of Jesus, and the object of his life. "In his heart was written: God is my Father and the Father of all men; all men are brothers. To this religion of humanity he dedicated his life, which he was ready wholly to offer up, if his religion might be that of all men. For it concerns the fundamental nature of our race—both its original and final destiny. Through it the weaknesses of mankind serve to call forth a nobler power; every oppressive evil, human wickedness even, becomes an incentive to its own defeat. The truest humanity breathes in the few speeches of Jesus which have come down to us; it is nothing else than humanity which he manifested in his life, and sealed by his death, just as the chosen name by which he called himself was the Son of Man. As a spiritual saviour of his race, he sought to train up men of God, who would labour from pure motives for the good of others and reign by their patience as kings in the realm of truth and kindness. An object such as this must evidently be the sole purpose of providence with our race; and all the wise and good on earth must and will co-operate to this end, in proportion to the pureness of their thought and endeavour; for what other ideal could man have of perfection and happiness on earth, save this universally operative humanity?"

According to Herder, therefore, the distinctive character of Jesus was, that he bore in his heart the ideal of man as the child of God, exemplified it in his life and death for our imitation, and at the same time trained up men of God and established a society of them, a kingdom of God among men, in which will be realised the purpose of providence with our race. The "Divine Sonship" of Christ is only another expression for this ideal "man of God," who knows God as his Father and all men as his brethren, and in self-sacrificing devotion to the good of men passively and actively fulfils the will of God. Was not this fundamentally Kant's meaning when he described Jesus as the pre-eminent representative example of the idea of a race of men well-pleasing to God? Herder, indeed, strongly denounced Kant's theory as "a romance, a mass of misleading fictions, an ignoble perversion of Scripture," etc.; but this denunciation was doubtless primarily due to the mistaken notion that Kant had wished to substitute a personified idea for the historic Jesus. Herder's mistake was rendered possible by Kant's method of expounding his position, as his constructive rationalism led him to start from the idea, and to connect the historical person of Jesus with it only as an example; while Herder started from the historical person as the source of the Christian religion of humanity, and portrayed the idea as the essence of the manifestation of this person. The latter method is undoubtedly more advantageous from the theological point of view; but we must not deny the philosopher the right of starting from the idea, with its basis in the reason, and of accentuating the distinction between it and the historical person in whom it is presented for imitation, though it does not derive from him its ultimate origin.

Again, just as Kant had distinguished the pure moral faith of the reason from the "statutory" faith of the Church, so Herder distinguishes the religion of Christ, identical with the pure religion of humanity, from the religion of which Christ was the object, or the "doctrines" about the two natures in Christ, the legal conflict between Christ and Belial, the satisfaction made by Christ's death, etc. Of these ecclesiastical dogmas, Herder speaks much more contemptuously than Kant, calling them childish questions, old second-hand phrases, masquerade and hypocrisy; for Kant had found a meaning even in these doctrines, by interpreting them as symbols of the inner processes of moral feeling. Herder's harsh judgment is no doubt to be partially explained by his practical experience as teacher, which showed him how many continue to cling to these husks of dogma, and so never reach the true kernel itself. But it was more especially the consequence of the optimism inherited by Herder from Leibnitz, Shaftesbury, and Rousseau, and shared by Goethe; he was convinced of the essential goodness of human nature, and could only look upon evil as a shadow, a weakness, which would of itself disappear with the development of man's powers. Like Goethe, Herder was incapable of appreciating the profound difference between idea and actuality, duty and inclination, or the struggle of the good and the bad principle, which was so important in Kant's ethics and religious philosophy. Hence both of them found Kant's doctrine of a "radical evil," which formed the basis of his moral interpretation of the doctrine of the atonement and justification, an incomprehensible stumbling-block. As the natural consequence of this unqualified antagonism to the dogmas of sin and salvation Herder found himself unable to explain them; he regarded them as purely "arbitrary doctrines, having nothing to do with religion, which is an affair of the heart," and even as "the tomb of religion." Herder did not sufficiently consider that they could never have arisen and influenced the Church, if they had not been the product and the expression,—however imperfect,—of the heart's religious energies, experiences, and needs; and this to a large extent explains the insignificance of Herder's direct influence on theology. Schleiermacher, on the other hand, whose philosophic views generally approached much more nearly Herder's than Kant's, was nevertheless able to adopt and assimilate the doctrines of sin and salvation, and was for this very reason in a position to carry out that reconstruction of Protestant theology at which Herder aimed.

Herder approaches Schleiermacher most nearly in his doctrine of the Holy Spirit, expounded in his discussion of the third article of the Apostles' Creed, in the essays, *Vom Geist des Christenthums*, and *Von Religion und Lehrmeinungen*. By tracing historically the development of the idea of Holy Spirit, he shows that its meaning in Christianity is nothing else than the spirit of Christ, as animating and guiding the Christian Church and uniting all nations in the Kingdom of God. He places it in contrast, not less to the dogmatic conception of a personal principle inspiring man from without, than to the philosophical idea of an autonomous legislation of the reason. The idea of magical inspiration he had already strongly protested against in his *Briefe über das Studium der Theologie*. Inspiration must not be conceived as either the depression or as the wild exaltation of our mental powers. "Can He who made the eye be compelled to blind us in order that we may see? Can the Spirit, who animates creation and all our powers, destroy them in order that in their stead he may produce light within us?" On the contrary, inspiration and enlightenment are the awakening of the noblest powers of the mind; perfectly undisturbed contemplation, calmest self-possession, the most quietly effective truth, clear thoughts, enlightened views, happy resolves, pure actions—these are the noblest gifts of the Spirit. The purest stage of revelation is to see things as they are, face to face, without figures and dreams. Least of all may we look for dark fanaticism in the revelation of him whom John calls light-giving Reason manifested on earth. His revelation, *i.e.*, the truth which he clearly saw and uttered, was deliverance from everything unnatural, the restoration of mankind to the full use of its powers. Wherefore what we have to do is to turn from everything unnatural, from all magic, all bibliolatry, to nature and truth, which is also the spirit of the Bible.

But, on the other hand, it is precisely this nature and truth which Herder cannot find in the abstractions of philosophy. "That egoism which of itself issues commands and derives all its power to obey the law from the might of its own proud formal dictatorship, can hardly be the Spirit of God; for in a formal legislation without contents, there is neither might nor blessedness, neither life nor spirit. But it is *life* that impels thee to what thou oughtest to do and to be. As in the realm of nature a universal law assigns to each impulse its limits, the observance of which limits leads to enjoyment, their disregard to discomfort; so the same law must be operative in the realm of man's spiritual impulses. Here too watches a beneficent spirit within us, awakening our slumbering powers, avenging their misuse, and saving us from excess. You may call it reason, conscience, etc.; the wise have ever recognised it as a voice of God." It was this pure impulse in man which was aroused by Christianity, not by the inculcation of virtue, for thereby no impulse is roused, but by awakening love. Every man has within him a good spirit, a divine voice, a canon and criterion of truth; not as a universal legislation for all rational beings, but, as a definite and perfectly individual ideal of what he himself is and ought to be. To become conscious of this ideal, to acknowledge it, to obey its active impulse and controlling limitations, this is living virtue; in it each finds himself united to others in a fellowship of mutual activity, for no impulse acts in isolation, and the noblest characteristic in man, the impulse of all impulses, is love, the basis of all social life.

Herder therefore maintains that the Christian spirit is neither the principle of magical inspiration nor simply the legislative reason, but the inward impulse to truth and goodness, as the power of enthusiasm, truth, and love, which does not merely command men to do the good, but is itself operative, which does not issue a universal imperative, but places before each his special individual ideal, and, as being the purest impulse in men's nature, necessarily unites them in social bonds. He opposed the abstractness and powerlessness of Kantian ethics on the same lines as those on which Schleiermacher, Fichte, Schiller, and others had tried to remedy the incompleteness of the categorical imperative and to restore to their proper place man's moral emotions and impulses and individual needs. In conclusion, we may sum up our view of the relation of Herder's philosophy of religion to that of Kant in the words of Haym (*Herder*, II. 654): "Not only was Herder's religion of equity, goodness, and loving-kindness larger-hearted than Kant's religion of rigid duty, but it also fitted itself much better to the original documents, and, in fact, to the historical elements of Christianity generally. Kant's religion of reason, with his principle of moral interpretation, did violence to the words of the Bible and the creeds; Herder's religion of humanity put itself by a little conciliation into accord with the words of Christ and the apostles. Kant primarily impressed upon the intellectual conceptions of the traditional religion a new moral form; Herder let intellectual conceptions alone, and, in opposition to all dogmatic theology and all philosophical formulæ, emphasised the inward contents of that religion, consisting in the emotions and dispositions of the heart. Both aimed at purifying and rationalising Christianity, the one by a morality of pure reason, the other by a morality not less emotional than rational."

CHAPTER III.

SCHLEIERMACHER'S PERIOD OF ROMANTICISM.

Two years after Herder's book on *Religion und Lehrmeinungen*, appeared the work of Schleiermacher, then a young preacher in Berlin, *Reden über die Religion an die Gebildeten unter ihren Verächtern* (1799). The object of the two books was essentially the same; they protested against religion being confounded with the opinions of the schools, whether theological or philosophical, and against its being mixed up with politics; in a word, against dogmatic and politico-ecclesiastical Christianity. They insisted, on the other hand, on the inwardness of the religious life, the immediateness of religious feeling, and especially on the free play of religious individuality. But the Romanticism of the younger writer led him so to exaggerate this common drift that it became unhistorical subjectivism and an exclusively emotional mysticism, which Herder's many-sided humanism and historical insight could never have approved. But in spite, or rather because, of this extreme one-sidedness, Schleiermacher's book made a deeper impression upon its time than Herder had been able to produce with his own more moderate writings, designed to effect a compromise between the extreme views. To-day, the mystical, poetical, rhetorical language of the *Reden* is hardly to our taste; but to the educated classes of his own time, whose thoughts and feelings were those of idealistic Romanticism, this language was intelligible, and well calculated to bring home to them the peculiar value of religion, and,—if not to accomplish the reconciliation of modern culture and the ancient faith of the Church,—at any rate to prepare the way and show its possibility. Though we can find but little in the paradoxical positions of these *Reden* which is permanent and valuable as it stands, they are still historically important, as containing the fertile germs, the refined and ripened products of which we shall hereafter meet with in Schleiermacher's great work on dogmatics, which accomplished the reconciliation of Herder's religion of humanity with the doctrines of the Church.

That Schleiermacher's system is much more akin to Herder's than to those of Kant, Fichte, or Schelling, is an indisputable fact, hitherto always overlooked only because Herder, standing mid-way between philosophers and theologians, has had the misfortune to be ignored by both parties as not belonging to either of them. In his attack on the chief positions of Kant's theory of religion,—the transcendental postulates of freedom, immortality, and God,—we find Schleiermacher in his earliest writings fighting side by side with Herder. As Herder had rejected a causality outside causality, and held freedom and necessity to be combined in the nature of the rational will, *i.e.*, the will determined by its own law (comp. *ante*, p. 34), so Schleiermacher, in an essay on freedom, substituted for Kant's dualism a psychological determinism, according to which the will is determined by the nature of the conceptions at any time present in the mind as a whole. As Herder had condemned Kant's procedure in basing his postulate of God on the conception of the supreme good, so Schleiermacher, in a subtle analysis of this idea,[1] showed the untenability of Kant's definition of it as the combination of virtue and happiness; for happiness is by no means a conception of the pure reason, being conditioned by time and sensation, and hence cannot belong to the "supreme good," either in a future world or in this, for the "supreme good" means simply "the totality of what is possible by the laws of pure reason." Moreover, as Schleiermacher elsewhere remarks, according to Kant's argument, which bases the belief in God and immortality upon impure motives derived from the interests of happiness, this belief must wane in good men as their motives wax in purity. Further, as Herder had resorted to an idealised Spinozism, as against the onesidedness of subjective idealism, so Schleiermacher felt the necessity of combining, as mutual correctives, Spinozism and the onesided idealism of Kant and Fichte which made the universe merely the reflection of our limitations, hoping thus to gain a "higher realism" as the foundation of religion. Thus Spinoza's *cognitio Dei intuitiva*

---

[1] In Dilthey, *Beilagen*, pp. 10-15.

lies at the root both of Herder's and Schleiermacher's conception of religion. Herder teaches that our reason must recognise God as the primal Being in all being, the primal Force in all forces, the supreme Reason in the world; he speaks of "a feeling of the invisible in the visible, of the one in the many, of power in its effects, as the root of all ideas of the reason" to which we must trace back the origin of religion. With this, Schleiermacher almost verbally agrees, pronouncing the "contemplation of the universe," and "the feeling of the infinite in the finite" the pivot of religion. But at this point appears a significant difference. Herder failed definitely to distinguish the intuitive perception and recognition of the revelation of God in the world and in men, either from thinking or in particular from moral willing and action; hence he gives so wide a meaning to religion that it is in danger of being lost in the indefiniteness of ideal humanity, and to a large extent becomes equivalent to morality; Schleiermacher, on the other hand, in order to ensure to religion its special sphere, drew so sharp a line between the immediate sight and feeling of the infinite and reflective thinking and the moral life, that religion seems to be confined to the mystical emotions of the individual, and its influence on the thoughts and actions of men, and therewith its power of forming communities, to be destroyed. With both thinkers religion is a matter of the *heart*, but it is so with Herder in the sense that the heart's emotion is one with conviction and purpose; with Schleiermacher it is so in the sense that the heart with its emotions withdraws into its own mystical depths, fearing any freezing contact with thought and purpose. This is the point of contact between Schleiermacher and Romanticism, in which the subjective idealism of philosophy had become the practical cultus of the ego, more specifically the apotheosis of the heart with its noble or ignoble feelings. Novalis was only expressing the views of Schleiermacher as he then was, when he said, "Religion arises whenever the heart comes to feel itself; when it makes itself into an ideal object, and all absolute feeling is religious."

In order to discover the origin of religion within the soul, Schleiermacher, in the second *Rede*, refers to the moment prior to all definite consciousness, in which the universe comes into contact with our sensibility, when sense and object are still one, not yet separated respectively into perception and feeling. In spite of the poetical description of this moment as "the direct betrothal, too holy for error or mistake, of the universe with the incarnate reason in creative, productive embrace," we cannot understand why in it should lie the origin specially of *religious* states of mind, since this moment is simply that of the direct affection of the senses, which is the source of *all* perception and sensation. This difficulty is not solved by what follows : " So far as your feeling expresses the life and being common to you and the universe, it constitutes your piety ; your sensations, and the effects upon you of all the life surrounding you, are all elements, and the sole elements, of religion ; there is no feeling which is not religious, save such as indicates an unhealthy condition of life." Here, as in the words of Novalis just quoted, feeling and religion are simply identified ; and the facts are overlooked, which can escape no impartial student of the religious life, that there are feelings which, without being unhealthy, have nothing to do with religion, and that religion has an active side of conception and purpose, in addition to a passive side of feeling.

But Schleiermacher speaks not only of feeling but also of intuitions (*Anschauungen*), which in the first edition of the *Reden* hold the first place, even though afterwards subordinated to feeling. The relation of the two is not clearly stated, but it is plain that Schleiermacher could not ignore the intuitions if he wished to state the definite contents of the religious consciousness, and not rest satisfied with the complete indefiniteness of feeling. The object of religious intuition is indeed the universe, yet not directly as such, but in its finite revelations in nature and human life. In nature it is not masses of natural or beautiful forms, but laws which reveal the divine unity and unchangeableness of the world, and which therefore affect us religiously. Yet there the question arises, whether the æsthetic view of nature is really so immaterial to religion, whether it does not affect the mind much sooner than the intellectual view ; further, whether the reign of law in nature is an object of direct intuition and not rather the result of reflective thought. The external world can only be understood by the internal, and this again only by the contemplation of self in the mirror of mankind at large; whilst the individual, when looked at from the moral point of view, is isolated and found wanting, as measured by the standard of the ideal, religion discovers even here a characteristic life and wonderful harmony of the whole. Leaving the whole and contemplating himself, the devout man finds there too the marks of the highest and the lowest, a compendium of humanity. Further, even when intuition fails us, imaginative presentiment can travel beyond nature and mankind, and reach further forms of the universe. With these intuitions are connected the religious feelings of humility, love, thankfulness, pity, remorse; feelings which, Schleiermacher holds, do not belong to morality but only to religion, since they do not exist for the sake of some action, but are their own cause and end, as factors of the highest and most inward life. These feelings have a peculiar complexion in each religion, comparable with the different styles and tastes in music; and the character of a religion is determined solely by this common element of feeling, not by a system of propositions deducible from each other and capable of logical concatenation. For this very reason, everything in religion is equally true, as far as it is the pure product of feeling and has not yet been moulded by thought. The distinction of "true and false," therefore, does not apply to religion at all; every religion is true in its own way, though it must not be forgotten that the whole realm of religion is boundless, and can assume the most diverse shapes. Religion is never intolerant, but only religious systems. The mania for systems repudiates everything foreign to each, while religion shuns the cold uniformity which would be fatal to its divine profusion. It is only the adherents of the dead letter, which religion rejects, that have filled the world with the tumult of religious controversies: they who have had a true vision of the Eternal were always peaceful souls, being either alone with themselves and the Infinite, or, if they looked around on others, gladly according to each his special characteristics. To a devout soul, religion makes everything holy and precious, even what is unholy and common, whether corresponding to its own thought and action or not; for religion is the sworn foe of all pusillanimity and narrowness. She cannot be held responsible for fanatical actions, simply because she does not of herself impel to action at all. Religious feeling is neither bound, nor permitted directly to influence action; it rather invites to peaceful, absorbing enjoyment, than impels to external acts. Feelings and actions naturally form two concurrent series, "nothing should be done at the instigation of religion; but everything *with* religion; religious feelings should accompany active life without intermission like a sacred melody."

We see that Schleiermacher is here pleading the cause of a mystical religion of the heart; a religion which is satisfied with the peaceful absorbing enjoyment of its own feelings, and does not think itself called upon to formulate either an intellectual truth or a consistent system of dogmas, or to take an active part in the world's life, thus with large-hearted tolerance giving free play to the thoughts and ways of mankind.

With all respect for this large-hearted humanity, we are compelled to ask two questions: Firstly, how far does the actual *history* of religion correspond to the description of it here given? Has any vigorous religion ever actually abstained from laying claim to the exclusive possession of the truth, or from giving expression to its emotions in corresponding deeds, in energetic action upon the world? Has not precisely the early youth of all religions, when their enthusiasm was most spontaneous and least controlled by reflection or confined in systems, been marked also by the most intolerant self-assurance, the most narrow exclusiveness, and the most passionate zeal in proselytising? And is the vehemence, distinguishing disputes about religious dogmas from other conflicts of opinion, due really to intellectual thought, and not rather to the pathos of the emotions finding expression in these dogmas? If it be rejoined that it was not Schleiermacher's object to describe the positive religions, but only the *ideal* religion, conceived by him as the goal of historical development, this would at once give rise to the further question, Can we accept it as characteristic of the ideal religion, that it should be the self-abandonment of each to the enjoyment of his individual feelings, without seeking at all to influence the thought and action of individuals, to say nothing of the community? In fact, the only conclusion to which we can come is, that this isolation, favoured by Romanticism, of the emotional religion of the individual heart is not less impossible, psychologically, than unhistorical, inasmuch as it destroys all the social elements by which religion has formed communities and become a power in history. Schleiermacher, it is true, could not escape the necessity of offering an explanation of the facts of the actual formation of religious conceptions and religious societies, accompanying every religion; but the way in which he does this serves rather to illustrate than to obviate the error of his principle.

The dogmas and propositions which experience shows to be connected with religion, are, according to Schleiermacher, simply the result of the comparison of the emotions, and the means of their expression and communication to others; for religion itself they are not necessary, but are only an adventitious creation of reflection. A man may have a great deal of religion without the aid of such concepts as "miracle, inspiration, revelation," but reflection on and comparison of his religious feelings necessarily put them in his way. Hence they have an unlimited right in religion, but only as religious expressions for subjective states of feeling, the meaning of which must not be extended to the sphere of metaphysics or morals. "Miracle" is the religious name for an occurrence; the religious man recognises miracles not in a few only, but in all occurrences. "Revelation" is any original and new communication of the universe and its inmost life to man, giving birth to a special class of intuitions and emotions. "Inspiration" signifies the feeling of higher enthusiasm and freedom. "Prophecy" is the presentiment foreshadowing and anticipating the further course of a present train of events. All these terms therefore denote subjective experiences essential to all religious life, and therefore present in some degree in every religious man. Hence, since each man can and ought to experience these things for himself, faith must not depend upon external authority, at any rate only temporarily. "Not every man who believes in sacred Scriptures has religion, but only he who has a living and direct understanding of them, and who, therefore, so far as he himself is concerned, can most easily dispense with them." Finally, Schleiermacher discusses from the same point of view the concepts, God and Immortality. These, too, he holds, are not presuppositions and conditions of religious feeling, but the product of reflection on it. Hence the form given to the concept of God is of secondary importance; it depends upon the bent of the imagination, whether we think of the Spirit of the Universe as free personality, or give up the personal idea of the Deity, in humble consciousness of the limitations of personality; in any case, whichever conception a man adopts, the main question is, whether he has a feeling of God, and this feeling of the

Divine will always be better than his conception of it. (The last point may certainly be conceded, although one may with good reason urge against the rest, that our idea of God is still of much greater importance to the content of religious feeling, particularly to its ethical character, than Schleiermacher was willing to admit.) To the ordinary idea of immortality our apologist for religion is not so much indifferent as hostile; it seems to him irreligious rather than religious, as betraying a clinging to the finite form of existence, whereas personality ought rather even here to be renounced from love to God, in order to live in the One and the All. "In the midst of the finite to become one with the infinite, and to be eternal in every moment,—this is the immortality of religion." (We may let the mysticism of this view pass without supposing that the last, or even a decisive, word has been pronounced on the question of immortality.)

The third Discourse draws a very dark picture of the age of the *Aufklärung*, the shallow utilitarianism of which stifled all sense of religion; and the fourth proceeds to speak of Church and priesthood, describing religious fellowship both as it is and as it ought to be. The actual Church Schleiermacher considers to be only an association of those who are still seeking religion, in which all are supposed to receive, and only one to give. It is therefore opposed in almost every respect to the ideal religious community. Though indispensable at present as an institution for scholars and learners, it suffers under unavoidable defects; the authority and the method of the transmission of religious doctrines inevitably produce sectarianism, superstition, adherence to ceremonies, and the distinction of priests and laity. All these evils are made intolerable, and the real ruin of the Church brought about by the interference of the State in the Church's life. Left to itself, its imperfect condition would have led to the separation of the true Church, the living members uniting in small societies around leaders chosen by themselves. But these true inspired members were excluded by the connection of Church and State from the leadership of the community, and their place was unworthily filled by officially appointed teachers, whose duty was to educate the citizens in the habits of thought favourable to orderly government. Besides this, articles of belief were settled, and ceremonies enjoined, and the whole degraded into a political institution. This state of things cannot be maintained. "Away with all such connection between Church and State! I shall continue, like Cato, to reiterate this oracle until the end, or until I see the connection annihilated." With the end of our artificial culture and social system will have come a time when, as in the sacred youth of the world, no other society will be necessary to help men to be religious than that of the devout home. There will no longer be any distinct office of teacher, no difference between teacher and congregation; the calling of the minister will be a private occupation, the temple a private room, an assembly of likeminded friends will form the Church. Then only will the exalted fellowship of truly religious souls spread in all directions, as an academy of priests pursuing religion as an art and a study, as a circle of brothers united by the closest ties of sentiment and mutual understanding. Such was the ideal Church of Schleiermacher in his early years, an ideal in which Moravian mysticism is combined with Romantic exaggeration in fantastic idealism. Herder, notwithstanding his equally great dislike of an official State Christianity, took a far more sober view of the functions of the Church in the moral education of the people.

The fifth Discourse treats of the Positive Religions. As something infinite, religion can exist in the world only under a multiplicity of specific manifestations, that is, in the various positive religions, and not as an empty abstraction, such as the so-called "natural religion" would be. The preference given to the latter in his time, Schleiermacher thinks, was due simply to the fact, that those to whom religion in general was obnoxious like that form of it best which is really not religion at all, and has the fewest of its characteristics. So-called "natural religion" is commonly so refined away, and so nearly akin to metaphysics and ethics, as to exhibit few of the characteristic traits of religion. On the other hand, every positive religion has a specific individual character. The character of such a religion is not determined by its share of the totality of religious views and feelings, for these may all be met with in some form in every actual religion; but each individual religion is produced when some special view of the universe is made a centre-point, and everything else subordinated to it. In so far as each man can do this for himself, there would naturally be as many individual religions as religious individuals. And, in fact, Schleiermacher explicitly says, Any man who can fix the date of the birth of his religion, and trace its origin to the direct action upon him of the Deity, *i.e.*, to "revelation," has his own special and real religion. Here everything is life and freedom and true natural development, whereas in "natural religion" everything is abstract, and its strength lies in the negation of what is positive and characteristic; it is like the soul that refused to come into the world, because it wished to be not a definite man, but man in general. This subjectivism, which resolves all connection between historical religions into accidental individual phenomena, was afterwards abandoned by Schleiermacher himself when he sought to combine the claims of individuality with the important functions of the social element.

The development of religion Schleiermacher conceives as following the successive stages (then erroneously accepted) of fetishism, polytheism, and monotheism. In this connection he has occasion to speak of pantheism, which he does not regard as a special form of religion, but as a speculative theory, quite reconcilable with true religious feeling, as long as we do not understand by it a masked materialism. The fundamental idea of Judaism Schleiermacher holds to be retribution, which was only possible in the narrow field of a limited national community; its importance as preparatory to Christianity he rates very low. "I hate in religion this idea of historical relations; each religion has its own eternal necessity, and has always its own independent origin"—a statement characteristic of Schleiermacher's want of historical insight, a defect from which even his later theology is never quite free. The fundamental idea of Christianity he considers to be, that the corruption of the world, consisting in alienation from God, is put an end to and a mediation is effected between the finite and God by individual points, scattered over the whole, in which both the Divine and the human are united. "Ruin and salvation, enmity and mediation, these are the two inseparably connected fundamental relations underlying this habit of feeling, and determining the shape of the entire religious content and form of Christianity." That presupposition of universal ungodliness is the cause of the polemical character and the sense of "sorrow" which, Schleiermacher thinks, are special characteristics of Christianity. But since Christianity at the same time discerns in history constantly new dispensations on the part of God for retrieving this ruin, ever higher revelations and mediators with a view of uniting the Divine and the human, it makes the history of religion itself the material of religion and so raises religion as it were to a higher power (just as, according to Schlegel, the poetry of Romanticism, by taking the given forms of poetry itself as its material, raises poetry to a higher power.) Of the founder of Christianity it is further maintained, that the wonderful thing about him was not so much the purity of his moral doctrine, which only expressed what is common to him with all men who have attained to full spiritual consciousness, nor his character, combining exalted power with touching gentleness; what was truly divine in him was the clearness of his idea of the necessity of a mediation between everything finite and God, or of the necessity of redemption for man imprisoned in the finite. "His consciousness of the directness of his knowledge of God and of his existence in God, and of his power of arousing it in others, was at the same time the consciousness of his mediatorial office and of his deity." "But never," adds Schleiermacher, "did Jesus claim to be the only mediator"; he never required men to accept his ideas for the sake of his person, but only the latter for the sake of the ideas; he never represented the views and feelings which he communicated as the totality of religion, neither did his disciples ever wish to limit the absolute freedom of the revelation of the spirit; and so neither does the Bible forbid any other book to be or become a Bible too. Christianity will last for ever in so far as there will never be a time when no more mediators are needed; but nevertheless it repudiates the claim to be the sole and sovereign form of religion; it wishes to see other younger, and, if possible, stronger and nobler forms of religion springing up beside it, and a prophetic mind could perhaps even now indicate the point which must be the centre of communion with the Deity for future generations. This view of the possibility of a more perfect religion than Christianity Schleiermacher afterwards limited to a continuous development within Christianity itself, just as in his later *Glaubenslehre* he no longer regarded Christ as one mediator among several, but as the only one whose consciousness of God was perfect and of unceasing efficacy for the whole race.

We can easily understand that so original and paradoxical a work as these "Discourses on Religion" would arouse much opposition on all sides; in the narrow circle of the author's Romantic friends only did it meet with approval, and even there it was qualified. Of the various criticisms none was more common, or more just, than that Schleiermacher had overlooked the essential connection of religion with morality and the basis of its importance socially. But any one who was inclined on this account to accuse our apologist for religion of lacking true regard for ethics, was at once corrected by the appearance of his *Monologen* (1800), supplying the moral philosophy corresponding to the religious philosophy of the Discourses. But the remarkable thing is, that while in the latter he taught a religion independent of morality, in the former he teaches a morality independent of religion. In both cases the formal principle remains the same, viz., the self-contemplation of the ego, freed from all extraneous hypotheses and limitations, the ego contemplating within itself the forms of the spirit's life in their individual development and also in their general laws. But in the first work the object of self-contemplation was the ego as intuitive and emotional, its passive relation to the universe being excited and determined by impressions from it; in the second, it is the ego so far as it is conscious of its absolute freedom and shapes its internal as well as the external world by spontaneous action. In the one he teaches, with Spinoza, the complete dependence of everything finite upon the One Infinite; in the other he makes, like Fichte, the ego itself the creative whole, of which even the world is only the self-created mirror. Common to both works is the individualistic form given to the ideal; in the one, it is required that every truly religious man should be conscious of special revelations of the Deity, or feel himself a special mirror of the universe; and in the other that each man should, in a manner peculiar to himself, represent in his own person the nature of humanity and determine his inward and outward action by the law of his own individual life with a freedom unrestricted by anything external. Free and harmonious culture by the independent development of our own capacities and glad recognition of the peculiarities of others, such is the principle of this theory of ethics, which seeks to overcome the Kantian antithesis of duty and inclination by conceiving the moral law, not as a universal imperative, but as arising in each individual as a special vital impulse which need only be followed purely and uninterruptedly in order to contribute a chord to the harmony of the moral world. It cannot be disputed that this æsthetic and humanistic ethical principle, adopted also by the Jacobis and Herder, Goethe and Schiller, embodies an important truth as against the one-sided rigorism of Kant; but it is equally indisputable that it does not contain the whole truth, and, if exclusively pursued, may lead to dangers of a different and more serious kind than did the Kantian ethics, especially when we remember the practical fruits of this principle in the circles of Romanticism, which cast their dark shadows even into Schleiermacher's life. The defects of the whole school may be stated in a few words : it fails to properly recognise the dependence of the individual on its historic conditions and the obligations of the individual towards the historic aims and objects of society. This indicates what is needed to supply subjective idealism with its true objective, *i.e.*, social, complement, and to correct the strange separation of religion and morals, as if unrelated to each other, inasmuch as religion shows the possibility of the reconciliation of both, as presenting in God the common source of individual freedom and social obligation.

The conversion of subjective into objective idealism was carried out by Kant's successors in various directions ; by Fichte in the direction of Ethical Idealism, the original ethical atheism of which afterwards became a mystical pantheism ; by Schelling in the direction of a philosophy of nature, which was afterwards transformed into theosophy ; by Hegel in the form of Logical Idealism, with the incorporation of the theory of historical evolution. Since these systems as philosophical theories, especially the two last, affected theology in various ways, it will be necessary for us to take a brief survey of them.

CHAPTER IV.

J. G. FICHTE'S ETHICAL IDEALISM.

THE years at the close of the last century in which Herder wrote his books against Kant, and Schleiermacher his *Discourses on Religion* and his *Monologues*, witnessed also the controversy on FICHTE's atheism. This controversy was both the occasion of the philosopher's removal from Jena, the stronghold of the Kantian philosophy, to Berlin, the stronghold of Romanticism, and, at the same time, of the reconstruction of his philosophy. It was provoked by Fichte's essay, *Ueber den Grund unseres Glaubens an eine göttliche Weltregierung* (1798), in which he affirmed that faith in our ethical vocation and in the moral order of the world, as the necessary presupposition for the accomplishment of our moral vocation in the world, is the only true faith, maintaining at the same time the impossibility of tracing this moral order back to God as its cause. Fichte followed in Kant's footsteps, in so far as the latter had based religious faith on faith in our moral vocation, which is at the same time the vocation of the world; but whilst Kant made man's inability to bring nature into harmony with his moral vocation the ground of the postulate of *God*, to supply this want of human power, Fichte considered this postulate not only as superfluous, but even as impossible, since a God acting in the interests of happiness would appear desirable to the physical man only, but would do dishonour to our moral reason, and therefore be really an idol. Hence in his *Appellation an das Publikum gegen die Anklage des Atheismus* (1799), Fichte declared that his accusers, who wished to have a God for the satisfaction of their desire for happiness, were the real atheists.

This rejection of Kant's dogmatic postulates was a necessary consequence of the logical rigour of Fichte's idealism, both practical and theoretical. From the autonomy of the practical reason he inferred that it was itself sufficient to work out its self-imposed aims, not needing to have its freedom supplemented by divine aid; and he gave full effect to Kant's assertion that the understanding legislates for nature; he set aside the "thing-in-itself" which had in Kant confined the independent activity of cognition by making it dependent on an object, and declared it the *self-imposed* limitation of the active ego. Thus the world which forms the content of our consciousness was made absolutely, in form and matter, the simple product of our consciousness, the unsubstantial image of our creative imagination. And just as the active ego, by its acts of reflection, is the free creator of its world, so its freedom or, what is identical with it, its moral vocation, is also the end and purpose of this world. The world, says Fichte, is nothing but "the material of our duty clothed in forms of sense," an object which, in itself unreal, is only conceived by the ego as the inevitable material for the action of its moral freedom. This thorough-going subjective idealism is quite reconcilable with ethical idealism as long as the non-ego created by the conception of the ego does not go beyond nature; for whether this is something real or only an unreal phantom of my imagination matters very little to ethical purpose and action; it might even seem conducive to the moral grandeur of mind to strip nature of its substantiality and degrade it to the unreal and impotent product of the mind's representative functions. But what if the non-ego include other human beings as well as nature? Are these also, as belonging to the content of my consciousness, only the product of my consciousness, only the self-imposed limitation and means of the employment of my freedom? Without doubt this pronounced "solipsism" would be the ultimate logical issue of subjective idealism; but it would also be the end of all moral convictions, for to theoretical solipsism could only correspond an unqualified practical egoism. It is extremely characteristic of Fichte's speculative thought, that it was not any theoretical consideration, such as the objection of unsophisticated common sense, but simply and solely this moral abyss that quelled the proud daring of his subjective idealism, and led to the introduction of a transcendental object.

We first meet with this change of view in the treatise on *Die Bestimmung des Menschen* (1800). In it too the final result of the philosophy of pure knowledge is still asserted to be, that the sense-world is only the conception in which all finite rational beings agree, depending upon the common limitation of their reason. But, he goes on to ask, what could limit reason except what is itself reason, and what could limit all finite reason except the infinite reason? This universal agreement with regard to the world of sense, as the sphere of our duty, and hence our necessary and antecedently given starting-point, is as incomprehensible as our agreement with regard to the products of our mutual freedom, and is the result of the *One eternal infinite Will*. But in that case belief in our duty is really belief in God, his rationality and faithfulness; *he* creates in our minds the feelings, perceptions, and laws of thought constituting the world of our consciousness. All our life is *his* life, our thoughts, so far as they are good and true, are thought in him. From this point of view the world too is seen in a new light: though the earlier idealism remains, with its negation of a dead mass, a material nature, and a blind destiny, it is no longer the ego that creates the world by its imagination, but it is the life of God that is visible to the religious eye, no less in the outer than in the inner world; the world is no longer the unreal shadow of my perfectly free and absolute ego, but the manifold appearance of the one divine life and light, of which I see the reflection within me and without, in the whole realm of kindred spirits with like conceptions and feelings. In this way subjective idealism is transformed into a mystical pantheism, most nearly akin to that idealised Spinozism found in Herder and Schleiermacher. But what in Herder was put forward dogmatically in opposition to Kant's critical philosophy, is in Fichte the result of the logical following out of critical idealism itself. Fichte's philosophy fell in with the tendency of the time, and helped on new developments of thought, whilst Herder's had the stream against it and remained unnoticed.

Fichte's change of view necessarily gave quite a new shape to his theory of religion. His former stiff moralism, according to which the only possible creed is a cheerful fulfilment of duty in active life, gave place to a religious mysticism quite averse to active life. In his *Grundzügen des gegenwärtigen Zeitalters* (1804), where the stern condemnation of the *Aufklärung* follows quite the track of Romanticism, religion is said to consist, not in any form of action, but in the view of the world as the differentiated manifestation of the one divine Being, or a metaphysic of the supersensible with the corresponding disposition of the heart; the love of the religious man is rooted in the one divine basal life, and hence he is raised both above the imperative laws and the low pains of nature, and every moment he is in immediate full possession of eternal life with all its blessedness. The nature of religion is more fully expounded and more definitely marked off from ethics and metaphysics in the work *Anweisung zum seligen Leben* (1806). In it Fichte distinguishes five ways of regarding the world: the lowest is the ordinary realistic view of the senses. The second is that of imperative law, finding the ground and purpose of the phenomenal world in a regulative law (Kant's position). The view of true morality ranks higher; according to it, the law is not merely imperative, but also creative, a vital impulse constituting the man swayed by it the image and revelation of the divine Being (position of Jacobi and the great poets). The fourth view is that of religion, which beholds in all manifestations of the true and good, the one life of God, and, by feeling, has experience of it, as the power of holy life and love. Lastly, the fifth view is that of science, which raises the connection of the finite with the one divine life, directly felt in faith, into a matter of knowledge, and makes it the object of clear conviction. Religion shares with this scientific view of the world the characteristic of not being directly active but contemplative, a peaceful view, remaining within the heart and not directly inciting to any definite action; religion is, however, superior to science in this particular, that it does not confine itself to contemplation but becomes a practical energy, the will to do all and every duty as the will of God for us and in us; religion is, in a word, the love of God, in which man feels God within him as a quickening spirit, and surrenders his whole personality to God. Fichte, it is true, describes this devout love of God, just like Spinoza, as absorption into God, as being fused and blended with him, so that it is really God's own love to Himself, which becomes conscious in man in the form of feeling. But even as this mystical oneness with God, Fichte's ethical idealism remains in so far intact, that the devout love of God is by no means exhausted in inactive emotion or calm contemplation, but is represented as the source of a joyful and active love of man; "moral action flows from it as quietly and calmly as the light from the sun." But this love founded on religion does not love everything in man without distinction; it hates everything base and mean, but believes in the existence and the development of the divine germ in every man, and so becomes the source of glad and hopeful labour for the elevation of the human race. Thus this warm and optimistic enthusiasm for humanity, based upon religious feeling, formed in the end the meeting-point of Kant's disciple Fichte and his opponent Herder; and in proportion as Schleiermacher rose above the æsthetic subjectivity of Romanticism, he too ranged himself definitely on their side; so that these three noble thinkers stand at the opening of the century as joint prophets of that truth which was to be the distinctive sign of the coming generations.

CHAPTER V.

SCHELLING'S PHILOSOPHY OF NATURE AND THEOSOPHY.

In the same year as Fichte's work on *Die Bestimmung des Menschen*, appeared SCHELLING'S *System des transcendentalen Idealismus* (1800), in which the objective idealism, first suggested in Fichte's work, was reduced to a system. This philosophy also claimed to be idealism, for it enunciated the principle, that all knowledge must be deduced from consciousness, by making the action of intelligence the object of intellectual contemplation. But just as Fichte had distinguished the absolute from the finite ego, which he conceived as the differentiated manifestation of the one divine life, so Schelling's Intelligence, by whose action the world is to be explained, is not only the human but the absolute Intelligence, and its action is not simply to produce ideal conceptions but to create the real world of nature and history. On the other hand, this divine Intelligence must not be thought of as apart from that of the human ego, but is related to it as the whole to a part or the original to a copy; and thus, Schelling holds, we can regard the functions of consciousness producing our ideal world as the copies and symbols of the forces and laws conditioning the generative process of the real world. If nature is visible spirit, and spirit is invisible nature, it appeared possible to explain the genesis of the real world, or nature outside us, by the contemplation of the action of the ego in forming propositions and definitions, in the same way as Fichte's theory of science (*Wissenschaftslehre*) had explained the genesis of the world of consciousness. This is what Schelling tried to do in the first part of his *System des transcendentalen Idealismus*. By the method of the Fichtean deduction of consciousness a philosophy of nature is propounded, in which the genesis of nature is traced in an ascending scale from the elemental forces of matter to the production of organic animal and conscious life. The second part supplies the corresponding practical philosophy, dealing with the action of human freedom in history. But in this action of individual free agents law or necessity prevails unconsciously, by means of which, from the play of the volition of individuals, there is ultimately produced an harmonious order, undesigned by them. This implies that all free action is ultimately based upon some common element guiding the orderly development of the whole. Such a synthesis, or pre-established harmony, of the subjective and objective, of conscious freedom and unconscious necessity, must depend upon something higher than either, which can only be the *absolute identity* of both. It is the "eternally unconscious" which is the root of all intelligences and the basis of law and order in their freedom, but which, being absolutely simple, can never be the object of knowledge but only of faith. At no point in history is it visibly manifested, but it is revealed continually throughout its whole course. But can we not somewhere get a direct intuition of this harmony of freedom and necessity? Certainly, answers Schelling, following Kant's Critique of Judgment, viz., in art. In artistic creation conscious and unconscious action so far coincide that the artistic product, though the work of freedom, is the end aimed at by nature's necessity. The infinite harmony striven after in the endless chain of historical acts, has become a finite manifestation in the beauty of the work of art. In æsthetic contemplation is objectively reflected the original identity of the conscious and unconscious, of nature and freedom, underlying all separations of them in consciousness.

When the absolute Identity had once been thus raised above the ego and nature as their higher unity and common basis, it was an easy step to formulate the new "Philosophy of Identity," in which consciousness was no longer taken as the starting-point, as in the transcendental philosophy, but the Absolute implied in it. Moreover, in his form of treatment Schelling went over from Kant to Dogmatism, as Fichte had gone over to Spinoza. As Spinoza in his Ethics begins at once without any deduction, with the definition of Substance, in order to draw deductions from it, so Schelling now starts with the proposition, that absolute reason is the indifference of subjective and objective. It is the end of all antitheses, it is the world as the eternal and unchanging unity of the real and the ideal. Hence the Absolute cannot be grasped by reflection, by analytic or synthetic thought, but only by "intellectual intuition," which, as the copy of the absolute, is likewise itself the unity of the ideal and real. By this method, which he pronounces the only truly philosophic one, Schelling attempts to derive differentiated Being from the unity of the absolute Identity. That this attempt was foredoomed to failure is manifest; if it lies at all within the range of our powers of knowledge, to trace the genesis of the world from the Absolute (which must be denied), this would in any case be rendered least possible by the assumption of this empty abstract conception of the Absolute as the simple indifference of opposites; how by its means the rich variety of the real world could be explained, is quite inconceivable. This was felt soon after by Schelling himself, and it led him to a theosophic reconstruction of his philosophy of Identity, though he only replaced one error by another, or rather substituted mythological poetry for philosophic thought. Before following this further step of Schelling's, we must glance at his theory of religion, as developed from the more sober point of view of the philosophy of Identity.

In his treatise *Methode des akademischen Studiums* (1803) Schelling has occasion to speak of religion, and treats it, unlike Schleiermacher, not from the subjective and psychological, but from the objective and historical point of view. In accordance with the then universally accepted philosophy of history, he makes history begin with a golden age of innocence, the unity of man with nature. Thereupon followed, after a universal fall, the epoch of disruption between mind and nature, of the painful consciousness of misery and guilt. The reconciliation of this disruption by faith in Providence began with Christianity, the central idea of which is God become man, in the sense that "the eternal Son, born of the being of the Father of all things, is the finite itself as it is in the eternal contemplation of God, and which appears as a suffering God subject to the conditions of time, who in his highest manifestation, that is in Christ, closes the world of the finite and opens that of the infinite, or the reign of the spirit." The Incarnation must not, therefore, be regarded as an individual event in time; it would in that case have no meaning, since God is above all time; but it is an incarnation from eternity; and though Christ is its highest point, and so also the beginning of its complete realisation, the perfect intelligibility, as historical events, of the rise of Christianity and of the person Jesus remains unimpaired thereby. Thus Schelling wishes in general clearly to distinguish the idea of Christianity, which can only be known from its entire history, from its first appearance as attested in the Biblical writings, and for this very reason advocates the free historical interpretation of these writings. Since the Christian idea is not dependent upon this one event, but is universal and absolute, it cannot, says Schelling, make any difference to its truth whether we consider the books of the Bible authentic or not, whether their narratives record actual events or Jewish myths, or even whether their matter conforms to the idea of Christianity or not; if Christianity had not always been considered a merely temporal phenomenon, we should have made much more progress towards the historical appreciation of the important documents relating to its origin. The task before us cannot be to restore these original forms, as the *Aufklärung* supposes, but to set the eternal idea free from the wrappings which have hitherto enveloped it, and to enable its ideal kernel to shape for itself new forms in the spirit of the present, a task to which the existing relations of philosophy and poetry to religion already point. In this distinction between the permanent idea in Christianity and its perishable envelope, and in the demand for the free development of the former out of the latter, Schelling is in complete agreement with Lessing and Herder, Kant, Fichte, and Schleiermacher; but whilst these thinkers found the idea of Christianity in moral or religious humanism, Schelling sought it in a speculative theory of the relation of the finite to the infinite, and thus entered upon the disastrous path of the intellectualistic theory of religion which was further developed by Hegel. Connected with this was Schelling's depreciation of the value of the historical side of Christianity, especially of the early Biblical records, which suffers him almost to sever all connection with ecclesiastical Christianity. Herder, with a true instinct, had already protested against a similar error on the part of Kant; and we shall see later that Schleiermacher's theology was indebted to this effort to effect a closer union between idea and history for its superiority over the idealistic philosophy of religion and for its profounder influence on the life of the Church.

The problem of the explanation of the finite from the infinite never ceased to occupy Schelling after the formulation of his philosophy of identity in 1801. The consciousness of his failure to solve it is already betrayed in his treatise on

Philosophie und Religion (1804), where the genesis of the world from God is explained by the aid of the Platonic myth of the declension of the ideas or souls from the divine unity. That this explanation explains nothing is evident; for the possibility of a declension presupposes the existence of the finite. The possibility of such a declension remained inconceivable as long as the conception of the absolute was adhered to as pure and simple identity. An alteration of this conception was therefore necessary on internal grounds, but it was actually brought about by Schelling's study of the theosophy of Jakob Böhme, one of the fundamental principles of which was, that God is not a simple but a living unity, comprehending distinctions within itself. From this new point of view Schelling wrote his *Untersuchungen über das Wesen der menschlichen Freiheit* (1809). The indifference of opposites, he now teaches, is not as yet God's actual being, but only its primal source (or *Urgrund*, to use Böhme's term). This unity differentiates God himself into the antitheses of nature and intelligence, which only when combined constitute the actual life of God. Moreover, nature in God, as in us, precedes intelligence as its Basis, and without it personality is as little conceivable in God as in us; for personality depends upon the combination of a self-contained principle with an independent Basis. This nature in God is as such simply a blind, unreasoning instinct. By it we can explain the residue of reality never resolvable into reason, the irregularities underlying all order in the world, as a chaos never wholly subdued. The desire for reconciliation on the part of this dark Basis produces reason, which, when united with the instinct of nature, becomes free, creative, almighty will, and reduces to order the forces of chaos. But since the blind will of this Basis continually reacts, and only gradually gives way to reason, the conversion of nature into spirit can only proceed by degrees in the various grades of the natural world. All beings, as springing from the dark Basis in God, have an individual will of their own; but, as also originating in God's reason, a universal will. From the increase and disunion of these two forces in man results evil, which has thus potentially its origin in the Basis of God, but actually in man's own act in separating himself from the Universal will by an act of self-determination out of time, and by that act simultaneously determining his individual character, which is manifested in his life in time. On the struggle of these two principles turns the world's history. After the primitive age of natural innocence, the will of the Basis, or natural self-will, obtains the supremacy in the age of heathenism, till the divine light, or the word of the divine Reason, appears in a personal mediator for the restoration of the connection of creation with God. Then the struggle between the divine and dæmoniacal kingdoms reaches its height; but in this struggle the physical glory of the old world passes away, and God reveals himself in the new world as the victorious spirit of the good. The goal of history is the reconciliation of the natural self-will and the universal will in love, which is the higher unity of both, and by which alone God can really be all in all.

While we must acknowledge that this theosophy contains profound ideas, which have influenced theological and philosophical thinkers (Baader, Martensen, Rothe, Schopenhauer), we still cannot deny that these ideas are mixed up with much mythological poetry, which fails to satisfy either philosophical thought or the religious consciousness. The notion of the divine Intelligence issuing from a dark Basis of nature and blind instinct grates upon religious feeling as a reminiscence of heathen theogonies, by which the spiritual and ethical purity of the Christian idea of God would be marred. This defect remains substantially uncorrected in the final form of Schelling's philosophy, though on this point the philosopher designedly adheres very closely to the terminology of ecclesiastical dogmatics. As this "philosophy of mythology and revelation" was only published after Schelling's death, about the middle of this century, and has had no influence upon the development of theology, any account of it is foreign to our purpose.

CHAPTER VI.

HEGEL'S LOGICAL EVOLUTIONARY IDEALISM.

HEGEL started from the earlier of Schelling's positions. He agreed with his fellow Swabian and fellow-student that the subject of philosophy is not merely phenomena, or the consciousness of the ego, but the Absolute, which unfolds the wealth of its content in the world of nature and history. Hegel, however, conceived the Absolute, not as the "indifference" of nature and spirit, but as spirit itself, which, as the rational source of nature, must be prior to nature; while, as the self-existent spirit of the conscious subject, it must have proceeded from nature. Spinoza had conceived the Absolute as Substance, Fichte as Ego or Subject, while Schelling had blended these antitheses in his neutral "Indifference." Hegel agreed with Schelling in his neutralisation of opposites in the higher unity of the Absolute, but argued that this unity must not be simply asserted without proof, "as if shot from a pistol"; but the thing needed was to show how Substance, or self-existent Reason, can become a subject, by evolving its correlate nature, and passing through it, generate itself as a subject or self-conscious spirit. Passive "indifference," excluding opposites, is thus changed into the self-development of spirit, passing through its opposite to a unity at once destroying and preserving the opposition. In conjunction with this change in matter there is an alteration in method. Hegel was indeed at one with Schelling as to the unsatisfactoriness of the philosophy of reflection, which proceeded from the antithesis of thought and being, and was accordingly incapable of apprehending being itself, and could never get beyond the antitheses of finite and infinite, appearance and actual being, world and God. But he was as much opposed to the "intellectual intuition" which Schelling wished to substitute for rational reflection as the sole philosophical method. This intellectual intuition, which is really an æsthetic condition of mind most nearly akin to Schleiermacher's religious intuition of the universe, cannot, Hegel argues, be the basis of philosophy, which is concerned with concepts, and is therefore the matter of thought. Only philosophic thought must not be something abstract, perpetuating the antitheses in their hostile exclusiveness, but something concrete, resolving antitheses and tracing concepts in their process through their opposite. If thought, according to the philosophy of identity, is one with being, and if the essential nature of the absolute Spirit consists in living development, then, Hegel infers, the philosophic method of thought must also consist in the dialectical development of concepts; hence the philosopher has to imitate in the dialectical method the self-development of the absolute Reason; or, more strictly, his attitude is that of a spectator observing the objective active process of pure thought, this self-development of the absolute idea through the process of the world's self-genesis. All the capriciousness of merely subjective thinking is thereby excluded; it is the logical necessity of absolute Reason, as it develops into reality, which is reproduced in the philosopher's thought. Herein, according to Hegel, consists the only truly "rational" thought, which combines the analytical reflection of the understanding with synthetic intuition, in order to carry the absolute unity of the one through the oppositions of the other up to the derivative unity of the "concrete idea." Hegel thus supplemented and corrected Schelling's intuitive method by Fichte's dialectical reflection; from Fichte's *Wissenschaftslehre* he took the general plan of his dialectic, the movement of thought through Thesis, Antithesis, and Synthesis; but what in Fichte was the movement of the subjective consciousness to the formation of its ideal world, became in Hegel the movement of absolute Thought, the self-development of which into the world of actuality repeats itself in the movement of the dialectical thought of the philosopher to the formation of his system. Here, as in Fichte, the world is simply the product of the development of logical thought, though not, as in Fichte, of the thought of the ego, but of the absolute Spirit; it is not subjective, but absolute logical idealism. But in contradistinction to Schelling, for whom the Absolute was passive identity and intuition the method of philosophical knowledge, Hegel's *logical idealism* is at the same time *evolutionary* in two senses; the actual is the evolution of the absolute Reason in and through nature and history, and philosophy is the imitation of this evolution in the dialectical movement of ideas.

The Hegelian philosophy was the most logical and most fruitful working out of the idealism which proceeded from Kant's *Critique of Pure Reason*, which made the understanding the lawgiver of nature. It was natural that this philosophy should produce an immense impression upon its time, and that it should be looked upon as containing the solution of all problems. It gave the thinking mind the exalted consciousness of perfectly comprehending the world, of fixing the place in its system of ideas for all the realities of nature and history, and of constructing *à priori* all the laws of phenomena in conformity with the laws of thought. And to the practical mind it gave the reassuring certainty that its sublimest ideas were not merely subjective postulates and imperatives never to be actually realised, but the eternal truths of reason, which, as the all-ruling Power, infallibly carries out its plans in the world of reality, and has realised itself in the past, and will continue to do so in the future. The proposition that the rational is actual, and the actual rational, expressed a more optimistic faith in the reign of reason in the world than any other philosophical system since Leibnitz had offered. In this ideal optimism a generation weary of endless discussion found the longed-for reconciliation of the intense but unpracticable and disappointed idealism of the 18th century with the actual forces of history, whose awful realities idealistic enthusiasts had been compelled, by the great events of the time, to remember and respect. If reason is everywhere the deepest basis and the guiding law of reality, it need no longer be looked for, as Kant taught, in a Golden Age of the future, in an Eternal Peace which seemed never coming, in a perfect condition of civil and political society, not as yet discovered; and equally little in a Golden Age of the past, in a happy state of nature, in which Rousseau and, to some extent, even Herder, had revelled. From all such supernatural and extravagant speculations, toward which an age of enthusiasm had directed its gaze in hope or sorrow, to the disregard of the historical world, Hegel called his contemporaries back to the firm ground of the historical life of man, and showed them how a loving eye might there discover undreamed-of stores of rational ideas and working ideals, in which at all times and in every nation the sovereign Reason of the world had been able to attain its lofty ends, half unconsciously to man himself; though each end, as soon as reached, must be seen to be but an imperfect stage in the development, and must serve as means to a yet higher end. From this standpoint a far profounder view could be taken of history, and a far juster estimate formed of its varied phenomena. In fact, no other branch of study owes to Hegel so much as historical inquiry. The arbitrary treatment of details which, in the case of Hegel and his immediate disciples, crept in, under the influence of his philosophical idea, had of course to be corrected by more exact historians; but the lasting gain is rich and manifold. It is a deeper insight into historical life generally, as an orderly development of the one common spirit of nations and ages, ruled by ideas, and aiming at necessary common ends; it is a more penetrating glance, through the confused play of phenomena, into the essence of man and things, into the dominant thoughts which are the controlling motives underlying even the apparent discord of individual passions; it is the unprejudiced appreciation of the necessity even of the oppositions and conflicts, the errors and passions of men, because, as Hegel says, with Heraclitus, war is the father of all things, and only through the strife of partial rights and one-sided truths can the whole truth of the idea gradually struggle into existence; it is finally an intelligent reverence for the heroic figures in history, in whom is embodied the genius of nations or ages, who, as instruments of a higher power, have roused the thought slumbering in the souls of all, have given it clear expression, and in mighty deed have summoned it to life. No such historians as Leopold Ranke, or Thomas Carlyle, or Christian Ferdinand Baur are conceivable without the Hegelian philosophy of history.

This profoundly suggestive conception of history has been of especial service in the departments of religious and ecclesiastical historical study. Hegel teaches us to see in the history of religion an orderly development of divine revelation in man's consciousness of God, a development in which no point is wholly without truth, though none has the whole pure truth; gradually divine truth reveals itself to the human consciousness in ever greater purity, but always veiled under imperfect conceptions and symbols. The positive religions are accordingly neither inventions of human caprice and cunning nor expressions of the accidental emotions of individual devout souls; but, like law and custom, art and science, they are necessary creations of the peculiar common spirit of the different nations, and can therefore be properly understood only in close connection with the general history of the development of human society. Christianity is so far an exception, that in it the spirit, not of a single nation only but of mankind as a whole, becomes conscious of its essential relation to God, and it is thus the absolute religion of revealed truth; though in it, too, this truth is always clothed and enveloped in conceptions which are more or less inadequate to the idea. When once the whole history of the pre-Christian and Christian religions is conceived as the religious spirit in the process of evolution, having divine reason for its source and human reason,—*i.e.*, man's true consciousness of his relation to God,—for its end, the opposition between rational faith neglecting history and historic faith contrary to reason,—which was the point at issue between the *Aufklärung* and its opponents,—is then perceived to be a misleading abstraction which must be replaced by rational historic faith and historical rational faith. Thus Hegel's philosophy of religion, like his philosophy of law and history, seeks to reconcile the claims of personal freedom of thought with the claims of an authority that has grown up in the course of history and acquired validity in society; it seeks to mediate between subjective and objective reason, between personal liberty and reverence for the social forces of history.

We must not, however, omit to look at the dark as well as the bright side of Hegel's logical idealism. The assertion of the rationality of everything actual was so one-sidedly optimistic as necessarily to produce the reaction of Schopenhauer's pessimism. Hegel's optimism led to a sluggish conservatism, a passive tolerance of the existing state of things simply because it exists; it could be fair and tolerant towards all historical phenomena except the *Aufklärung* and its rationalistic criticism of tradition; its dislike of abstract subjectivism might be carried so far as to reinstate faith in every authority, no matter how irrational; and these results of his system were so obvious that, though not intended by Hegel himself, they at once showed themselves in his school and disastrously perpetuated and increased the confusion of ideas produced by Romanticism. But apart from these practical consequences, the question arises, Is the foundation of this absolute logical idealism sound? Is the position tenable, that thought and being are identical and the whole world only the self-evolution of pure thought? Hegel makes the transition from logic, the region of pure thought, to the world of reality by means of the proposition that the idea externates itself and evolves nature from itself as its correlate; but this is really a phrase that explains nothing, to which Schelling (like Fichte) unanswerably replied, that it is impossible to deduce the real from a mere idea. But if this proposition is untenable, the whole foundation of logical idealism is cut from under it, the identification of the real evolution of the world with the logical evolution of ideas is made impossible, the dialectical method based on the identification is a failure, the whole system which stands or falls with this method is doomed, and a radical reform of idealism unavoidable. To this extent the reaction of post-Hegelian empiricism was fully justified, provided only that it did not go so far as again to deny altogether the ideal element in knowledge and philosophy, and so surrender the lasting results of the Kantian critical philosophy. We shall return again to this point in another connection.

The exclusively logical character of Hegel's philosophy, with its resolution of all life into conceptual relations and processes of thought, is the ground of the weakness of Hegel's theory of religion, viz., its intellectual character, its exclusive accentuation of the religious concept, and its failure to see that religion is essentially a matter of the heart. According to Hegel, religion has the same subject-matter as philosophy, yet not, like the latter, in the form of logical concepts, but of intuitions (*Vorstellungen*) in which the truth is conveyed for the world at large; religion is therefore to a certain extent an exoteric philosophy for the general community, while philosophy is the esoteric knowledge of the truth of religion. The common content of both is "the knowledge possessed by the finite spirit of its nature as absolute spirit," which also presupposes "the absolute spirit's knowledge of itself in the finite spirit," a self-communication or revelation of the divine spirit in the human. But man's knowledge of the God revealing Himself in him is not reached at once in a final and complete form; it is developed in a gradual advance of the consciousness from the worthlessness and slavery of our natural existence to the truth and freedom of a spirit at one with God. This necessary process of self-deliverance from bondage to nature, of coming to oneself and becoming conscious of our divine nature, furnishes the proof of the truth of religion and of its foundation in man's nature. In his description of this development of the religious consciousness Hegel distinguishes three stages—feeling, intuition, thought (*Gefühl, Vorstellung, Gedanke*). Feeling he describes as the immediate form in which a content of consciousness is made ours; and he is far from disputing that the true content of religion, in order to be our personal possession, must be an emotion, must be in the heart, as the permanent seat of feeling and willing. But this direct form, feeling, must not be regarded as the whole of religion, or as its distinctive excellence. For this form can have the most various contents, the basest as well as the highest, the truest as well as the most worthless. "As the object of feeling, God is in nothing superior to the worst thing; the kingliest flower springs from the same soil as the most rampant weed." Feeling Hegel does not even regard as specifically human, but as the sense-form of consciousness common to men and animals; in it only the individual subjectivity asserts itself, desiring merely its own enjoyment, instead of forgetting self and living in objective thought and action. Hence feeling, though the necessary lowest grade in consciousness, is one that must be overcome and superseded by intuition and thought. (This view of feeling is clearly based upon a false psychology, connected with the fundamental error of logical idealism; instead of recognising the co-ordination and interaction of the emotional and the rational side of our spiritual nature, the former is made a subordinate stage of the latter, which is plainly contrary to all experience and eminently prejudicial to a true appreciation of religious experience.)

By intuition, or inward perception, consciousness, according to Hegel's further description of the religious process, converts the content, with which it was directly united in feeling, into an object distinct from the subject. Intuition uses sense-forms derived from direct perception, but in order to convey spiritual truth, a higher rational sense; it is therefore truth under sense-symbols. It presents spirit, which transcends time and space, as subject to the conditions of time and space (*e.g.* in sacred history), or under a multiplicity of contradictory conditions (*e.g.* man's freedom and dependence), each of which taken by itself is accidental and irrational, since only in their unity can we perceive their truth as phases of the one Spirit. Hence intuition is an inadequate form of truth, and must be replaced by conceptual thought. But in thought Hegel again distinguishes the reflection of the understanding from truly rational or speculative thought. The former perpetuates the opposition of infinite and finite, nature and spirit, etc., and cannot effect their union. But thereby the infinite, conceived as outside and beyond the finite, is itself limited and so made finite; and the ego, conscious of itself as the author of this act of limitation, appears itself to be the Infinite; the antitheses change places, the humble consciousness of finiteness becomes proud self-deification (comp. Feuerbach's anthropologism). But religion demands a point of view which shall be both the negation of the ego in its self-centred isolation and at the same time the affirmation of its true self in God. These conditions are fulfilled by speculative thought, which includes the finite, as an element of the divine life, and the infinite, as the living process by which it first becomes and then ceases to be finite. If the absolute self-conscious spirit thus appears from our finite point of view as a result which has been brought about by nature and finite spirit, in reality it is the Alpha, the necessarily presupposed basis of the finite world. God is the unity of the natural and the spiritual, yet not such a unity as to place the two on an equality, for the unity is spirit, not some *tertium quid* in which both are neutralised. God is, on the one hand (as finite) one side of the antithesis, and again (as absolute) that which includes the other side, and so is the unity of both (nature and finite spirit). This clearly indicates the difference between Hegel's speculative idea of God and Schelling's Absolute as the identity of spirit and nature; the latter is the neutral identity in which both sides of the antithesis are equally absorbed; Hegel's Absolute is the spiritual principle which creates and dominates the antithesis, not so as to be related in the same way to both sides, but so as to make nature, as its own correlate, an instrument for the purpose of the spirit in which it reproduces itself. It cannot be denied that this conception of God is at least more allied to theism than to what is generally understood by "pantheism." So far undoubtedly Hegel was to some extent justified in maintaining that there was no material contradiction between his philosophy and Christian dogma; though we cannot deny that he optimistically underrated the difference.

Hegel's Philosophy of Religion most nearly approaches Christian doctrine in the profound chapter on worship, which he regards as the active union of man with God by the voluntary surrender of himself to the divine revelation experienced within him. Worship is primarily an inward act, or faith, this living communion of the ego with God. It may begin from some external witness or authority, but then it is only formal faith; true faith has as its basis and subject-matter nothing accidental or merely traditional, but the living witness of the spirit. "The non-spiritual cannot by its nature constitute the subject-matter of faith. If God speaks, he speaks spiritually, for spirit reveals itself to spirit only." The end and aim of worship is self-sacrifice, self-renunciation, and the appropriation of the divine grace as the real strength of our own goodness, as the Holy Spirit. This inward sentiment then finds its expression in moral action also; hence religious faith and worship have everywhere the profoundest influence upon the habits and laws of society; want of freedom in religion leads to want of freedom in the State; freedom in the State and not in religion leads to conflicts, such as have arisen between the modern State and the Catholic Church. In this recognition of the historical and social importance of religion Hegel's religious philosophy compares favourably with Schleiermacher's subjective mysticism.

After discussing, in the first part of his Philosophy of Religion, the nature of religion in general, Hegel proceeds in the second part to speak of "specific religion," *i.e.*, religion in its pre-Christian forms. These various positive religions are partial representations of special elements in the idea of religion, not indeed adequate to it, but necessary stages in its evolution. Hegel distinguishes immediate religion, or the religion of nature, corresponding to the childhood of humanity; then the religion of spiritual individuality, corresponding to the period of youth, or of growing spiritual freedom; to this class belong the religion of the sublime (the Jewish), of the beautiful (the Greek), and of the expedient (the Roman). Finally comes "the absolute religion," or Christianity, in which the idea itself finds manifestation; Hegel also calls it "the revealed religion," because in it God is known as He who reveals himself in our spirit as truth and love; and again "the religion of truth and freedom," because in it the spirit recognises itself in its true nature and thus at the same time attains its freedom. In his account of Christianity he treats of God, firstly, *per se*, as He is in eternity (kingdom of the Father); then in His manifestation in history (kingdom of the Son); lastly, in His return from manifestation into Himself, in the process of reconciliation, or as the spirit of the Church, which is the eternal in time. We must look rather more closely at this philosophy of Christianity, as we shall often meet traces of it in the history of theology.

Hegel regards the Church's doctrine of the Trinity as supplying the stages of the speculative idea of God; the self-contained unity, self-differentiation, and the absorption of the difference into the concrete identity of the differentiated one. Of the three Persons, he expressly states that they must not be taken literally, but as the figurative expression of the true thought—that God is not abstract unity, the identity without difference conceived by the understanding, or the supermundane omnipotence of the Jewish religion, but "eternal love," which is itself when in its correlative. This nature of God is a mystery to the sensuous mode of thought and to the understanding, clinging to differences as final, but not to the reason, which finds in all life a continual generation and destruction of contradiction, and therefore an analogy of the triune life of God. It is easy to see that this speculative interpretation of the Trinity is nearly identical with that given by Lessing and Schelling, according to which the Son is the world as an object of the divine thought, the intelligible world, called also in Philo the Son of God.

The element of difference, already implicit in the nature of God, comes into definite existence in nature, the correlative in which spirit alienates itself, and completes itself in man as conscious disunion. The orthodox doctrine of the original state and fall of the first man, Hegel says, must be taken as the symbol of what holds of man generally as such. The idea of man, his design and function, is to be spirit, to think and to will rationally, to learn to know God and nature; but if this idea of man is imagined to be his original condition in time, this is a mythical notion. For by its very nature spirit cannot be actually existent from the beginning. At first it is still absorbed in nature, and must, therefore, in order actually to become rational thought and free will, withdraw itself from nature and come into conflict with it. An original direct union with nature, so far from being a condition of superiority, is the condition of barbarism and wild desire, unworthy of spirit, and diametrically opposed to its higher vocation. To this animal insensibility, to the want of moral consciousness, must be ascribed the innocence of man as the child of nature. The loss of this was therefore not at all an irremediable misfortune, but a divine necessity. The ever-recurring history of man's freedom is that of his progress from this insensibility of his earliest years to the light of consciousness, or more particularly, that he learns to know good and evil. This advance from *naïve* consciousness to moral consciousness, with its contradiction between will and duty, its guilt and remorse, its discipline and labour, does indeed at first seem to be a calamity; but this is only one side of the matter; the other side is, that within this calamity lies the source of the remedy. Evil therefore did not spring from the accidental act of the first man, nor is it transmitted by inheritance to his descendants, but is involved, without any mediation whatsoever, in the freedom of each individual as the first mode of its appearance. For freedom arises solely through consciousness, and consciousness is the act of the disunion of the ego, as individual will, from the universal and rational will. In this disunion within, and in relation to everything else, both freedom and evil have their seat; it is the source of moral disease and also of its cure, of the reconciliation of the contradiction.

Like the contradiction, the reconciliation can only take place by a process within the human spirit. Still Hegel finds a sufficient reason for its being conceived in the creed of the Christian Church as the external history of the incarnation of God in Christ, as the atoning death of the God-man. For the reconciliation cannot be produced from within man himself, by his subjective will and action, which never gets beyond the contradiction; but the consciousness must be brought to look at and in faith appropriate the reconciliation as a supposition certain in itself, as the objective truth of mankind's actual reconciliation with God and by God as reconciling love. Man can feel himself reconciled with God and received into union with Him only when he sees in God a being no longer foreign to himself and keeping mankind at a distance, but Spirit and Love, in which man's nature as spirit and free is also affirmed. But this unity of the divine and human nature can become an immediate certainty in the religious man only when it takes the form of God appearing to him as man and man as God, and indeed in the contemplation of a concrete person in whom both are conjoined; thus the orthodox conception of the deity and humanity of Christ, is explained as an inner necessity of the religious consciousness in its Christian stage. Still Hegel is by no means of opinion that the historical Christ was really a supernatural being in the sense of the dogma of the two natures, but he holds the historical Jesus to be essentially a man, who was conscious of being himself one with the divine will, and in this consciousness of union with God proclaimed, in the language of inspiration, the highest religious truths; by his teaching and life he brought home to men, as the truth and the necessary foundation of their religious consciousness, the doctrine that God is not supermundane and far off, but present in his kingdom, that He is love, and that the certainty of this must be realised in each man's own breast. But it was by faith only that the words of the man Jesus were rightly and spiritually understood; and this spiritual faith was the fruit of Christ's death. His death was the crucial point in the development of the Christian consciousness, when the great transition was effected from faith in a mere man to faith in the God-man, for it brought clearly before men's minds the truth of the unity of the divine and human natures. And it was just because this consciousness of the reconciliation of God with the world, so fundamental to the Christian faith, dawned upon the Church in its full spiritual significance only after the death of Jesus, that Christians came to regard this death itself as the central point of the reconciliation, and beheld in it the absolute love, which in the finite itself overcomes the finite—death, and so negatives again this negation.

But though it was intelligible and, looked at historically, necessary, that the Christian Church should contemplate the idea of reconciliation in the form of a particular occurrence in history, it was nevertheless an incongruity to conceive what was really eternal and of universal validity as having happened once only and in the case of one individual. This incongruity was in the first instance partially corrected by the two additional doctrines of Christ's second advent and of the mission and perpetual presence of the Holy Spirit. By these two conceptions the limitation to one external event put upon the idea of reconciliation in the history of Christ was removed, the reconciliation being made universal, perpetual, and inward, just as the one fall of the first man was supplemented by the idea of all men's inheritance of Adam's sin. This addition was indeed only an external correction, one partial conception being added on to another equally partial. The essential thing, the real advance from the outward to the inward, can only come to pass by individual Christians personally going through this history or process, which they conceived at first as a divine history external to them and enacted for their sakes. By the enactment of the reconciliation as a subjective process in individuals themselves is realised the Christian Church. The Church is the institution having for its object that men come to the truth, and that the Holy Ghost become in them a living power, the knowledge and desire of the truth. The means of attaining this object is doctrine, in which the Church develops into conceptions (dogmas) the truth originally given as the direct witness of the spirit. Baptism declares that the world into which the child enters is not a hostile one, but the Church, in which evil is, as such, already overcome and God reconciled. It only remains for the individual to form himself upon the Church, by education and practice, and to habituate himself to the goodness and truth already existing in it. This constitutes his regeneration. The spirit is not directly and without mediation what it is designed to be ; the natural heart, by which man is held captive, is the foe to be striven against. The work of the Church is this very education of the spirit, so that truth may become more and more inwardly one with the man, with his will, and so his own personal knowledge and volition. Here we have no mere naked obligation, progress without an end, endeavour never to be fulfilled, as in the Kantian philosophy. Here evil is known to be in itself already overcome in the spirit (the Holy Spirit of the Church) ; and if the individual only makes his own will good by means of this Spirit, by believing in the reconciliation already accomplished, evil has for him personally disappeared and sin is felt to have been forgiven. This act is, on the one hand, the act of the individual, who sacrifices his self-will (dies with Christ), on the other, the act of the divine Spirit within him, which is the spirit of the individual so far as he has faith. In the Lord's Supper the Church celebrates this presence of God in the immediate self-consciousness of believers. But this reconciliation, accomplished in worship, as an inward certainty in the depths of the soul, must make itself felt in the world of nature and society. Moreover, the freedom of the spirit reconciled to God must be active, not merely a negative, monkish renunciation of the world, but must work positively, in permeating all secular interests with the Holy Spirit, and in moulding the world after the pattern of eternal truth. The harmonising of true religion with true secularity is effected in morals and science, which are the realisation of reason in the will and knowledge of society.

Thus the Hegelian philosophy of religion ends as it began, with the conviction that religion and Christianity, if taken in a deep and free spiritual sense, so far from being antagonistic to secular culture and knowledge, really form their source, foundation, and motive power, and, on the other hand, find in them their consummation, confirmation, and choicest fruit. Kant's idealistic philosophy had started with the emancipation of thought from the fetters of external authority, demanded by the *Aufklärung*, and with his sketch of "a religion within the limits of pure reason." But even Kant, bold critic as he was, had warned men not to confound *Aufklärung* with radical revolution, but to seek it in a just and orderly use of the understanding; and he had arrived by his investigation of the laws of reason at a point of view which was so far superior in ethical depth to the popular philosophy, and so essentially in touch with the Christian view of the world, that he was even able in his theory of religion to undertake what was really a defence of Christian doctrines, at any rate in respect of their ethical contents. Herder and Schleiermacher did justice to religious emotion and intuitive imagination, which Kant had slighted, and at the same time attempted to connect ideal religion more closely with the historical facts and the Biblical records of Christianity; still these thinkers (we are here speaking only of Schleiermacher's early period of Romanticism) were too much shut in by the horizon of a subjective piety to attain to a full appreciation of the historical development of Christianity. This was the side from which Schelling attacked the problem; like the ancient Gnostics, he tried to explain Christianity, from the most comprehensive point of view, as a phase of the general development of the world, not however without falling again into the Gnostics' error of resolving religion into cosmo-mythological processes. Hegel carefully avoided everything like Gnostic mythology, but carried on the great task of applying an objective historical method to the study of religion. Herein lay his strength and his lasting importance, while he was weak in the psychological analysis of the religious consciousness and the emotions influencing it. But though his theology, and even more that of his disciples, needed to be supplemented in this respect by the school of Schleiermacher, it was of great importance that Hegel clearly pointed out that the history of religion is a development of the rational spirit, under the guidance of ideas, and a development in closest connection with all other sides of social life. He thus accomplished what Herder had demanded, and an advance of the abstract subjectivity and the poor external pragmatism of the *Aufklärung* was thereby finally checked.

BOOK II.

THE EVOLUTION OF DOGMATIC THEOLOGY UNDER THE INFLUENCE OF IDEALISTIC PHILOSOPHY.

CHAPTER I.

THE THEOLOGY OF THE SCHOOL OF KANT.

THE Kantian philosophy influenced the whole theology of its time, but in very various ways, according as the one or the other of the tendencies of thought involved in it was followed by theologians,—whether it happened to be the sceptical, or the moral and rationalistic, or the theological utilitarian side of the system. The theological postulates based on utilitarian considerations, in which Kant, sceptic and rigorous moralist as he was, made conciliatory advances to popular thought, offered both to the conservative supernaturalists and the Wolfian neologists of the *Aufklärung* a welcome means of approaching this new philosophy and connecting themselves with it. In other respects the former of these parties adopted the scepticism of Kant's theoretical critique, and made it the foundation of their historical dogmatism, while they either simply rejected or else greatly limited the autonomous rationalism of the practical reason; the neologists, on the contrary, adopted Kant's rational ethics and ethical theory of religion, though they toned down the rigour of his ethics, on the lines of theological and philosophical utilitarianism, and tried, with more or less success, to bring the rationalism of his religious system into closer connection with historical Christianity. Hence originated the various shades of the *Rationalistic theology* derived from the school of Kant. It alone concerns us here; while the use made of the Kantian criticism in the cause of ecclesiastical and Biblical orthodoxy was so foreign to the spirit of this philosophy, and had so little influence on the development of theology, that we are justified in dismissing it with a passing mention.

We may notice as a curiosity that many theologians, both Protestant and Catholic, beheld in Kant's distinction between phenomena and noumena and his limitation of knowledge to the former, the means of rescuing the orthodox system from the onslaughts of neological doubt. Though in the world of phenomena three persons are not equal to one person, and one person cannot have two natures, still, they argued, the possibility of this cannot be disputed in the case of the Divine Persons, since they belong to the noumena, of which we know nothing except that in this realm everything is in all respects different from what prevails in the case of phenomena. A similar position was held by STORR and his colleagues and disciples, the so-called older Tübingen school, who exercised greater freedom with regard to ecclesiastical dogmas, but held all the more strictly to Biblical supernaturalism, which they rested upon the traditional theory of inspiration. They maintained their Biblical system against all the objections and doubts of the *Aufklärung* by an appeal to the Kantian philosophy; since, according to the critical philosophy, reason itself admits its inability to know anything of the supersensible, it has logically no right to protest against what has been made known to us concerning supersensible things by historical revelation; with regard to the practical reason, Kant himself allows that it demands a requiting Deity for the satisfaction of our desire for happiness, and is therefore in its own interest called upon to receive upon authority the historical revelation concerning God and his government of the world. Hence the truth of the Biblical doctrines stands higher than the critique of the speculative reason which confesses its own incompetence, and accords with the demands of the practical reason; it has therefore nothing to fear and nothing to expect from philosophy, but rests entirely upon the positive authority of a supernatural revelation, which has only to be first historically proved and then reduced to a system. Storr did this by putting together a dogmatic system, in the fashion of a mosaic, from detached Biblical texts, without caring for any other proof of his propositions, either by appealing to philosophy or to the religious consciousness. We cannot but recognise the strength of this position, which meets all rationalistic objections by a sceptical depreciation of reason; in all periods this standpoint of faith, founded purely upon authority, has been popular, but especially in those when philosophic thought was at a low ebb owing to the overweening flights of previous speculation. Its weak point is the unhistorical arbitrariness with which individual passages of Scripture, torn from their context, are used in proof of a system which is foreign to them, because unknown to any of the Biblical writers. This method of using the Scriptures as one uniform code of doctrine quite ignores the peculiarities and variety of the religious habit of thought of the Biblical authors, so different in point of time, place, and character. Hence this Biblical dogmatism could not survive a really historical examination of the Scriptures, such as was undertaken by the later Tübingen school. History had been the sole basis of the system of the older Tübingen school, and by means of history it was overthrown by the younger Tübingen school. Profound thinkers, like the youthful Schelling, had, indeed, before this clearly perceived how little this application of the Kantian philosophy to the service of theological dogmatism accorded with its real meaning and spirit; his ridicule of these pseudo-Kantians was not undeserved; and dislike of this movement may well have been one of the motives which soon began to lead Schelling himself to subordinate, and this too absolutely, the critical to the speculative side of Kant's system.

The thinker whose position was nearest that of Kant's philosophy of religion was the theologian and philosopher TIEFTRUNK. He held that the only possible foundation for a religion with any claim to universal truth is the consciousness of unconditional freedom and autonomy, by which we raise ourselves above the world of sense and become members of a world of spirits, or, indeed, even gods, as he says in the hyperbolical language of the then prevalent idealism, and differ from God, the supreme head of all intelligences, only in degree, not in kind; we have the same will and the same law as God, our existence and independent activity are alike unconditional, and we have by our own will an infinite object in our holiness, wisdom, and blessedness, which is also the object of God. But whilst God is pure intelligence and therefore his power of good is equal to his will of it, we are at the same time creatures of sense, and our power of execution on that account falls short of our autonomous reason. Thus the law of reason becomes a command to which both our sensuous inclination and the external world of sense are often opposed. Hence as intelligences we are supreme, and have no other reason for obeying the moral law than the demands of the dignity of our own personality. If we *could* satisfy this law in its infinitude, we should be all-sufficient in ourselves and have no need of a God. But as in reality it is our personal worth only that wholly depends upon our own will, while our circumstantial well-being is not in our own power, inasmuch as though we ought by merit to claim happiness we cannot accord it to ourselves, we are led to acknowledge God, who solves the contradiction between our ethical sovereignty and our natural dependence by making all things subsidiary to the end of created spirits and assigning them a natural condition corresponding to their personal merit. Here, just as in Kant, the existence of God and his government of the world are postulated to make up for our want of power over nature, while our moral nature, taken in itself, is conceived as so absolute as in its self-sufficiency to have no need of God. It is true that from this point of view faith in God, as thus established, our reason itself, and its autonomy, are traced back to a divine origin, but still the relation of the pre-supposed sovereign autonomy to the divine legislation is not made clear; ethical idealism and the religious mode of thought have no necessary connection, but move in parallel lines, sometimes supplementing and sometimes restricting each other.—Though the idea of God cannot be established by speculation, its certainty is grounded on ethical necessities of thought, for it forms the condition of the possibility of the supreme good, in which we are by our moral nature compelled to believe. Nor, again, is the further determination of our idea of God possible by the methods of ontology, but by those of ethical analogy—by our reasoning analogically from our own moral causality to the relation of the divine causality to the world, whereby we are able, at any rate symbolically, to describe the action though not the nature of God, his moral attributes, holiness, justice, goodness, and wisdom being first inferred, and then the ontological ones deduced. The doctrine of the Trinity is interpreted, with Kant, of the threefold relation of God—as Creator and Lawgiver, as Ruler, and as Judge. Further, the belief in immortality is rested, in Kantian fashion, upon its being the condition of the possibility of endless moral progress.

These doctrines, according to Tieftrunk, make up the essential contents of every religion, no religion being universally valid save as it rests upon the principle, cognisable by reason, of freedom and the moral law. From this he infers that Rationalism alone meets the requirements of religion; for religion does not originate in feeling, but solely in the spontaneity of the knowing faculty, and is therefore valuable only when the product of perfect insight and thorough conviction. "Religious feelings must be produced by knowledge, and not *vice versa*; the perception of the moral law, of the existence of God, and of our own immortality, is the first step, and produces in us an interest, which, as resulting from our recognition of these truths, we can call a religious emotion." But the theologian Tieftrunk could not rest satisfied with this formal and self-sufficient Rationalism. He endeavoured to find an opening for historical religion and its claim to revelation. In the first place, he showed in general that a revelation is logically conceivable and morally probable on the supposition of a declension of human morality so profound as to be remediable only by a direct divine proclamation of the moral law, together with the necessary outward means of securing its observance. Among the latter he includes miracles wrought on nature, which are considered quite possible, as the sensible effects of a supersensible cause, as our own free will operates in the world of sense as intelligible causality. When once supernaturalism, after its repulse at the hands of arrogant Rationalism, had thus been re-admitted by a back-door, it maintained its position, at any rate so far as the Christian religion is based, upon the historical testimony of the Biblical writings. Since these satisfy the moral criteria, *à priori* necessary, of a divine revelation, their acceptance may be regarded as rationally justified. Still, Tieftrunk is far from constructing upon this foundation a positive system of Biblical dogmas after the manner of Storr's. On the contrary, he holds that the content of revealed religion is the same as that of natural religion, inasmuch as the essence of the teaching of Jesus consists in the love of God and of our neighbour, which is equivalent to Kant's "joyful recognition and observance of the moral law as a divine command." He cannot however but see that even the revealed religion of the Bible (not to speak of the theology of the Church) contains some things beyond natural religion. Though in what this addition consists, and what is its value and importance for us, are questions to which this Rationalism can give only confused and indefinite answers.

The Rationalists AMMON, BRETSCHNEIDER, WEGSCHEIDER, and RÖHR sought to keep in closer touch, to some extent, with the historical theology of the Protestant churches, and were thus enabled to exercise a more widespread influence on the thought of the churches. In their theological manuals it was their custom to begin with an historical sketch of the development of the various doctrines in the Bible, the Fathers, and the Protestant creeds, and only then to state their own view in the form of a final judgment. This method had several advantages: in the first place, it involved a full historical statement of the facts of the case, and thus put the student in a position to form an independent opinion from his knowledge of the actual materials; and secondly, it brought clearly out the mutability of dogmatic conceptions, and their dependence in every case upon contemporary thought, and thus destroyed a *naïve* faith in the infallible authority of a particular form of doctrine, and established the right of the present to form an opinion, from its own point of view, on the dogmatic decisions of past ages, and to restate them in more adequate forms. This procedure constitutes both the justification and the historical merit of these theologians, who have been too unceremoniously and disdainfully dismissed by the later conservative theology. By their learned and impartial presentation of the history of dogmas they trained up a generation of scientific and liberal-minded theologians such as we do not afterwards meet with in equal numbers. And with regard to the conclusions they themselves drew from the history of doctrine, we must recognise not only their intelligent clearness and manly honesty, but also their profound moral earnestness, their sincere piety, and their living trust in God; in other words, a disposition of mind which could justly claim to be Christian piety, even though it did not adequately represent the specifically Christian doctrines of salvation, and on that account could not satisfy profounder religious needs. In any case this theological school has as much historical justification as any other, and it is undeniable that its representatives in the first half of our century presented Christianity to the great majority of the German people in the form most intelligible to them, and did better work in the cause of quiet, practical Christianity than many of those who from the proud position of a reactionary theology, artificially conformed to the creeds, assumed the right to condemn these men.

By its juster appreciation of the importance of the historical element in religion, this post-Kantian Rationalism contrasts favourably with Kant's unhistorical Rationalism. While Kant had held everything positive which goes beyond the moral faith of reason to be simply "statutory," the product of man's imagination and caprice, Ammon pronounced the positive religion of the Bible divinely revealed, inasmuch as, while not contradicting natural religion, it still did not originate solely in the reason common to all men, but was imparted by divine Providence through definite historical persons and events to supplement and confirm the truths of natural religion. Hence the relation of natural to positive religion resembles that of the universal moral consciousness to the definite morals and laws of individual nations, or that of the common constitution of men as men to the special unfolding of it in history. From this very useful point of view Bretschneider explained the relation of a general and a special revelation: the former lays the foundation of religious knowledge in the constitution of the world and of our nature, the latter extends and develops this foundation by gradually educating us to a higher wisdom. The need of special revelation is owing to the mind's need of education, or to the fact that our knowledge of God, as well as our knowledge of the world, can only gradually arise and be made perfect. Revelation and reason come from the same source—the divine Logos, and hence cannot contradict each other. But revelation is related to reason as religious education is to the individual: it does not give religious ideas all at once in their complete form, but at first only in general outlines and without a clear perception of their foundations, as truths to be received on authority; but by degrees reason, led and growing strong in the leading strings of authority, attains to a clearer and purer comprehension of religious ideas, and to a perception of their inward truth and agreement with the nature of the world and of man. The very fact that immediate revelation harmonises with the universal revelation, and really develops further religious ideas, is the final proof of its divine origin; while its possibility cannot, according to Bretschneider, be denied, since the Spirit of God pervades all creation, including therefore the human spirit, and hence is able to impart illumination to it, though this is always conditioned by men's general culture and knowledge of the world.

Whilst therefore Ammon and Bretschneider, neither of whom remained uninfluenced by the advanced thought of their time, held the idea of revelation in such a way as to avoid an absolute antithesis between the divine immediateness and the historical medium, and so between the supernatural and the natural, Wegscheider and Röhr, who were unable to escape from the narrowing abstract rationalistic habit of thought of the 18th century, pressed the antithesis to the point of direct contradiction, denying altogether supernatural revelation. Their reasons were psychological and metaphysical: man possesses in his reason a power adequate for the knowledge of everything required by his vocation. It is the renunciation of the true dignity of man to suppose, with a denial of that rational power, a foreign and supernatural authority. To call in a supernatural cause contradicts the laws of our thought, according to which we are compelled to trace all phenomena to a cause within the natural connection of things, and are unable to state any indications whatever of any other cause. Any supernatural interference would be a magical disturbance of the rational connection of our thought and of our mental life generally, would expose us to all kinds of fanaticism, and also in particular lame or destroy our moral activities, which are based upon rational conviction. Finally, the supposition of supernatural interference, by which the orderly course of nature would be interrupted, is opposed to the true idea of God—his unchangeable omnipotence and infinite wisdom, which have so arranged the world that it needs no miraculous interventions and improvements. The notion of a supernatural and direct revelation must be ascribed therefore to men's way of regarding things, when they do not know the natural causes of certain occurrences, and on that account deny their existence, whilst improved knowledge shows in every case that what was supposed to be supernatural can be quite well explained from natural causes. The idea of revelation is nevertheless retained, but it must be conceived as mediate and natural, being founded in the constitution and government of the world, in creation and providence. Thus the true religion, Christianity, in particular, is based upon an historical arrangement of divine Providence, under which Jesus preached the idea of a reason inspired by true religion, and personally represented, as it were in a mirror, the divine reason. Accordingly between Christianity and Rationalism there exists complete accord,

It cannot be questioned that these reasons for Rationalism, if the antithesis between it and supernaturalism is once accepted in this absolute form, have been logically thought out, and they retain at all events their validity in opposition to abstract supernaturalism, which sets aside the laws of reason and the creation. The only question is whether that exclusive conception of the relation of the natural and the supernatural is required, and whether in it the characteristic experiences of the religious life are taken into account. Or whether these facts, when conceived as they are, do not rather point to a view of God's relation to man and the world such as allows man to experience the action of God within the natural and spiritual order of the world, the supernatural and the natural thus ceasing to be exclusive, and only different and complementary aspects of the religious relation. But the unyielding intellectuality of a Wegscheider and Röhr was in its self-satisfaction impervious to this deeper view of the matter which might have reconciled the antitheses. And the unyielding intolerance of the two men toward new and deeper tendencies in theology (Schleiermacher, Marheinike, Hase) has done much to discredit Rationalism in the public view, and to give currency to an opinion of it which really did it injustice by superciliously failing to recognise its relative truth. In this is conveyed the lesson, which it is well to lay to heart, that the religious consciousness of the churches has no sympathy whatever with the domineering arrogance of any heresy which seeks to proclaim its own frigid intellectuality as the one valid canon and the infallible authority in matters of faith. This will be repeated in every period when a doctrinaire pedantry tries, with the ridiculous claim of possessing the only true system of doctrine, to force itself upon the churches. And we must add that it is precisely true theological science which, perceiving the irreconcilability of any such claim with the proper nature of theology, must most thoroughly justify the protest and the practical consciousness of the churches.

The inspiration of the Scriptures Wegscheider finds in the fact that their authors, under Divine guidance, committed to writing their teaching on religion, which, like their good thoughts generally, they traced back with devout feeling to God's will and operation; and these their writings, although designed only for the readers of their day, are of such a nature that the doctrines of the Christian religion can still be drawn from them, even though they must be adapted to the enlightenment of a more educated age. Jesus himself (John vii. 17) declared that the doctrine communicated by him was divine, in so far as its divine nature can be readily perceived and understood by the truly devout and upright. It is, however, divine also because it was first discovered and handed down *non sine numine*. For the Omnipresent God is far from no one who earnestly seeks him and is prepared to carry out his counsels. And who was ever more deserving of his help, or ever enjoyed more marked proofs of the favour of divine Providence, than the founder of the Christian religion? As regards the person of Jesus, the Gospel story of his supernatural birth must be considered a pious legend of Jewish origin, having also its parallels in many other nations; and with it all assertions of the miraculous nature of Jesus fall to the ground; but this is not the case with the conviction that his remarkable endowments and powers, as well as the conditions of the age favourable to their development and employment, must be ascribed to God as their cause. Of the ecclesiastical doctrine of the two natures in Christ, there are, Wegscheider does not wish to deny, some germs in the Biblical writings; but since in its developed form the doctrine gives no assistance to virtue, and in fact is in the highest degree detrimental to the influence of the example of Jesus, which was given for our imitation, besides wholly contradicting sound reason and some plain passages of Scripture, it is best to adhere to the more simple form of doctrine by revering and imitating Jesus as truly a Divine delegate, interpreter of the Divine will, prototype of men destined to be filled with true religion and virtue, who was himself full of the Divine (*numen*, θεῖον), and placed before us in this capacity a dignity not without God. Against the ecclesiastical doctrine of the substitutionary satisfaction of the death of Christ, the objections of a theological and moral character which had been urged from the time of the Socinians are brought forward, and to them others are added of a cosmological nature: it is difficult to suppose, he holds, that in the second person of the Trinity God himself, the Governor of innumerable sidereal systems, should have determined to descend in a human form to this earth, such a tiny part of the universe, to suffer death at the hands of the Jews, and thereby to offer himself as a propitiatory sacrifice to himself. A thought which gives expression to the undoubtedly just feeling that the Christian consciousness has not remained uninfluenced by the Copernican theory, and must abandon antiquated mythological ideas. Moreover, Wegscheider is sufficiently unprejudiced to perceive that the doctrine of satisfaction cannot by fair exegesis be wholly eliminated from the Scriptures; he looks upon it as conveying Christian truth in a form suited to the times of the apostles, and to which a certain pædagogical value still attaches for some minds, while on the other hand more advanced minds are entitled, on the ground of other forms of Scriptural teaching, to regard the doctrine as a mere symbol, intended to indicate that by a faithful observance of the religion taught by Jesus and attested by his death, we shall be pleasing to God without any further sacrifices and ceremonies. The doctrine of the atonement may also be interpreted as a symbol of the love of God and Christ to men, or of the consecration of a new religion as a new covenant between God and men. With regard to these criticisms of the doctrine of the atoning work of Christ, we must allow, as undoubtedly just, that various religious motives are represented in it which we can accept as valuable, though we are able to give expression to them in another form. Moreover, precisely the deepest religious element in the doctrine, which was also adumbrated in the Pauline germs of it, had been previously much better expressed by Kant in his ethical idealistic version of the dogma, than by any of his successors amongst the theologians, who none of them penetrated so far as he beneath the mere surface of the matter. The same was the case with respect to the doctrine of salvation. Presupposing the fact of a "radical evil," Kant had pronounced not merely a reformation of morals, but a change of mind and principle, or a "regeneration" of the entire man, the condition under which we may hope to be regarded by God as good, the Searcher of hearts accepting the good principles instead of the actual perfect goodness which can never exist: and with this Kant had connected the Protestant doctrine of justification by faith. The theologians of the school under consideration continued, it is true, to lay great stress upon feeling and disposition as opposed to external and individual acts, and looked upon this as the pivot of Protestant soteriology; but that this good disposition is something profoundly different from the natural selfish mind, and is based upon a radical transformation of the mind, they did not teach, because, unlike Kant, they regarded men as by nature essentially good and only in part morally enfeebled and impeded by sensuous-ness or bad example. By this view the Biblical and ecclesiastical distinction between the natural and the new man was in their case softened down to a gradual moral reformation, under which a man may feel assured of the Divine approbation according to the measure of his worthiness. And it can hardly be disputed that but poor provision is thereby made to meet either the moral earnestness of ideal requirements or the religious need of an assured salvation and a quieted conscience—two objects which the Protestant doctrine of justification by faith is intended to secure. Kant's teaching was more profound and was in closer touch with the Protestant soteriology than the post-Kantian Rationalism; as Fichte and Schleiermacher show, a development of Kant's moral and religious philosophy in the direction of religious mysticism was possible; but from the Kantian Rationalists it was rather a retrogressive turn in the direction of the popular philosophy that it actually received.

This school could not for long satisfy the newly awakened and deeper religious feeling, and had accordingly to make room for a more profound mode of thought. At the same time, it had not merely done good service in its day in freeing the churches from the curse of an intolerant dogmatism, but there is conveyed a lasting lesson, worthy to be laid to heart now not less than then, in the words of Wegscheider, in the preface of his *Institutiones Theologiæ:* "In the interpretation and criticism of the opinions and doctrines of early times, theologians ought to take greatest care to combine the use of sound reason with the results of the learning of so many centuries. Then only will they follow in the footsteps of the great Reformers, who in their noble struggle against so many injurious errors never claimed themselves to have made an end of all inquiry, and never grudged to their successors progress in religious knowledge. The teachers of the Church ought particularly to endeavour to communicate to the people the teaching of Christ and his Apostles regarding God and duty in all its purity; to show that the truth of this teaching does not depend on ancient dogmatic formulas and pedantic interpretations of Biblical passages, but is borne out by the properly developed nature of our own mind; to no longer try to defend forms of doctrine which were adapted only for the thought of certain people and times, but gradually to lay them aside and adopt a simple form of teaching, such as is indicated in the New Testament itself; to permit the sparks of true morality and piety to flash from the light of genuine Christian doctrine, instead of offering the smoke of ancient opinions as the light of knowledge!" We honour the genuine Protestant love of truth which finds utterance in such words; we still acknowledge the vocation proposed to theology by those men; but, certainly, in the meantime we have learnt that the fulfilment of this vocation is far more difficult than they thought, that it presupposes both more thorough historical inquiry and more profound insight into the facts and laws of the religious and moral life than they could command. For this reason we have not only grown more cautious in our criticisms of what is old, but also more patient with its adherents, than was the habit of the Rationalism of the Kantian school.

The transition from the rationalistic theology of the Kantian school to the theology of Schleiermacher was made by DE WETTE, who adopted the philosophic standpoint of the semi-Kantian Fries, who desired to complete the Kantian critical system in an anthropological direction. All our knowledge, Fries and De Wette taught, is limited to the world of phenomena, which is directly perceived in space and time, and has to be reduced to concepts by the understanding. But this "philosophy of the understanding" is not the true one, for beyond it is the world of ideas demanded by the reason; these ideas are not objects of knowledge, but of faith: namely, the idea of imperishable being, or of the soul, of absolute independent power, or of freedom, and of the unity of the absolute Whole, or of all-conditioning cause—God. These ideas have no connection which can be philosophically proved with the phenomenal world which is the object of our knowledge, but they are in complete contradiction to it, since our experience presents everywhere only the finite and incomplete, nowhere the eternal and infinite. Nevertheless we feel that these ideas have full truth and unconditional certainty. It is true they must never be assigned a place in our philosophy of the understanding, which has to do solely with the mechanism of finite causes and effects; but they form the foundation of our higher or "ideal philosophy," which arises when we, by means of emotional presentiment, bring those ideas to bear upon the world, and judge of the world æsthetically and religiously in their light. The religious ideas are of themselves, when conceived by the speculative faculty, without life, inasmuch as they arise only by the negation of finite limitations, that is, by means of the abstraction of reality; but they obtain their positive significance, and become of value in life when they are taken up by the emotions, and clothed in the picture-language of the poetic and symbolising imagination. All religious propositions with which theology is occupied must therefore be carefully distinguished from intellectual knowledge, as they are part of the ideal view of the world, and only the symbolical expression of surmising feeling. It is to the erroneous confusion of this ideal philosophy, expressing itself in symbols, with intellectual knowledge, that all dogmatism and scholasticism must be ascribed. And dogmatism misunderstands as much the nature of religious feeling as of knowledge, whilst to it is owing the endless conflict between faith and knowledge, which can be set at rest only if both are completely separated,—knowledge being confined to the world of experience, faith being directed to the ideal world, and comprehended under the æsthetic view of things. In particular three kinds of æsthetico-religious feeling must be distinguished: *enthusiasm*, kindled by the idea of the personal dignity and immortal destination of man, and also by the view of the beauty of nature, and of the reign of purpose in history; *submission*, which, under the feeling of one's own imperfection, rises above the evils of the world to faith in the higher spiritual realm of things, which blooms in eternal undimmed beauty beyond the imperfections and fragments of terrestrial things; lastly, the feeling of *worship*, which quickens the idea of God into the idea of eternal Goodness, guiding all things for the best, and rectifying all confusion; while for the understanding the idea of God is nothing more than the empty form of absolute Unity. To these three religious feelings, to which correspond, De Wette holds, the æsthetic ideas of the epic, the drama, and the lyric, all religious statements must be referred, in such a way as to be symbols of the feelings, and find in them the test of their truth. In this consists the true function of theology. It is not its business to substitute for dogmas its own speculations or mere moral doctrine (after the manner of the Kantians), but in the first instance to give an historical account of them, and then to interpret them in accordance with their religious symbolism. Figures and symbols must not be dispensed with, for we always want them in the representation of religious feelings, and do best to adhere to the figurative language which we have inherited. But it must be set free from the fetters of intellectual abstractions, and restored to æsthetic intuition. This is the goal at which Protestantism must finally arrive. When scientific criticism has succeeded in releasing religion from the misleading influence of the understanding, it leaves it to the rule of religious feeling and its handmaid—art.

De Wette has laboured to recast dogmatic theology from this point of view in such a way that we cannot withhold from him the praise of having done his best to reconcile the just claims of religious feeling with those of rational thought, although it must be confessed that his attempted reconciliation was led too much by subjective considerations of taste, without the needed objective foundation, to hold its place beside the theology of Schleiermacher, with its profounder structure. At the same time, it is well worth while even now to take a glance at his mode of treating the leading ideas of dogmatic theology.[1]

Divine revelation we find in every religious phenomenon which so impresses us with the power of the religious truth and beauty conveyed in it as to make us feel ourselves lifted beyond ourselves and our own spiritual capacity. That Christianity is a divine revelation, is an ideal judgment, which cannot be proved by evidence of the understanding, though theological reflection has to show its general necessity; just as a judgment of taste regarding the beauty of a work of art cannot be proved, though it can be so far established as to be shown to satisfy the requirements of art. In doing this the content of this revelation must be first examined, to see what relation it holds to reason, with which nothing good and beautiful can be in opposition, as otherwise man would come into collision with himself. Inasmuch, therefore, as it will be found that nothing has been prescribed in Christianity but the eternal ideas of reason in their greatest purity and fulness, the belief in it as a revelation is thereby justified. Rationalism is accordingly itself nothing else than the philosophical view of faith in revelation, in so far that we must acknowledge a revelation in whatever furthers in an important degree the

---

[1] We follow his work, *Ueber Religion und Theologie*, 2nd ed., 1821.

historical development of the religious mind, such as has been the case with Christianity in the very highest degree. The doctrine of inspiration is likewise only a form of expressing the fact that the Biblical writers were animated by holy enthusiasm, without however possessing infallible wisdom, which, moreover, is a matter belonging to the understanding. Canonicity, in the religious sense, may be ascribed to those writings which contain divine truth, and is therefore independent of the historical view of the Biblical books.

The part of dogmatics which deals with general principles must be criticised strictly in accordance with the speculative and ethical ideas of philosophy. Definitions of the Divine attributes must be referred to the philosophical ideas of God, without sacrificing their virtue as popular symbols. The Mosaic myth of the creation may pass as a figurative representation of the truth that the world is eternally postulated by the divine omnipotence. Angels and devils are mythological figures which may be retained in sacred symbolism and art, though neither historical nor metaphysical truth may be looked for in them. The doctrine of the Trinity must be interpreted as the forms of the revelation of God, whether in the world generally, when Son and Spirit can be referred respectively to the formal and the real principle of the universe, or in the Christian revelation in particular, the doctrine then containing the truth of the different views of God (though in the false scholastic conception of these views as persons), giving expression to the superiority of Christianity to Judaism and Heathenism. Of the anthropological doctrines, the myth of the Fall must be regarded as a symbol of what is always taking place in each man. On the one hand, it is correct that we must look upon our propensity to evil as guilt, and that we are unable, with all our moral effort, to attain to inward peace, inasmuch as we cannot rise to true holiness. On the other hand, it is a dogmatic exaggeration to deny that man has any power to do good; such a doctrine overlooks the fact that there is in man an inward moral power, which, it is true, requires to be aroused from without in order to act. In so far, therefore, man stands in need of salvation, of divine grace. Yet the Holy Spirit and human reason must not be conceived as opposed to each other, but the latter subordinated to the former; grace and freedom are two views taken from different standpoints, the former belonging to faith, the latter to observation and reflection, while both are correct and are not mutually exclusive. Election and reprobation is at the same time the work of God and man, though God's not according to his absolute will, but according to his relative operation within the historical world of sinful men. The dogma of the two natures in Christ as a conception is a contradiction, but easily admits of reduction to these two views: in relation to nature, Jesus is a man, but regarded æsthetically and in relation to the ideal, he is God; and as both ways of regarding him are at bottom one, so he is but *one* person, the God-man, not two persons. "Away, therefore, with those barren dogmatic formulas, of which, moreover, the Bible and the people's faith know nothing! Let Christ be regarded as a divine messenger, as God-man, as the image of God; let us not be too stingy with our glorification of him, let us not too anxiously weigh our expressions! At the same time, we must not forget that we are dealing not with truths of the intellect, but simply with religious ideality (*Schönheit*), and whoever speaks of this subject to the people, let him never do it without the elevation and the warmth of devout enthusiasm." While hitherto the history of this dogma has been occupied with the conflict of truth with beauty, from this time forth "the period must follow in which beauty will maintain its claims side by side with truth." (De Wette correctly perceives that the essence of Christological controversies is about the relation of the historical and the ideal, but the problem is not solved by the simple comparison of the intellectual, or true, and the ideal, or æsthetic view.) The doctrine of the atonement is only a beautiful, æsthetico-religious symbol of the thought that Christ has restored to our sin-troubled hearts inward peace, so that we can look up to God, the holy Judge, with confidence. As in Christ all ideas take an historical and personal form, so also this highest idea of atonement, in order that the whole life of humanity might be mirrored in him. As in his death, suffered for us, he represented the highest moral perfection and the complete victory of the spirit over the flesh and sin, we may make this our own by faith in him; he raises us to his own height, as we with him set ourselves free from the rule of the flesh; and this assurance gives us peace of mind, so that we no longer dread God, but are sure of his grace. The idea of sacrifice in this connection is to be understood only in the sense of a moral example and type of purified and pardoned humanity. The doctrine of justification by faith contains the religious truth, unrecognised by modern moral theology, that man cannot be saved by his own merit, which is as nothing before God's holiness, but alone by the grace of God. The doctrines of eschatology must be interpreted as symbolical mythology, which have at their basis the truths of anthropology and soteriology (eternal life, the victory of good in the kingdom of God).

It appears from these dogmatic views, as well as from the excellent hints for practical theologians, that De Wette occupied as free a position as the Rationalists with regard to the literal authority of the creeds of the Church, but that he sought to give their due value to the religious feelings, which the Rationalists had not done, and, with a more unfettered mind towards history, to maintain the connexion of the present life of the Church with the past. It may be regarded as a defect from the point of view of a scientific theology, that he tried to effect this only by means of an æsthetical treatment of the dogmas in question, which was often somewhat confused; but for the practical purposes of theology, which he always kept in view, the advantages of his method of treatment may well have exceeded its disadvantages. In this respect De Wette occupies a position nearest to Herder in his relation to the Rationalists; and, of our contemporary theologians, Hase is the spirit nearest of kin to him. And in the prosperity of the churches of Thuringia lies the best proof that the prospects of that church are not unpromising, which follows in the course marked out by Herder, De Wette, and Hase.

CHAPTER II.

THE THEOLOGY OF SCHLEIERMACHER'S "GLAUBENSLEHRE" AND HIS SCHOOL.

WHILST Rationalists and Supernaturalists carried on their warfare with each other, without either side being able to gain the victory, because both represented a partial truth and shared false premises, a stronger than either came upon them, who struck into new courses. I refer to SCHLEIERMACHER, from whose work, *Der christliche Glaube nach den Grundsätzen der evangelischen Kirche im Zusammenhang dargestellt* (1st ed., 1821; 2nd ed., 1831), dates an epoch in the history of modern theology. The error common to both of these contending parties had been that they conceived the Christian faith as a number of traditionary doctrines which appeared to stand in such hopeless opposition to the rational thought of modern times that one of the two must make room for the other; the endless contention being—which of the two must yield, and how far? Schleiermacher took the ground from under this contention by removing its main pre-supposition. The Christian faith, as he showed, does not consist in any number of positive doctrinal propositions such as have arisen from intellectual reflection upon that faith; this faith is not a doctrine, or a system of doctrines, but a condition of devout feeling, a fact accordingly of inward experience, neither produced by thought nor depending on its existence, but, like all experience, simply an object to be observed and described. He took up, therefore, a position opposed to the standpoint of the Supernaturalists, on the one hand, by conceiving the Christian faith not as a doctrinal authority given us from without, but as an *inward* condition of our *own self-consciousness*, which must be connected with the remaining contents of our consciousness and the laws of our mind. On this point Schleiermacher occupies completely the position of modern idealism, for which there can be no truth that does not rise out of and answer to the human mind. On the other hand, he maintained, in opposition to the Rationalists, the view that the Christian faith is not a product of rational thinking, but a condition of the heart, a feeling preceding thought and supplied independently of it; moreover, a feeling not of the devout individual only, but of the Christian, or specifically of the Protestant, Church; accordingly a fact not merely of individual experience, but of the common experience of a historical community; an experience, therefore, which, like all positive experiences in history, must be received and intelligently described, while it cannot and may not be reasoned away.

From the basis of religious experience, therefore, Schleiermacher seeks to give an account of the Christian faith, supposing all along that his own religious experience is essentially the same as that of the Christian Church, at all events in the Protestant form of it. That this supposition can be taken as correct only with very considerable limitation, is what might be expected in the case of a man whose religious nature had been in his youth nurtured in the peculiar form of piety of the Moravian community, and whose mind had been formed by the study of Plato, Spinoza, Kant, Fichte, Jacobi, Schelling, and who in his first work, his *Discourses on Religion*, had appeared as a disciple of Romanticism, with its thoroughly modern form of thought. It may be allowed that in the two decades which lapsed between his Discourses and his *Glaubenslehre*, Schleiermacher had thrown off the extravagances of Romanticism, and had brought his entire mode of thought much more into accord with the faith of the Church: still, it cannot be doubted, and his *Glaubenslehre* shows it most plainly, that the varied elements of his rich education had a far-reaching influence upon his religious consciousness; so that his religious feeling differed from that of the Church in some characteristic points. Accordingly, in spite of all his honest effort to harmonise and bring into one the individual and the common elements, his *Glaubenslehre*, which proceeds from this subjective experience, retains everywhere a marked individual character which could not make any direct claim to general acceptance in the Church. However, we must not on this account reproach Schleiermacher, when we remember that the same objection would in some degree have to be made to every attempt to give an account of the Christian faith from the standpoint of the present; in fact, it must be pronounced really one of Schleiermacher's merits, that by his example he

asserted the claims of *individuality* to a place in theology also, and put an end to the miserable delusion of a sole and exclusive possession of the truth. It is true that the perception of this is yet far from being universal; but I venture boldly to assert that in future it will be regarded as a principal criterion of true theological education, that the theologian should remain conscious of the individuality of his way of looking at things, and should renounce all claims to doctrinal authority of universal validity.

The individual character of Schleiermacher's theological system appears forthwith in his definition of religion, which had great influence also upon his doctrine of God. Religion, he teaches, is "the feeling of absolute dependence"; in our relation to the world our consciousness is always divided between a feeling of relative freedom and a feeling of relative dependence, according as our active or passive states of mind predominate; but when we rise above the interchange of these relative states of feeling to the unity of the higher consciousness, we get the feeling of an absolute dependence, which is one with the consciousness of God; inasmuch as the source of *this* feeling, in which the antithesis of relative freedom and dependence vanishes, can only be the unconditioned cause of all conditioned interaction of beings, that is—God. Acute as this deduction is, it cannot be said that it describes accurately or fully the nature of the religious feeling, particularly in its Christian form. The religious feeling of reverence contains, together with the sense of dependence on God, the sense of obligation towards him, and of relationship and of exaltation to him; in this devout consciousness there is in addition to the feeling of passive dependence also the feeling of moral alliance, and accordingly of a free relation of the will; whereby the idea of God also obtains a much richer content than that of mere causality; at the same time the immediate religious feeling can receive a different *qualitative* characterisation, as the basis of the difference in relative value of the feelings belonging to various stages of religion; whilst in the case of Schleiermacher's simple feeling of dependence nothing more is possible than a *quantitative* difference in the degree of strength possessed by the religious feeling in proportion to the secular consciousness. But it is clear that a merely quantitative estimate of the religious feeling, according to the strength of its presence in consciousness, is not sufficient for the determination of its qualitative value; otherwise the devout feeling, for instance, of a Mohammedan would be equal to that of a Christian. If we ask how Schleiermacher came to give such a meagre account of religious feeling, emphasising what may be called the physical side of dependence on an infinite cause, to the neglect of the moral side, represented in the feeling of alliance with a voluntary power related spiritually to ourselves, we can hardly be wrong in tracing the origin of this defect to the influence of the philosophy of Spinoza, whose *cognitio Dei intuitiva* is nothing else than the reference of all finite phenomena to the necessary causality of God,—that is, the feeling of our dependence upon it. This supposition is confirmed by Schleiermacher's doctrine of God, which is connected with his imperfect theory of the nature of religion.

Having based his system of belief upon devout states of feeling, of which he is conscious as a member of the Church, for Schleiermacher the questions with which apologetics had usually been occupied lose their relative importance and appear in an entirely new light. Above all the Scriptures cannot, from his position, be any longer regarded as the foundation of faith. In the introduction to his dogmatic system, Schleiermacher hardly comes to speak of them at all, but deals with them under the head of the Church's means of grace. He regards them as a product of the Holy Spirit in as far as the latter is the common-spirit (*Gemeingeist*) of the Church. This spirit has borne witness to Christ in the apostolic writings, not essentially otherwise than in later writings, only more at first hand, and more under the immediate impression of the Apostles' personal acquaintance with Jesus, such as the men of a later generation did not enjoy. On this account the writings of the New Testament possess a special dignity as normative for all subsequent accounts of Christianity; but not so the writings of the Old Testament; since the connexion of Christianity with the religion of the Old Testament is, according to Schleiermacher, only very loose and indirect. Speaking generally, it is not the reputation of the Scriptures upon which faith in Christ rests, but this faith must be pre-supposed before a special reputation can be assigned to the Scriptures. Least of all may this reputation be based upon their inspiration, for supposing even that the latter could be proved from the New Testament writings, the conviction of it would still be very far from Christian faith, and could by no means directly produce it, since this faith can proceed only from the total impression of the personality of Jesus. The normative dignity of the New Testament writings rests solely upon the fact that that impression can be obtained from them, that they, therefore, truly transmit the image of Christ. On the other hand, the reports they contain of external miracles, which Jesus is said to have done or been the subject of, are matter for criticism. The miracles cannot be regarded, according to the usual habit, as supports of Christian faith, for the simple reason that they presuppose the latter, and must be understood by means of it. For as Christian faith finds in Christ the highest revelation, miracles may reasonably be expected of him (though they can be called such only relatively, as containing something extraordinary for contemporary knowledge of the connexion between physical and mental life), without at all taking them out of the realm of the regular and orderly phenomena of nature. Though Schleiermacher nowhere offers an express critique of the traditional doctrine of miracles, whether of the actuality or the possibility of the recorded miracles, he still lays down the general principle that in the interests of religion the necessity can never arise of regarding an event as taken out of its connexion with nature in consequence of its dependence on God. Even the miracles at the beginning and the end of the life of Jesus, which are so often looked upon in the Church as the foundation of faith in Christ, do not form, according to Schleiermacher, an essential part of faith in the person of Jesus, since his disciples already possessed this faith, although they still knew nothing of those particular miracles.

At the same time Schleiermacher does not altogether reject the idea of the miraculous, or the supernatural, or revelation. All these terms represent in his view facts of religious experience which exceed ordinary experience ; but inasmuch as they are experiences of the religious emotions, which, it must be remembered, are part of human nature, they must also have a side related to nature, and can accordingly be supernatural only in a *relative* sense. By revelation he understands the originality of a religious phenomenon, whether it be in a personality or in life, of such moment as to form the foundation of a religious community : this definition excludes both external communication and tradition, and also intentional invention and reflection, while it includes divine communication and promulgation. Only this communication must not be regarded as in the first instance a didactic influence upon the mind in the form of knowledge, but as the peculiar and extraordinary effect produced by the total impression of a personality upon the general consciousness of those who come within its range; which does not exclude direct instruction, but includes it only as one factor amongst others. In heathenism, too, such personalities must be looked upon as revelations of God, in whom the divine is likewise typically made known in an original manner, and such as cannot be explained from the immediate historical surroundings. Yet every such revelation is still only something relative, since only the universe as a whole could be called the absolute revelation, every individual phenomenon, however original it may be, being intelligible only from the general condition of the community to which it belongs. In any case, therefore, no claim of absolute truth can be made for any revelation, since this would involve a manifestation of God as he is in himself, whilst an effective manifestation of him can only give expression to what he is in his relation to us. This is true also of Christianity. Its origin in the person of Jesus is supernatural in so far as the peculiar spiritual contents of his person cannot be explained from the natural surroundings of his life, but can have proceeded only from the general source of spiritual life by a creative act of God. But this supernatural origin is at the same time natural, in so far as the rise of a higher original life must be conceived as the effect of a power of development inherent in the race, a power which finds expression, in conformity with divinely ordered laws, though laws hidden from us, in certain men at certain points, that by them the rest of mankind may be helped onwards. As the highest development of the spiritual power of our race, the unique phenomenon of Christ is not an absolute, but only a relative miracle. In the same way, that which is "above reason" in Christianity consists only in its transcending the ordinary human reason, not in its exceeding the rational faculties of mankind at large, Christianity being in reality their highest perfection. And, again, the doctrinal propositions of the Christian faith are in so far beyond reason as their religious content is not evolved from rational reflection, but is given as a special experience, which, like every other similar experience, can be received only by a love willing to behold it; but they are at the same time perfectly rational, in as far as they must conform to the same laws of logical thought to which all other propositions are subject.

In these statements the relation of Schleiermacher to Rationalism and Supernaturalism is very plainly presented. With the former he rejects the absolute miracle, and looks upon Christianity as a product of human nature, of its original spiritual energy, yet—and thereby he goes over to the position of the latter—not as the product of ordinary thought and reflection, but as an original creation of the highest development of man's rational nature; and moreover, as an unique historical phenomenon, which is embodied in the person of the Saviour, and has accordingly to be acknowledged as a positive fact of revelation. Christian faith is, therefore, according to Schleiermacher, not merely faith in universal religious or moral truths, but in the historical person of Jesus as the Saviour, whose characteristic influence is to produce in us the Christian consciousness of salvation. And hereby the business of Christian theology becomes for Schleiermacher even more positive than for the Supernaturalists of that time: it has, according to him, to describe faith in Christ as the Saviour, as given in the Christian Church, and to draw it out connectedly into the various doctrinal propositions therein implied: but it has nothing to do with other sciences and philosophy. Dogmatic propositions, he demands, ought to be "the outcome of the observation of religious states of feeling," and ought on no account to be mixed up nor confounded with speculative propositions which are due to quite different interests. "Dogmatic theology will never stand as firmly upon its basis as the physical sciences have long done upon theirs, till the separation of the two kinds of propositions is so complete that such a strange question, for instance, as whether the same proposition can be true in philosophy and false in theology, could not arise, for the reason that a proposition cannot occur in the one in the same form as it occurs in the other, but the difference must be presupposed however great the similarity may seem to be." "The Protestant Church is convinced that the special shape peculiar to its doctrinal propositions is quite independent of all schools of philosophy, and does not owe its origin at all to any speculative interest, but solely to the satisfaction of immediate self-consciousness by means of the genuine and unadulterated institution of Christ." Neither will Schleiermacher admit that at the beginning of the formation of

Christian doctrine speculation had any influence on the subject-matter of dogmatic propositions; an opinion with which no historian of the present day will agree, seeing the influence of Greek speculation is plain enough in the theology of Paul or John!

We have not here to ask whether the rigid separation of theology from philosophy demanded by Schleiermacher is possible, but whether he himself fully carried it out. So far as the form of his doctrinal propositions goes, this is undoubtedly the case; he carefully avoids all reference to philosophical matter, and all direct and declared dependence on philosophical schools and systems. Still, no one can fail to see that not only his own philosophical education generally, but also a definite philosophical system, exerted a profound influence upon his theology. Nor could his critical distinction between the form of ecclesiastical doctrine and its religious subject-matter, his appeal from the traditionary objects of faith to the religious subject's own inner life as the source of their origin, be conceivable apart from the school of critical idealism. And how could we explain the wide departure of Schleiermacher's doctrine regarding God and the world from that in vogue in the Church, and its close approach to the doctrine of Spinoza, if it had really been deduced simply from the consideration of the religious feelings of Christians? Strauss, we must allow, was right when he said,[1] "None of the leading propositions of the first part of Schleiermacher's *Glaubenslehre* can be fully understood save as they are re-translated into the formulæ of Spinoza, from which they were originally taken. The relation of God to the world (which forms the basis of his entire theology), according to which both God and world are conceived as equal magnitudes, only that the former is the absolute and undivided unity, while the latter is the unity divided and differentiated, can be explained only from the relation of the *natura naturans* to the *natura naturata* of Spinoza."

In a note in his *Glaubenslehre*, Schleiermacher incidentally throws out the passing but pregnant remark, that pantheism is consistent with religion if it is only meant to represent some form of theism, and the word is not simply a masked materialistic negation of theism. "If we keep pantheism to the customary formula, One and All, even then God and the

---

[1] *Charakteristiken und Kritiken*, p. 166.

world remain distinct, at least in point of function; and therefore a pantheist of this kind, when he regards himself as part of the world, feels himself with this All dependent on that which is the One." There can be no doubt but that Schleiermacher has here characterised his own view of God and the world, as it is presented best of all in his *Dialektik*, but plainly enough in his *Glaubenslehre*. At the beginning of his work, in the deduction of the idea of God from the feeling of dependence, Schleiermacher lays emphasis on the point that the word "God" is only an expression for the "whence" of our absolute dependence, but is by no means given or to be conceived as an object: to conceive of God apart from the world would be empty mythology. God is the correlative unity to the multiplicity presented as the world. Creation and Preservation are forms of expression for the eternal causality or omnipotence of God, which is so completely represented in the totality of being, that in the divine omnipotence there is no excess of potentiality beyond the totality of the actual, nor in the latter anything in excess of the former. Omnipotence and the totality of natural causes are commensurate, the former never coming in the place of the latter to meet a defect, but everything exists and arises solely and wholly by means of the natural system of things; so that each thing existing by virtue of all, and all things entirely by the divine omnipotence, all things undivided subsist through one. This is, in fact, an exact formulation of the "immanence" of God as taught by Spinoza. But Schleiermacher holds not only Spinoza's theory of immanence, but also his idea of substance, with its simple unity of being and operation to the exclusion of all definitions. In his view the divine attributes do not denote any distinctions in God, or even so much as an objective difference in his relation to the world; which would be to conceive God as a multitude of functions, and therewith, Schleiermacher thinks, to bring God into the region of antitheses; but they denote only the various modes in which we refer our feeling of dependence to God, different aspects in which God's causality (in itself simple) presents itself to our consciousness. That is, as neither in time nor space, but as conditioning both, this divine causality is his omnipresence and eternity; as in extent one with the totality of natural causes, though differing in form, it is his omnipotence; as living or spiritual causality, it is called his omniscience; in relation to our moral conscious ness, it is his holiness or justice, inasmuch as together with sin we have conscience, and connect the feeling of guilt with evil—and both in virtue of divine arrangement; in relation to the consciousness of salvation, the divine causality becomes love and wisdom. All these distinctions, therefore, are confined to the human consciousness of God, and have no foundation in the objective nature of God, which does not admit of any distinctive qualifications, as they would only contradict the infinity of God, according to Schleiermacher; in full agreement with Spinoza's canon, *Omnis determinatio est negatio.* An absolutely simple causality of this kind, in which there is no distinction between *posse* and *facere*, *facere* and *velle*, *velle* and *scire*, nor any succession of acts and states, but everything is simply one eternal act, is at all events not a personality, nor can it scarcely be thought of as spiritual being, having nothing in common with anything which constitutes for us the spiritual; it is in reality simply operative power, like Spinoza's substance. From the first it has been remarked that this conception of God fails to meet the need of the Christian religious consciousness; nor was Schleiermacher able to bring it into harmony with the religious consciousness in any other way than by reducing the latter to the mere feeling of dependence, thereby detracting from its moral side as we saw above (p. 105). It is therefore certain that Schleiermacher cannot be regarded as the unprejudiced interpreter of the universal, still less of the Christian, religious experience, in his treatment of the primary ideas of religion and God, but that he has reduced them to the dimensions of his philosophical system.

And how did he possibly find a transition from this basis to the Christian faith, and make the account of this, rather Spinozistic than Christian, conception of God a description of the religious consciousness of the Christian community? By identifying the antithesis between the consciousness of God and sense-consciousness (answering to the opposition in Spinoza of the reason to the imagination) with that between sin and salvation of the Christian consciousness. This identification was effected thus: the predominance of the sense-consciousness over the consciousness of God, or the hindrance of the latter by the former, becomes to us the consciousness of sin and religious unhappiness, or the need of salvation; while, on the contrary, the predominance of the God-consciousness over the sense-consciousness, in which every act of the latter is determined by the former, becomes to us the consciousness of the removal of that hindrance, or of salvation, of the strength and blessedness of the higher self-consciousness. Between the one and the other of these two states of feeling lies the entire life of the religious consciousness. But while the condition of the hindered consciousness of God is the general experience of mankind, the condition of the delivered and unhindered consciousness is the special experience of the Christian Church, and is the operation of its Founder. Thus what is primarily a difference within consciousness becomes likewise an objective difference between mankind in its natural condition, as needing salvation, and mankind as Christian and saved. It is easy to perceive that these conditions, described by Schleiermacher as "sin and salvation," are really what Spinoza described, in the last two books of his *Ethics* as the *servitus et libertas humana*, and what is by Kant called the supremacy of the lower, sensuous, and of the higher, rational, desires. The difference is simply that the transition from the one condition to the other is in the view of the philosophers made as a psychological and ethical process within the consciousness and by virtue of its natural human constitution; whilst in the system of our theologian the change appears as an historical process in the consciousness of human society, having its origin and effective cause in a definite point of human history. If it is true that the human race is the macrocosmic type of individual life, the right to identify the various states of the religious personal consciousness with the different phases of the historical development of humanity cannot be disputed; but then neither can the logical inference be avoided, that the same laws and forces which condition the change of states in the individual will also produce the analogous change in the historical life of the race, without calling in the aid of special and unique causes alien to all customary experience. We shall subsequently see what treatment this inference met with in Schleiermacher's theological system.

The antithesis of sin and salvation, or grace, is made by Schleiermacher the basis of the disposition of the second or special part of his treatise, after he had in the first part treated of the religious consciousness without reference to this antithesis, or the fundamental questions of God and the universe and the original perfection of man. In each part the materials are arranged so that the religious consciousness as such is first described, and then the doctrines concerning the world and God that are therein implied. As regards the doctrine concerning God, there is the disadvantage in this arrangement, that the doctrine is nowhere dealt with connectedly, but only in fragments here and there; which, it must be allowed, offered the advantage of veiling the want of an objective conception of God. In other respects this arrangement involves a number of difficulties: for instance, the Christology falls under the account of the Christian consciousness, whilst it ought surely to have an historical object as its subject-matter; again, the doctrine of the Church is placed under the declarations of the Christian consciousness regarding the world. The eschatology is handled in loose connection with the rest of the work as a "prophetic article."

Sin, Schleiermacher describes as the opposition of the flesh to the spirit, as the hindrance of the higher self-consciousness, or God-consciousness, by the lower, sensuous or finite consciousness. It has its natural rise in the priority of man's sensuous development to his spiritual development, and of his intellectual development to his power of will. It is therefore the inevitable outcome of human nature as such, and not an external inheritance from Adam. By the first sin of the first parents no alteration of the nature of the human race was brought about, which would have been impossible, but that first sin was only the first appearance of the sinfulness which is a property of human nature as such, and was to be looked for in the first parents. The ecclesiastical doctrine of two consecutive states, *status integritatis* and *status corruptionis*, must therefore be interpreted as the two sides of man's original perfection, both of which always belong contemporaneously to our nature, or of the endowment with God-consciousness and of an original sinfulness, or sensuous weakness. Rational as this re-interpretation of the traditional doctrines of the primitive state and the fall undoubtedly is, it must be remarked that Schleiermacher's view of the nature of sin is as unsatisfactory as the essentially similar view of Spinoza, according to which evil is only defective power in the reason over sense-affections; whereas a true analysis of the moral consciousness, uninfluenced by philosophical prepossessions, will always discover in evil a conflict of the selfish individual will with the obligations of the law of the whole, and therein a self-contradiction within the mind itself, not merely a contradiction between mind and sense. With great dialectical acuteness, Schleiermacher brings the other traditionary articles under this head into accord with his totally different premises. He adopts without reserve the position that the sinfulness inherent in the nature of the human race must be regarded as a total inability to do good, which, while it must not be exaggerated so as to cancel the capability of salvation, is still so far infinite that it cannot be completely removed even by the power of salvation. Guilt must also, according to Schleiermacher, attach to original or hereditary sin, it being reckoned not to each man in his individual capacity, but to the race as the common guilt of a common act; so that the consciousness of it always involves at the same time the general human need of salvation. Finally, Schleiermacher goes even a step beyond the traditionary doctrines in maintaining that actual sin proceeds to such an extent from original sin, that in the entire sinful race not a single moment occurs in which contradiction of the God-consciousness is wholly absent. Accordingly the difference in point of merit amongst men must not, according to him, be sought in the various degrees of their sin, but solely in their nearer or more distant relation to salvation; an assertion in which appears the same subordination as in Spinoza of the moral point of view to that abstract levelling conception of evil as the general *malum metaphysicum* of the finite.

Schleiermacher's soteriology starts from the position, that we are conscious in the Christian community that our God-consciousness constantly advances so as to gradually overcome the hindrances proceeding from the sense-consciousness, attended by the corresponding approach to the condition of blessedness. But since this advancement cannot originate in the life of sin common to humanity, where nothing but unhappiness is developed, it must, Schleiermacher argues, have its origin in the new common life of the community founded by Jesus, and be accordingly traced back to the saving activity of Jesus as its cause. The question arises therefore, To be the cause of such an effect, what must the person of Jesus have been? The answer is: Our experience as Christians of the increasing strength of our God-consciousness could proceed from the person of Jesus only if this consciousness was actually present in him in absolute measure; that is, only if the ideal type of religion was in him historical, and his entire life was that of the religious model, person and idea in his case perfectly corresponding. As this typical, model man, according to Schleiermacher's exposition, Christ was distinguished from all other men by his essential sinlessness and absolute perfection, which excluded not only all actual sin, but also all possibility of it, and accordingly everything like a moral struggle; and further, by his freedom from error, having never himself originated an erroneous notion, nor adopted one from others as one of his convictions. This perfect God-consciousness of Christ must be regarded as properly God in him, and as the one perfect revelation of God in the human race. In this respect his person was a miraculous phenomenon in the common life of sin, not to be explained by that life itself, but only by a new creative act of God, which may be called a second creation, or rather completion of creation, being really one with the first creation, as part of the same universal system of nature. It is this only—that the phenomenon of Christ had its cause in a creative act, or an original attainment of the human race as unaffected by sin,—which Schleiermacher regards as the true essence of the doctrines of the supernatural origin of his life; while, on the other hand, the suspension of the natural parental participation in the origination of his life adds nothing of essential moment to the matter. In general, the miraculous in the person of Jesus must not be conceived in such a way as to negative the sameness of his nature and ours. Though it may trace its origin to the miraculous (in the above sense), the complete historical character of his subsequent life must still be held fast. To this belongs the gradual unfolding of his powers, including the spiritual ones, save that this will have proceeded without contradictions and struggles, as the constant and regular passage from the innocence of childhood to full spiritual vigour; further, his specific nationality, the qualification of his ideas and actions by the habits of thought of his nation and his age, although it is not allowed that his personal activity, but only his receptivity, was subject to this limitation. In so far, Schleiermacher grants that further progress in advance of the historical form of the appearance of Jesus, as this was conditioned by temporal and national limitations, is not only possible, but a fact; but this is not an advance beyond his essential nature, which will, on the contrary, be only more and more fully brought out by the progressive development of the Christian world. Schleiermacher thus makes evidently the well-known distinction between the ideal principle which was revealed in Jesus and the form the principle takes as a historical phenomenon. In the communication of the principle itself consists the work of Christ: his work as Saviour is that of imparting to others the strength of his consciousness of God; his work as Reconciler is the communication of the happiness of this consciousness; effects which were at first the immediate work of Christ, but subsequently could only be produced by the continued operation of his spirit and example in the mind of believers. To the ecclesiastical dogma of vicarious satisfaction, Schleiermacher attaches the following meaning : Christ made satisfaction in so far that a source of inexhaustible blessing was opened in his person and activity as Founder of the Church; but this satisfaction is not vicarious, inasmuch as the blessing of it belongs only to those who also enter into fellowship with Christ ; to his sufferings, on the other hand, a vicarious character attaches, since by virtue of his sinlessness, his own person would have been beyond the reach of the universal calamity connected with sin ; but this form of substitution is not satisfaction, individuals in the Christian community having, as we all know, still themselves to suffer. In other words, Schleiermacher rejects the idea of a transcendental reconciliation through the atoning sufferings of Christ as the representative of mankind before God, and puts in its place the historical view of the matter, according to which Christ by the total impression of his personality had such a strengthening and beatifying influence on men's religious consciousness that they felt themselves saved and reconciled, that is, delivered, or gradually being delivered, from the hindering and miserable contradiction between the higher and lower self-consciousness. It is this stronger consciousness of God, proceeding from Christ, which, as the consciousness of the Christian community, is the "holy Spirit." As the God-consciousness of Christ is the divine in him, so the holy Spirit " is the union of the Divine Being with human nature in the form of the common spirit of the community, as animating the collective life of believers." The holy Spirit, therefore, is the same saving principle in the community that primarily appeared in the person of Jesus in the form of an individual life ; and the saving work of this principle is the production, in those individuals who open themselves receptively to it, of a life of invigorated and felicitated God-consciousness similar to that which was typically present in Jesus. In this consists "conversion and justification," the two aspects of "regeneration," in which a new religious consciousness is produced in the believer by the common Christian spirit of the community, and a new life, or "sanctification," is prepared for.

Looked at from this point, Schleiermacher's soteriology does not in principle differ from Kant's philosophical doctrine, and that of his followers, according to which the victory of the good principle over the bad, or of reason over sense, is effected by "faith in the ideal Son of God,"—that is, by the reception of the divine idea of man into the heart and the quickening of the divine spirit in man. In both systems salvation is an inward process in man, the deliverance of his higher divine being from the hindrances of his lower nature; and both agree also in regarding this inward deliverance and renewal in the individual life as evoked and sustained by the moral community, the foundation of which must be traced to Jesus. There is, finally, agreement in regarding this common spirit of the higher religious and moral life as having proceeded from the Founder of this community with original energy and purity, and as therefore to be beheld in his person as in a typical example for imitation. But while the philosophers generally go no further, and see no cause for supposing that the relation of this ideal principle to the human personality in the person of Jesus was essentially different from what it is in other men, Schleiermacher feels obliged to trace the origin of this common Christian spirit to a personality of unique perfection, or sinlessness and freedom from error. But he has failed to show either the congruity of this supposition with the sameness of Christ's nature and ours or any good ground for the logical necessity of the supposition itself. For all that he alleges with regard to the experiences of the Christian community as to the common spirit of a strengthened and felicitated God-consciousness—experiences which confessedly never go beyond a *relative* approximation to perfection and felicity—by no means presupposes an origin of *absolute* quantitative perfection of God-consciousness, the psychological possibility of which is exceedingly problematic; but that experience is fully accounted for on the supposition of the inward qualitative truth of the God-consciousness which is present in the community as a fact of experience. Schleiermacher had previously himself acknowledged that the inward qualitative truth of a religious principle must not be at once confounded with the personal perfection of its first preacher. In his *Discourses* he had pronounced the confounding of the fundamental fact in which a religion takes its rise with the fundamental idea of this religion itself a "great mistake," which has misled almost everybody and given a false direction to the view of almost all religions. But it cannot be denied that this mistake lies at the basis of his own dogmatic theory of the ideal person of Christ. That he could thus deceive himself on this point may be psychologically explained from the peculiar personal wants of his religious nature, in which the Moravian impressions of his early days continued to operate. And for the practical value of his theological system that error worked advantageously, without doubt, helping as it did to bring it into line with ecclesiastical tradition. It is true that what was in Schleiermacher's case an inconsequence, based on individual peculiarities, was made by others the principal thing and the starting-point of a positive retrograde movement in dogmatics.

It remains to state the chief points of Schleiermacher's doctrine of the *Church*, its essential characteristics, and its origin and consummation. He rejects the traditionary distinction between the visible and the invisible Church, as contradictory terminology; for what is invisible is not actually the Church, and what is the Church is not invisible. The proper meaning of this distinction he finds very justly in the relation of the operative Christian spirit in the Church to the natural, sinful elements, or the world, still present in it,— that is, in the opposition of the spirit and the flesh, transferred to the whole body of the Church. It is only to the first aspect of the Church that the predicates of unity, universality, sanctity, and infallibility are to be applied; to the historical form of it, on the other hand, only so far as it is actually approximating to its ideal. Amongst the means of grace, "prayer in the name of Christ" is admirably handled. It represents the common desire and will of the Church as directed to the consummation of the kingdom of God, and its presentiment of what is truly salutary, having in so far the promise of being heard. But this must not be conceived as involving anything approaching a magical influence upon the divine will, such prayer having simply a strengthening effect upon the praying community itself. The sacraments are treated from the standpoint of the union of the Lutheran and the Reformed (Calvinistic and Helvetian) confessions; with a rejection of extreme views, various forms of the idea of a sacrament are admitted; Schleiermacher's own view approaches most closely the spiritual form of the Reformed confessions. Under infant baptism, the addition to the rite, which has importance primarily for the Church only, of a personal confession on the part of the candidate on reaching the adult age (confirmation) is demanded, as necessary for completing the sacramental means of grace.

To the most subtle and acute portions of his work belongs his treatment of the doctrine of election. As early as 1819, Schleiermacher had published an essay in defence of the Calvinistic doctrine on this head, the fundamental ideas of which are worked out in his *Glaubenslehre* in a somewhat modified form and with more of an eirenical than apologetic purpose. The distinction between elect and non-elect is based certainly upon "divine predetermination, which may not be made dependent on foreknowledge, as thereby the divine causality would be made conditional; at the same time the articles of predetermination and foreknowledge have equal right to be retained side by side, inasmuch as they represent simply different ways of looking at the same thing." (This reminds us of the way in which Spinoza, in his *Theologico-Political Treatise*, explains the divine determination as identical with the divine knowledge.) Nevertheless, Schleiermacher relieves the harshness of the Calvinistic doctrine by limiting the dualism of elect and non-elect to the historical form of the kingdom of God, and denying its validity as the definitive end of things. In the course of historical development, it is a necessary law that all cannot be at the same time received into the Christian community, but some are preferred to others, who are for the time put back. This distinction is founded on the general relation of the kingdom of God to the world, and is accordingly presupposed in the divine order of things. But it is not an absolute, but only a relative difference, between an earlier and a later reception into the sphere of the operations of divine grace. This temporary difference will sometime cease in a final universal salvation; with this consolatory outlook faith rises above the apparent harshness of the doctrine of election, without in any way letting go the unconditionality of the divine decrees.

With these prophetic glances into the future of the consummation of the Church, "the prophetic articles," as Schleiermacher entitles his eschatological sections, are occupied more closely. At the commencement he makes the general observation, that the description of the perfected condition of the Church, since it does not arrive in the course of human life on the earth, is directly of use only as the model towards which we ought to approximate. He then proceeds to say of the belief in personal immortality, that it is not connected in general with faith in God, for it was possible to expound the latter without reference to it. It is also possible to conceive a resignation of individual immortality based, not upon a materialistic denial of the spirit, but upon a humble consciousness of the limitation of all individual life; with such a view, the supremacy of the God-consciousness would be perfectly consistent, while it would also require the purest morality and spirituality of life. On the other hand, there may be an irreligious, eudæmonistic form of faith in immortality: for instance, "whenever the faith is postulated on behalf of retribution only." "If, therefore, it must be admitted that the continuance of personal existence may be rejected in a form prompted more thoroughly by godliness than is the case with other forms of its adoption, the connexion of this belief with the consciousness of God as such cannot be maintained." But though faith in immortality is not directly connected with faith in God, it is still connected with faith in Christ, in so far as Christ's promise of the lasting fellowship of his followers with himself presupposes, not only his, but also our own personal immortality (but this is probably only a less simple form of the truth, that the hope of immortality is based upon the Christian consciousness of the indestructible salvation of the devout children of God). As regards the conceptions of the Church as to the future life and the consummation of all things, in Schleiermacher's opinion, they ought to have a place in dogmatic theology only as "tentative efforts of an insufficiently authorised faculty of surmise (*Ahnungsvermögen*), in conjunction with the reasons for and the considerations against them." The difficulties of the doctrines appear to him especially that the conceptions formed of the consummated condition of the whole Church, and again of the perfected condition of individual souls after death, nowhere fully agree together; it is as difficult to conceive of the consummated Church, after the analogy of the present one, as in continual development, as it is to think of it as completed and so without movement, the latter condition presenting no ends for active work for one another. The only course left for us, therefore, in this matter is to put the imagination, to whose sphere all these things that are foreign to our present experience pertain, under the protection of exegetical science, and to work up the materials which it supplies.

At the end of the work is added a section on the Trinity. It follows of itself from what has already been said on Schleiermacher's doctrine as to the divine attributes, that he could not acknowledge hypostatic distinctions in the Divine Being. His dialectical critique of the ecclesiastical doctrine of the Trinity is as admirable as the historical estimate of the various motives which led to the construction of this doctrine is unsatisfactory. It is undoubtedly correct that the doctrine is not a direct utterance as to the Christian self-consciousness, but only a combination of several of such,—namely, of our union with God by the revelation of Christ, and by the common spirit of the Christian Church. Schleiermacher explains, therefore, the Trinity modalistically of the various forms of the revelation of God, and justifies his procedure by an appeal to the early example of the Sabellians.

The entire theology of the last half-century, as far as it seeks at all to remain in touch with critical thought, has been in some degree or other influenced by the theological system of Schleiermacher. But of the numbers who called themselves disciples of Schleiermacher, it has been only a very few who have succeeded in maintaining that combination of keen logical thinking, inward devoutness of feeling, and close sympathy with the life of the Church, which constituted the chief characteristics of the master. In the case of the majority, the requirements of their personal devout feeling, and still more regard to the real or supposed wants of the churches, prevailed to such an extent as to lead them to put on one side the critical element in the theology of Schleiermacher, and to use his formulæ rather for the purpose of hiding or modifying the difficulties of the supranaturalistic theology than to encourage them to advance beyond the old standpoint along the new paths of the master. It is true this "positive mediating theology" (*positive Vermittlungstheologie*) rendered the service to Church life of softening the old antitheses, of bringing parties nearer to each other, and, in opposition to the narrowness of strict confessionalism, of giving effect in the Church to a certain breadth of religious views, together with warmth of devout feeling. But as regards scientific theology, it marks, in general, not so much an advance beyond as a falling back behind Schleiermacher, even though we must admit that in some points its divergence from him was justified.

In the *System der christlichen Lehre*, by Carl Immanuel Nitzsch, in the *Dogmatik* (left unfinished) of Twesten, in Ullmann's works on the Sinlessness of Christ and the Nature of Christianity, in Julius Müller's book on Sin, and in other representatives of this school, the prevailing aim is to save as much as possible of the traditional matter of the ecclesiastical dogmas, while softening down their offensive features by forms of expression borrowed from Schleiermacher's theology. Nor in this effort was there wanting, on the part of the above-named theologians, either learning or dialectical ingenuity : what they lacked was critical power and simple thoroughness and consistency of logical thought. The one amongst them who possessed most independence of thought was NITZSCH; but his desire to be profound caused him to sacrifice clearness, and his affected brevity often issued in oracular ambiguity. He took as his starting-point the fundamental thought of Schleiermacher, that religion is not doctrine but life, direct consciousness, feeling. At the same time he sought to bring religious feeling into closer connexion with knowledge and volition than Schleiermacher had done ; he laid special stress —and justly—on the recognition of a necessary and radical union of religion with morality, treating both dogmatics and ethics together accordingly in his *System der christlichen Lehre*. In his exposition of the idea of revelation, the originality, the new beginning of a religious phenomenon in the life of humanity, is made the prime feature, and then follows what promises to be an extension of the idea so as to embrace heathen religions, as far as they can be conceived as an education for Christianity ; but, after all, this preparation for Christianity was only negative and ideal, while the positive and real preparation is to be found only in the facts and events of Old Testament history. With the supranaturalists, Nitzsch places miracles and prophecies principally amongst the specific facts of revelation. Miracles are to be regarded as supernatural, creative acts; yet not as unnatural or contrary to law, but only as a higher nature in the lower one. Indeed, he does not hesitate to say, "Miracles and nature, though distinct, cannot be separated; for the complete idea of nature involves that of miracle, and the true idea of miracle that of nature." Irreconcilable conceptions are to be reconciled by thus playing fast and loose with words! So with reference to prophecy, at first the rational point of view is presented, that prophecy has essentially to do with the divine in history and relates to the kingdom of God as a whole, not to the details of outward events. Nevertheless, prediction of single events of the future, though only to a "moderate" extent, must not be excluded from prophecy. The fulfilment of prophecy, however, must not be conceived as a complete "consequence," but as an analogical or typical correspondence, which admit also of a repeated and gradual fulfilment. That is, we have the confusion of two totally opposite points of view: on the one hand, development in accordance with law, and on the other, a supernatural prediction of accidental details. For Scripture, too, Nitzsch demands a "completely unique union of the divine word with the human, a quite peculiar economy," by which the miraculous character of an infallible authority is secured to the Bible. Thus in his Prolegomena, to go no further, the standpoint of Schleiermacher is absolutely put back to that of the supranaturalists; and the same thing occurs in the body of the work, especially in his *Christology*. TWESTEN, it is true, excels Nitzsch in the formal clearness of his reasoning, though the material weakness of his incongruous principles is thereby made only the more obvious. His *Dogmatik der Evangelisch-Lutherischen Kirche*, of which, however, only the first part, as far as the doctrine of the angels, has appeared, is a surprising attempt to deduce the ideas of the orthodoxy of the seventeenth century from the religious feelings of the modern consciousness, in which attempt not all the arts of a sophistic scholasticism avail to bridge the wide chasm which parts the two points of view. In JULIUS MÜLLER the scholasticism was carried so far as to revive the ancient Gnostic theory of the fall of man before all time, a theory which found no favour amongst his theological friends. Other representatives of this supranaturalistic

Mediating Theology will come before us subsequently, either amongst the apologists in opposition to Strauss, or amongst the speculative eclectics.

The only theologian among the immediate pupils of Schleiermacher who has taken up his ideas in their purity and developed them with independence, is ALEXANDER SCHWEIZER. The significance which he ascribes to his master's *Glaubenslehre*, and the direction in which he seeks to further develop it, he has clearly stated in the introductory paragraph of his own *Christliche Glaubenslehre nach protestantischen Grundsätzen* (1863-73). "The distinctive nature of Schleiermacher's theological system is a subjectivity open and free towards the true objectivity, or an objectivity such as can really live in the devout subject and make itself felt as the truth. That which marks the present stage of our development in the Church, which has been far more widely reached than is openly confessed, is not Schleiermacher's person and his dogmatic labours, but the freedom in appropriating traditional dogmas which was evinced by him as an obligation upon our time generally, and which has since Schleiermacher been still more urgently imposed upon us as a duty. Unmistakably our age needs and demands a free development of theology as well as of piety, of congregations as well as of the Church, a free, independent sphere for the religious life, a system of religious belief which represents the faith that is really believed and believable, a conscious advance beyond dogmatism and dogmatics." Theology must not take its matter merely from the Scriptures, nor merely from the ecclesiastical creeds, nor again merely from the reason, in so far as it has not been brought under the influence of Christian experience; but from the faith itself of the Protestant Church, that is, the devout consciousness, as far as it has been brought under the influence of the general experience of the Protestant Church in its historical development. The common Christian life of the churches is the sphere in which alone Christian experiences can adequately arise. Our faith is based upon Christian experience. It is accordingly never merely feeling, but always likewise thought and impulse, *i.e.*, tends to pass into doctrine and action, especially as the feeling itself arises in consequence of doctrine and action, or is produced and determined in us as Christian feeling. Although religious feeling is the primary and original element of subjective piety, on the other hand it is neither an isolated thing, inasmuch as it can only be made intelligible by its expression in doctrine and practice, nor is it what it is save through the influence of the religious practices and teaching by which we are surrounded. As little as the non-ego can be construed from the pure ego can a definite, clear, and complete system of faith be deduced from the devout ego, that is, from the emotions of the ego which we call feelings, without the incorporation, consciously or unconsciously, of the objective experiences of the Church which are represented in its doctrines. It is true that Schleiermacher desired this, but he identified his own devout feelings too much with those of the Church. It is an excellence of Schweizer's *Glaubenslehre* that a definite distinction is drawn in it between subjective and objective faith, and a mutual interaction and regulation of both is maintained. Connected with this is a further difference by which Schweizer gave fuller development to the theology of Schleiermacher on the speculative side. If devout feeling is the source from which doctrines are derived, it cannot be also the canon by which these doctrinal statements are to be judged. For this purpose devout feeling is an element too indefinite, variable, purely subjective, with regard to which it is impossible to be sufficiently certain either as to the measure of its agreement with the feeling of the Church or as to its intrinsic truth. Not only must its place in the development of Christian piety be in each case proved, a condition which Schleiermacher did not sufficiently observe, but it must also be determined from another side than the historical one—by the ideal of religion itself, since we are by Christian experience placed in a position to find and recognise that ideal. The moral and religious perfection of man is an ideal which lives within our souls, having been aroused and fostered by Christian experience especially, and taking definite shape in our conceptions, it helps to determine our religious feelings also. Whatever contradicts this ideal in our traditional religion cannot be to us the truth; Christianity, whatever impure and perishable accretions may have sometimes accidently adhered to it, is essentially one with the ideal of perfect religion, and must therefore take the form called for by this ideal as well as by Christian experience. As in objective knowledge generally, the truth is established by the agreement of empirical observation with the idea obtained by the speculative method, so in religion certain truth is reached by the agreement of experience with the religious idea. The excellence of Christianity, which guarantees for it imperishable duration, is that in its essential matter it coincides with the idea of perfect religion, and simply seeks to realise it. Christianity comes to its true self, not in the reason of rationalism, but in the ideal of perfect piety. The one proper canon of truth, to be followed by theology in its criticism of traditionary matter, is to compare the historical form with the idea, and to require the approximation of the former to the latter. It is precisely the excellence of this canon of truth that it is not one so definitely formulated as, for instance, the Apostles' Creed; for no period is in a position to produce an infallible formula to serve as the canon of truth for all the future. This canon must be itself subject to improvement, advancing with universal and Christian knowledge. The ideal of perfect godliness will be perceived more purely and fully in proportion as Christian experience advances, since our ideals are brought to life and full consciousness by means of the experience that answers to them. Guidance into more truth takes place in the interaction of progressive Christian experience and of the ideal of absolute religion and morality, rendered growingly perfect through that experience, so that whatever does not satisfy that ideal cannot be genuinely Christian, however long it may have dogmatic currency.

These are the principles of genuine Protestantism, and at the same time of genuine modern scientific theology. The ideal factor, the idea which lives within us of the perfect religion, is recognised, together with the factor of experience in the consciousness of the Church, as the canon of truth in the construction of theological doctrines, and it is at the same time acknowledged that this religious ideal is not always the same, or to be put into an exact formula for all time, but develops, advances, and deepens. Such principles cut the ground from under dogmatism in every form, not only the dogmatism of orthodoxy, but also of rationalism and speculation, while they clear the way for a treatment of theological doctrines which is both conservative and free, in which the valuable elements of past development are preserved and the course is opened and the direction shown for progressive development in the future. Schweizer accordingly declines to place dogmatic theology (as Schleiermacher desired) in the division of ecclesiastical statistics, as a historical science, but assigns to it, no less than to ethics, as essential the duty of preparing for and directing the future development of faith.

In accordance with these principles, Schweizer puts the various doctrines in a form which is not less productive religiously than rational. The dignity of Scripture, he maintains, must be asserted in opposition to ecclesiastical tradition, to fanatical claimants of special illumination, and to abstract reason uninfluenced by Christianity. But if this authority is carried to excess and urged against reason generally, even when brought under the influence of Christian experience; or if it is applied to scientific matters, whether in the department of historical criticism or of the physical world, it must cease to serve the truth, and could only give rise to error by presenting non-religious matters as religious, and thereby promoting superstition. The Scriptures supply what is necessary for salvation, in a form abundantly recognisable by the Christian community in its free development, precisely when exegesis acknowledges no binding canon in tradition. Nor is the authority of the Scriptures based upon a mechanical, or any other supernatural inspiration of their contents, but simply upon their recognisable value and the historical position of their authors.

In Schweizer's hands the doctrine of God likewise takes a more satisfactory form than in Schleiermacher's system. Instead of going back, as his master had done, to the philosophy of Spinoza, Schweizer recurs to the theology of the Calvinistic Church, in which the unconditioned and universal causality of God, as the basis of the certainty of salvation, is made the centre point of the theological system. Schweizer had previously traced minutely the historical development of the central doctrines of the Reformed Church, and makes use of his historical and critical inquiries in his *Glaubenslehre*. He defines God as the living cause whose operation is the foundation of the world as one of law and order. The world of nature and the world of moral order, with the life of salvation in the kingdom of God, are absolutely dependent on God; and they are thus dependent as ordered worlds, so that their order is never interrupted by their dependence on him, but is caused and preserved thereby. In the order of nature, God's omnipotence and omniscience, eternity and omnipresence, are manifested; in the order of the moral world his holiness, truth, and righteousness ; in the life of salvation in the kingdom of God, his paternal love and wisdom, which called into existence by Christ the religion of salvation, prepared for by the religion of nature and the religion of law, and which guide and consummate its course in conformity with a necessary historical order. The truth of the doctrine of predestination is found in the unconditional dependence upon divine grace of the entire course amongst men of the Christian life of salvation ; but the Augustinian and Calvinistic doctrine of the divine decrees, with its particularism and definitive dualism, must be given up. For the grace of the religion of salvation is in its object and effect designed for all mankind, though it is made particular in its historical realisation, not producing effect all at once upon all, and the same effect upon all, since, as its operations are spiritual, it exerts no compulsion, but allows of resistance. But notwithstanding this particularism in its historical operation, the divine grace, which is in itself universal, cannot suffer a final dualism of the saved and the unsaved. This Judaistic conception must not interfere with the Christian hope of the perfect consummation of the appropriated salvation in eternity. In this monistic consummation of the divine work of salvation, Schweizer recognises the true logical consequence of the position taken by Zwingli as to the preordination of sin in the eternal purposes of God, in view of salvation, in support of which Romans ix.–xi. may be quoted.

Schweizer's Christology is, like Schleiermacher's, based upon the Christian consciousness, but with a much more cautious use of the historical documents. He starts from the position, that according to the supposition underlying our Christian consciousness, Christianity is that historical religion in which the idea of religion is presented and realised, so that in that idea nothing is contained which could not be realised in Christianity. Thence he infers that the idea of man as one with God must be embodied in Christ, must shine unchecked through his whole manifestation, so that with and in Christ the ideal of religion is brought home to our consciousness. "We behold in him the pure image of the divine life in human form, without going so far as to identify absolutely the ideal and the historical Christ." For the Hellenistic conceptions of a divine and human nature, and of three persons in the Godhead, must be substituted those of our modern thinkers—idea and manifestation, eternal and temporal, being and historical realisation. If we apply these ideas to Christology and Pneumatology, our definitions will become much more intelligible, harmonising both sides of the relation without the surrender of the one or the other, or the confounding of both. Not until dogmatic Christology and Pneumatology have passed in our belief into an ethical and religious Christology and Pneumatology, will this problem, proposed from the very first by the Reformation, find its solution. A special point on which Schweizer worked out more definitely suggestions of Schleiermacher's is the parallel between Christology and Pneumatology, the Holy Spirit bearing just the same relation to the Church as in Christ the idea to its manifestation. The Church then appears as the Christ widened into the historical life of the community, Christ as the original representation of the common spirit of the Church, or of the ideal religion. When it is added that this religion was founded and historically prepared for in mankind from the beginning, it follows that in Christ the ideal destination of humanity first reached full realisation, and that Christianity is therefore essentially one with the ideal of human nature; a view to which Zwingli had already prophetically pointed, and in which the thought of Protestant philosophers and theologians is found in full accord.

CHAPTER III.

SPECULATIVE THEOLOGY.

HEGEL'S religious philosophy was from the first a *Janus bifrons*, from which accordingly the theology to which it gave birth was developed in two contrary directions. The assumption of the identity of religious and philosophical truth produced a strongly conservative attitude towards ecclesiastical dogma; while if stress was laid on the distinction between them—that religion gives us truth only in the imperfect form of intuitions or percepts, but philosophy in the perfect form of concepts,— the obvious inference was that religion, as the lower stage, must be resolved into and replaced by the higher stage of philosophy. The conservative attitude was exclusively taken by Hegel's school during the master's lifetime, and was predominant for long afterwards. "This school," according to Baur's admirable critique,[1] "was enamoured of the opinion, which it either entertained itself, or wished others at all events to entertain of it, that between its philosophy and Christianity there was an affinity and harmony such as no other philosophy had been able to boast of. If this philosophy had its Trinity, why should it not likewise have its Incarnate God, its Reconciliation, and similar dogmas? To speak of an Incarnate God sounded to the Hegelian school speculatively as profound as it was edifying to the Christian; while Schleiermacher had spoken only of a "Saviour," now the Hegelian school, as if conscious of a certain priestly dignity, put its profoundest significance into the doctrine of a "God-man." But how little the chasm separating the God-man of philosophy from the God-man of the Church was realised, may be best seen in the theology of Marheineke. After speaking philosophically of the unity of the divine and human nature, of the former as the truth and the latter as the reality, he makes the transition to the historical personage in perfect good faith, by simply saying that

---

[1] *Kirchengeschichte*, vol. v. p. 378.

"the unity of God and man was historically realised in the person of Jesus Christ." So too in Daub's *Theologumena*, the incarnation of God and the redemption of the world is in the first place deduced as an eternal truth from the idea of God in the following manner: God's eternal self-contemplation must be identical with human reason, and God's eternal activity consists in bringing back the world from its finiteness, the result of its apostasy, to the unity of his infinite Being,— the world of nature by the natural method of the death of the individual, but mankind by the spiritual method of religion, as exaltation above the emptiness of the finite to the infinite. The importance of Christ, Daub considered to be that he exhibited this eternal incarnation of God and redemption of the world in his own person, as an historical fact, on which account he was himself the God-man in a unique sense, his death the sacrifice redeeming the world, his life a continual miracle and full of miracles. It was quite after the style of this romantic and uncritical speculative method to connect the metaphysical ideas, which had been arrived at by means of philosophical dialectic, directly with the persons and events of the Gospel narratives, thus raising these above the region of ordinary experience into that of the supernatural, and regarding the most absurd assertions as philosophically justified. Daub had become so hopelessly addicted to this perverse principle that he deduced not only Jesus as the embodiment of the philosophical idea of the union of God and man, but also Judas Iscariot as the embodiment of the idea of a rival god, or Satan. We of this generation find the confusion of ideas underlying such deductions so incomprehensible that it is hard to avoid unfairness in our estimate of the individual theologians of this class, especially when they carry their disdain of the sound human understanding so far as to ascribe with Daub, in the very title of his last book (1833), rational doubts respecting the dogmas and legends of the Church simply to criminal self-seeking.

The credit of having chased away the mists and clouds of dogmatic illusions such as these, and of restoring to the critical understanding its rights, belongs to the Swabian theologian, DAVID FRIEDRICH STRAUSS. Two previous works upon Immortality, the authors of which, Richter and Feuerbach, were reckoned among the Hegelian school, had indeed, by the radically negative conclusions therein reached by the application of this philosophy, shaken the confidence generally felt in Hegelian orthodoxy; but since the other adherents of the school were active in protesting against these negative inferences, such isolated efforts produced no very important effect. When, however, Strauss brought the heavy artillery of his criticism, distinguished equally by learning and penetration, to bear first on the historical foundations of dogma and then on dogma itself, the unsubstantial fabric of Hegelian dogmatism was within a few years completely destroyed. The first and greatest shock was given by Strauss's work on the life of Jesus, which will occupy us in the next book. As the polemical literature which his Life of Jesus provoked was chiefly occupied with dogmatical reflections and speculation, rather than with historical criticism, Strauss was induced to supplement it by a further critical work on the history of Christian dogmas, bearing the title, *Die christliche Glaubenslehre in ihrer geschichtlichen Entwickelung und im Kampf mit der modernen Wissenschaft*" (1840–41). The strong point of the book is its acute and ingenious application of the principle that the history of dogma is its destruction and the story of the process of its dissolution. Strauss himself, in his preface, characterises his method in the forcible words: " Individual subjective criticism is a water-pipe which any boy may close for a time; objective criticism, as it is accomplished in the course of centuries, advances like a foaming torrent against which all sluices and dams are powerless." In the same preface he thus describes the object of his work: " Its purpose is —if the profane figure is allowable—to do for the science of dogmatics what the balance-sheet does for a commercial house. If the firm is not made directly the richer by it, it learns exactly what its resources are: and that is often as valuable as an actual increase of them. Such a survey of our dogmatic property is in our days rendered the more urgently necessary in proportion as the majority of theologians entertain the greatest illusions on the subject. The depreciation of the old theological stock-in-trade made by the criticism and polemics of the last two centuries is greatly underrated; and on the other hand, the doubtful assistance supposed to be derived from the emotional theology and mystical philosophy of the present century is much over-estimated. It is generally imagined that the greater part of the lawsuits which are pending with regard to those depreciations have been won, and that there is certainty of the greatest profits from these newly opened resources. But it is not impossible that these suits should all be lost in a *single* day, and if then these new mines should also disappoint expectations, failure would be inevitable. Reason enough, surely, to know in time, after careful calculation, the relation of the credit to the debit side of the account!" The result of this balancing of accounts, Strauss declares to be the complete bankruptcy of the Christian faith; neither is it merely the dogmatic formulæ of the theology of the Church that are subject to this process of dissolution, but, Strauss holds, that with them the Christian religion must pass away, and even religion in general. This marked precipitation was only possible in the case of a man in whose nature religious feeling was much weaker than critical intellect, and who had besides grown accustomed in the Hegelian school to that intellectualism which makes knowledge everything and all other vital functions nothing, and in which particularly religion was regarded only as theoretical and bound to stand or fall with a particular theory. Strauss's study of Schleiermacher might have preserved him from this gross error; but great as was his acumen in descrying Schleiermacher's dogmatic weaknesses, he was quite unable to understand the importance of Schleiermacher's theory of religion, and the justice of the distinction between religion and theology. In general, the overweening self-confidence of "absolute knowledge" fostered in Hegel's school had materially tended to accentuate the negative radicalism of Strauss's criticism. Whoever imagines himself to possess the key to all the riddles of the world in the formulæ of his philosophical school, will very naturally pass a much more negative sentence upon all attempts to form a conception of the world from a religious point of view, than the man who humbly recognises the relativity of all our knowledge and is under no illusion with regard to the value of the formulæ of all systems. The absolute and irreconcilable antagonism between philosophy and theology which Strauss tries to show, in the case of each dogma, is the final result of the historical process, arises unavoidably then only when both the philosopher and the theologian make the same mistake of embracing a dogmatism which propounds its formulæ as infallible truths. This is indisputably the case to a marked degree with the Hegelian-Straussian philosophy of "absolute knowledge." But since this dogmatism is the opposite of scientific, the radicalism of Strauss's History of Dogmatics evidently cannot decide the general question of the relation of religion and science.

The final consequences of Strauss's position were inferred by Feuerbach. Strauss did not go beyond an idealistic pantheism, which, while it gave up the God of religion, at least assumed a universal spiritual principle, an "idea" which realises itself in the finite, evolves nature from itself, and becomes conscious of itself in man ; and in this Feuerbach recognised a remnant of mysticism which must be got rid of ; the Absolute above man he declared to be an empty abstraction, the really Absolute or Divine is man himself. All and every system of theology, not excepting speculative theology, must therefore be superseded by anthropology. But if man alone is divine, how can he come to believe in and worship a God? Feuerbach answers that the conception of God is an illusion, formed of the wishes of the heart and of the poetic imagination. The gods are *Wunschwesen*, i.e., the wishes and ideals of the human heart objectified by the imagination. In them man contemplates his own nature, not as it really is, held in by the limitation of the world, but as he wishes it to be, as the unlimited omnipotence of feeling. Religious faith is the self-assurance of the heart demanding the satisfaction of its desires. A miracle is the realisation (of course the imagined realisation) of a supernatural wish. Christ is the omnipotence of subjectivity, the reality of all the wishes of the heart ; the conception of an incarnate God is the disclosure of the truth, that the nature of God is simply man. So also the Christian heaven means, just like the Christian God, the fulfilment of all wishes. Immortality is the testament of religion, in which it makes its last will ; as heaven is the unfolded nature of the Deity, it is also the frankest declaration of the inmost thoughts of religion.

Feuerbach stands at the head of those who hold religion to be an idealistic fiction without actual truth, viz., the modern Positivists and Agnostics. But while the latter with cautious scepticism decline to deal with the metaphysical questions as to the origin of the world and of man, Feuerbach only abandoned the idealistic dogmatism of his Hegelian school to adopt that of materialism. He held that only what is cognisable by the senses, what is material, is real ; even in man the spiritual is only an effect of the sensible, the sole reality ;

"*der Mensch ist, was er isst*," man *is* what he *eats*, was finally Feuerbach's watchword. It follows of course that from this cynical point of view religion can only be regarded as a foolish aberration, a kind of mental disorder; but since by the same hypothesis the other objects of man's spiritual endeavour, morality, art and science, must lose all their meaning and value, this position is really self-destructive. For if man is only a material product of nature, like a plant or an animal, it is inconceivable why he should come to form moral ideas of any kind, or to propose scientific views on any question. The naturalistic point of view adopted by Feuerbach could logically lead only to the rejection of *all* ideas and ideals, or to pure nihilism and solipsism, as is clearly shown in Max Stirner's notorious book, *Der Einzige und sein Eigenthum*. The same holds good of the last book in which Strauss laid before the world his final confession of faith, *Der alte und der neue Glaube*, 1872. Like Feuerbach, he abandoned the dogmatism of idealism for that of naturalism, undeterred by the logical inconsistencies of naturalism and the difficulties of Feuerbach's theory of knowledge. On the principles of modern natural science, he now believed himself able to explain the world as a mechanism of blind material forces, without any final cause, and hence without any spiritual principle; nevertheless he sought to acknowledge reason and goodness in the universe, and honour them with a certain piety. Man he considered a part of nature, developed from the ape by Darwinian selection; nevertheless he required him never to forget that he was man, and not merely a part of nature, that in him nature had not merely striven upwards, but even to surpass herself; he must therefore be guided in his action by the idea of the race, and by the consciousness of mutual obligation seek to mitigate the cruel struggle for existence, although as a part of nature he cannot wholly avoid it. It comes to this then, man is a part and again not a part of nature; the product of an aimless mechanical natural process, and yet a product in which nature has striven to surpass herself! The struggle for existence, the right of the stronger, is the only law ruling the world, and yet man is bound to be guided by the altruistic principle of the idea of the race! The new creed which includes such gross contradictions, without even attempting their solution, can hardly claim more scientific importance than any one of the old confessions of faith. In point of fact, both philosophy and theology soon passed from Strauss's last book to the order of the day. His earlier contributions to historical criticism ought not however to be forgotten. We shall speak of them in the next book.

But neither the right nor the left wing of the Hegelian school permanently enriched dogmatic theology, owing to the weakness of the former in historical criticism, and of the latter in the appreciation of religious facts. On the other hand, we have to mention a number of men who, avoiding these two extremes, tried to gain by the aid of speculative philosophy a profounder conception of the Christian faith. The most important works in this connexion are three: *Biedermann's Christliche Dogmatik*, *Weisse's Philosophische Dogmatik*, and *Rothe's Theologische Ethik*. Their common feature is a speculative theism and a theistic and theological view of history, in which the facts as well as the ideas and ideals of Christianity find a place.

At the time of ALOIS EMANUEL BIEDERMANN's youth scientific and ecclesiastical circles had been deeply stirred by the Hegelian philosophy and Straussian criticism. Both profoundly affected him and greatly enriched his thought, without robbing him of his freedom and individuality. He never was an Hegelian in the strict sense of the school, but from the first regarded Hegel's characteristic method of *à priori* dialectic as an error and as the untenable weakness of the system, and tried to correct it by a less ambitious departure from experience. Still, he saw profound truth in the fundamental principle of the Hegelian philosophy, that reason is in everything which exists and occurs, and must, as the creative nature of things, be comprehended by our own rational thought. He likewise recognised the great importance of Strauss's critical labours, although he early perceived that the limitation of Strauss's powers lay in the fact that he could not rise above the critical dissolution of the conceptions of ecclesiastical tradition to the speculative recognition and presentation of the religious truth contained in them. Biedermann regarded criticism, in which he was equal to Strauss in point of rigour, as only one half of the problem to be solved ; the other, and certainly not less important half, being to formulate as conceptual knowledge the content of religious truth after it has been purified in the crucible of critical analysis. To make this positive addition to Strauss's negative results, he regarded as his own life-work, to the accomplishment of which he devoted the labours of his best years. The result of these labours is contained in his chief work, *Die Christliche Dogmatik*, the first edition of which appeared in 1868, and the second in 1884-5, enlarged by a philosophical introduction in which is expounded the theory of knowledge underlying his metaphysics and theology.

This theory of knowledge occupies a peculiar position intermediary between Hegel's logical idealism and Spinoza's parallelism of extended and thinking Being as the two sides of the *one* substance. Biedermann holds firmly to the Hegelian principle that the substance of spirit is logical Being, and hence can be wholly and entirely comprehended in logical categories, both in respect of the infinite spirit, or God, and of the finite spirit, or man. But he does not hold that the logical Being of spirit includes within it all Being, and that the world is only the development and manifestation of the absolute logical idea ; nor does he think that we can construct and logically deduce the world by means of an *à priori* dialectic. On the contrary, he teaches that spiritual or ideal Being is never given us other than with and in sensuous or material Being, and only in such a way that they are by nature antithetical—the one, logical Being, is outside space and time ; the other, material Being, spatial and temporal, but both are combined with and in each other to form the *one* whole reality. The problem of cognition accordingly is, in the case of any content of consciousness, so to distinguish the ideal Being from the material Being, in combination with which it exists, as to make clear both the antithesis of their respective natures, and at the same time the indivisible unity of their substance. This abstraction of logical Being from material Being, and the comprehension of the former, as the ideal content of experience, in purely logical categories, is what Biedermann means by "pure thought." This theory of cognition is the foundation of his metaphysics ; from it follow, in his view, the answers to the most important questions regarding soul and body, God and world. On this very account we must not refrain from stating the grave objections to which the theory is open. In the first place, we must observe that the conception "ideal Being" is ambiguous, since it denotes sometimes thinking Being[1] (spirit, consciousness), sometimes

---

[1] denkendes Sein.

Being thought[1] (conception, relation, law). Now it is certainly wrong to say that thinking Being, *i.e.*, being which thinks, is *merely* logical Being, since the same Being which thinks also wills and feels; for this reason we cannot antecedently expect that this thinking Being, or spirit, will be comprehended purely and entirely in logical categories. Neither can we assent to the proposition that ideal or spiritual Being is timeless, while temporal Being as such is physical or material; Being thought, as the idea of a triangle, of spirit, or of history, is indeed timeless; but thinking Being, or spirit itself, is never given us in experience as timeless Being, but always as the consciousness of our ego taking place in time. Whether this peculiarity of occurring in time, which always attaches to the Being of spirit in our experience, is accidental and can be dispensed with in thought, is a difficult question, and has been variously answered; but whatever answer be given, at any rate the identification of spiritual with timeless Being can never be taken for granted as an unquestionable axiom. Further, with regard to the fundamental principle of this theory of knowledge, viz., the parallelism of ideal and material Being as the two inseparable sides of one substantial reality, I remark, firstly, that this view, derived from Spinoza, cannot be deduced from the analysis of our consciousness, since direct experience is always entirely a phenomenon of consciousness, and hence ideal Being, from which we afterwards mediately infer the existence of an external material Being. Secondly, as a psychological hypothesis this theory is not calculated satisfactorily to explain the relation of body and soul without doing violence to the facts of experience. Thirdly, as a metaphysical hypothesis it is equally unfitted to explain the relation of the world to God; for if the world is both spiritual and material Being, we cannot see how it should have its foundation in a purely spiritual God; *vice versâ*, if with Biedermann we accept the latter hypothesis, we should expect the reduction of material Being in some way to spiritual Being, and not the co-ordination of the two as from the first opposite in nature. Hegel's monism of absolute Spirit, and Spinoza's dualism of Thought and Extension, are theories too contradictory to admit of combination in a single system. Biedermann most likely recognised the one-sided

---

[1] gedachtes Sein.

character of absolute logical idealism, and its need of amendment from the side of actual experience; but in having recourse, with this object in view, to Spinoza's dualism of thinking and corporeal Being, he grafted a foreign and antagonistic shoot upon the trunk of idealism, and left unremoved Hegel's fundamental defect, his abstract logical formalism. Still, by this alteration Biedermann attained one object—a more definite distinction between God and the world, thus the substitution of theism for pantheism, though still in too abstract a form; and to do this was an essential condition for a right view of religion.

The investigation of the nature of religion was improved in the second edition of Biedermann's work by the psychological description of it being placed before the inquiry into its metaphysical basis. Biedermann defines Religion as the endeavour of the human ego to rise above the limiting negations of the world as the scene of its natural life by appealing to a Power raised above such limitation, in order by its help to obtain deliverance; it is produced by anything which discloses the opposition between man's demands of life and the limitation he experiences. The psychical form of this endeavour is Faith, in which all the elementary functions of the personal spirit are harmoniously combined: a feeling of dependence and mundane limitation as the point of departure, and of freedom as the goal of the act of appeal, a conception of an infinite Power above man, a desire to rise to this Power, with a longing for deliverance from the cramping limitations of the world. This whole act of the man, theoretical and practical in one, constitutes real "religious faith"; while "faith" in the sense of mere theoretical belief is not a religious act at all. Precisely because religious faith is something other than a mere form of secondary knowledge, it can never be rendered obsolete and replaced by any higher kind of knowledge, such as philosophy. Philosophy can exercise a purifying influence upon the theoretical side of religion,—on the various modes of conceiving the contents of faith,—but can never replace the distinctly religious act of faith itself—the practical elevation of the man to God. By this means Biedermann secured himself against the Hegelian confusion of religion and philosophy, which had led Strauss to the fatal step of annulling the former by means of the latter, and strictly guarded the indefeasible rights of the religious life against all encroachments on the part of knowledge.

But Biedermann does not end with the psychological description of religion. Though this has its proximate source in the nature of man himself, as finite spirit, the appeal of his soul to God is incomprehensible without the metaphysical supposition of relations on God's part with man; the fact of religion presupposes the existence and self-revelation of God. The legitimacy of this presupposition, of which the religious consciousness has an immediate certainty, is shown by the reasoning intellect in the "proofs of the existence of God"; and then the idea of God is put into a "pure"—*i.e.*, abstractly logical—formula, as follows: "The absoluteness of the spiritual Being of God consists therein, that the *actus purus* of his self-sufficient existence within himself is the non-temporal and non-spatial condition, *i.e.*, the eternal and omnipresent source, of the temporal and spatial process of the finite world." God is the source of the world, not by temporal act of creation out of nothing, but in that by a non-temporal method he produces from himself the material being of the world, and makes it external to himself. The latter expression is intended definitely to provide against any pantheistic confusion of God and world; but, it must be confessed, the conception of the absolute Spirit producing from himself, and making external to himself, a material world, the nature of which is antithetical to his own spirituality, is as unrealisable in thought as the Church's idea of creation, which lays no claim to logical truth. Moreover, in Biedermann's case this claim rests upon a delusion; the categories of (*Insichseins*) existence within self, and making external to self (*Aussersichsetzens*), evidently belong to the intuition of space, and are therefore by no means purely logical, but figurative expressions, which are not purer but only much less significant than the expressions usually borrowed from the analogy of the human spirit. Biedermann's rejection of this one possible way of arriving at positive (though, of course, always relative) statements about God, ostensibly in the interests of "pure thought," which, it is said, can lay claim to absolute appropriateness, was not the strength but the weakness of his theology, betraying his bondage to the logical formalism and dogmatism of the Hegelian school.

Biedermann discusses at length the nature of divine revelation. It is a process within the human spirit, effected by God, in which man's spiritual activities are not set aside but raised above their finite limitation, so as to experience the divine.

More particularly, we may distinguish three elements in the divine revelation: it appears as the basis of man's spiritual life in his bent to rationality (*Vernunftrieb*), as the law of his spiritual life in his conscience, and as the force securing its normal realisation in his religious and moral freedom. This latter is the properly religious revelation, which takes place in the faith of the religious man as illumination, blessedness, and sanctification. These *inward* experiences of the religious spirit are the effect therefore of direct divine action or revelation, and in this consists the *only* revelation properly so called; on the other hand, things lying behind or outside them, whether external events or history or sacred scriptures or ceremonial observances, are in themselves only phenomena of *man's* life of faith; though a natural confusion of the external and derived with the inward and primary causes them to be looked upon as direct divine revelations, and gives them in the faith of the Church a position of unchangeable *divine* authority given once for all. Hence we have the principle of supernatural authority common to all positive religions, and their tendency to strictly preserve anything traditional as having ostensibly come directly from God. This failure of supernaturalism to recognise the natural side of historical religion is corrected by Rationalism, which calls attention to the natural historical conditions of all religious phenomena, but on the other hand exaggerates the truth of this observation by treating everything in religion as a merely natural product of the human mind, and quite dispensing with the divine factor. The problem of critical and speculative theology Biedermann considers to be to preserve such a mean between the two extremes that the supernatural or divine, and the natural or human come to be recognised as the two inseparably united sides of *every* revelation and throughout the *whole* history of religion. Biedermann has also applied this principle to the Christian tradition and to the solution of the great questions of Christology, of the nature and value of the Bible, and of the creeds of the Church.

The Christian religion, he teaches, had its historical source in the person of Jesus, while its essential nature or principle is to be found " in the religious relation as it is presented to us in the religious consciousness of Jesus as a new fact of revelation determining his whole personality and at the same time creating faith in that personality." We can therefore call the religious personality of Jesus the essential principle of Christianity, meaning by this that the new saving influence on mankind with this new object of faith, was simply the characteristic religious consciousness of this person, which took the form of the consciousness of sonship to the heavenly Father. Undoubtedly this personal consciousness of Jesus points to a divine revelation, and so far was miraculous, but only in the relative sense, not as something transcending the constitution of humanity, but as itself the highest fulfilment of the religious and moral destiny of the race ; in Jesus the religious truth that we are all called to be sons of God became, with immediate freshness and force, the content of our knowledge and feeling and a motive-power in our will ; in this sense he is the Son of God and the Saviour κατ' ἐξοχήν. But when the Church converted this relative miracle of the original religious personality of Jesus into a miracle pure and simple, the superhuman person of the God-man from heaven, it did so in consequence of the above-mentioned psychological "law of identification," according to which the divine source of revelation gets directly identified with the human means of its manifestation. Biedermann considers it to be the business of dogmatic Christology to correct this optical illusion from which all its difficulties spring, to discriminate between the *person* of Jesus and the Christian *principle*, the spirit or the ideal of life, the idea of Christianity, and to do this in such a way as neither to confound the two nor to abstractly separate them, but rather to present the person as the historical embodiment of the principle, and the principle as the ideal significance of the person. In this idea of the business of Christology, Biedermann is in substantial accord with the theory of Alexander Schweizer above noticed, though the theories are somewhat differently formulated.

Our theologian adopts a similar course in describing the Reformation. Here too he distinguishes the principle from its historical manifestation in the formation of the Reformed churches. The former consists in a fundamental tendency of the Christian spirit, which always exists in the Church, because belonging to the essence of Christianity—the tendency to react against its own misrepresentation in the Church, and to maintain its peculiar truth in contradistinction to the lower stages represented by the religions of nature and of law. The Reformation gave dogmatic expression to this tendency in the "formal principle" of the sole authority of the word of God, and in the "material principle" of justification from grace alone and through faith. But when the Churches of the Protestant confessions were formed, it was only the practical religious importance of this principle that was recognised, and the consequences involved in it were not worked out. It was indeed historically unavoidable and justifiable in itself to go back for a knowledge of Christian truth behind the tradition of the Church to the Scriptures as historically the original source of this knowledge. But this historical appreciation of the Scriptures did not suffice; they were regarded as "the word of God" absolutely, and infallible divine authority was consequently ascribed to them. Thereby the traditional Catholic theory of authority was in principle still adhered to, and only the *form* of the authority changed, though in a way which might be regarded as an advance. But there was only a relative difference between the Protestant's principle of Scripture and the Catholic's principle of tradition. Equally opposed to the essence of Protestantism was the elevation of ecclesiastical forms of doctrine of historic growth to the position of symbolic statements of unconditional authority. What is really Protestant is simply the continual regeneration of doctrinal theology out of the living principle of Christianity by means of the scientific criticism of the previous development of dogma.

This is the task of theological science which must not be hindered by any theory of inspiration. On the contrary, theology has to distinguish in the Scriptures, no less than in the creeds, between the ideal truth as the lasting kernel and the historically conditioned wrappings in which it appears in the Biblical and ecclesiastical forms of doctrine. Biedermann has sought to do this. He gives an account first of the whole system of Biblical theology, and next of the theology of the Church with its central christological dogmas; he then proceeds to critically analyse these dogmas, and finally presents their pure ideal content in a systematic form. This mode of treatment has the advantage of furnishing a strictly objective account of the Biblical and ecclesiastical doctrines, the historical account being kept separate from the theologian's own critical and speculative estimate of it; but it combines the double disadvantage, that each individual doctrine is treated of in various parts of the book, thus rendering a connected view less easy, and that the positive result, the pure logical essence of the historical subject-matter and its critical analysis, proves to be very much too meagre and vague to help the Church of the present day to understand its faith. It is true that this defect is the consequence, not only of the form of treatment, but also of the theory of knowledge before considered. The metaphysics and psychology based upon this theory exercise also an influence for evil upon the matter of his eschatology: a consequence of it is the denial of the immortality of the soul, since according to this theory the soul must be conceived only as the ideal side of the body and together with it, but not as an independent entity. It is clear that the Christian Church cannot accept this theory without cutting itself off from its whole past history; and such a demand may be the more readily rejected in proportion as it is also scientifically inadmissible,—for it depends upon the undemonstrable assumptions of a philosophical dogmatism. This dependence is the weak side of Biedermann's work, which in other respects contains so much that is excellent.

CHRISTIAN HERMANN WEISSE also belonged at first to Hegel's school, but probably perceived the error of logical idealism, and tried to correct it in a manner which bears close resemblance in many respects to the theosophy of Schelling's later years and of Baader, while his system is not without the originality of genius, and contains an abundance of profound and fertile thoughts. The fact that his *Philosophische Dogmatik oder Philosophie des Christenthums* has notwithstanding had no important influence upon theology, may be explained partly by Weisse's heavy style, partly by the little sympathy his purely deductive method meets with in the bent of our time towards empirical induction. To do Weisse justice, it must not be forgotten that his speculative reasoning, in all departments, including religion, commands a wide knowledge of the empirical subject-matter, and that he succeeds in working up this into his deductive statement in a most suggestive manner.

Weisse's *Philosophische Dogmatik* begins with a speculative construction of the nature of God, in which his departure from Hegel's logical idealism at once becomes apparent. The divine Reason, in which the eternal and necessary truths of reason are contained as an intelligible world, is, according to Weisse, not the whole nature of the Deity, but only the first element or stage of it, the primary possibility of all Being, but not as yet reality. To reason and its necessary thoughts we must add the divine Heart (*Gemüth*), in which the divine life, as sentient and perceptive, begets a profusion of forms which prefigure the ideal types of the world; and from this profuse creation of inward thoughts and figures there arises, thirdly, the divine Will, which freely works upon this given material, and so actualises the nature of God as personality and love. The identification of these three elements, or stages, with the Persons of the Trinity is a concession to dogmatic theology for which Weisse could quote precedents from the history of dogma; but the conception of the self-realisation of God as a process in time preceding the creation of the world, is open to graver objections, and reminds us strongly of Gnostic mythology. The creation of the world, too, Weisse represents as a series of acts beginning and continuing in time, the first of which was the formation of matter, or the chaotic fundamental forces, which proceeded from the divine Will by its action on the ante-creative products of his "nature" (or his heart), and formed the material for God's further organising and shaping activity as creator. From the nature of matter thus conceived Weisse explains the metaphysical necessity of evil in the world. The matter of the world, as the externalised will of God, which has put itself in antithesis to his personal will, possesses a distinct spontaneity of creature-existence which passes into a real antagonism to the inwardness and blessedness of God, and hence is the common root of both physical and moral evil. Just as matter, though generated by God, presents notwithstanding, as something relatively independent, an antithesis to his personal will, so God cannot all at once and by a fiat of will put an end to the evil involved in matter, but can only gradually end the misery unavoidably involved in every fresh birth of living creatures, by the progressive creative activity of his loving will, and transform it into gladness. To this prehuman evil, having its final metaphysical source in the self-will of the creature as such, Weisse refers ideas commonly held of the devil. Similarly the first origination of sin in the personal creature is, according to him, not to be sought so much in conscious acts of will, as in the genesis before time of the personal will out of the natural spontaneity of individual beings. These are, at any rate, profoundly suggestive thoughts, which a serious and earnest theology cannot pass over with indifference.

The process of creation, which reaches its climax in the generation of rational creatures, is continued in the process of the history of civilisation and religion, which must be regarded as a continual "incarnation of God," in the sense that human nature is transformed from earthly nature to one in the image of God, and the ideal "Son-Man" is realised in the human race. The history of religion Weisse conceives as beginning in a consciousness of God, which in its essence is spiritual and with an ethical content, but vacillates between unity and plurality, spirituality and a sensuous form. From this undetermined beginning, either monotheism or polytheism might be developed. The fact of the priority of the latter development in heathen national religions is explained by the psychological law that the activities of the imagination and the heart are earlier in the ascendant than those of the conscious will. Progress in the mythological age consisted partly in the refinement of the æsthetic form of the myths—in conjunction with the general development of each people—partly in the ethicising of their religious contents. From the first the physical and ethical permeated mythology, it is true; but while at the beginning the physical predominated, the emphasis was afterwards laid on the ethical; the sensuous materials of the intuitive imagination were more and more freely melted down into the form of their ideal content, quite independent of the direct phenomena of nature; the gods of nature were personified and brought into connection with man's moral life. Hence we cannot deny the moral and religious value of the mythological religions, particularly the Grecian; Weisse does not hesitate to say that in them was already at work the same power of God to save and sanctify which ecclesiastical dogmatism wishes us to regard as the sole property of the so-called revealed religions in the stricter sense. And he rightly adduces in favour of this broad human view the early Christian doctrine of the pre-Christian mission of the divine Logos. Though the religion of the Old Testament is a revelation in a higher sense, yet it is not this in such a way as to justify the exclusion of the polytheistic religions from the common idea of the incarnation of the divine. But what from the first distinguished the Hebrews' conceptions of God was their subordination of the imagination, the source of myths, to the ethical power of will, the source of history. The legislation of Moses was a typical act of liberation, inasmuch as it showed mankind that its divine vocation was to rise above nature to a moral order of life. This conception of God was then freed from its national limitation, and the universal religious ideal prefigured in the teaching of the prophets, which may be compared to the teaching of Greek philosophy and of the Mysteries; for this too had risen in the Platonic "Idea of the Good" to the rank of a monotheistic principle, and in the doctrine of immortality of the Mysteries to an ethical spiritualisation of religious hopes and ideals.

This universal historical process of the incarnation of God, or the realisation of the "Son-Humanity," is consummated in Jesus, who combined and gathered up the historical conditions into an act of personal consciousness. This permeation of the human nature by the divine, whereby the man Jesus became above all other mortals the instrument of the highest revelation of God, the personal "Son-Man," must not be understood mythically as a physical event, but as an ethical miracle accomplished in the soul of this unique personality. The peculiar characteristics of the personality of Jesus may be summed up by saying that he was endowed with *genius* in the highest sense of the word, analogous to that of all those historical personalities who have been originators in the realm of religion, in particular the prophets of Israel, though in the case of Jesus we must suppose an extraordinary intensification of the gifts of talent and genius. Religious experience was intensified in him to the absolute power of an inward revelation which first raised the historical revelation of God in the human race to its summit of perfection; for this revelation, for the first time concentrating in consciousness the whole truth of the idea of God, completely permeating the heart and will of the entire personality, presented a person before the eyes of the world, who, within the limits of humanity, exhibited purely and completely the image of God. This is the same Christology as that of A. Schweizer and Biedermann, above described; with the latter Weisse shares the speculative framework of his Christology, and with the former the more definite delineation of the historical character; common to him with both is the rejection of the mythically supernatural, and the translation of it into ethical ideality in the domain of history.

Very closely allied to Weisse's speculations is RICHARD ROTHE's *Theologische Ethik* (1st ed. 1845-8; 2nd ed. 1864 sq.). His method also is deductive construction by means of speculative ideas, resulting in a Christian system of philosophy, to which the supernaturalism of the Bible, the theosophy of Schelling and Oetinger, and the theology of Schleiermacher have been made to contribute. The combination of these diverse elements in a systematic whole forms a work of art of too peculiar a character to admit of its being used as a general authority, but the charm of which consists in its being the product and reflection of a rich and noble mind, a profound thinker, a vivid imagination, and a truly devout soul.

Rothe himself describes his method as follows: speculative thought, when engaged in speculation, closes its eye absolutely to everything without, and looks solely into itself; it follows only the dialectical necessity under which every idea produces new ones from its own fertility. It is not till afterwards, when speculation has completed its construction, that the consideration of reality has to be added, as the test of the conformity or nonconformity of the results of speculation with the actual condition of the world; if the latter be the case, the mistake must be looked for in the manipulation of the ideas. Rothe therefore fully shares the formal principle of the Hegelian school—its dialectical method; his results however differ widely from those of this school, and approximate very closely to Schelling's theosophy and Schleiermacher's theology; and this is owing partly to the peculiar distinction drawn by him between philosophical and theological speculation, according to which the contents and drift of the latter are from the first quite different from those of the former. Philosophical speculation must, Rothe thinks, start from the pure consciousness of the ego, from this formal act of thinking self, abstracted from all content; theological speculation, on the contrary, must start from the consciousness of God, which in its immediate certainty is co-ordinate with self-consciousness, and is therefore adapted to be the starting-point of an independent system of speculation entirely parallel to the philosophical one; an assertion which is exposed to the objection of being an unfounded *petitio principii*, and has nowhere found acceptance. We must however see how Rothe constructs his system on the basis of this principle professedly free from assumptions.

The conception of the absolute as the "self-determined" involves the distinction of potentiality and actuality. Hence we must think of pure potentiality, indeterminate and indifferent Being, as the first thing in the Deity. From this hidden source the actuality of God springs in the double form of personality and nature; and originally Rothe had made nature in God the cause and therefore the antecedent of his personality; but in his second edition he makes God's personality rise directly from his potentiality and determine the further process of his self-actualisation; though, it must be acknowledged, that a clear conception of this is impossible, since we have no analogy in man's personality to guide us. The similarity of this speculative conception of God to that formulated by Weisse is at once evident, though Rothe does not wish, like Weisse, that the three elements or stages of the divine nature should be identified with the three Persons of the ecclesiastical dogma of the Trinity, but pronounces the connexion to be altogether remote and unessential. From God's affirmation of himself as ego, Rothe further deduces his simultaneous affirmation of his non-ego, at first, as existing involuntarily in thought only; but when God actualises this imagined non-ego by a free act of will, it becomes pure matter. This is for God a limitation of his absoluteness (though created by himself), which as such he strives to abolish, but cannot simply negative, since it is necessarily implied in his ego. Hence his active relation to matter can only consist in introducing spirit into it, thus raising it to the position of his *alter ego*, created spirit. This fashioning of undivine matter into the organ of the divine spirit is the continuous process of creation, which may be conceived as the continuous "becoming of the world" (*Weltwerdung*), or, in relation to its goal, as more definitely "the incarnation (*Menschwerdung*) of God within the limits of material existence." But inasmuch as this creative activity in organising matter is at each stage dependent on the previously created things as its means, and in the last instance on matter as its substratum, it cannot be purely absolute. This is the ground of the want of completeness in every stage of the world, and of the imperfection of its condition at all times. All evil in the world, including moral evil or wickedness, has its final source therefore, according to Rothe as well as Weisse, in the never wholly vanquished antagonism which the distinct life of matter presents to the will of God. And this is true not only of the present epoch of the world, but of all future ones; for every new period of creation will again have to contend with the dross of matter inherited from the one before it. Hence Rothe, like Origen, maintains that the end of the world is always followed by a new period of creation.

Rothe's conception of the ethical vocation of mankind is closely connected with these cosmological speculations. Just as the spiritualisation of material elements is the purpose of the perpetual creative work of God, so the ethical vocation of the personal creature is the appropriation of material nature by means of his self-determination determining nature. Man is by self-determination to become a personal character, but at the same time by cultivating nature he is to become lord of the world. Hence if God's purpose with the world is identical with the progressive civilisation of historical humanity, the normal ethical action of the latter must be identical with religion, for it is action performed in fellowship with God, who influences and directs man's growing personality, and for the purpose of God, whose will is to occupy the world as personality. From this Rothe infers that morality and piety in their normal development are co-extensive, and that a piety without morality would be an abstract, phantom piety. In particular, "Christian piety is absolutely identical with pure and complete morality," and hence its community, the Church, is identical with the ethical community, the State. At present, it is true, as the moral has not reached its true normal condition, and the ethical community has not yet fully developed into a universal organism of states, this is only an ideal to be aimed at, and not immediately realisable; but even now it must be the final end determining our moral and religious development.

These fundamental principles of his theological speculation Rothe consistently followed out in relation to practical church politics. He opposed every form of ecclesiasticism that lacks moral stamina, that pietistically shuns the world or is hierarchically hostile to it, and insisted on practical Christianity; with fine breadth of mind he recognised all that is true and good in modern culture, in art and science, in the intercourse of nations, and in cultivated society; Christianity and true humanity ought not only to form a close alliance, but Christianity ought to become absolutely moral and human, and humanity absolutely religious and Christian. Undoubtedly noble principles, which in any case retain their truth, even if we object to the formula of the "absolute equivalence and coincidence of religion and morality, Church and State," on account of the psychological and social difference of the two spheres, and though we regard Rothe's eschatological forecast of the future as a transcendental fiction.

For in spite of the rationality of Rothe's view of the moral vocation of mankind, he still distinctly accepts the supernaturalism of the Biblical and ecclesiastical doctrines. Though regarding sin as an unavoidable passage in the course of the moral development of personality out of nature, he still believes that pre-Christian humanity fell a prey to an abnormal development, to sinful depravity, from which it could only be delivered and restored to its normal moral condition by a miraculous act on the part of God, resuming the interrupted creation and beginning it afresh, viz., by the sending of the supernatural person of the second Adam in Jesus of Nazareth. This second Adam, Rothe held, had necessarily to come into the world in a purely supernatural way, springing indeed from natural humanity, yet not called into being by its own development and in the ordinary way, but by a creative act of God upon it, which was absolutely miraculous; the Saviour had to be born of a woman, though not begotten by a man, but created by God. Only thus, Rothe thought, could he be the second Adam and begin the normal moral development of mankind. He was not indeed from the first actually a divine person, but became such in the course of his life in consequence of his supernatural birth. For from the first moment of his personal life God entered into a relation of real union with him, in order by means of his moral development to dwell in him in ever closer approximation to absolute unity. The course of his life was therefore a continual process of Man becoming God and God becoming Man. This was completed in the resurrection and the elevation of Christ to the divine sovereignty of the world, which he at present exercises by his spiritual presence in Christendom, until on his visible return to earth he will establish the perfect kingdom of God. Together with Christ will appear the saints, clothed then with a spiritual body, the bodies of the pious upon the earth will be made spiritual, while the ungodly will be given up to judgment, *i.e.*, to total destruction. Finally, the terrestrial world will also be spiritualised and placed in communication with the heavenly spheres. Thus the kingdom of earth becomes the kingdom of heaven.

We shall not here inquire how far these doctrines are consistent with the speculative premises of the system. It is certain that Rothe's heart and imagination clung as firmly to this miraculous world of faith as his energetic ethical mind insisted on moral action and the reconciliation of Christianity with the culture of our time. We may say there dwelt two souls within his breast; yet the two were united in him so as to form a complete harmonious personality, and it was just this which enabled him to generously tolerate and acknowledge the very various tendencies of the Christianity of to-day. "To the pure all things are pure," and Rothe was one of the purest.

CHAPTER IV.

ECLECTIC MEDIATING THEOLOGIANS.

UNDER this head I include a series of theologians, belonging to the most recent past and the present, who in spite of the difference of their results possess the common characteristic of trying to reconcile the faith of the Church with their own thought and that of their contemporaries, without making their faith dependent upon the hypotheses and formulæ of a definite philosophical system. At this point I wish expressly to premise that I do not in any way use the adjective "eclectic" in a derogatory sense. In philosophy, it is true, the word has usually such a sense, because from a philosopher we are wont to demand a harmonious system based on a definite fundamental principle, and giving a scientific account of the world, and hence we regard the eclectic method of philosophising, which tries to combine thoughts derived from various quarters, as defective. Even in the case of philosophy, however, we might object, that precisely the most important and fruitful contributions to it have derived the most varied elements from previous philosophers, and have never been more than partially successful in thoroughly combining them; so that even in philosophy our unfavourable judgment ought not to condemn the eclectic method as such, but only unsatisfactory attempts to reconcile contrary modes of thought. Much more will this hold in the case of theology, which is not intended to construct systematic scientific explanations of the world, but to exhibit the belief of a particular Church for the practical purposes of its ministers at a particular time. If we consider that the theology of the Church is the product of its history during eighteen centuries, enriched with contributions from the most various minds, we must admit at all events that here, in a much greater degree than in philosophy, systematic unity can never be more than an approximately attainable ideal. If we further consider that the needs of the Church of to-day, for which the theologian must work, are of the most various kinds, and that their variety grows with the Church's wealth in individual religious life, we shall come to the conclusion, that a theology sacrificing this diversity of religious interests and forces in an attempt to work out in systematic form a definite and limited principle, fulfils its task worse than a theology maintaining an eclectic attitude towards the various philosophical systems, and contenting itself with rendering the Church's belief intelligible and useful to the general educated thought of the day. This is confirmed by experience. In proportion as a theology is dependent upon one particular philosophical system, it is certain to be wrecked upon the limitations of the latter, for its influence is confined to the narrow circle of the adherents of the system, and to the short period it is in vogue. The more, on the other hand, the theologian succeeds in giving expression to the religious and ethical ideal existing in the mind of the Church with a breadth of view and a freedom of treatment which recognises fully the (relative) justice of the claims of the various existing modes of thought and belief, the greater will be his success in presenting to extended circles the means of a common religious understanding, a symbol therefore of the community of faith, which always exists in spite of all differences. It is, however, evident that the theological works which aim at eclectically reconciling the old and the new, according to the needs of the Churches of to-day, must not be measured by the standard of strict theological science. These theologians are right in so far as they succeed in finding for the faith of the fathers an expression intelligible and acceptable to the present generation; where they are wrong is when any of them confounds the conditional truth of his dogmatic statements with an unconditional and universal truth, and in his dogmatic arrogance disputes the equal justification of other presentations of it. I shall therefore, I think, be justified in confining myself to an objective review of the characteristic opinions of the individual theologians of this class, without attempting a critical estimate of them. I also purposely refrain from arranging them according to their dogmatic schools: the only difference of a general nature among these mediating eclectics is that with some of them a conservative fear of breaking with ecclesiastical tradition is predominant, and with others a free recasting and development of this tradition. But this is an altogether indefinite distinction; for even the conservative reproduction of ecclesiastical dogma necessitates in some measure a recasting of its original meaning, and even the liberal development of it is not intended to break the continuity of the historic growth of the Church's creed, and involves therefore to some extent an " accommodation " to tradition. I shall begin with those mediating theologians who have the greatest affinity with the speculative theologians already discussed, while differing from them in that their speculative thinking is not so much an end in itself as the form in which the given ecclesiastical dogmas can be best exhibited with such modifications as the times demand.

The most important of these theologians, and the type of the whole school, was indisputably ISAAC AUGUST DORNER, who possessed a deeply reflective Swabian nature, profound religious earnestness, and a vivid sense of the need of sounding by thought the depths of the truths of Christianity dear to his heart. His youth was passed during the time of the great disturbance in the Church created by Strauss's *Leben Jesu*. While he was repelled by the negative result of this criticism, his love of truth and fairness was equally opposed to the tumultuous mode in which its opponents replied to it, with their superficial apologies, or even appeals to ecclesiastical and political force. His view was that the business of scientific theology is to bring the Christological problem, propounded by Strauss, nearer to a solution. From the historical researches undertaken for this end came his great contribution to the history of Christology, *Entwicklungsgeschichte der Lehre von der Person Christi* (1856), a work in which the author's profound learning, objectivity of judgment, and fine appreciation of the moving ideas of history were shown, as was universally acknowledged. This book was followed later by another important historical work, his *Geschichte der protestantischen Theologie* (1867). Like Alexander Schweizer, Dorner developed and elaborated his own convictions by his diligent and loving study of the history of the Church's thought and belief. He gave these convictions permanent form in his two principal treatises, *Christliche Glaubenslehre*, and *Christliche Sittenlehre*, the former of which appeared shortly before his death (1879-81), while the latter was posthumously edited by his son (1886).

Dorner's *Glaubenslehre* is a work extremely rich in thought and matter. It takes the reader through a mass of historical material by the examination and discussion of the various opinions of ancient and modern teachers, and so leads up to the author's own view, which is mostly one intermediate between the opposite extremes, and appears as a more or less successful synthesis of antagonistic theses. Of his method, Dorner speaks as follows: "The method of Christian dogmatic theology must be not simply productive, but rather reproductive ; still it must not be merely empirical and reflective, but also constructive and progressive. When the enlightened Christian mind is in harmony by its faith and experience with objective Christianity, which faith knows to be its own origin, and which is also attested by the Scriptures and the scriptural faith of the Church, then such a mind has to justify and develop its religious knowledge in a systematic form." This is practically the same principle as that adopted by Alexander Schweizer ; and the considerable difference in the results of the two men only proves that this method, while a very valuable one, allows great latitude of individual opinion as to what constitutes objective Christianity, and from the nature of the case must always do so. The arrangement of Dorner's book is singular. After a lengthy introduction, a kind of religious phenomenology, leading successively through the different points of view of doubt and of hesitation to that of Christian faith, there follows, in the first part, the discussion of the general fundamental Christian doctrines—God, his nature and relation to the world ; man, his nature and original condition ; and finally, religion, as the unity of God and man, resting on divine revelation, realised in the historical religions, and perfected in the historical appearance of the God-man Christ. Then comes, in the second and special part, the doctrine of sin, its nature and origin, and its connection with the devil and death, and of Christian salvation, based on Christ's person and work on earth and in heaven, realised in the Church or the kingdom of the Holy Spirit, and to be consummated in the eternity beyond. It is characteristic of Dorner that he treats the doctrine of Christ as the God-man among the general fundamental doctrines, placing it before the special doctrines concerning the historical Christ and his work of salvation. The incarnation of God (*Gottmenschheit*) he regards as a speculative idea of the nature of an *à priori* truth, following from the nature of God and man, which would necessarily have been realised in history, if there had been no abnormal development of mankind in sin, which was not therefore the condition of the appearance of Christ the God-man, but only of his historical mission of salvation. This arrangement has, however, the disadvantage of breaking up the doctrine of man, the accounts of his original state and of his sin being separated by the description of the historical development of religion and revelation until the appearance of the God-man.

The doctrine of God is treated by Dorner with special thoroughness, and contains valuable thoughts. He rejects the idea of the complete cognisability, as well as of the absolute incognisability of God; our knowledge of God is always incomplete, growing, and relative, but is not therefore untrue. Again, the scientific examination of our belief in God is neither impossible nor unnecessary; what is indeed primarily an immediate religious certainty, can and ought to be raised to a conviction with a scientific justification. This falls to be done in the section treating of the so-called proofs of the existence of God, though these must be so presented as to contain at the same time the doctrine of the divine nature and attributes. At each stage of the line of proof the idea of God is enriched with some new element, from the metaphysical attributes of infinitude, omnipresence, and eternity, to the wisdom involving moral purposes, while each successive aspect thus gained of our conception of God is also shown to be the determining principle of some particular religion—the processes of dialectic and history being thus made to run parallel, evidently owing to Hegelian influences. Of the details we must notice Dorner's view of the eternity of God, which he says must not be so conceived as to imply that for God time does not exist, making history a mere semblance without truth; but the unchangeableness of God's nature does not exclude a changed relation to changes in time, a variation of his knowledge in the course of time; the immutability (*Sichselbstgleichheit*) of God must not be understood in so abstract a sense as to negative his life. Of the spiritual attributes of God justice is placed first, and defined as God's maintenance of his honour, which, as the absolute standard of all value, is the source of right in the world; God's justice consists in the ethically good as the absolutely valuable, and secures for it its absolute and unique rights. Absolute intelligence, or omniscience and wisdom, is represented as derived from ethical perfection, to indicate that, like everything else, intelligence in the last resort is only a subordinate instrument of moral goodness. The question as to the compatibility of God's self-maintenance, as absolute intelligence and personality, with his self-impartation and immanence in the world, leads to the doctrine of the divine Trinity, which is precisely the Christian synthesis of this antithesis of transcendence and immanence, or of God's just self-maintenance and his loving self-impartation to the world. The essence of every religion is expressed in its conception of God, and thus Christianity by its doctrine of the Trinity has secured itself against both the abstract monotheism of Judaism and the polytheism and pantheism of heathendom. The two Unitarian heresies, Arianism and Sabellianism, were the effects of the imperfections of Jewish deism and heathen polytheism, the former denying the true communion of God and man, the latter the holy exaltation of God above the sinful world. Christian Gnosis rose above both these errors by its conception of the holy love of God, of which the doctrine of the Trinity is the exposition. From this point of view Dorner constructs an ethical Trinity: the ethically Necessary, the ethically Free, and the Love uniting both, form the three aspects of the one absolute Personality; each of these three "modes of being" participates in the personality of God, but is not itself a separate personality, for the absolute personality can only be *one*. In this way the ecclesiastical dogma of the Trinity is interpreted from the point of view of a speculative theism, bearing the closest resemblance to that of Weisse.

The eternal love of God creates a free world, distinct from God, to establish a communion of love with itself. Being an organism with varied elements, this world is intended to be the copy of the triune life of God. The creation out of nothing means that the matter and form of the world are alike wholly derived from God; but this derivation must not be conceived as having had a beginning in time. The conceptions "creation" and "preservation" must neither be confounded nor separated from each other. Preservation is the continued action of the divine creative will, though in such a way that the secondary causality imparted to the creature itself becomes the means for its own self-reproduction, so that the created world, by reason of the all-pervading omnipotence, is also the cause of itself. If we define creation and preservation teleologically, they lead to the conception of a Providence partly ruling existing things, partly creating new ones. Its final end is a kingdom of moral spirits, governed by holy love; the freedom of the creature, not fettered by the universal plan, but, as foreknown, is made a part of that plan. Man, on the one hand belonging to nature, and on the other rising above nature as an immortal spirit, is in the image of God, partly as his original birthright, and partly as his true destination; he cannot therefore be a mere product of nature, but his existence presupposes a fresh creative act of God. Man, though good by his original creation, became the cause of evil by an act of freewill, of which no further explanation can be given; the evil became the permanent corruption of human nature, and as such was by the laws of heredity transmitted from the first parents to all mankind. This inherited racial sin involves a general need of salvation, but is not personal guilt, and does not decide a man's definitive merit or final destiny, which depends upon his personal decision. The restoration of the image of God, marred by sin in the human race, was only possible by the incarnation of God in the Son.

But this incarnation, as the completion of the revelation of God, was also necessary in itself independently of sin, since mankind was from the first created to arrive at perfection by communion with God. Hence Dorner had previously connected with the doctrine of man's nature, as created in the image of God, the doctrine of the unity of God and man in religion. God being love, imparts himself to man, and man is spiritually able to receive the communication; the reality of this impartation and reception affirmed as a unity is religion. Religion is primarily realised not in one of the spiritual faculties, but in the man as a whole, or in the heart; as Dorner very characteristically seeks to prove, not by psychological considerations, but from the fact that God as personality is an indivisible spiritual whole. To God's manifestation of himself in his sovereign power and his will, there corresponds on man's side a primary consciousness of absolute dependence upon God and devotion to him, by reason of which man is filled with divine life in knowledge, freedom, and blessedness. Since religion is not simply a subjective action, but presupposes an approach of God to man, it implicitly contains the idea of revelation. Revelation is a creative act of God upon the human heart, and its distinctive marks are originality or novelty, constancy and universality, positiveness and gradual growth. The ideas "supernatural" and "natural," "immediate" and "mediate" in relation to revelation must not be thought of as exclusive and contradictory, but, as from Schleiermacher's point of view, as the two aspects of every revelation. As regards its form, revelation is partly the outward manifestation of the divine power as interfering in the system of nature (miracles), partly its inward working upon the human spirit (inspiration). The possibility of miracles must be conceded for the sake of the freedom of God in relation to the world, and in virtue of the breadth and elasticity of natural law; their necessity follows from their importance in authenticating revelation. Very characteristic of Dorner's mode of thought, which is emotional and poetical rather than strictly intellectual, is the sentence, "Every uncorrupted soul rejoices in the miraculous. It is the part of prose to hate the miraculous, of poetry to love it; of true poetry, of course, which does not create vain phantoms of the imagination, but loves to contemplate the realised ideal, the higher, more perfect, and therefore poetical stage of spiritual freedom, when it is in harmony with nature:"—a sentence which reminds us of the utterances of Romanticism, *e.g.*, the "magical idealism" of Novalis. Inspiration is the spiritual miracle performed on the spirit as a whole, increasing its strength and purity, or, more particularly, it is enthusiasm (*Begeisterung*) and enlightenment with regard to truth, for the purpose of establishing permanent religious fellowship. The primary seat of inspiration must not be sought in books, but in men, and must not be separated from the general history of revelation. But though no specific difference can be proved between men endowed with the spirit and inspired men; still of the latter it is a distinctive and indeed unique characteristic, by virtue of their being vehicles of revelation, that without being personally absolutely incapable of error, they are yet preserved from it in their teaching and preaching, and proclaim only unerring truth, even in historical details, as the word of God. Thus after approaching a freer rational view, Dorner returns to the old ecclesiastical doctrine of the absolute inspiration and infallibility of the Bible, a concession to ecclesiastical dogma which was fatal to his position with regard to scientific Biblical criticism.

Revelation, and therefore religion too, reaches in the first instance perfection in a single being, who, as the "absolute God-man," is the Revealer pure and simple; but as the perfect man after the image of God, is the instrument of securing the perfection of the world. The necessity of the incarnation does not depend merely upon sinful humanity's need of redemption, but is demanded apart from it by the vocation of mankind to reach full communion with God, and to form a united organism under a central head; for such a universal head, in whom all the limitations of human individuality are done away, can only be a man in whom God's communication of himself to mankind is absolutely and universally realised, or in whom God as Logos has become man. Indeed, the God-man, as the absolute pneumatic personality of universal spiritual power, is not merely the head of men, but also of angels, his kingdom includes all ranks of spirits, and perfects their conscious unity. Finally, Christianity claims to be the absolute religion, which necessitates an absolute God-man as the permanent centre of this religion. That this intrinsically necessary incarnation actually took place in Jesus of Nazareth is historically proved by his holy personality, his witness to himself, and his work, as well as by the changes still being wrought in mankind by his influence. The question as to the *manner* in which God's incarnation in Jesus must be conceived as taking place, is the business of theological speculation to answer. On the basis of the historical development of Christology, Dorner constructs a theory of his own, of which the following is an outline. The subject of the incarnation is "God as Logos," *i.e.*, not a personal Logos hypostatically distinct from God the Father, but God himself in his loving will to reveal and communicate himself to mankind. That the Logos "became flesh" must not be understood to mean that he assumed human flesh as a garment, or even changed himself into a man, for he would then only have acted the part of a man, without having become a man; it rather means that God, as Logos, bestowed not merely his own power, but his absolute self, upon the human person of Jesus, from the moment of his birth in ever-growing measure, while the personality of Jesus received this impartation of the divine life with increasing power and receptivity in the course of his free personal life, becoming ever more completely possessed and filled by God, till his human being became at last absolutely and indissolubly one with the divine mode of being of the Logos. The conscience and the Christian witness of the Spirit—that is, of course, the moral and religious consciousness in its Christian ideality—is mentioned as having analogy to this union of human knowledge and will with the divine : whence we might infer that the person of Christ must be conceived as the first and archetypal manifestation of the Christian ideal of piety and morality. But this inference, however natural, would not quite represent Dorner's view, according to which Christ is not a mere individual like others, but differs from all empirical individuals in representing the general idea of the human race, freed not only from sin, but also from the limitations and incompleteness of other individuals ; in a word, he is "the central individual," ordained to be the centre, not only of humanity, but also of the whole realm of spirits, being in consequence the eternal celestial sovereign, and the personal judge of the world at his second coming to consummate the kingdom of God. The motives of this Christology of Dorner are plain ; he wishes to do fuller justice than is done by the ecclesiastical doctrine to the human and ethical side of the person of Christ, and at the same time retain as much as possible of its transcendental metaphysics ; whether he has satisfactorily accomplished this, in particular whether a central individual coincident with the idea of the race is conceivable in actual history, is a question I will in this place only suggest. The same holds good of Dorner's treatment of the doctrine of the work of Christ, in which he follows the ecclesiastical tradition still more closely than in his doctrine of Christ's person, not only *formally* in the doctrine of three offices, but *materially*, especially on the central point—the atonement by vicarious satisfaction. Dorner teaches that when Christ put himself in the place of mankind, in order, in his own feeling of pain, to bear the divine displeasure against the guilt of the race, he made himself an offering for us to the punitive justice of God, and thereby became for the world the perfect surety, for whose sake God can grant, not only freedom from punishment, but even blessedness.—That Christ's three offices are perpetuated in the corresponding offices of the Church, is a valuable remark of Dorner's, which might naturally have suggested a retrospective modification of his doctrine of Christ's work.—Finally, we must mention that in his doctrine of justification, Dorner defended the strictly Lutheran theory against Hengstenberg's more rationalistic form of it. We can, however, trace a certain hesitation on Dorner's part with regard to the decisive question, whether the ground of justification is the objective merit of Christ to which the believer's relation is simply receptive, or not rather subjective faith itself, as the frame of mind pleasing to God, and, therefore, in principle, the beginning of a new life. Dorner's concern as a churchman for the objectivity of the work of redemption, inclines him to the former view; his personal concern for the *ethical* conception of the Christian life of faith to the latter.

On the latter point characteristic words of Dorner's are found in his correspondence with Martensen: "The *ethical idea* is now all-important. . . . More and more I see Schleiermacher's peculiar greatness, and his unique position among modern princes of science, in virtue of his thorough blending of ethics and dogmatics. This will be a mine of wealth for the times which are now at hand." What Dorner commends in Schleiermacher characterises also the fundamental principle of his own theology; he tried to blend dogmatics and ethics, and renovate theology and the Church by the ethical idea of personal freedom in God. In this he is in complete accord with Rothe. The excellence of this object, and the purity and fervour of his devotion to it, will keep Dorner's memory in honour, however we may judge of the success of his attempts at dogmatic mediation and the tenability of his particular doctrinal views.

The Danish theologian MARTENSEN, with whom Dorner was connected in a long and close friendship, represented a similar mediating speculative position, but differed from Dorner in his way of treating theological doctrines. Dorner had arrived at his results by the process of dialectical reflection upon the various forms of doctrine of ancient and modern theologians; but in Martensen the historical method is put quite into the background in favour of independent speculation, which indeed everywhere presupposes the ecclesiastical dogmas, specially those of Lutheranism, but tries to skilfully combine them with the ideas of Böhme's and Baader's theosophy. The problem of dogmatic theology Martensen holds to be the synthesis of the Christian consciousness of redemption and revelation, or the reproduction of revealed divine wisdom in our conception of the Christian idea of truth, which ought to comprehend the subjective and the objective, the human and the divine side of Christianity. This idea dogmatic theology has to grasp and develop, showing not only the coherence of its given matter, but also its possibility and basis, and logically reconciling the antitheses in the unity of the idea. This method was suggestively pursued by Martensen himself, though we cannot deny that his efforts at reconciliation often suffer much from obscurity of conception, owing to the want of a rational introductory criticism. We often get the impression of brilliant speculative fireworks, throwing a peculiar light on the Church's dogmas, without making obscure questions really plainer. With the antitheses of nature and spirit, ethical and cosmical, personal and impersonal, he presents a dialectical exhibition which rather confuses than instructs the sober understanding. A few of the chief examples will serve to characterise this method.

On the one hand, the fact is specially emphasised that Christianity is an ethical, historical religion, belonging to the world of spirit, language, conscience, freedom, and personality. Christianity is essentially Christ himself. But on the other hand, Christ must not be conceived as essentially an ethical (or, to use our author's usual term, moral) and historical being simply, not as simply the new Adam, but as the centre of the whole world, of all spirits, and of nature. Schleiermacher's error lay in overlooking Christ's trinitarian pre-existence and his cosmical position. The Logos is, it is true, primarily, in Martensen as in Philo, simply the ideal world of the divine consciousness; but he maintains that the superiority of Christianity lies in its making this idea as thought into a thinking principle side by side with God, into the second hypostatical ego of the Son; just as the will, which raises the necessary content of thought to the freedom of love, must be conceived as a third ego, the hypostasis of the Spirit. Thus the Trinity is constructed by the discrimination of different elements in the divine life, and the transformation of them in the process into independent persons. Dorner had proceeded more cautiously.

In his doctrine of the creation, Martensen well remarks that we must combine the heathen point of view of cosmogony, or the world's evolution of itself, with the Jewish view of its free creation; the world is both nature and creature; regarded as the former, it is eternal and necessary; as the latter, it had a beginning in time, and was the product of freedom, so that in its further development also it is exposed to the free interference of divine miraculous power. How this conception of the supernatural side of creation can be combined in thought with the idea of nature, or the self-evolution of the world, Martensen did not succeed in explaining.

Very characteristic is Martensen's doctrine as to angels and devils. They must not be conceived merely and primarily as personal, but as ideas and powers in the life of nature and of peoples, intermediate between imagined personifications and real personal beings, but sometimes becoming real persons, ministering spirits in the kingdom of God. In particular, the devil is really the universal principle of cosmical self-existence in its antagonism to God; being a principle, he has not a self-existing personality, but has only a nascent personality, which "as such is intermediate between existence and non-existence, personality and personification, actuality and possibility, 'being' and 'signification.'" The principle only reaches personality in individual creatures, though not merely in human, but also in superhuman spirits; among the latter is one in whom the principle of evil is so hypostatised as to make him its central revelation, and therefore the personal centre and head of the kingdom of evil—the personal devil or Antichrist of the Bible. He may be regarded as the younger brother of the Son of God, Christ, and his personal rival throughout the history of revelation. In the snake of the Garden of Eden he was still as it were in swaddling clothes; then his strength grew more and more, until simultaneously with the revelation of the Logos in Christ, he gained possession of the sovereignty of this world. Although already conquered by Christ, he will continue to exercise his power and craft until the last decisive struggle with the returning King of heaven. Thus our Gnostic theologian regards the personifications, by means of which the poetical imagination vividly realised the warring forces of the world's history, as objective realities, though he cannot quite forget their origin in the creative power of the imagination; the "hovering" of these strange figures between personification and personality is the mark of this theology, with its oscillation between poetical imagery and really definite thought.

The temptation of the first parents in Paradise he explains psychologically, by the antagonistic fundamental impulses of human nature, and also metaphysically, by the contrary superhuman powers—God and the cosmical principle. The Mosaic account of the Fall we must regard as "a combination of history and sacred symbolism, a figurative description of an actual fact," that is, not merely as the symbol of a general, ever-recurring event, but as an historical fact from the earliest times; though, again, not as this fact itself, as it actually occurred, but only as an emblem or symbol of it. This justifies the free allegorising of all the individual features of the narrative, while still preserving its character as traditional history in opposition to the mythological interpretation in current criticism. How these two conceptions are to be united is however not made clear.

In his Christology, Martensen vigorously demands the reality of the incarnation of God and the union of the two natures in the God-man, as against all mythical and mystical rationalism and idealism. But in order to secure the unity and gradual development of the person of Christ, Martensen revises the ecclesiastical doctrine, partly by postulating (with Liebner) an act of self-renunciation (*kenosis*) on the part of the Logos, whereby his divine attributes were reduced to the measure of the human, and partly by maintaining (with Dorner) a gradual growth of the germ of divine life planted in the human child from the unconscious possibility to the conscious reality of an ego at once human and divine. This certainly avoids the stumbling-block of the ecclesiastical doctrine of the two natures, a twofold life in Christ, but substitutes for it a "twofold life" in the Logos, in that "as the pure Logos of the Deity it works throughout nature, which is filled by its presence," and at the same time, as the Logos incarnate in Christ, has a humanly limited form of existence, and only gradually rises from the unconsciousness of the potential ego to the consciousness of itself. It is not clear how this life that is humanly developing and that life eternally existing are combined in the unity of the same personal Logos; but the purpose of this artificial reasoning is to show that we must recognise in Christ not merely an ideal man, but the "centre of the universe," the cosmical mediator of the consummation of the whole kingdom of nature and of spirits, which is of importance to our author on account of his doctrine of the sacraments and his eschatology. He further teaches that Christ's birth was both truly human and also a true superhuman miracle; that his life as man cannot be conceived without a national colouring, but that he was without the natural limitation attaching to every nationality; that, since he was subject to human temptation, we must assume the possibility of his sinning, though, on account of the divine source of his life, this possibility could never become actual, and was therefore in fact equivalent to the impossibility of his sinning. The work of reconciliation belonging to Christ's high priestly office must be interpreted not merely as a reconciliation of man to God, but as a reconciliation of God himself. Reconciliation may be defined as the removal of an antithesis in the process of God's revelation of himself, viz., the antithesis between his love and his justice. "Although these attributes are essentially one, there is on account of sin a certain disagreement between them in the divine nature. For, in spite of God's eternal love of the world, his actual relation to it is not one of love, but only one of holiness and justice, an antithetical relation, since the unity it involves is hindered and kept down." This contradiction can be removed only by the vicarious satisfaction of the Son of God. The necessity of such an objective vicarious expiation is, it is true, again rendered problematical by the subsequent discussion, according to which the subjective consciousness of reconciliation is the effect of the new birth, and of faith, which Martensen regards as the germinal beginning of the new man. Accordingly, the actual reconciliation appears as a psychological process in consciousness, in consequence of the ethical change in the human mind; so that, after all, the necessity for a reconciliation once for all by Christ's satisfaction is not made clear.

The same hesitation between an ethical and non-ethical point of view recurs finally in a specially surprising form in Martensen's teaching on the Sacraments. Baptism is primarily the pledge of divine grace in view of future faith; but it is more than this: it is also, in truth, the beginning of the Christian life, since it "involves, not indeed personal, but substantial and essential regeneration." It is an objective mystery, in which creative grace establishes a new relation of being between God and man, "incorporating" the latter's unconscious nature "into Christ, not psychologically merely, but organically, not figuratively only, but essentially." Since in the case of a child this cannot, of course, be done by ethical means, a physical influence is the only remaining method, and accordingly Martensen does not hesitate to speak of "a holy nature-mystery." How this mystery is to be conceived without having recourse to magic is not explained. In the same way, Martensen sees in the Lord's Supper "the inseparable union of a holy spirit-mystery, and a holy nature-mystery," since not only Christ's spirituality, but also his corporality is offered as food, not only for the soul, but for the whole new man, accordingly for that future man of the resurrection also, who is already germinating in secret, and this food is received by all, including the unbelieving. To the old objection of the Zwinglian school, that we cannot think of Christ's body as omnipresent, he returns the not very luminous answer, that we must conceive of heaven as where the glorified Christ is; not as a material place, a "where" according to the ideas of our present sense-perception, but still as "a more definite 'where,'" where cosmic life is completely filled by God.

We see that Martensen's method of speculation never belies its character; it dazzles by its brilliant antitheses and bold syntheses, but generally leaves us wholly uncertain as to how we are actually to combine the contradictory sides in thought; dogmatic thought and imaginative contemplation combine to form a Romantic twilight, from which the critical understanding departs unsatisfied.

Of much greater value than his *Dogmatik*, is Martensen's *Ethik*, in two volumes, in which the versatile theologian's wide knowledge of life and the world is shown in an attractive form. The general lines of this book are best characterised in Martensen's own words in a letter to Dorner: "The onesided views against which we have to contend are those of onesided ecclesiasticism, and onesided individualism. Both negative the great problem of the modern age—the living union of Christianity and humanism. For a nomistic ecclesiasticism which suppresses all intellectual, and especially all scientific freedom, and an individualism which tries to isolate Christianity, and separate it from the varied spheres of human life, are alike un-Christian and inhuman. The problem will continue to be the presentation in life and doctrine of this union and combination of Christianity and genuine and free humanity."

From Martensen, we pass to the theologian most nearly resembling him in spirit, JOHANN PETER LANGE, a man of rich imagination and varied culture, who tried to defend and renovate ecclesiastical dogma by theosophical speculation. His *Dogmatik* (1849–51) contains many fruitful and suggestive thoughts, which, however, are hidden under such a mass of bold figures and strange fancies, and suffer so much from want of clearness of presentation, that they did not produce any lasting effect. He affirms the true principle that theology must start from a knowledge of man's nature. But his procedure consists rather in an ingenious playing with analogies than in logical inference from ascertained facts. In the pneumatic, or regenerate man, he finds a threefold consciousness, and therein a copy of the Trinity, the Persons of which are to be conceived as threefold forms or centres of consciousness; each form of consciousness is the whole consciousness of the divine nature, yet each is fundamentally different from the others; regarded ideally, it is another person, but regarded really another form of personality. Since religion is deducible from our conceptions of God and man as their real interaction for the purpose of their union, the incarnation is an eternal truth which influenced the whole history of mankind, being as it were gradually realised, until it found its absolute reality in the individual God-man Jesus. Hence, in order rightly to understand the religious importance of this person, we must consider his historical life altogether in the light of the absolute idea. The possibility of the incarnation must be explained from the nature of man: " Man in the God-man is not an individual man, but the man who takes humanity up into himself, just as humanity has taken nature up into itself. Only so does he come into coincident relation with the divine as self-conditioned, and as the Son of God with human conditionality. The man in the God-man comprehends the eternal Becoming of the whole world, as it proceeds from God, according to the potentiality of his nature. He is, therefore, essentially the real transition of the process of being through the completed Becoming to absolute Being, and hence the fit organ of the Son of God after his ideal entrance upon absolute Becoming. He is conditioned unconditionality, which is identical with unconditioned conditionality, the divine man who takes up into himself the human God." It cannot be said that this explanation makes the matter very plain. Peculiar to Lange's Christology, is the reference to the psychological distinction of "day and night consciouness" and the related idea of "genius." Genius, he well remarks, is a permanent form in which the "day consciousness" receives inspirations from the "night consciousness," which, as a rule, is a closed world to the ethical "day consciousness," and makes its existence known only in certain special influences. The application of this analogy from the general theory of the soul to the person of Jesus was calculated to explain several points; but Lange leaves the matter in considerable obscurity, when he says, "The ethical consciousness of Christ's human development was based on the infinitude of his night consciousness, like the lotos flower on the lake; and this latter consciousness was not the eternal form of consciousness of the Logos *per se*, but it was the night side of the universal human consciousness which the Logos had assumed with his incarnation. It was the infinite plastic educative thought of the Son of Man in his personal conditionality, that is, the human form which the eternal Son could assume, without suffering any obscuration of his eternal consciousness." In spite of all analogies from general experience, in spite of all the ideal and real preparation and mediation, Lange leaves the individual person of the God-man Jesus as "the absolute miracle," and his life on earth as a series of miracles. Lange deduces seven chief miracles from the seven-fold miraculous nature of the God-man. In discussing them he lays stress on the ideal, spiritually symbolical meaning of the narratives, but insists equally upon their proper historical character, because, as he holds, the ideal would otherwise be conceived in a false abstraction, without the real. He follows the same method in the case of the Old Testament legends. The garden of Eden, for example, is ideal nature in general, but at the same time a definite place; the tree of knowledge in the garden is an actual historical tree, no less than an ideal symbol of the seductive charm of the pleasures of nature; the cherub with the flaming sword was both a real angel, with an ethereal celestial body, and a symbol of lost innocence; and in general, Christianity presupposes, not only the subjective, but also the objective truth of the appearances of angels and demons. The devil, in Lange's, as in Martensen's view, is an ambiguous term: on the one hand, the symbol of absolute evil as a principle, and on the other, a personal evil spirit, or fallen angel, and as such not absolutely evil, but only evil in a great and ever-increasing degree. The Apocalyptic eschatological world-drama is, of course, interpreted by our theologian quite realistically.

In Dorner, Martensen, and Lange, speculation and ecclesiastical dogma preserved a certain equilibrium. But neology spread among members of those circles which had undertaken the defence of ecclesiastical, and in particular of Lutheran, dogma; so that they too must be included, to some extent, among the Eclectics. It is especially on the doctrines of Christ's person and work that the Erlangen Lutheran theology deviated from orthodoxy.

The perception of the inconceivability of the complete humanity and human development of Jesus on the supposition that the divine Logos in his full personality was present in him, led the Erlangen theologian THOMASIUS to the so-called "Kenotic Christology." He held that with the incarnation, the Logos renounced the relative attributes of deity, which he considered as not necessarily belonging to the divine nature—omnipotence, omnipresence, and omniscience, in order to assume the limited form of the existence of Jesus; only in the course of the life of Jesus did the Logos make an actuality the absoluteness of action and knowledge which had been voluntarily surrendered or reduced to an inoperative potentiality. But inasmuch as during this kenosis the Logos is supposed not to have given up his personal ego, nor ceased to form part of the Trinity, we get the difficult conception that, though in Jesus the divine self-consciousness of the Logos existed, it was not as divine, because it is supposed not to be omniscient and almighty. Hence Gess was more logical in maintaining a kenosis on the part of the divine Logos to such an extent that he completely renounced his self-consciousness, and converted it into the human soul of Jesus. By virtue of his subordination to the Father he was, it is said, able to surrender to him his personality, and by virtue of his kinship with the human soul, which is in the image of God, he was able to convert himself into such a soul, which potentially bears within it the fulness of all the divine powers, but can only by a gradual development become actually able to use them. Jesus, therefore, was from the first a potential but not actual God, and was consequently capable of a human development. During this development, his Logos-consciousness occasionally flashed through the human limitations, in recollection of his pre-existence, but ordinarily it remained only the latent ground of the development of his human consciousness, which rose step by step to complete identity with the divine Logos-consciousness, whereby, and not before, the man Jesus was received into the complete unity of the life of the Trinity. The opponents of this theory rightly remarked that it deviated widely from the orthodox doctrine of God and Christ, in representing the life of the Trinity as interrupted and deprived of its second person by the conversion of the Logos into the human soul of Jesus during the latter's life on earth, and in regarding Jesus as only a potential but not actual God-man; but for us the chief interest lies in the fact that the theory is evidently on the point of quite breaking away from the ecclesiastical dogma, and taking the side of the speculative theory, according to which the universal capacity for the divine, the innate destiny and vocation of every human soul, was typically realised in Jesus.

Still further removed from orthodoxy was the teaching of the Erlangen theologian, CHRISTIAN VON HOFMANN. His doctrine of the Atonement was the most prominent though not the only instance of his heterodoxy, and hence was the first object of attack on the part of orthodox theologians. Hofmann, indeed, only wished to teach old truth in a new form, but a glance at his system shows the serious extent of the neology in his teaching. A vein of modern Rationalism runs through his theology, but it is concealed, by means of an artificial dialectic, behind a supernaturalism rather Biblical than ecclesiastical. His theological system is given in his two chief works, *Weissagung und Erfüllung* and *Der Schriftbeweis* (1852–56), to which may be added his collected *Schutzschriften*, containing an exposition and defence of his system against ecclesiastical attacks.

Hofmann, exactly like Schleiermacher, bases his theology upon the inward experience of the facts of personal Christianity. This experience he attempts to develop into a system of organically connected statements, in which every individual fact is to find its definite and necessary place as an historical presupposition or inference. And the *Schriftbeweis*, or proof from Scripture, he holds to consist precisely in showing that Biblical history and doctrine as a whole finds its proper place in the systematic development of the facts which make us Christians ; it is not that certain dogmatic propositions are to be proved by individual texts of Scripture, but the Biblical history of revelation as a whole, from the creation to the consummation of the world, is to be explained from the point of view of the necessary premises of our experience of Christianity, and inferences from it. It need not be said that the subjective conception of Christian experience thus acquires fundamental importance in the interpretation and explanation of the history, and that arbitrary and violent expedients are not always avoided in the case of important points. At bottom this *Schriftbeweis* is the supernaturalistic counterpart of Hegel's *Philosophy of History;* both pursue the same method of deducing history from *à priori* ideas, philosophical ideas in the one case, theological in the other ; both connect historical events with transcendental relations : the one, with the movement of the idea through the antithesis of its elements to the unity of the concept and of reality ; the other, with the movement of the Persons of the Trinity through antithetical modes of existence to the unity of love and blessedness.

The fellowship with God into which we know that we have been admitted through Christ has, Hofmann teaches, the divine Trinity as its eternal condition. For the self-determination of the divine love beyond itself, having for its object the gradually evolving man of God, *i.e.,* historical humanity, presupposes an eternal self-determination on the part of God within himself, having as its object the eternal man of God, or the Son of God (who is accordingly not really God at all, or a Person in the Trinitarian nature of God, but the preexistent ideal man, something like the Pauline Christ). God's eternal will of love, or his inward divine relation to his Son, is accomplished in the history which transpires between him and mankind. This history has a threefold beginning : one given to it by God, one given to it by itself, and one a fresh beginning, annulling the latter and completing the former, God having appointed his Son for this. Since the final end of the divine will is the man Jesus, mankind necessarily began in a single man, Eve being taken therefore from her husband. The original state of mankind was a state of actual and true, though only incipient, holiness and blessedness, not excluding the possibility of self-determination in opposition to God. The source of the first sin, however, did not lie in man, but outside him, in the temptation of Satan, who was able to deceive the woman. This brought mankind into a state the reverse of life from God, under the necessity of death and the seductive influences of Satan. Still there existed the possibility of divine counter-influence, prophetically testified to in the revelation of God to Israel, and fully realised in the incarnation of the eternal Son. His entrance into the humanity derived from Adam was for it the realisation of God's eternal will of love, since he was the beginner and originator of perfect fellowship with God for the same humanity which had in its sin made a beginning opposed to the holiness of God, and frustrating God's work of love. At the same time, however, his inward divine relation to the Father became involved in the most extreme antithesis possible to it without cancelling itself. For as having become a member of Adamite humanity, the Son was bound to an obedience to the Father which involved undergoing the consequences of God's anger inflicted upon the sinful race. But the sinfulness of the human race inherited from Adam could not possibly be shared by the Son, from the fact that his incarnation was a deed of holy self-determination, to the accomplishment of which nothing was necessary on man's part except obedient faith in the divine word of promise on the part of the woman destined to conceive him. His human action could then only be the continuation, by means of a sinless human nature, of the holy self-determination by which he had become man.

The acquisition of righteousness for mankind by Jesus was the effect of his entire holy life, from his incarnation to his death. It began by his assuming human nature in a sinless state as his own, thus making a new beginning in opposition to the sin of Adam. It was continued in the harmony of all he did with the will of God, expressed in consequence of sin in the form of the law, which demanded obedience to the various ordinances of man's social life. It was consummated by enduring the enmity of men in his fidelity to the divine will, preserving his holiness to the end in suffering as well as in action. The death of Jesus was therefore not a vicarious atoning sacrifice to the divine punitive righteousness, but an "occurrence" resulting from the historical position of affairs, and which became the deed of Jesus by virtue of his voluntary submission to it. But just as this thing which happened to him was not the suffering of what sinful humanity would have had to suffer, so the thing which he accomplished was not what humanity ought to have done, but it was the obedience of the divinely ordained Saviour to his own vocation. The abandonment of the Son by the Father to the hostile power of men and the devil brought the history transacting between God and the second beginner of mankind to a conclusion, which was at the same time the conclusion of the previous history of mankind conditioned by sin. For in his maintenance of the office of mediator in opposition to the enmity born of sin lay likewise his deed of satisfaction for the sin of Adamite humanity, that is, the actual realisation of the relation to God which had been desired and brought about by God, a relation for which sin no longer exists, and which is holiness alone. This whole act of God we call the redemption of mankind, irrespective of its effects upon individuals, because it sanctified and glorified human nature in the person of Christ. Its sanctification was its salvation from sin; its glorification its salvation from death. This glorification was accomplished by the raising of Christ from the dead, by which he entered upon a new kind of human life, in which his human nature was the perfect instrument of his unconditional fellowship with the Father. Christ's work of salvation was an expiation of sin, not in the sense that the Triune God had claimed something as a recompense for the wrong done him, but in the sense that for the benefit of the human race he displayed his eternally holy love, which seeks not its own, but what is another's. The salvation of the world is not based upon the Triune God having been appeased, but upon the Son having accomplished that in relation to the Father which only the Holy One was able to accomplish, but not sinful mankind for itself. Only in this sense can his work be called vicarious. The result of this history, commencing with Christ's incarnation and completed by his death and resurrection, is that the relation of the Father to the Son is henceforth also the relation of God to the humanity beginning anew in the Son, a relation which is henceforth not determined by the sin of the race of Adam, but by the righteousness of the Son. But participation in this new relation to God is open to us only when, by virtue of the working of the Holy Ghost, which makes us certain of this change accomplished once for all, we are resolved to belong to the humanity begun afresh in Christ, and therefore to make our own, not only the forgiveness of its sins, but also its life unto God. It is the righteousness of the Son which renders mankind the object of the divine approval; and it is by acting up to the relation to God existing in his person that the individual man becomes certain of its existence, and its existence for him. What he thus becomes certain of is the beginning of a new humanity, though this only becomes such for him by his attaching himself to it as soon as he is certain of its existence.

The near kinship of this theory of salvation to that of Schleiermacher will be at once perceived. The fundamental principles are the same as those recurring in all rationalistic theology since Kant, only here they are, by a somewhat artificial dialectic, so interwoven with Biblical supernaturalism as to appear to be the result of the *Schriftbeweis*. We may even admit that they have points of support in Biblical teaching, although not exactly in accord with true Pauline doctrine. At any rate, we must admit the theologian's right to emphasise some sides of Biblical teaching neglected by ecclesiastical theology, and to make use of them for his own rational conception of the dogma. But Hofmann's opponents were quite right in asserting the essential difference between his theory of the Atonement and that of Anselm and Luther; and Hofmann's wish to represent his teaching as essentially in accordance with the dogma of the Confessions can only be called a piece of strange self-deception. But this want of honesty towards himself and others, this concealment of the heresy of which he was really guilty, is so general a weakness among theologians, that we must not press it too much in relation to individuals.

The lines of Hofmann are followed by DANIEL SCHENKEL in his *Dogmatik* (1858–9), though he is a step further removed from ecclesiastical dogma. He starts from man's self-consciousness as involving the three fundamental facts of man's need of salvation, the divine bestowal of salvation, and the completion of salvation in the Church, these facts being directly given in experience. He blames Schleiermacher for emphasising the subjective side of the truth of salvation, the facts of the religious consciousness, to the detriment of the objective side, the facts of God's personal bestowal of salvation. (Though how the "facts of salvation," which are only historically known, can at the same time be directly given in the religious consciousness, Schenkel does not explain, and throughout his book we can trace the effects of this failure to distinguish between direct facts of the religious consciousness and their conditions, which are only indirectly inferred or historically knowable.) The truth of the facts of salvation can be established in three ways: first, by their answering to a human need of salvation; secondly, by their containing a fresh communication of himself by God to man; thirdly, by their being the basis of a progressive development of the Christian community with regard to salvation.

Above all Schenkel, not without reason, maintains that theology requires a thorough revision of the idea of religion, which lies at the root of all its propositions. In spite of Schleiermacher's great merit in distinguishing religion from knowledge and conduct, his definition of religion is unsatisfactory, as confusing the religious and æsthetic functions by the identification of religion with emotion, and so overlooking its ethical character. Schenkel, for his part, thinks he has discovered a specifically religious organ in the conscience, quite distinct from reason, will, and emotion; for while in the latter our self-consciousness involves only relation to the world, in the conscience we are conscious of ourselves in primal and direct relation to God. The primary religious function of conscience is the consciousness that God is personally present in us, but that our original normal relation to God is disturbed by the distracting consciousness of the world, and that we therefore stand in need of the restoration by God of our normal relation to him. It is plain that this theory represents religious convictions of a very complicated origin as the original content of conscience, and from the first substitutes dogmatic presuppositions for a psychological analysis of facts; but, setting aside his totally inadequate deduction, we must recognise the justice and value of Schenkel's attempt to show "the synthesis of the religious and ethical factors" from the nature of the religious spirit itself, and thus to secure from the first the indissoluble connexion of religious and moral truths.

In treating of revelation, Schenkel complains of the want of a distinction in the older dogmatic theologians between the act and the record of revelation; for while the former is a direct working of God on the human conscience, this absolute divine act of communication becomes, by its incorporation with human activity, a human and historically conditioned record of revelation, which on that very account can never be absolutely perfect, nor completed in past history, since God's revelation of himself is always continued in the historical development of salvation. Of "miracles," Schenkel speaks very variously: on the one hand, he says, with Schleiermacher, that from the religious point of view all phenomena depend upon the divine causality, while from the rational point of view they are at the same time explicable from the uniformity of nature, thus doing away with miracles in the proper sense; on the other hand, he maintains that specific miracles are creative modifications by God of the uniformity of finite nature, mysteriously introducing something new into the world, though it afterwards obeys natural laws, since, *e.g.*, the loaves miraculously multiplied stilled the people's hunger like ordinary bread. Schenkel was evidently not clear as to the essence of the question; his objection to Schleiermacher is unmeaning. Of inspiration, Schenkel says that it originates directly from God, but is continued through human instrumentality, so that we must admit the imperfection of the individual inspirations during the formation of the whole record of revelation. Still it is not enough to say that the Scriptures contain the word of God; we must also say that they are the word of God, though not all the individual words of the Bible are this, but the Bible as a whole. Schenkel's method of proof from Scripture corresponds to this conception of its authority; he interprets the passages in the Bible so that they agree with the affirmations of his "conscience," and where that is impossible, he has recourse to the supposition of the Biblical teacher's accommodating himself to the conceptions of the people, *e.g.*, in the doctrine of the devil; an unprejudiced historical estimate of the Bible is unknown to Schenkel.

Accordingly the historical truth of the whole Biblical history from the creation of the world onwards is maintained by Schenkel for conscience' sake. In speaking of the Fall he does indeed quote Nitzsch, to the effect that it is "a true but not an external history"; nevertheless it must be regarded as having taken place as an external fact at some time. In particular the belief in the historical trustworthiness of the Gospel narratives of miracles, from the supernatural Birth to the Ascension, is represented as a demand of "conscience," and thus historical criticism is indirectly charged with want of conscience! Schenkel does indeed, as a fact, allow himself several departures from Biblical statements of doctrine, but he always endeavours by artificial interpretations to produce the appearance of complete agreement (*e.g.*, in the case of the Johannine Christology, of the Pauline doctrine of sin and atonement). On the other hand, he in many points openly and expressly opposes ecclesiastical dogmas, and censures others, *e.g.*, Hofmann, for trying to conceal their heterodoxy, forgetting that he is himself in precisely the same position with regard to the Scriptures.

Schenkel sees the fundamental error of the ecclesiastical Christology in the fact that it has never been able to acknowledge the real humanity of Christ; and the source of this error he holds to be that it assumed the personal Logos, the second Person of the Trinity, to have been the principle constituting the person of Christ. Hence he begins his reconstruction with the doctrine of the Trinity. It is not a triple personality in God which is testified to by conscience and Scripture, but a triple relationship of God to the world, and hence a triple consciousness of God in relation to the world. "God as the Father rests in the eternal source of creation; as the Son he issues from his absolute source and enters the life of the world, without himself becoming finite, and reflects the eternal image of the world within himself; as the Holy Spirit he transforms the life of the finite back into his absolute source, in such a way that this life ceases to be solely for the finite and comes to be for God, *i.e.*, for divine and eternal purposes." The Logos is therefore not a person, but the idea of the world eternally thought in God's self-consciousness, reaching its highest form in the idea of a perfect man. Only in this ideal, not in a real personal, sense can we maintain Christ's pre-existence, and only in this sense must we understand the Biblical statements with respect to it. "Christ had indeed an eternal pre-existence in God, in so far that the Father had chosen him from all eternity to represent the idea of man within the limits of the historical development of the human race. The Logos, as the eternal, conscious, divine idea of humanity, really became flesh, *i.e.*, had historical existence as a human person." The perfected archetype of humanity and the complete image of the deity realised themselves historically in Christ. In respect of his personal nature, Christ did not differ from other men, as would have been the case if he had had within him the personality of the Logos with absolute attributes. Still he is as an individual different from others, in that he is the spiritual centre in which mankind is eternally one; in him God conceives and contemplates mankind from all eternity as a whole, as a logical and ethical unity. Hence in the conception of Christ's true humanity is involved that of his true Deity. For just as it is the prerogative of every man to be historically in time related to God in his conscience, so it is Christ's prerogative above all other men to be *eternally* directly related to God, and to be conscious of himself as the man in whom the idea of humanity is realised as it was known and willed in God before all time. In this sense we may say that God himself, and nothing less, became man in Christ, because he is the self-revelation of the eternal God, that is, of his eternal will directed towards the world and humanity. As the self-revelation of God within the limits of a human life, he is the representative of Deity to mankind; as the personal exemplification of a true and perfect man, he is the representative of mankind in relation to Deity; in conjunction with both, he is the eternal mediator and surety, binding mankind to God and assuring it of salvation.

The atonement wrought by Christ consisted in the restoration of the fellowship of mankind with God, disturbed by sin, and the cancelling of the effects of sin, guilt, and punishment. This result was only possible by the manifestation in his own person of the ethical perfection of human nature, and especially by his condemnation of sin in its weakness, and revealing his divine self-sacrificing love in all its glory by his suffering and death. God regards this ethically perfect sacrifice not simply as an individual act, but as the common deed of mankind generally as represented in Christ, and hence looks upon mankind in general as if the normal development begun in it by Christ were already finished; which is the more natural as this atonement was eternally willed and historically accomplished by God himself. Thus Schenkel rejects, with Hofmann and Schleiermacher, the ecclesiastical doctrine of a vicarious satisfaction made to the punitive divine justice, and holds that the atoning element was rather that Christ by his holy life, attested by his death, made amends for the sin of mankind, *i.e.*, actually overcame it and destroyed it at its root, and thereby gave God the pledge of a life of humanity well-pleasing to him. This triumph over the supremacy of sin put an end to the cause of the discord between God and mankind, and rendered it possible for God to look upon mankind as if the new development of life, begun in principle, was already actually accomplished. Christ's deed was vicarious only in the sense that his suffering and action exemplified by anticipation what we are bound to suffer and do in fellowship with him. But when the work of atonement has once been comprehended, "with the help of the conscience," as a truly ethical deed, salvation, *i.e.*, the individual appropriation of the effects of the atonement on the part of each individual, must necessarily also be ethically conceived. Salvation can no longer be supposed to consist in the imputation to a man of another's merits, faith being merely the passive acceptance of this justifying sentence of God. On the contrary, the new life won, in principle, for mankind by Christ, must be practically realised in each individual; and this is done by faith, inasmuch as faith is the central activity of man's conscience in relation to God. Faith is the subjective condition of justification, inasmuch as the man by virtue of this change in his conscience, participates in the atoning personal life of Christ, and has received into his heart the new divine principle of life exemplified in Christ. This beginning of a new life in the believer, God imputes to him as if it were already completed; he regards it on account of the perfection of the principle active in it (the personal life of Christ), proleptically, as if it were itself already perfect.

The close connexion of this doctrine of atonement and of justification with the fundamental principles of Kant's philosophy of religion is very plain; the difference is only that what Kant called the ideal of a humanity pleasing to God, Jesus being the conspicuous example of it, is here identified with the ideal person of Christ; but in both cases it is by receiving this ideal into his own heart that the man becomes good in principle, and thus righteous before God, in spite of his asting empirical imperfection. That Jesus was not only the model but also the creative cause of this ethical and religious process, while the society which he founded was its social mediate cause, is the theological addition to the Kantian theory made as early as Schleiermacher, and which we have met with in various phases in the discussion of this group of theologians.

Most nearly akin to Hofmann and Schenkel is the theologian ALBRECHT RITSCHL; with Schenkel he lays special stress on the ethical element, with Hofmann he emphasises the historical and social element, and claims with him to be a true Lutheran; he is distinguished from both by the peculiarity of his epistemology and his method, which he eclectically derived from Kant and Lotze. In his book, *Metaphysik und Theologie*, he very emphatically opposed the "bad epistemology and metaphysics" of previous theology, and offered his own as the foundation of an altogether new theology.

On a closer inspection, however, this, his famous theory of cognition, is seen to be only a dilettante confusion of the irreconcilable views of subjective idealism, which resolves things into phenomena of consciousness, and common-sense realism, which looks upon the phenomena of consciousness as things themselves, admitting no distinction between phenomena as perceived by us and the being of things in themselves; a confusion to which the nearest parallel is the semi-idealistic, semi-materialistic theory of the Neo-Kantian Lange, author of the *Geschichte des Materialismus* (2nd ed. 1873), which enjoyed a brief celebrity as having supplied, it was thought, a justification of the sceptical tendencies of the time. We may, moreover, conjecture that Ritschl did not make this theory of cognition the basis of his theology from the first, but rather propounded it subsequently, in its defence. In spite of its intrinsic worthlessness, it is well calculated to furnish this theology, in its wavering between the subjective dissolution of the objects of theology and the affirmation of their objective reality, with an appearance of scientific justification having a certain attraction at least for amateurs in these questions.

Ritschl expounded his theological system in the third volume of his principal work, *Rechtfertigung und Versöhnung*, of which the first and second volumes had contained the history of the dogma and its Biblical-theological premises respectively. The third volume appeared in three editions, between 1874 and 1888, differing in some points from each other. Indeed, a careful comparison of the later presentations with the earlier shows an increasing advance in the direction of speculative scepticism and historical dogmatism.

Religion was defined by Ritschl in the first edition as the "common recognition of the dependence of man on God," or, more precisely, "as our view of the world from the basis of the idea of God and our estimate of ourselves from our sense of dependence upon God in relation to the world." The peculiarity of the religious view of the world he holds to be that it involves the conception of a whole, while theoretical knowledge in philosophy and the special sciences is limited to the general and particular laws of nature and spirit, and cannot by its methods of experience and observation attain to the conception of the world as a unity and a whole. Wherever philosophy has claimed by its methods to construct a view of the universe, we should rather discern an impulse of religion, which philosophy must distinguish as specifically different from its own object of systematic knowledge. Conflicts between religion and science are to be avoided by religion retaining as its privilege the right of viewing the world in its unity, and by science limiting itself to the particular phenomena of the world. Afterwards, on the other hand, Ritschl admitted that philosophy also treated of the world as a whole, with the object of comprehending it under one supreme law. Hence the distinction between religious and scientific knowledge is not to be sought in its object, but in the sphere of the subject, viz., in the difference in the attitude of the subject towards the object. For religion, he now states, "is occupied with judgments of value (*Werthurtheile*)," *i.e.*, with conceptions of our relation to the world which are of moment solely according to their value in awakening feelings of pleasure or pain as our dominion over the world is furthered or checked. "In all religion, by the help of the sublime spiritual Power which man adores, the solution is attempted of the contradiction in which man finds himself placed as a part of the natural world and as a spiritual personality with its claim to sovereignty over nature. For in his position he is a part of nature, in subjection to it, dependent upon and checked by other things, but as spirit he is moved by the impulse to maintain his independence against external things. In these circumstances arises religion as a belief in superior spiritual powers by whose help the deficiencies in man's own power are supplied." All religion seeks to supplement, by means of the idea of God, man's sense of personal dignity in the face of the hindrances of the world; this idea of God is "the ideal bond between the particular view of the world and the vocation of man to attain goods (*Güter*) or the highest good (happiness.)"[1] The thought of God must be treated in Christian theology solely as a judgment of value, or as a conception valuable for the attainment of goods. This is the same theory of religion as the well-known one of Feuerbach: the gods are the "*Wunschwesen*," invented by man from his practical need of a supplement to his own powerlessness over nature. But while the pathological explanation of the idea of God by motives of human feeling was intended by Feuerbach to deny the truth of this idea in an objective sense, and to affirm its purely imaginary character, the theory is directed by Ritschl to the exactly opposite conclusion, that the emotional value of the conception of God for the preservation of man's sense of personal dignity is also the warrant of its truth. That *this* warrant is not sufficient to insure to theology a knowledge of speculative truth and the character of a science, had indeed been formerly fully recognised by Ritschl himself, who had therefore in his first edition still held the necessity and possibility of an independent proof of the existence of God, founded upon the general data of the human mind; as such he had regarded the ethical proof as stated in Kant's *Critique of Judgment*, and had expressly declared that the "acceptance of the idea of God on that proof was no practical belief (as Kant had thought), but an act of speculative cognition," by which the general rationality of the Christian view of the world is established and thereby the possibility of a scientific theology secured, while such a theology would be impossible if the idea of God could not be established to the satisfaction of speculative knowledge also as its necessary basis. In the third edition, on the other hand, this position is altogether abandoned; we now read "this acceptance of the idea of God is, as Kant remarks, a practical belief, and not an act of speculative cognition." In justification of this change of view, it is alleged that it is the work of theology to preserve the distinctive character of the idea of God, that it is allowable to use it *only* in judgments of value. Hence theoretical proofs of the idea of God are doomed to failure, "because their professed results, even if true, do not accord with the Christian thought of God, in that

---

[1] Seligkeit.

they fail to express its value for men, in particular for men as sinners." Thus while Ritschl formerly recognised that a scientific and universally valid justification of the belief in God, and consequently of theology, cannot consist merely in an inference from the religious view of the world to its inner coherence, but must be based upon independent and universal data of the human mind, he now, on the contrary, pronounces the theoretical method of proof objectionable in not being confined to Christian judgments of value, or in aiming to be not only simple practical belief, but also independent theoretical knowledge. We see from this how, from the subjective conception of religion, is deduced the limitation of the science of religion, or theology, to the sphere of judgments of value, or subjective truth, and the abandonment on principle of all attempts to attain objective truth valid for the knowing mind in general.

In accordance with his principle that the Christian thought of God must be put forward only in judgments of value, Ritschl teaches that God should be thought of only as love. All metaphysical statements regarding God's absoluteness, his existence through himself, in himself, and for himself, must be rejected as "heathenish metaphysics," connected with the false theory of knowledge which maintains the existence of things irrespective of our conception of them. The idealistic subjectification of the idea of God on the lines of Feuerbach seems a necessary consequence of this. Such is not, however, Ritschl's intention; on the contrary, he seeks to conceive of the personality of God as objectively real. That this involves the assertion of an absolute existence of God in himself, as distinguished from his existence in relation to us, or his love, is plain, but is not admitted by Ritschl. He says that the attribute of personality is only the form for God's love. If this proposition were taken strictly, it would finally come to mean that our conception of the personality of God is the form under which we personify love as "God," which is the view of Feuerbach and the Positivists. But Ritschl does not mean this; indeed, he speaks also of an "intrinsic purpose of God,"[1] into which God takes up the purpose of the world, or which he realises in the education of the human race for the kingdom of God. But such a purpose is a relation of the

---

[1] Selbstzweck Gottes.

will to itself, and therefore presupposes a being which is not solely love, that is, existing for others, but exists also as a subject in and for itself. This inner self-subsistence of God, with his loving communication of himself, is not merely a necessary metaphysical conception, but also of great religious importance, since it is the foundation, as Dorner has well remarked, of the Biblical conception of God's holiness and righteousness, which in the teaching of the Bible and the Church is inseparable from that of his love. But this side of the idea of God is altogether neglected by Ritschl. He says: "In comparison with the conception of love there is no other of equal value. In particular this holds of the conception of holiness, which in its Old Testament sense is, for several reasons, not valid in Christianity, and the use of which in the New Testament is obscure." And with regard to God's righteousness, in which, according to Biblical doctrine, his holiness is actively shown, Ritschl (like Hofmann) considers that it is "his action for the salvation of the members of his religious community, and is identical in fact with grace."

This is connected with Ritschl's peculiar doctrine of sin. He altogether rejects the idea of original sin, because it assumes that there is a will previous to its individual acts; an assumption related to the false doctrine of things in themselves, and because the hypothesis of an innate evil tendency makes both responsibility and education impossible. The latter demands the exactly opposite hypothesis, "that the general though still indefinite impulse towards good exists in the child, although it is not guided by a general insight into the good, and not yet tested by the various relations of life." For the conception of original sin we must, therefore, substitute that of the "kingdom of sin," *i.e.*, of the collective unity of free actions opposed to the purpose of the kingdom of God, and of the inclinations acquired thereby. The law of sin in the will is not a natural loss of its freedom, but is a consequence of the necessary reaction of every act of the will upon the direction of the power of volition. Accordingly the unchecked repetition of selfish determinations of the will produces a tendency to selfishness, and the sin is then transmitted from one individual to another by the interaction of their conduct in society. Ritschl has not indeed shown how any selfish determinations of the will at all can be explained, if there exists in the child by nature only an indefinite impulse towards good;

for the attempt to explain it from ignorance is certainly unsatisfactory. Ritschl holds, namely, that ignorance, as experience proves in the case of children, is "a very momentous factor in the origination and development of sin;" and further, that it is "the essential condition of the conflicts of the will with the order of society as the rule of goodness, and also the condition of the fixity of the will in its resistance to this order." It may easily be seen how little this explanation accords with experience, of which a very different account is given even by the heathen poet (*Nitimur in vetitum*), and above all by the Apostle Paul (Rom. vii.). In Ritschl's case also, this treatment of sin as ignorance is not so much the result of actual observation as a postulate of his doctrine of God and reconciliation. To the regulative conception of God corresponds, he says, the distinction between the two stages of sin—an imperfect stage, not excluding the capability for redemption, and a completed stage, consisting in a final purpose of opposition to the known will of God. Since the latter is only a hypothetical possibility, of which we can nowhere assume the reality, all actual sin of mankind is confined to the former stage, and this is regarded by God as "the relative stage of ignorance." The artificial method by which Ritschl tries to harmonise his theory with the statements of the Bible, may be here passed over as valueless.

The correlative to the love of God is the kingdom of God, inasmuch as it is the union of men for mutual and common action from the motive of love, which action, as correlative to the purpose of God himself, and as the specific operation of God, is the perfect revelation of the fact that God is love. In the precise development of this thought there is again a noticeable difference between the first and the later editions of Ritschl's work. In the first the *Christian* idea of the kingdom of God is the *highest* stage of ethical society among men, though removed from the earlier preparatory stages to no greater degree than these from each other. It is more perfect in virtue of its greater extent, but is not essentially different in kind, since the pre-Christian forms of society (family, friendship, nationality) originated in love. And since, as is then stated, this union of men, *wherever* realised, must *always* be regarded as dependent upon God, and as the effect and revelation of His love, the conception of a universal revelation of God throughout all human history is evidently presupposed, since this history has never been without ethical fellowship and love. In the later editions, on the other hand, the comparison of the Christian kingdom of God with the preparatory stages of ethical society in history is omitted, and the love of God is exclusively confined to the historical Christian Church, which, by acknowledging Christ as its Lord, itself comes to stand in the same relation as he to God. Whereas it was formerly maintained that "God loves the *human race* from the point of view of its vocation to the kingdom of God," we are now told that "God is love as revealing himself through his Son to the *Church* founded by the latter in order to educate it for the kingdom of God"; and whereas we were then told that all ethical union originated in love, and that all action from love must always and everywhere be regarded as dependent on God, and as the effect of the revelation of his love, it is now stated that "All love of man originates according to Christian ideas in the revelation of God in Christ." From these statements it would directly follow that before Christ there was neither a revelation of God nor an ethical association of men. If that be so, from what source were religion and morality in pre-Christian humanity derived? This Ritschl has never explained. Simply to deny that it had any religion or morality, would lead to a pessimism more extreme than that of Augustine, and would strangely contradict Ritschl's optimistic view of the goodness of human nature. Finally, it is evident that the limitation of the divine revelation solely to the person of Jesus, whose historical connection with the religion of Israel is undeniable, verges close upon the denial of revelation altogether. Thus ultra dogmatism in the end leads to the opposite extreme, as has actually been exemplified in Ritschl's disciple, Bender.

In his Christology, Ritschl starts from the principle that in a personal life what is real and actual consists of spiritual effects and nothing else. By this means the Christological problem is much simplified. Not only the dogma of the two natures, but the whole metaphysical background of ecclesiastical Christology is thus got rid of, even more decisively than in Schleiermacher's theology, and replaced by an historical view of the subject. In strange contrast with this, Ritschl nevertheless continues to speak with orthodox theology of the deity of Christ. It is true this term has for him an altogether different meaning. It is the expression of our estimate of

Jesus, of our trustful acknowledgment of the unique value of what his life effected for our salvation, but is not meant to predicate any metaphysical characteristic of his nature whatever, or any transcendental unity of his nature with God. The predication of the deity of Christ sums up his unmistakable importance as the perfect revealer of God and as the manifest type of spiritual supremacy over the world. Our religious estimate of Christ must be tested by the connection of his action in the world with his religious convictions and with his ethical motives. It has no direct reference to his presumptive possession of innate qualifications and capacities, for Christ does not influence us thus, but morally and religiously only. Jesus is the representative of the perfect spiritual religion, standing in a reciprocal relation of union with the God who is the originator and final end of the world. This involved his recognition of God's divinest purpose, the union of men by love, as the task of his own life, whereby he experienced that independence of the world which the members of his Church ought to come to share with him. The peculiar value of his life on earth gains the character of a permanent rule by serving as a pattern for our religious and ethical vocation. This authority, which either excludes all other standards or else subordinates them to itself, and which is also the ultimate regulative principle of all human trust in God, is equivalent in value to his deity. On the other hand, metaphysical attributes of deity cannot be ascribed to him for the simple reason that they are altogether outside the religious method of cognition, which is concerned only with judgments of value. So too the passages of Scripture from which Christ's personal pre-existence has been inferred, are only to be understood in the sense that, in the thought and will of God, Christ from the beginning was the head of the community of the kingdom of God, which is the object of the world. The Johannine formula of the Word becoming flesh, means that the Word, which is the general form of divine revelation, became in him a human person, *i.e.*, that he is the perfect revelation of God.

While it follows from this that the doctrine of Christ's work must not be separated from that of his person, Ritschl further rejects the usual dogmatic distinction of his threefold office as prophet, priest, and king. In order to form a single comprehensive conception of Christ's work, we must regard it from the point of view of his vocation. Now, this vocation was the foundation of the kingdom of God, or of the universal ethical association of men as the divine object of the world. But since, as the founder of the kingdom of God in the world, or the representative of God's moral sovereignty over men, he is unique in comparison with all other men who have received from him the same purpose, he is the factor in the world in whose intrinsic purpose God, in a creative way, gives effect to, and manifests his own intrinsic purpose, so that all his actions in fulfilment of his vocation constitute the revelation of God, present and perfect, in him; or, in other words, he is one in whom the Word of God is a human person. This theory gives the consistent ethical and religious estimate of Christ, and thus the christological problem of theology is solved. It is not the business of theology to inquire how the person of Christ came from God, and came to be that which is the subject of our ethical and religious estimate, especially as the problem lies beyond the possible range of inquiry. The grace and faithfulness of Christ in the fulfilment of his vocation, and the elevation of his spiritual aims beyond the limited and natural motives of the world, constitute the elements of his historical appearance which are comprehended in the attribute of his deity. Looked at with reference to man, this patience and faithfulness of Christ is the result of his devotion to his calling of realising the kingdom of God among men as their supermundane destination, supported by his special knowledge of God; with reference to the divine Being, this human life appears as the completed revelation of God, since the final purpose of the world, to which Christ's life is devoted, is founded in God's inner purpose, or in his will of love. For the complete definition of Christ's deity the further supposition is required that his grace and faithfulness and world-subduing patience have produced as their effect the society of the kingdom of God, with analogous attributes. This is evidently equivalent to saying that the "deity" of Christ consists in the original exemplification and communication of the same true piety and morality in which consists also the "deity," or better, the fellowship with God, the divine sonship and divine likeness of Christians. This is the same thought as that found in the whole of Schleiermacher's school, except that the latter usually express it more simply, being less painfully anxious to keep to the ecclesiastical term, to which from this position, really no just claim can be made.

There can be no such thing as special priestly functions on the part of Christ which are not included in those of his general vocation. If Christ is to be conceived as priest, he is so fundamentally because as the Son of God he stood in the closest communion of purpose with God, and carried this out in every moment of his life, since every act and word in his life's work, until his voluntary and patient suffering of death, sprang from his religious relation to God. The juridical conception of a satisfaction of God's punitive righteousness offends against the design of religion, since law and religion are contradictory standards of action, and the assumption that in God righteousness and grace tend in opposite directions, is *irreligious*, the unity of the divine will being the inviolable condition of all trust in God. Even if we agree with Ritschl's rejection of the theory of satisfaction, we cannot approve of his unsympathetic judgment of the Pauline and orthodox doctrine of the atonement ; we cannot but see in this an illustration of that Rationalistic dogmatism which is neither able nor willing to appreciate objectively, from a given religious point of view, the historical and psychological conditions of dogmatic conceptions, or to admit their relative validity for such a point of view. In respect of this intolerant dogmatism, Ritschl's theology marks a return to the weakest side of that Rationalism which he has so severely censured.

Not specially the death of Christ, which is only the comprehensive term to express his religious union with God, as preserved throughout his life, but his work in his vocation generally, brings about the forgiveness of sins, or justification, or atonement. These synonymous conceptions are predicable of the Christian society in the sense that in it there exists a union of men with God, in spite of their sins and of the accentuation of their feeling of guilt. The standard and historical source of this union is Christ's union with God, which he preserved in the faithful execution of his vocation to found the kingdom of God. For the grace and faithfulness of God, which is the ultimate efficient cause of the forgiveness of sin, is made manifest solely by the purpose which controlled all Christ's work of conducting men into such a relation to God as should save them from sin and gather them under the moral rule of God. From this point is first deduced the formula, that God makes the union of the members of Christ's Church with Christ the condition of admitting them to a union with himself. But this proposition (which agrees with Schleiermacher's doctrine of salvation) receives forthwith in Ritschl an important modification. He maintains (though on the basis of very arbitrary exegesis) that it is historically certain that Christ conceived not individuals but the society to be founded by him and represented in the twelve apostles, as the direct object of the forgiveness of sins which he was to grant. Hence he pronounces Schleiermacher's formula wrong, that in Protestantism the relation of the individual to the Church depends on his relation to Christ, while in Catholicism the converse holds good; for in the case of Protestant Christians also the right relation to Christ is conditioned, not only historically (which is self-evident) but ideally, by the fellowship of believers, since no action of Christ upon men is conceivable except in accordance with the antecedent purpose of Christ to found a society. Schleiermacher's formula is only the reflection of the pietistical disintegration of the idea of a church, which dated from the individualistic theory of salvation in the Lutheran theology, but was not in harmony with Luther's own view (according to his Short Catechism). As in the purpose of Christ the guarantee of a universal forgiveness of sins and the foundation of his Church were equivalent ideas, so in the result of his work it is the same thing to be certain of having one's sins forgiven and to belong to Christ's community. The forgiveness of sins or reconciliation is possessed by the individual only as a member of the religious society of Christ, in consequence of the immeasurable interaction of his own personal freedom and the determining influence of the society. It is not by an individual imitation of Christ that we become assured of salvation, as pietists and mystics held, including Schleiermacher and his followers, for all imitation of Christ in the proper sense is rendered impossible by the difference of the special conditions of his life from those of the members of his Church; but we are warranted in the assurance of being children of God by belonging to the society founded by Christ. Moreover, love to God and Christ is not an apt description of the religious function of the individual, for we might understand by it "an imaginary private relation to God and Christ," bearing the character of indifference to the world or of fleeing from it. In these statements Ritschl's social positivism and his dislike of the mystical element in religion is carried to such extremes as plainly to do violence to essential interests of Christian piety.

The justification possessed by the Christian as a member of Christ's community is attested practically by his freedom or dominion over the world. This is not to be understood in the empirical sense but ideally, though not therefore any the less a reality. It is, in general, in faith in God's providence that the religious dominion over the world is exercised; for in the view of the world as a unity, under the idea of God as our Father, and in the corresponding estimate of ourselves, all things and events are regarded as means to our good. Under this Christian belief in providence Ritschl appears to include also the hypothesis of "miracles." He puts both in contrast, as the general teleological and the miraculous view of the universe, with the scientific view, and he seeks to deprive the opposition of the latter (which is however not directed against the teleological, but *only* against the miraculous view) of its force by reference to the incompleteness of our scientific knowledge of the world and to the immediate certainty of the feeling of personal worth expressing itself in the belief in providence. He warmly opposes the view of the theology of the *Aufklärung*, that the belief in providence is a part of natural religion or of general scientific culture. He holds that, on the contrary, confident trust in God is exclusively the contribution of the Christian religion, since it rests upon the assurance of Christ's Church of our reconciliation to God; a statement which, considering the innumerable expressions of trust in God in non-Christian religions, particularly in the Old Testament, requires considerable modification; it is related to the statement above considered, that God has revealed himself as love only in Christ; in this case, as in others, a difference of degree is made an exclusive peculiarity, which is simply unhistorical dogmatism. There are however several good points in Ritschl's detailed account of the Christian belief in providence: as that it must approve itself in patience and humility amid all the vicissitudes of life, and that it is shown in Christian prayer, which is chiefly thanksgiving or humble recognition of the divine rule. Finally, the moral perfection of the community of the kingdom of God is deduced from its religious view of the world, and it is shown that it manifests itself primarily in the faithfulness of the individual to his calling, since moral action in a calling is the form of each man's total contribution to the kingdom of God. In this way freedom is realised in law. But freedom is identical in kind with the religious functions of belief in providence, patience, humility, and prayer, in which, in consequence of the Reconciliation, the individual becomes assured of his value as part of a whole in comparison with the world. The two spheres of morals and religion are so connected that neither can exist without the other. In the religious dominion over this world lies the present blessednesss of eternal life. But the moral formation of character also has eternal life for its object, since the certainty to the person of the indestructibility of spiritual existence is always connected with the experience of the value of the ethical and religious character. Thus it is equally important to assert that the eternal life is given by God in the reconciliation through Christ, and that the completion of our salvation is attained by the development of the ethico-religious character and by the perfection in its kind of our life-work in our vocation. In spite of all this the moral and the religious sides of Christianity are not brought into a perfectly harmonious unity by Ritschl, as is seen in the remarkable statement that we *must take both points of view alternately* (viz. that of moral freedom and that of dependence upon God), an evident admission that the two are mutually exclusive. This is the inevitable consequence of his conception of religion as *supplementing* our freedom. The external dualism between moral freedom and the religious feeling of dependence thus introduced from the first runs like a red thread through the whole of his theology, and is in particular the real cause of his dislike of religious mysticism, in which freedom is felt in experience to be realised not *along with* but *in* dependence, the difference of the two being thus brought into a harmonious unity.

Among the opponents of Ritschl's theology, LIPSIUS occupies a prominent place, and all the more that, to a certain extent, he shares Ritschl's epistemological principles. He maintains with Kant the limitation of our knowledge to the realm of experience, to our external and internal perceptions and their logical combination so as to form regular relations of natural and spiritual existence ; and he denies the possibility of a metaphysical knowledge of the transcendental, which, he holds, inevitably involves contradictions. But while Ritschl's school constructs an insurmountable barrier between our theoretical knowledge of the universe and our ethico-religious certainty, Lipsius demands a connected and consistent theory of the universe, which shall comprehend the entire realm of our experience as a whole. He rejects the doctrine of dualism in a truth, one division of which would be confined to "judgments of value," and be unconnected with our theoretical knowledge of the external world. The possibility and necessity of combining the results of our scientific knowledge with the declarations of our ethico-religious experience, so as to form a consistent philosophy, is based, according to Lipsius, upon the unity of the personal ego, which on the one hand knows the world scientifically, and on the other regards it as the means of realising the ethico-religious object of its life. The former is effected by the study of the causal connection of external and internal events, and the latter by referring them teleologically to the ethical subject and its vocation. Neither of these modes of looking at things can be reduced to the other, neither employed indifferently to supplement the deficiencies of the other; only in their mutual relation do they yield the whole of reality for us. Moreover, they must not be placed externally side by side in such a way that the one would be limited to the life of nature, and the other to that of history, but the sphere of teleology extends likewise into nature, and that of causality into history. Nevertheless, it is the sphere of the historical and ethical life of humanity which first elevates the teleology imperfectly traced in nature to the position of a prime factor in the construction of our philosophy of things. No one can be compelled by the method of scientific proof to recognise the teleological unity of the world; it is the personal feeling of moral obligation which leads to the belief in a moral order of the world superior to the order of nature. But this ethical certainty must not be allowed to make us indifferent to the natural conditions of the moral life, which can only fulfil its vocation by their means. This justifies the rule as to method, as rigidly keeping the causal, or empirical, and the teleological, or ideal, view of the world clearly distinct, as, again, of connecting them as the two sides of the same thing. By the application of this method by Lipsius to dogmatic theology, it assumed in his hands the form of an ethico-religious philosophy of life and the world, which as such is throughout teleological, but which must also remain in thorough harmony with the empirical or causal point of view of theoretical science.

Lipsius defines religion as the solution of the riddle presented by the contradiction of our empirical determination by nature to our ethical vocation. Religion does not primarily concern society, but the individual, though the individual only in virtue of his necessarily seeking religious fellowship; it is thus the most individual and at the same time the most universal of man's concerns. Its empirical motive lies in man's instinct of self-preservation, which seeks help from a supernatural power, and for this purpose enters into a personal relation with it, ranging upwards from reverent dread to childlike trust and thankful love. But the ultimate source even of the elementary form of the feeling, as well as of its advance from natural to ethical religion, is the supersensible nature of man, or his "transcendental freedom," which both determines the entire course of his ethical development, and also leads him to enter into religious relations. For this freedom can only be realised in a transcendental dependence upon a free Will, such as contains both the creative source of man's capacity for transcendental freedom and the power to realise it by rising above the determination by nature. Inasmuch as the religious man, by rising to a Will above nature, becomes conscious of the action of this same Will in his own spirit, we have here the root of all belief in revelation. On its metaphysical side, therefore, religion is a real mutual relation between God and man, the home of which is the personal spiritual life of the latter; revelation and religion are therefore convertible terms. The reality of this mutual relation consists in a personal fellowship of faith, experienced in the intercourse of prayer; its *manner* lies beyond the analysis of the understanding, and constitutes the mystery of religion. As stages of religion, Lipsius distinguishes natural religion, ethical religion in its legal form, and the religion of salvation, in which the divine Will is revealed not merely as an imperious law, but as love delivering from sin and evil. This highest stage is realised in Christianity.

In Christianity we must distinguish between the characteristic fundamental religious relation and the fundamental historical fact; the former is made actual by the latter,—that is, in the historical person of Christ; but the value of the latter to us lies in its being the vehicle of that fundamental relation, —that is, the sonship of man to God, which as such involves his participation in the kingdom of God as God's final purpose for the world. His sonship to God is subjectively conditioned by penitence and faith, and is objectively based upon God's reconciling and redeeming grace. This is, therefore, the specifically religious good, to the acquirement of which Christianity is the vehicle, and it is primarily the highest good for the individual. The ethical association of men under the idea of the kingdom of God, which is the ethical and social side of Christianity, is subordinate to its religious and individual side. The Christian's religious experience of his sonship to God is the subject-matter of the Christian faith with regard to God, man, and the world; this contains no theoretical truths as to the objective nature of God and the world, but primarily only descriptions of the experienced relations of God to the religious man and to his world, though including declarations as to the supersensible realities of which faith is assured. This faith, with its declarations, is derived from the teleological contemplation, peculiar to the Christian, of the divine action in nature and history, and the course of his own life, a way of regarding the divine activity which, though it does not rest on speculative (causal) knowledge, must not be inconsistent with it. Theological doctrines are therefore not mere descriptions of subjective devout states of consciousness, nor mere judgments of value, with no corresponding judgments of being; but they are descriptions of objective relations between God, man, and the world, based upon subjective religious experiences, which are associated with the feeling of their being of the highest value for the subject.

All the declarations of the Christian faith have their objective foundation in the revelation of God in Christ, of which the New Testament writings are the documentary authorities. Revelation is God's manifestation of himself for man. It takes place by various stages—in the order of nature, in the moral order of the world, and in the order of salvation, which stages must be conceived as included in God's eternal plan of the world. The subject-matter of the highest, or Christian revelation, is not the kingdom of God, the announcement of which was not brought by Christ as something new, but it is God's saving and reconciling designs towards man, including the ethical idea of the kingdom of God as the necessary consequence of the fellowship of love between God and his children. Nor does the guarantee of the truth of the Christian revelation consist in the individual being a member of the community which possesses reconciliation and redemption, but in his personally appropriating by faith these saving blessings revealed in the Gospel, and thus obtaining the immediate personal experience of his reconciliation to God. This immediate personal certainty of salvation, in virtue of its resting upon the witness of the spirit, is the true centre and heart of Christian piety, its mystery not to be theoretically proved, but practically experienced, like the experience of the moral law, which is equally undemonstrable empirically, and yet is the foundation of the whole moral life. Still, the individual certainty of salvation is preserved from the suspicion of being subjective self-deception by its known agreement with the similar experience of the whole Christian society.

These are the fundamental principles of Lipsius' theology, as expounded in his *Abhandlungen zur Dogmatik*, and in his work, *Philosophie und Religion*. From his more special treatise (*Lehrbuch der evang. prot. Dogmatik*, 1876; 2nd ed., 1879) we may here notice his treatment of the dogmas [1] of *God, Christ, Justification*, and the *Church*.

The divine Trias of revelation must have its foundation in the divine nature. But our thought has no possible means of arriving at any logically tenable conclusion as to internal distinctions in the transcendental divine nature, much less as to personal distinctions in the Trinity. All such attempts lead to mythological conceptions. Similar difficulties arise from the application of the idea of the Absolute to the Christian idea of God. It is, it is true, an unavoidable necessity of our thought to conceive God as in fact absolute, *i.e.* as raised above the world of time and space; only as the absolute cause is he the almighty creator and ruler of his world. But the ethical view of the world demands, again, that we should conceive the absolute source of the world as personal, *i.e.* according to the analogy of our human consciousness. For the source of the world of nature and of spirit cannot be less than spirit, and real spirit is personal, self-conscious, and self-determining spirit. Nevertheless, it is impossible for our thought to show how personality can be consistent with absoluteness. Personality is arrived at *via eminentiæ*, absoluteness *via negationis*; but these two methods yield no coherent

---

[1] I do not give his exposition of these doctrines in the words of the text of the above work, but according to the author's most recent personal explanations.

conception, but a double series of statements, which we cannot see how to bring into unity. A personal consciousness and will, not confined by the limitations of time, is as inconceivable to us as it is impossible for us, on the other hand, to think of the divine knowledge and will as conditioned by time. Space and time are indeed the forms in which God reveals himself, and which are therefore for him no more mere appearance than the variety of his particular acts of will. But our thought cannot reconcile the participation of the divine knowledge and action in the temporal and spatial distinctions of earthly life with the elevation of the divine nature above the world and time. The pretended speculative solutions of this and similar difficulties are only apparent. We can therefore apply the conception of the absolute to God only as a critical canon or rule which serves to prevent us, in our figurative use of human analogies, from making finite our idea of God, by continually reminding us of the purely symbolic validity of these statements about God. The idea of an infinite consciousness and will remains indeed a necessity of our thought, but is only a *Grenzbegriff*, a conception containing no adequate knowledge of God's nature and attributes. The religious value of the theological ideas of the divine attributes consists, on the other hand, in their being descriptions, based on religious experience, of the action of the divine Will upon us and our world. The Christian faith regards the existence and course of the world from the teleological point of view as the means of securing the divine purpose of the world—without prejudice to the scientific causal theory of the world. The same course of the world must be placed entirely under the point of view of natural causation, and also entirely under that of a divine purpose, since the divine teleology manifests itself as the power immanent in the course of nature. This distinction between the causal connection of all events and their teleological control by the overruling divine Will justifies also the religious belief in miracles, which as such are never empirically demonstrable, but from the teleological point of view are an actual proof of a special divine intervention. The belief in providence is indeed inseparably connected with every religious theory of the world, and therefore not peculiar to Christianity, but it reaches its perfection only by means of the Christian consciousness of salvation. Not that the Christian was the first to refer every event to the purposes of the divine kingdom—that was done in the Old Testament—but because he first recognised the infinite value of every human soul as an object of special divine care.

In the doctrine of the person and work of the Saviour, the empirical must likewise be distinguished from the religious mode of regarding them. The former regards the Saviour as the historical founder of the Christian religion, the personal representative and source of the new religious principle animating the Christian Church. The latter recognises in him the personal revelation of God's will to save the individual and human society. For the former, Jesus Christ is only historically important; for the latter, he has also a direct religious significance. The object of faith is always primarily the eternal good which God, by Christ, gives to believers as their own. It is not, however, an eternal idea or truth of the reason that is illustrated in the person of Jesus, but God's eternal will of love become in Christ an historical act of love. The revelation of saving and reconciling grace in Christ is not merely a proclamation but a revelation by deed. The reconciliation is not simply the liberation of the human spirit from its mistrust of God, arising from its ignorance, but primarily the reconciliation of God to man, an actual new relation entered into by God with mankind, and revealed by him in the consciousness of believers. This new relation is eternally based upon God's plan of salvation, the goal to which the divine governance of human history has always been directed; but it was only historically realised when the historical conditions were given. These were on the one hand the actual realisation of a perfect life of harmony with God (perfect righteousness), and on the other, humble submission to the connection between sin and misery established by God for the common life of the human race, and the consequent recognition of the divine sentence upon sin (perfect satisfaction). The Christian faith affirms both to have been vicariously accomplished in Christ's sufferings and death, not in the sense of legal substitution, but in the sense of action and passion on the part of the new humanity in its personal head. As the head of the new humanity, Christ is its representative with God; mankind is reconciled to him in so far as it enters by means of faith into communion with Christ. On the other hand, Christ, in virtue of the reconciliation of God and man being actually accomplished in him, is the representative of God in relation to men, the bearer of the divine revelation to them, proclaiming as a fact the reconciliation actually accomplished by him. This position of Christ as mediator between God and man is described in ecclesiastical tradition by metaphysical statements about the union of the divine and human natures in Christ's person, and about a transcendental work of reconciliation accomplished by Christ in relation to God, by which God himself was delivered from a conflict between his mercy and justice. In both points these theories transgress the limits imposed upon human knowledge; and it is of minor importance that the philosophical means used to establish these theologoumena were borrowed partly from Platonic eclectic speculations, partly from the legal conceptions of the middle ages. These theologoumena must be employed in theology simply as figurative expressions, and any higher claim necessarily turns them into mythology. The Christian faith is content to speak of God being in a unique manner in Christ, in the sense that in his personal consciousness and life-work was actually accomplished the revelation of the love of God as seeking the salvation of mankind. Historically considered, Christ's life-work must be regarded from the ethical point of view of his personal vocation to found the society in which is realised the kingdom of God, by life in harmony with God gradually overcoming the power of sin. Reconciliation thus appears as the consequence of salvation. But the Christian faith is not content with this. That the founder of the society is its pattern has not been historically demonstrated, the "sinlessness" of Christ remains from this position a mere possibility. On the other hand, from the teleological point of view it is simply included in the statement of the belief that Christ is the personal revelation of the divine love. For God can be perfectly revealed only in a man religiously and ethically perfect, and one, therefore, altogether fitted to be the pure organ of his revelation. This holiness of Christ is the specifically religious miracle. God reconciles the world to himself by creating in Christ a new man, in whom mankind appears in the perfection desired by God, and therefore as reconciled to God. This reconciliation involves salvation, viz. the foundation of a new moral and religious life of humanity, in which the power of sin and the world is gradually vanquished.

The appropriation of salvation is accomplished from the

empirical point of view as a psychological ethical process, the chief elements in which are penitence and faith. The religious and teleological description of this process is that it is the self-attestation of the divine spirit in the human spirit, which the latter experiences as the communication of divine comfort and strength. As distinguished from the idea of the kingdom in the Old Testament, the society of Christ's kingdom is based upon the believer's personal sonship to God ; to make his *personal state of grace* sure is the first concern of each individual believer, membership in the kingdom of God being involved in this. In the state of grace justification denotes the religious side, the appropriation of reconciliation ; regeneration the ethical side, the appropriation of salvation. Justification, regarded as a divine act, is the declaration of the will of God that the penitent and believing sinner shall not be excluded from communion with him ; but this act of justification is identical with the consciousness of justification in the soul of the believer ; these are the two inseparable sides of the same process, which consists in the acceptance of the Gospel message of grace. Regeneration, as the fundamental ethical renewal of the man, is—logically, though not temporally—the consequence of his justification. From the psychological point of view, a change of mind must have begun before the faith to appropriate justification could exist ; nevertheless we are right in teleologically regarding regeneration as the fruit of justification, viz. as the inward working of the same spirit of God that had before assured man of his sonship to God ; for only from this assurance can spring the power of joyful fulfilment of the divine will and the religious freedom of elevation above the world. The witness of the Holy Spirit, and being led by the Holy Spirit, are connected as cause and effect. The fellowship of the believer with God, viewed empirically, is simply a harmony of will, but teleologically considered, it is the actual indwelling of the divine spirit in man, *unio mystica*.

With regard to the Church also we must distinguish between the empirical or historical conception of it, as the society of those confessing the Christian faith, organised in external forms, and the religious and teleological idea of the communion of saints, which is an object of faith. The identification of the former with the latter is the fundamental error of Roman Catholicism. The Church can never be called a divine institution in any other sense than that of being a community in which the Spirit of God, by means of the word, produces and fosters the Christian life of salvation. As the educator of individuals into the Christian faith, she is the mother of believers. Only those who, under her educating influence, have attained to a life of personal communion with Christ and God, are living members of the community of believers; thus (Ritschl notwithstanding) Schleiermacher's statement holds good, that according to the Protestant faith, communion with the Church is conditioned by that with Christ, and not *vice versâ*. In the ministration of the word and sacraments we have from the empirical point of view, ecclesiastical functions which are signs and symbols of the faith animating the Church. From a religious or teleological point of view, they are signs and pledges of divine grace, by means of which the Holy Spirit produces faith, and communicates the blessings which the signs signify. The kingdom of God is primarily a divine gift, and only secondarily a human vocation; it is, therefore, not an empirical but a religious conception. The peculiar blessing possessed by the members of the kingdom is sonship to God, attained by justification and regeneration; the personal certainty of this brings with it participation in the kingdom of God, but membership in the Church is not identical with membership in the kingdom of God. In actual history, the kingdom of God appears in the advancing moral organisation of the whole of human life under the guiding principle of love to God and the brethren. Beyond the historical and always relative realisation of the kingdom of God, faith pictures the ideal of its eternal consummation, both for the individual and for the race. As to *how* this is to be, we can have no conception, and therefore no possible knowledge. Individual immortality can be scientifically neither proved nor refuted. But viewed teleologically the belief in immortality has its roots in the same self-assertion of the ego in opposition to the forces of external nature as gives birth to both the moral and the religious theory of the universe.

The similarity of Lipsius's theology with that of De Wette is obvious; Lipsius, thanks to a profounder analysis of the religious spirit, presents, however, a more subtle and satisfactory method of harmonising the two distinct methods of looking at the phenomena than did his predecessor. The reconciliation of our present knowledge of nature and history with the religious faith handed down in the Church, and imparted to us in our education, will remain in the future the perpetual problem of theology. It is evident that its formulæ, from the very fact of their having this practical object, cannot claim to be scientific propositions, valid universally and for all time. A sound tact, giving prominence to what is for us religiously essential, and putting into the background what is antiquated, will, perhaps, prove better able to solve the problem than a rigorously systematic method. In this respect, we must finally mention Hase's *Evangelisch-protestantische Dogmatik*, the six editions of which are sufficient proof of its usefulness. Its value lies partly in the full and judiciously chosen historical materials prefixed to each dogma, and partly in the skill, caution, and tact, with which the permanent religious significance of various dogmas is discussed. This allows, it is true, large latitude to the personal taste of the author, with his high religious and scientific culture. But where was this otherwise with a theological manual, which was not intended to be a mere book of the symbols of the Church? The proper and strictly scientific work of modern theology does not and cannot lie in the field of dogmatic theology, but in that of historical research.

BOOK III.

BIBLICAL AND HISTORICAL THEOLOGY.

CHAPTER I.

NEW TESTAMENT CRITICISM AND EXEGESIS.

THE year 1835 marked an era in our scientific knowledge of the Biblical foundations of Christianity. In it appeared David Friedrich Strauss's Life of Jesus, Christian Ferdinand Baur's work on the Pastoral Epistles, and Wilhelm Vatke's history of the religion of the Old Testament, three works containing the germs of the researches of our own day into the Old and New Testament writings. These works did not of course come down from heaven, but were to a certain extent the result of the labours of older critics. Still, the difference between them and earlier works is so fundamental, the new element in them is so predominant and of such moment, that we are justified in dating from them the special character of the Biblical criticism of to-day. We shall first take a brief glance at the state of New Testament criticism in the first three decades of this century.

The principle enunciated by Semler, Lessing, and Herder, that the books of the Bible must be read and criticised as human productions, was systematically applied by Eichhorn. He saw that the New Testament epistles were not all written by the apostles whose names they bear, that 2 Peter and Jude are not genuine, and that the Epistles to Timothy and Titus do not come direct from Paul. Of special importance was his hypothesis as to the synoptic Gospels. The problem as to how their frequent verbal agreement in conjunction with their discrepancies can be explained, he believed himself able to solve by the hypothesis of a primary Aramaic Gospel, of which various translations and editions were at first current, and from which at a later time sprang our canonical Gospels. Instead of this primitive written Gospel, Gieseler regarded oral tradition as the common source, an hypothesis which explained the differences between the Gospels more easily but made their agreement in details more difficult. Schleiermacher combined both hypotheses, by assuming along with the oral tradition a number of small written accounts ("*Diegeseis*"), by the collection and combination of which our synoptic Gospels were formed. The Gospel of Matthew even does not, in his view, come directly from the Apostle Matthew as its author, but is only based upon a collection of speeches made by him (the λόγια of Papias). The Gospel according to Mark is derived from Matthew's and Luke's Gospels, both of them being used alternately. The Johannine Gospel only is the authentic production of one author, and was composed by John the apostle and eye-witness; and as the earliest authority for the life of Jesus it is always to be preferred to the synoptists. The authority of the great theologian Schleiermacher secured for this theory for a long time wide acceptance. It must however be remarked, that of all conceivable combinations it is the most erroneous, and is a complete subversion of the real state of the case, since Mark's Gospel is not the latest but the earliest, and John's Gospel not the earliest but the latest, and throughout dependent on Mark and Luke. Historical instinct was not Schleiermacher's strong point, and his preference for the Fourth Gospel did not rest upon historical grounds but upon his theological postulates and his sympathy, as one of the Romanticists, with the Johannine idea of Christ. Schleiermacher ought to have learnt better from Herder, who, though he regarded the Fourth Gospel as apostolic, still possessed enough historical insight to see in it "the echo of the earlier Gospels in a higher key," while he regarded Mark's Gospel and that of the Hebrews as the earliest, from which was derived first Luke's and then Matthew's Gospel (after the destruction of Jerusalem), and finally, a generation later, the Gospel of John. Herder was, in my opinion, perfectly right in this determination of the order (though not of the date) of the Gospels; that his view was ignored by theologians was a great hindrance to the clearing up of this important problem; on this, as perhaps on other points, that Herder was eclipsed by the overwhelming authority of Schleiermacher had injurious effects upon the healthy development of German theology. So too Schleiermacher's denial of the genuineness of the first Epistle to Timothy, while he accepted the second and the Epistle to Titus as genuine, must be considered a very doubtful service to science, when we remember that Eichhorn, and still more De Wette, had a truer perception of the un-Pauline character common to the three plainly connected epistles. De Wette was, after Semler and Herder, the most important Protestant Biblical critic before 1835. He was the only critic quite free from dogmatic prejudices, and unequalled for profound learning, keen insight, and fine linguistic perception. Yet neither was he able to arrive at satisfactory and thoroughly consistent results. His critical method was too purely subjective and formal, founded upon matters of taste and individual considerations such as might be met by others of pretty much the same weight; he paid no proper regard to the general character of a book and its place in the history of the early development of Christian doctrines. Hence he generally remained in doubt, unable to arrive at any final result; this was the case with the problem of the Gospels. Ephesians and the Pastoral Epistles he considered as certainly not genuine, as also the Apocalypse and 2 Peter; but what was the advantage of knowing that these works do not come from the authors whose names they traditionally bear, if nothing positive was ascertained as to their date, or character, or the ecclesiastical circle to which they belonged, or the purpose they were intended to perform for their time and surroundings? In fact this critical method, which was employed by De Wette in its best form, was purely negative, and was therefore only preliminary to the main aim,—a positive insight into the historical origin of the various New Testament writings and their importance in the history of primitive Christianity. This was accomplished by the critical labours of Baur and the investigators directly or indirectly stimulated by him.

Along with the investigation of the origin of the New Testament writings, a critique of the Gospel narratives was carried on by Rationalistic theologians. But neither was this more satisfactory in its method or its results. Dr. Paulus, the best known representative of the Rationalistic interpretation of the Gospel narratives, started from the principle that in the Gospels we must look for nothing but actual facts, not for poetry or legends, and that these facts were natural and not supernatural events, and that they had acquired the appearance of supernatural occurrences, or miracles, partly through the errors of commentators, partly through the erroneous apprehension and judgment of the narrators. The task of the scientific commentator is to get rid of this false appearance and to see in the stories of the evangelists simple events with natural causes. The execution of this task by Dr. Paulus himself was such that we do not know whether to wonder most at his learning and ingenuity or his ineptitude and want of taste. He turns the finest of the Gospel narratives, the blossoms of the noblest religious poetry, by his "natural" interpretation, into the most trivial, commonplace incidents, without any deeper meaning or religious significance. Indeed, in not a few places he is even guilty of an absolute meanness in his interpretations, almost on a par with the notorious theories of a "priestly fraud." Thus the narrative of the supernatural birth of Jesus is reduced to a deception cunningly practised upon the Virgin Mary. The occurrence at Christ's baptism was that the clouds just then accidentally opened and a flying dove appeared in the blue sky. The devil that tempted him in the wilderness was an *agent provocateur* sent out by the Pharisees. The plan of Jesus was essentially the political one of restoring the temporal splendour of the Israelitish theocracy and placing himself as the Messiah-king at its head; it was not till after the failure of this attempt that he confined himself to an ethical kingdom of God. His miracles of healing were successful cures, the medical means applied being generally ignored by the narrators. The instances of restoration to life were only from apparent death. The walking of Jesus on the sea was his walking by the sea on the shore. The miraculous draught of fishes was the result of the good advice given by Jesus to the dispirited fishermen. The multiplication of loaves at the feeding of the multitude in the wilderness was the effect of the good example of Jesus in giving away his store of food, which was followed by the rest of those present who had any. The change of the water into wine at Cana was a marriage jest, Jesus giving the present of wine he had brought for the married pair in this humorous way. The resurrection of Jesus himself was an awakening from an apparent death by tetanus; his ascension, his retirement in his subsequent illness into the summit of the mountains, the mist serving to take him from the sight of those beholding his departure.

That this interpretation of the Gospels, which everywhere retains the husk and surrenders the religious kernel, was countenanced even by orthodox theologians in many instances, and accepted, at any rate partially, by Schleiermacher too in his lectures on the " Life of Jesus," can only be accounted for by remembering the difficult position of the theologians of that time, whose general culture made a naïve belief in the reality of actual miracles impossible, while their historical criticism was still fettered by the supposition that at least one or the other of the Gospels came direct from an eye-witness and had therefore to claim an historical character for all its narratives. The rescue of theology out of this blind alley by a thorough and consistent, instead of a halting criticism, getting rid of the fettering suppositions and clearing the way for a scientific study of the origins of Christianity, was the work of Strauss.

In the preface to his *Leben Jesu*, STRAUSS places his own position as the "mythical" in contrast with the positions of orthodoxy and Rationalism in the following terms : " Orthodox exegesis started with the twofold assumption that the Gospels contained firstly history, and secondly supernatural history ; then Rationalism rejected the second of these assumptions, only to cling more firmly to the first—that these books had in them pure, though natural, history. Science cannot stop thus half-way, but the first assumption also must be dropped, and the question examined whether and how far we stand in the Gospels upon historical ground." The mythical theory, he continues, had already been variously applied to the gospel history, but neither in its pure form nor to its full extent ; too much history was always expected in details, in spite of the acknowledged mythical character of the Gospels in general. Moreover, the application of this theory had always been too limited ; mythical elements were, indeed, admitted in the narratives of the childhood of Jesus, and again at the close of his life, but not in the intermediate narrative, the history of his public ministry. This limitation is untenable ; it is not permissible to enter the evangelical history by the splendid portal of myth and leave it by a similar one, and for what lies between rest satisfied with the crooked and weary paths of a natural explanation. " The author's method is to apply the principle of myth to the whole extent of the story of the life of Jesus, to find mythical narratives, or at least embellishments, scattered throughout all its parts."

In justification of this method, Strauss appeals to the similar allegorical interpretation in the ancient Church, *e.g.* in Origen. While the method of natural explanation of the Rationalists and Naturalists sacrificed the divine content of the sacred story and clung to its empty historical form, the mythical, like the allegorical, method prefers, on the contrary, to sacrifice the historical reality of the narrative and keep its absolute (eternal and spiritual) truth. If Supernaturalists cannot make up their minds to this, they only prove that, like children, they much prefer the painted historical shell, even if emptied of all divine contents, to the richest content when divested of its coloured covering. He then goes on to defend this method against objections which were partly due to misconception of the nature of myth, as if it were an artificial product of intentional invention, and partly based on the supposed incredibility of unhistorical legends becoming incorporated in Gospels composed so early and in part by eye-witnesses. This objection would, Strauss says, be a serious one if the assumption as to the Gospels were correct. But the assumption rests neither on internal nor on external grounds, since neither in the case of the first nor of the fourth Gospel do we possess testimony early enough to assure us of their authorship by the apostles Matthew and John. In the absence of such testimony we are at liberty to assume an interval of at least thirty years between the death of Jesus and the origin of our Gospels; and that this interval is sufficient to explain the rise of myths is placed beyond all doubt by the actual analogy of profane history (*e.g.* Herodotus). If any one still insists that an historical period like that in which the public life of Jesus was passed renders the formation of myths concerning it impossible, the reply is, that a great personality, especially if connected with a revolution profoundly affecting the life of man, soon becomes the centre of an unhistoric halo of mythical glorification, even in the most matter-of-fact period of history. "Conceive a recently established community, revering its founder with all the more enthusiasm on account of his unexpected and tragic removal from his work; a community impregnated with a mass of new ideas which were destined to transform the world; a community of orientals, chiefly unlearned people, who therefore could not appropriate and express those ideas in the abstract conceptual forms of the understanding, but only as symbols and stories in the concrete fashion of the imagination. When all this is remembered, one can perceive that under these circumstances there must necessarily have arisen what actually did arise, viz. a series of sacred narratives fitted to bring vividly before the mind the whole mass of new ideas, started by Jesus, and of old ones, applied to him, cast in the form of particular incidents in his life. The simple historical structure of the life of Jesus was hung with the most varied and suggestive tapestry of devout reflections and fancies, all the ideas entertained by primitive Christianity relative to its lost Master being transformed into facts and woven into the course of his life. The most abundant material for this mythical ornamentation was furnished by the Old Testament, in which the first Christian community, composed chiefly of Jewish converts, lived and breathed. Jesus, as the greatest prophet, must have gathered up and surpassed in his life and deeds everything that the ancient prophets had done and experienced; he, as the restorer of the Hebrew religion, could not be in anything inferior to the first law-giver; in him, finally, as the Messiah, must have been fulfilled all the Messianic prophecies of the Old Testament; he had inevitably to meet the ideal of the Messiah as already conceived by the Jews, so far as the departures from this ideal which were made in known historical actions and speeches allowed. It ought in our time to be unnecessary to remark that this transference of what was expected into the history of what actually took place, and in general the mythical embellishment of the life of Jesus, was not the work of premeditated deceit and cunning invention. The legends of a people or of a religious sect are in their genuine elements never the work of a single person, but of the generalised individual of the community, and hence are never consciously or intentionally produced. The imperceptible growth of a joint creative work of this kind is made possible by oral tradition being the medium of communication."

I have given Strauss's description and defence of his method in his own words, in order at the same time to give a specimen of the lucidity and beauty of his style and exposition. This mastery of form has no doubt contributed much to the profound and far-reaching effect of the book; this was, however, much more due to the inexorable logic with which the critic worked out his task in all parts of the gospel history. "In this book all previous critical researches into the life of Jesus meet; but they are at the same time completed, more exact, more pointed, and reduced to one fundamental principle. This iron necessity of the method, carried through like a process of nature, this cold, passionless objectivity, in which the author is sunk in his work and is only the calculator setting down and summing up the various accounts before him, was what made the book so impressive, or perhaps rather so terrible. It had about it the cold indifference of fate; in the criticism of the gospel history the balance had been struck, and the verdict was bankruptcy. The gospel history had from all sides already felt the teeth of criticism; it was here shown that its very heart had been reached. The effect of this work was immense."[1]

Such an effect Strauss himself had not anticipated. The panic of the theological and lay world, which saw in Strauss's criticism nothing less than the destruction of the Christian faith, was all the more surprising to him as he had not intended anything of the kind. According to his assurance in the preface, which deserves full credit, his conviction had rather been that the inner kernel of the Christian faith was quite independent of his critical investigations. "Christ's supernatural birth, his miracles, his resurrection and ascension, remain eternal truths, however much their reality as historic facts may be called in question. This certainty alone can lend to our criticism calmness and dignity, and distinguish it from the naturalistic criticism of former centuries, which thought to overturn the religious truth with the historic fact, and had therefore inevitably a frivolous character. The dogmatic content of the life of Jesus will be shown to be untouched in an appendix to this work. In the meantime, may the calmness and coolness with which in the course of it criticism undertakes apparently dangerous operations, be attributed solely to the assured conviction that none of these things harm the Christian faith."

The appendix to the second volume, thus announced, undertook the dogmatic restoration of what criticism had destroyed. Unlike the naturalist and freethinker of earlier times, the critic of the nineteenth century should be filled with reverence for every religion, and should in particular be conscious of the identity of the highest religion, the Christian, with philosophical truth. There then follows a critical sketch of the historical development of Christological dogma, the truth contained in which is finally given in the following speculative form:—
"When mankind is once sufficiently developed to have as its

---

[1] Schwarz, *Zur Gesch. d. neuesten Theol.*, p. 97, sq.

religion the truth that God is man and man of divine race, this truth, since religion is the form assumed by truth for the ordinary mind, must be shown in a manner comprehensible by all as a sensible certainty, *i.e.* a human individual must arise who is regarded as the present God. Inasmuch as this God-man unites in himself the heavenly divine nature and the earthly human ego, he can be said to have the divine spirit as his father and a human mother; inasmuch as his ego reflects itself not in itself, but in the absolute substance, seeks to be nothing for itself, but to exist for God alone, he is the sinless and perfect one; as a man of divine nature he is the power over nature and the performer of miracles; but as God in human form, he is dependent upon nature, subject to its wants and pains, is in the condition of humiliation. Will he have to pay nature the last tribute also? Does not the fact that human nature is subject to death falsify the belief that it is one with the divine? No; the God-man dies, showing that God has not shrunk from becoming man fully; that he does not disdain to descend to the lowest depths of the finite, since he can find the way back to himself even thence, and in the most complete self-abnegation can yet remain identical with himself. More precisely, since the God-man as man's spirit reflected in its infinitude, stands in contrast to man as clinging to his finiteness, this involves an opposition and conflict, and the death of the God-man is necessarily made a violent one at the hands of sinners, physical suffering being thus supplemented by the moral pain of insult and accusation of guilt. If God thus finds the way from heaven to the tomb, there must also be a way to be found for man from the tomb to heaven; the death of the Prince of Life is the life of mortal man. By his very appearance in the world as God-man, God showed himself reconciled to the world; or more exactly, by laying aside in death his subjection to nature, he showed the way by which he eternally accomplishes the reconciliation, viz. by emptying himself and voluntarily assuming subjection to nature, and then annulling it to remain identical with himself. Since the death of the God-man only puts an end to his self-abnegation and humiliation, it is really his elevation and return to God; thus in the nature of things death is followed by resurrection and ascension."

We can well understand that Strauss, as the disciple of Hegel, could honestly believe that by this allegorical interpretation of Christ's appearance as a figure of humanity and its metaphysical relation to the Absolute, he had restored "dogmatically what he had destroyed critically," but we can understand equally well the energetic protest of the Christian world against such a compensation for its loss. Strauss had in fact deluded himself, and his case had in it a tragic element, in that he shared this delusion with the chief philosophy of his time, and cannot therefore be made personally responsible for it, while its disastrous consequences were borne by him personally more than by any other man. It was the fundamental error of the Hegelian philosophy to suppose that the truth of religion consists in the logical consciousness of metaphysical relations, thus totally overlooking its actual nature, consisting, as it does, in emotional and volitional processes; and this error led Strauss to think he had found the essence of faith in Christ in metaphysical statements about the human race, which really did not so much as touch the sphere of religious faith, much less exhaust its highest truth. Strauss's mistake did not therefore lie in regarding the gospel stories of miracles as symbols of ideal truths—that they are really this could be easily proved from the New Testament itself; but his mistake lay in looking for these truths outside religion, instead of within it, in metaphysical categories of doubtful value for knowledge, instead of in the facts of the devout heart and moral will, in which the saving and gladdening effects of our religion are found. If he had paid more regard to these religious and moral truths, the "deliverances of the devout consciousness," as Schleiermacher called them, this would of itself have led him to see further, that the historical Jesus was not merely an accidentally chosen type and example of these truths, but their original creative type and their historic source. If the historical Jesus had been thus brought into an inner and essential relation to the religious and moral idea of Christianity, as its pioneer and prophet, justice would have been done to his religious importance, which is quite lost sight of in Strauss's allegorising, since there is no sort of inner connection between the philosophical ideas in which he looked for the essence of the belief in Christ and the person of Jesus himself. However, if Strauss, after the critical disintegration of the legends of miracles, had given us a positive picture of the ideal life of Jesus as a religious and ethical character, and had offered this to Christendom as the permanent kernel in place of the husks which criticism had destroyed, his scientific work would of course still have been attacked, but not with that passionate bitterness which proved so disastrous not only to Strauss's outward life, but also to his inner development, alienating for ever from Church and theology a man of great talent and a courageous spirit of inquiry. We of to-day, separated by half a century from those years of the Straussian movement, can only look back upon it with unfeigned regret at the tragic fate dooming such a powerful and noble mind to failure, partly because the time was not ripe properly to receive what was true and valid in Strauss's critical labours, partly also because he was himself still fettered by the false, and in this case fatally mistaken, assumptions of the philosophical intellectualism of the time.

Of the mass of polemical literature evoked by Strauss's work, only three books are important for our purpose: Neander's *Leben Jesu* (1837), Ullmann's *Historisch oder mythisch?* and Weisse's *Die evangelische Geschichte, kritisch und philosophisch bearbeitet* (1838). The first two of the writers just mentioned belonged to the mediating school of Schleiermacher, which, with all its supernaturalistic leanings, made too many concessions to criticism to be able to condemn Strauss's line of procedure unconditionally. Strauss offered as a motto, aptly descriptive of Neander's book, the words, "Lord, I believe, help thou my unbelief." NEANDER, unable wholly to accept or to dispense with miracles, takes refuge in an emasculated conception of miracle; a miracle he holds to be not anti-natural but supernatural, as resting on higher laws, at present unknown, the sign of a higher order of creative forces acting in our nature, which the ordinary order of nature has by the divine wisdom been eternally predestined to receive. We must also assume various degrees of the supernatural, a less degree in miracles of healing than in some other kinds. Yet even these latter are a little softened down. The water at Cana was not changed into actual wine, but properties merely like those of wine were imparted to it, in the same way as mineral waters have them. In the cases of raising the dead there is always (even John xi.) the possibility of only an apparent death. The miraculous star of the Magi is explained as a natural conjunction of planets, which only gave occasion for the journey, but did not show the way. The phenomenon at the baptism of Jesus is represented as a vision, the story of the temptation as an allegory. In this way the most striking miracles were either partially or entirely got rid of, though others were still retained, in particular the resurrection of Christ himself. Such an illogical method of procedure was evidently no refutation of Strauss's criticism; the book was important only as showing how impossible a naïve belief in the gospel narratives had become for a theologian affected by the thought of the time, and how important it had therefore become for theological science to take up a fresh position with regard to these records.

ULLMANN penetrated more deeply than Neander into the heart of the question. He admits that in the Gospels legends of an essentially symbolic character do occur, but it does not follow from this that everything is mythical; it is precisely the problem to determine exactly the boundaries of the historical and the mythical. Ullmann holds—and without doubt rightly—that Strauss's work failed chiefly in not doing this, but in confining itself to the mere negation of the traditions. Strauss's net result, as Ullmann acutely remarks, amounts to this, that the Church invented Christ; but this makes the history of Christianity incomprehensible. We ought rather to infer from this actual fact, which has changed the course of the world, that there was a corresponding cause, which can only be found in the personality of Christ, the Founder of the Church. Strauss, Ullmann argues, had underrated or ignored this personality, because his own philosophical assumptions involved the antecedent conviction that the idea does not fully manifest itself in a single individual, but is only unfolded in the race as a whole. In reply to this assumption, it must be urged, that as an historical fact geniuses do appear from time to time in all departments of mental life, in whom ideas are embodied typically and perfectly, the idea of art, for example, in some of its forms. In a Homer, Sophocles, Dante, Shakespeare, Raphael, Handel, etc., the idea of their respective arts is fully given in a single example, and a supreme standard is set up for all who come after to aim at. Much more must this be possible in the sphere of religion. Though revelation may be common to all nations and times, it necessarily tends to concentrate itself at one supreme point of the religious development of mankind, and this point is the ideal, sinless Christ.

Amongst all the books written against him, Strauss treated that of Ullmann with the most respect, making, in fact, some not inconsiderable concessions to it. To the dilemma propounded by Ullmann, whether Christ created the Church or the Church invented Christ, Strauss replied, not without reason, that the alternatives are not mutually exclusive; even if the Church had been created by the power of the personality of Jesus, it might still, in return, have transformed and adorned the idea of Christ by the aid of its mythical conceptions and hopes. Nevertheless, in his book, published shortly afterwards, *Vergängliches und Bleibendes. Zwei friedliche Blätter* (1838–39), Strauss allowed the justice of Ullmann's objection so far as to admit that man's religious life is related to the rest of his life as the centre of a circle to its circumference, and that in religion Christ was supreme, and was so far above other founders of religions as to be unsurpassable for all time. For it was in him that the unity of the divine and human first became a matter of consciousness, and this with such creative power as to supply the need of all who came after him. He therefore now, with Ullmann, recognised Christ as a religious genius historically unique, only he refused to follow Ullmann and Schleiermacher in converting this uniqueness of genius into absolute perfection, thus raising it altogether above the plane of history. But assuming that this position of Strauss was in itself a tenable one, its weakness lay in his method of proving this grandeur of Christ; for it is clear that the philosophical consciousness of the unity of the divine and human can scarcely be ascribed to the Johannine Jesus, and at any rate not to the historical Jesus of the synoptic Gospels. The error, which was bound to prove fatal to this eirenical position, lay in the attempt to find Christ's greatness in a philosophical idea, instead of in the unique character of his religious and moral consciousness and work. And in order to be able to ascribe that philosophical consciousness to Christ with an appearance of historical justification, he was guilty of the blunder of admitting the possible genuineness of the Johannine Gospel and of treating it as an historical authority. This produced a wavering uncertainty in the third edition of his *Leben Jesu*, in unpleasing contrast to the unflinching logic and clearness of the earlier editions, while the possibility of thus creating a favourable impression upon the theological public was lessened by the not unfounded suspicion that personal motives of expediency had helped to produce these partial concessions. Strauss himself retraced this false step in the fourth edition, which appeared shortly after, and thus brought the question back to its original position. But this wavering had at any rate shown the totally inadequate treatment by Strauss of the fundamental question for a life of Jesus, as to the historical value of the documentary sources, and their relation to each other. The necessity therefore was shown of a scientific investigation of the question.

This was first supplied, and in a very thorough manner, by HERMANN WEISSE. He says in the preface to his *Evangelische Geschichte* (1838), that he had from the first welcomed Strauss's work as not an injurious one but a helpful contribution to true Christian knowledge and insight, which belongs not to the past but to the future, inasmuch as the book had carried through the unpleasant task of destructive criticism so thoroughly as to give us all the more courage for the attempt to substitute something positive for what criticism had swept away. With this view, Weisse starts with a detailed investigation of the literary relations of the Gospels, and comes, to his own surprise, to the conclusion that Mark's Gospel must be placed before the others in point of originality and age; a conclusion so opposed to the then universal view that it required considerable courage to make it the basis of an account of the gospel history. The same view was simultaneously defended by a compatriot of Weisse, the Saxon clergyman Wilke, in an exhaustive treatise. Still the view could only slowly and with difficulty make any way at first against the twofold prejudice in favour of John and Matthew, and afterwards against that in favour of Matthew; it has now been accepted by the majority of theologians; and the acceptance of the priority of Mark and the late origin of the Gospels of Matthew and of John as among the assured results of Biblical criticism is apparently only a question of time. Notwithstanding Weisse's success in determining the relation of the synoptic Gospels to each other and to that of John, he took up an untenable half-way position with regard to the latter. He considered it to be the work of a disciple of the apostle John, having no claim to direct historical accuracy, but still based, in its speeches at any rate, upon historical reminiscences of the apostle, which, however, received a strong subjective colouring both in the apostle's mind and in the process of literary composition by his disciple. The unity and symmetrical plan of the whole composition of John's Gospel were not recognised by Weisse; Baur's indication of them sealed the fate of Weisse's semi-critical hypothesis. But while Weisse was certainly corrected by Baur on the question of the Fourth Gospel, he was as certainly superior to Baur in taking the right view of the synoptists.

In his estimate of the evangelical narratives Weisse fully agrees with Strauss in the negative conclusion, that everything really miraculous, in which the laws of nature, valid for all history, are alleged to have been broken by the absolute spirit, is to be regarded as unnatural and on that account as unhistorical. "Before an act of the Deity completely violating the laws of nature and history, before a miracle in this properly unhistorical and anti-natural sense, we could only take up an attitude of vacant unreasoning resignation." Weisse, too, believes that in these narratives we must look for religious myths. But he is by no means satisfied with Strauss's explanation of them; they are not to be explained, as Strauss thought, by a mechanical transference to the Messiah Jesus of conceptions and legends already given in the Old Testament, but they are the special product of the religious spirit of Christianity, which expressed in them symbolically its ideal truth, as the fulfilment of all previous Jewish and heathen anticipations. Thus Weisse interprets the stories of miracles purely as religious allegories, involuntarily invented by the imagination of the primitive community, which did not distinguish between the poetic form and the ideal content. Weisse rightly urged that this method of exegesis is much less offensive than Strauss's to the religious feeling of the present time. "For whatever is illustrated in a legend permeated with the true subject-matter, with the *idea* of the sacred history, must be itself religious, essentially sacred. The historical revelation of God in the Gospels loses not a whit of its sacred content if a part of this content ceases to be regarded as an immediate fact of such a kind that the Deity appears in it as treating his own noblest work rather in jest than in earnest. On the contrary, this revelation gains when the Gospels are recognised as the productions of rich spiritual genius, in which the circle of men, to whom the divine revelation of Christianity was first addressed, deposited a productive, creative consciousness of the divine spirit, descended into their midst, and of the manner of his working. It was a consciousness such as this which found its thoroughly appropriate expression in the sacred legends." It is certain that this way of looking at the Gospel narratives, in conjunction with a penetrating investigation of the literary relations and value of the authorities, first indicated the course by which theology might hope to leave behind it Strauss's purely negative criticism and obtain a positive understanding of the Gospels. The further pursuit of this method by the *Tübingen School* led to very important results.

The best, most just and most thorough estimate of Strauss's book was that given by his Tübingen teacher, the famous critic and ecclesiastical historian, FERDINAND CHRISTIAN BAUR, in the introduction to his book, *Kritische Untersuchungen über die kanonischen Evangelien, ihr Verhältniss zu einander, ihren Charakter und Ursprung*. Baur finds both Strauss's strength and his weakness in his thoroughly logical negative criticism, which revealed the baselessness of our supposed knowledge of the Gospels, and showed us our ignorance of the real historic truth, thus preparing the way for true knowledge. To quote his own words, " Like all works of true originality and genius, Strauss's book has the great merit of being before and yet the child of its time. It gathered up the critical inquiries on the life of Jesus with their results from every quarter, in order to present their naked ultimate issue and form them into a single whole, by a more vigorous method of proof, by defining what had been left indefinite, and by supplying existing deficiencies. Thus the book became the living centre of the whole critical movement of the time, which alone explains its immense effect. Strauss was hated because the spirit of the time could not endure its own picture, which he held up to it in faithful, clearly drawn outlines. In this reflection of itself the age became conscious of much of which it before had had no distinct idea, coming to perceive its contradictions and inconsistencies and false assumptions ; in a word, its complete want of true knowledge. Let us frankly admit the facts of the case, and rest assured that, instead of going on for ever with vague and empty polemics, it is time to look at Strauss's criticism as a product of its time, and to understand how, in the then existing stage of criticism, it was not only a possible but also a necessary phenomenon. What result could be reached from the investigations then carried on into the origin and mutual relation of the Gospels, except a purely negative one? One opinion was opposed by another, taken together the opinions were mutually contradictory and destructive, and any certainty was impossible. It was, in fact, just as Strauss himself said, in the darkness produced by the extinguishing of all supposed historical lights by criticism, the eye had gradually to learn to distinguish individual objects. Strauss's work was intended to begin this process, by leading men out of the general darkness into the clear day of historical knowledge. But it introduced a new era not in virtue of this positive but of its negative side; its chief merit lay not in the knowledge which it brought to light, but in the want of knowledge of which it made men conscious. This is the truly historical importance of Strauss's critique. Its greatest merit will always consist in having shown the condition of historical knowledge of the gospel history at the time, and in having done this from a pure love of truth, without prejudice or assumption, without mercy or consideration, and it must be allowed with cold severity. Every step the work takes beyond this seems to lie outside its true province. But the spirit of an age resists with all its might the proof of its ignorance in a matter of its knowledge of which it had long been so certain. Instead of recognising what had to be recognised, if any progress was to be made, all possible attempts were made to create fresh illusions as to the true state of the case, by reviving long antiquated hypotheses, by theological charlatanism, by using all the motives of a false party spirit. But a higher certainty as to the truth of the gospel history can only be attained by recognising, on the basis of Strauss's criticism, our previous knowledge as no knowledge at all. When all our previous knowledge is self-contradictory and self-destructive, certain knowledge can only come from the examination and classification of details. But these details formed the limit of Strauss's criticism."

In order to get beyond Strauss's negative results, the criticism of the gospel history must become the *criticism of the documents* which are the sources for this history. And if this is not to continue to consist of mutually exclusive hypotheses, but is to be placed upon a firm basis, the special characteristics of each Gospel must be exactly ascertained, the literary features and objects of its author must be investigated, and its relation determined to the general circumstances of the time out of which it arose. This had been attempted, after a fashion, before F. Chr. Baur by Bruno Bauer, Weisse, and Wilke, who put the evangelist Mark in the place of a general indefinite tradition, as the original evangelist, and derived the other Gospels from him. This view was carried to the most extreme lengths by Bruno Bauer, who regarded Mark not only as the first narrator, but even as the creator of the gospel history, thus making the latter a fiction and Christianity the invention of a single original evangelist. In spite of the evident absurdity of this "phantasmagorical view of history," we must recognise a grain of truth in Bruno Bauer's opposition to Strauss, when he asked whether the mysterious myth-creating consciousness of the community could produce its Gospels without having hands wherewith to write, or taste to compose, or judgment to connect related and exclude alien matter? This touched, in fact, a weak place in Strauss's method, viz. his ignoring the subjectivity of the authors of the Gospels. But it was precisely this subjectivity, as F. Chr. Baur remarks, which deserved the primary attention of historical criticism. "Since all history, before it reaches us, passes through the medium of a narrator, in our criticism of the gospel history, the first question is not, What objective reality is possessed by this or that narrative *per se*? but rather, What is the relation of the narrative to the mind of the narrator, through the medium of whom it becomes for us an object of historical knowledge?" We must, therefore, in the first place know the aim and purpose of the writer, his motive in writing as he does, and the influence of this motive on his account; and this question can only be answered by as exact an investigation as possible of the historical conditions under the influence of which the author wrote. Every author belongs to the time in which he lives, and the greater the importance of his subject for the struggles, parties, and interests of the time, the safer the assumption that he must bear the impress of his age, and that the motives determining the form of his narrative must be sought in the circumstances of the time. This holds also of the Gospels; hence the first question in the criticism of them will be, What was the aim and purpose of each of their authors? Thus only can we gain the firm ground of concrete historical truth. Since a special motive (*Tendenz*) is most apparent in the fourth Gospel, Baur took this Gospel, which had hitherto offered the stoutest resistance to all the attacks of criticism, as the point of departure for his inquiry.

But before we trace this inquiry further, we must glance at his previous critical works. I have begun with the above discussion in the introduction to his book on the canonical Gospels simply in order to make clear his relation to Strauss. Baur himself, which is characteristic of his method, started not from the Gospels, the most complicated problem of New Testament criticism, but from the Pauline Epistles, where the questions are comparatively simpler. As the fruit of his exegetical lectures on the Epistles to the Corinthians, he published in 1831 the essay, *Die Christuspartei in der korinthischen Gemeinde, der Gegensatz des paulinischen und petrinischen Christenthums in der ältesten Kirche, der Apostel Petrus in Rom.* He had here proved that Paul had to contend in Corinth with a Jewish Christian party, which disputed his apostolical authority and wished to set up a particularistic Jewish Christianity, in opposition to his universal Christianity. He had then pursued the traces of the same division of parties in the post-apostolic age, down to the Clementine Homilies, and attempted to explain by its means the legends of Simon Magus and of the episcopate of Peter in Rome. In these ingenious, if at times rash, theories lay the germs of his later view of primitive Christianity, but his literary criticism had not yet reached an independent position. The full and unique importance of this was first seen in the work, *Über die sogenannten Pastoralbriefe*, which appeared in the same year as Strauss's *Leben Jesu* (1835). His researches into the Christian Gnosis, published in the same year, had led Baur to look for traces of this phenomenon in the New Testament also, and he then discerned that the false teachers opposed in the Epistles to Timothy and Titus could be no other than the Gnostics of the second century, in particular the Marcionites. This gave a firm footing of objective historical value for the criticism of these epistles in place of the previous vague subjective hypotheses. Other peculiarities of these epistles, in particular those respecting ecclesiastical offices and arrangements, were set in a clearer light by the circumstances of the second century, and this at the same time served to support the hypothesis based on his characterisation of the false teachers. Individual critics, such as Eichhorn and De Wette, and also Schleiermacher, had previously doubted the authenticity, at any rate of 1 Timothy, and not only were these doubts now fully justified by Baur, but, what was the main thing, the positive result was reached that these Epistles originated in the opposition of the Catholic Church to Gnosticism in the middle of the second century, and were intended to establish the Church's tradition and hierarchy against heretics. The importance of this work of Baur's went far beyond the question directly treated of, inasmuch as it substituted for the first time *objective criticism*, based on a wide general conception of the conditions of primitive Christianity, for the subjective criticism hitherto adopted—*a new method*, of the great importance of which Baur in his preface shows himself well aware. This critical method he applied during the following years to the Pauline epistles and to the Acts of the Apostles, and collected the results of these researches in the work, *Paulus, der Apostel Jesu Christi, sein Leben und Wirken, seine Briefe und seine Lehre* (1st ed., 1845 ; 2nd ed., 1866). In the first part of this work, Baur describes the life and work of Paul, as the apostle who first gave Christianity its universal historical importance, and freed it from Judaism, which was not accomplished—as was hitherto held in conformity with the Church's tradition—with the concurrence of the elder apostles and the primitive Church, but in opposition to and in conflict with them. He here subjects the account given in the Acts to a thorough critical investigation, which leads to the result that this book differs from the authentic testimony of the Pauline epistles in so many and important points that it can be regarded as of only quite secondary historical value ; the author's aim was not to write history, but to give " a defence of the Apostle of the Gentiles against the attacks and accusations of the Judaisers." With this view he represented Paul as quite a different man from the actual Paul of the genuine Pauline Epistles ; he minimised his divergence from the Jewish Christians in the same way as he made Peter more Pauline than was really the case. The writer's motives for doing this must be looked for in the circumstances of the time, in which " Paulinism had been so put in the background by Jewish Christian efforts as only to be able to maintain itself by entering into a compromise with the powerful Jewish Christian party, and by an attitude of conciliation softening down all the harshness and directness of its opposition to Judaism."[1] The second part of the work gives an analysis and criticism of the Pauline Epistles, of which only those to the Galatians, Corinthians, and Romans, are accepted as genuine. The third part gives an account of the Pauline theology from the point of view that it represents Christianity as the absolute spiritual religion in opposition to Heathenism and Judaism. There is no doubt much in these two latter parts, as in the former one, capable of being disputed and needing amendment, but the great merit of the book remains, of having clearly set forth with an emphasis, never approached before, the epoch-making importance of the Apostle Paul in the history of Christianity, the originality of his conception of Christianity, and the magnitude of the struggle by which he carried out his ideas in spite of the Jewish prejudices of the primitive Church.

Equally important, for a right understanding of primitive Christianity, with Baur's work on Paul was further his Criticism of John's Gospel, first given as an essay (1844), which he afterwards incorporated in his book on *Die kanonischen Evangelien* (1847), as its first and most important part. He does not start in the customary way with the question as to the author, which only concludes the investigation. The question he starts with is, on the contrary, that of the idea and purpose guiding the author in his peculiar presentation of the gospel history. Baur finds this in the idea of the Logos presented in the prologue; since the Logos, as the divine principle of light and life, appears bodily in the phenomenal world in the person of Jesus, and enters into conflict with the darkness of the world, the whole history of Jesus turns on the development and solution of this antithesis of metaphysical and ethical

---

[1] This view of the Acts of the Apostles was further developed and put into a more extreme form by Zeller. It regards the Acts as an "offer of peace" made by a Paulinist to the Judaisers with a view to the union of the two parties: but it cannot be maintained: for (1) the supposed extremity of Paulinism in presence of an all-powerful Jewish Christianity is unhistorical; (2) the Acts, on the contrary, exhibits a Gentile Christianity energetically asserting itself against Judaism; (3) the inexact account of Paulinism given in this book cannot be the result of intentional misrepresentation, since it was not peculiar to the author but common to Gentile Christians of the second century; (4) finally, the theory altogether overlooks the real and undoubted object of the writer, viz. to defend Christianity in view of the Roman power as a religion not violating the laws of the State, and with a claim to the same toleration as Judaism.

principles, light and darkness, truth and falsehood, belief and disbelief, children of God and children of the devil, life and death. Thus John's Gospel contains a Christian gnosis akin to though not identical with the heretical gnosis, clothed in the form of an historical account of the life of Jesus. That such an account, completely dominated by *ideal motives of a doctrinal nature, does not possess historical truth, and cannot and does not really lay claim to it*, is self-evident, and is then further proved by Baur by a critical comparison of the Johannine and synoptic Gospels, the superior historical probability being always found on the side of the latter. In particular it is shown, in opposition to the attempts to divide the Gospel, that precisely the Johannine speeches serve the dogmatic purpose of the author and stand in the closest connection with the narratives, and in general that the whole Gospel shows a systematic unity of composition which excludes all possibility of distinguishing between genuine and not genuine—or better, between historical and purely fictitious elements. At last the question as to the author of the Gospel is investigated and his identity with the Apostle disproved, partly by the unhistorical character of so many of the narratives, in which the Gospel is inferior even to the writings of Mark and Luke, who were not eye-witnesses, and in particular by the ignorance shown of places and conditions in Palestine (*e.g.*, i. 28; v. 2; ix. 7; xi. 51; xviii. 13); partly by the attitude of the author to the question of the Passover, which is the exact opposite of the view which the Church in Asia Minor claimed to derive from the Apostle John; partly also by the contrast between the entire dogmatic character of the Gospel and that of the Apocalypse, which exhibits, in accordance with Galatians ii., the Apostle John as still quite enthralled in Jewish Christian conceptions, which the author of the gospel has left far behind. But if it be asked how it was possible for a non-apostolic gospel to be regarded by the Church as a work of the apostle, Baur finds the explanation in the peculiar spirit and character of the Gospel. By its spiritual nature, that pneumatic character attributed to it even by the ancients, it exercised a peculiar charm on men's minds; and since, in virtue of its later origin, it represented a more developed form of Christian consciousness and life, it offered all the more points of contact with the time of its origination and diffusion. It contains references to all the conflicts of the time, and yet nowhere bears the definite mark of a temporal or local opposition. The most important of these elements of its time are the Gnosis, the doctrine of the Logos, Montanism, and the question of the Passover. To all these movements and questions of the age the Gospel stands in a special relation; we cannot say that they presuppose the Gospel, and yet neither is it conditioned by them; it comes into contact with them, and yet remains in this respect free and independent. It is the peculiar characteristic of this Gospel to be connected with all shapes of the consciousness of the age, and yet only in so far as at the same time to maintain an independent attitude towards all, harmonising the antitheses into a higher unity."

While particular points in Baur's argument may be impugned, his view of the Fourth Gospel has as a whole not been refuted by later researches, but always confirmed anew. And when we consider how this very Gospel had previously stoutly withstood all criticism, and how difficult this *non liquet* had made a scientific investigation of the gospels, and so of the origin of Christianity generally, we must admit that Baur's discovery deserves to be called the beginning of a new era and a fundamental achievement for all future investigation of primitive Christianity. The same cannot be said of his criticism of the three synoptic Gospels. However natural it was for him to think that he ought to apply to the other gospels the key which had proved so useful in the case of John's Gospel, viz. the discovery of a dogmatic purpose, it was this very fact that prevented him from seeing their literary relation to each other. Only thus can we explain Baur's resting content with Griesbach's altogether mistaken hypothesis that Mark's Gospel consists of extracts from Matthew and Luke, when Wilke and Weisse had already clearly and irrefragably proved the priority of Mark as the source of both the others. It is the common fate of scientific discoverers to be led into fresh extremes and errors by the exaggerated application of their newly found principles. Baur did not escape this fatality; that his keen critical eye failed him in the case of the Gospels of Mark and Matthew and of the Apocalypse is only to be explained by the apparent agreement in these cases of the traditional view with his theory, derived from Paulus, of the perpetuation of the opposition between the Judaic and Pauline parties in the post-Pauline age

A more exact appreciation and a less prejudiced critical analysis of these three books might have led to a limitation of the scope of this theory. Baur's further labours in the history of the Church and of dogma will be described in a later chapter.

Baur was as great a teacher as he was an author. He prosecuted scientific research as a sacred service in the temple of truth; he combined the lofty comprehensive glance of genius with the laborious industry and careful accuracy of the scholar, and imparted the truth he discovered with the straightforward openness of a conscience freed from selfishness and party spirit; he thus exerted an influence over intelligent and receptive young men of the depth and intensity of which the present generation can form no idea. No wonder that Baur from the first decade of his academical activity continued to gather round him a band of disciples who followed intelligently in the footsteps of their master, and soon became his co-workers by their independent prosecution of his researches.

The first of these was Strauss, who had shot ahead of his teacher by his *Leben Jesu*, considered above, and who had supplied if not the impulse yet the proximate occasion of the epoch-making critical investigation of the Gospels. He was followed by Eduard Zeller, Albert Schwegler, Karl Planck, Karl Köstlin, and others. The common organ of this "Tübingen School" was the *Theologische Jahrbücher*, edited by Zeller, still of special interest as the monument of one of the most active and fruitful periods of modern theology. A glance at the essays and studies therein collected suffices to show how entirely Baur's disciples and friends were free from the slavish dependence, narrow-mindedness, and dull uniformity which are wont to form the unpleasing darker side of "schools." Essentially agreed in their critical method, Baur's disciples differed from the first not a little in their critical results.

ZELLER, in his critical essays on the Acts of the Apostles, which first appeared in the *Theologische Jahrbücher*, and were afterwards collected in a volume, made some valuable contributions to the exegetical interpretation and historical criticism of the Acts; even those who, like myself,[1] hold that he carried out Baur's theory of an intended reconciliation of Paulinism and Jewish Christianity in a one-sided and much exaggerated

---

[1] Comp. *ante*, p. 229 note.

manner, to the neglect of other essential points, will not deny to Zeller's book the merit of having by its incisive criticism brought out the problem of early Christian history into the full light of day, and of having thus contributed to its solution, even though this does not accord with his own.

Even more than of Zeller's *Apostelgeschichte*, we must say of A. SCHWEGLER's book, *Das nachapostolische Zeitalter in den Hauptpunkten seiner Entwickelung* (2 vols., 1846), that, in spite of all the ingenuity often shown in the just appreciation of details, it must be regarded as on the whole a failure. Baur's view of the original opposition and gradual reconciliation of the primitive Christian parties is here exaggerated into a caricature. Christianity before Paul, Schwegler considered to have had no lofty ideas at all, but to have been a narrow, rigidly ascetic and legal form of Judaism, closely related to Essenism, which, as "Ebionitism," maintained the upper hand even against Paul's universalistic teaching, so that the principles of the latter could scarcely anywhere prevail; until the age of Irenæus ecclesiastical Christianity remained more or less an Ebionitic Jewish Christianity, which by degrees developed into Catholicism. This point of view guides Schwegler in his estimate of the whole of early Christian literature; everything in it really, or presumedly, un-Pauline is at once taken as a proof of the Jewish Christian character of the book in question; the possibility is never considered of the existence of Gentile Christians with un-Pauline and even anti-Pauline views, not from Judaising tendencies, but because they found much in Paul's theology which was unsuited to the comprehension and needs of the Gentile Christian Churches. It seems as if Schwegler, hypnotised as it were with the one idea of early Christian "Ebionitism," was completely blind to all the varied thoughts and interests which moved that age and also influenced the life and belief of the Christian Churches. The dangerous tendency, to be seen, it must be confessed, in Baur, of insisting too exclusively on a new point of view as the only true one, was carried in Schwegler to the most extreme lengths.

It is, however, of importance to note that a protest was immediately raised against this one-sidedness from within the Tübingen School itself. Planck and Köstlin, in several excellent essays, still worth reading, in the *Theologische Jahrbücher* (1847 and 1850) endeavoured to correct Schwegler's theory. Its principal error, PLANCK holds to be, that it made Paul the real author of the new principle, and therefore the founder of Christianity, leaving unexplained how he was enabled to arrive at this new knowledge and to connect it with the person of Jesus. We must rather start from the position that the new principle was actually conceived, if not fully developed, by Jesus, being contained in his idea of the true righteousness as perfect self-renunciation and the surrender of the human will to the divine will, thus combining the perfect fulfilment of the law with its translation into the spirit, and the cancelling of its purely external character. Paulinism therefore only developed into full consciousness the principle implicitly contained in primitive Christianity. The true righteousness of self-surrender to God, which Jesus spontaneously exemplified and so experienced as an immediate fact of his own consciousness, became in Paul the quickening " grace," or power of the " Holy Spirit," coming to us from without, from Christ. In this appears the difference between the dependent and the creative mind, between the systematising theologian and the original religious genius. Since the older apostles did not, like Paul, prosecute dogmatic reflections, they failed indeed to see so clearly the difference between the new Christian principle and Judaism, but they still possessed this principle in the form, directly derived from Jesus, of deepened righteousness and practical piety. This Christianity, Judaic only in form, was not opposed in principle to Paul's anti-Judaic Christianity; and hence a reconciliation of the two was possible, without external concessions, by means of an inward approximation of each to the other. It should be mentioned that Planck held with Schwegler, that the development was wholly on the Jewish Christian side, while Paulinism stood apart as a stimulating principle but one incapable of growth.

KÖSTLIN likewise censures Schwegler for not distinguishing between the later extreme Ebionitism and the original apostolic Jewish Christianity. The latter was from the first, in point of fact, though without being clearly aware of it, in advance of Judaism, and was then stimulated by Paul to a development in two directions; on the one hand, it advanced to ecclesiastical unity, and, on the other, retrograded to heretical Ebionitism. To Köstlin also belongs in particular the credit of first seeing that Paulinism and Gentile Christianity must not be forthwith identified. The failure of the Pauline doctrines of righteousness by faith and of the annulling of the law to find permanent acceptance, is to be explained not, as Schwegler thought, by the preponderance of Jewish Christianity, but by the fact that the Gentile Christians themselves were without the speculative conditions and practical needs necessary for the comprehension and adoption of these doctrines. They did not need, like Paul, the disciple of the Pharisees, deliverance from the law, but the discipline of the law; the law did not seem to them, as it did to Paul, a negative stage of development of transitory validity, but the permanent standard of a pure and thoroughly ethical life for the community. The natural desire to form fixed Christian *morals* was what made the acceptance of Paul's doctrines of the law and of justification a practical impossibility to the Gentile Christian Churches, even if they had been understood. Even Paul had recognised this desire of his Churches so far as to speak of a "law of the Spirit," according to which Christians ought to live. Nevertheless his teaching lacked the legal precision desiderated by the Church; it was too ideal to be directly made use of by it. The need was felt of supplementing this ideal Paulinism on the side of the actual morality of works, and this found expression in the combination of Peter with Paul, or in the appeal against the one-sided party watchwords of the heretics to the authority of *all* the apostles—*i.e.* of Christ himself.

The lines of Planck and Köstlin were further pursued by ALBRECHT RITSCHL, until from being an adherent he became an opponent of the Tübingen school. In the first edition of his book, *Die Entstehung der altkatholischen Kirche* (1850), his disagreement with the theories of Baur and Schwegler was only partial, but in the second edition (1857) he declared his total antagonism to their fundamental principles. Like Planck and Köstlin, Ritschl holds that in the person of Jesus and the belief of the first apostles we have the common neutral starting-point of the various later parties. The attitude of Jesus towards the law, he maintains, was an essentially independent one—superiority to the externality of the ceremonial law in the ethical principle of love to God and man, while observing a conservative attitude in outward religious life. Accordingly Ritschl considers that the first apostles no longer regarded the law as religiously binding, but only continued its observance as a national custom, a view for which he appeals to the Epistles of Peter and James, the genuineness of which he ventures to maintain against the doubts of criticism. Though we must admit this to be too great a concession to conservative apologetics, we recognise a valuable advance on the older Tübingen theologians in Ritschl's tracing the development of Catholic Christianity, not like them from Jewish, but from Gentile Christianity, which he distinguishes from Paulinism. He rightly points out that Paulinism had a neutral basis in common with Jewish Christianity in the doctrines of God, angels and demons, the present and future world, Christ's second coming, the resurrection and judgment; to which we must add that the specifically Pauline doctrines of reconciliation and justification have their roots in Jewish (Pharisaic) theology. The earlier Tübingen theologians were distinctly in the wrong in almost completely overlooking Paul's Jewish side in exclusive attention to his anti-Jewish tendencies, and thereupon explaining every departure from his teaching by a reference to Judaistic motives, while, reversely, it must be explained for the most part from the anti-Judaistic habit of thought of the Gentile Christians. Ritschl is right in maintaining that "Catholic Christianity is a distinct stage of religious thought within the sphere of Gentile Christianity; it is independent of the conditions of Jewish Christian life, and opposed to the fundamental principle of Jewish Christianity; it does not, however, depend merely upon the authority of Paul, but rests both upon the Old Testament and the sayings of Christ, and also upon the authority of all the apostles, represented by Peter and Paul." But when Ritschl goes on to explain the conversion of Paul's teaching into the Catholic Christianity of the early Church by the failure of the latter to understand the Old Testament, and condemns it as a "degeneration," the objection presents itself that Paul's doctrine of justification is not found in the Old Testament, which, as the Epistle of James shows, offers rather the means of its refutation than of its proof. Ritschl was unacquainted with the sources of the Pauline theology, and hence cannot satisfactorily explain its post-apostolic development. A second serious defect is his total neglect of the other chief factor in the evolution of the theology of the Church, and even of that of the New Testament—viz. Hellenism. This explains his strange inability to deal with such an important phenomenon of early Christianity as the Gospel of John, and his omission of all reference to it in his book, with the exception of a brief and meaningless note. Beyond question this gospel can be explained neither by means of Jewish Christianity nor of Paulinism, least of all by a superficial Gentile "degeneration" of the latter, since it is purely a product of Christian Hellenism. The very existence of this single book (irrespective of others, *e.g.* the Epistle to the Hebrews) is a proof that no history of early Christianity can be regarded as complete which does not take account of the important factor of Hellenism, which Ritschl, in a much more striking degree even than the other Tübingen critics, has failed to do.

With Ritschl are connected several other opponents of the Tübingen school, of whom we may here mention the more important: MEYER (*Commentar zum neuen Testament*), BLEEK (*Einleitung in das N. Test.* and *Commentar zu den synoptischen Evangelien*), LECHLER (*das apostolische und nachapostolische Zeitalter mit Rücksicht auf Unterschied und Einheit in Lehre und Leben*, 2nd ed., 1857), WEISS (*der petrinische Lehrbegriff; der johanneische Lehrbegriff; Biblische Theologie des Neuen Testaments; Einleitung in das Neue Testament*), REUSS (*die Geschichte der heiligen Schriften Neuen Testaments*, and *Histoire de la Théologie chrétienne au siècle apostolique*), EWALD (*Geschichte Israels*, vols. v. and vi.; *Geschichte Christus*, and *Gesch. des apostol. Zeitalters*), HASE (*die Tübinger Schule. Ein Sendschreiben an Dr. Baur*). It would lead us far beyond our limits to give the views of all these theologians in detail, and we shall therefore be content to mention summarily their objections to the Tübingen theory. They first dispute the sharp antithesis affirmed by this theory between Paul and the original apostles. A certain difference in tendency is indeed admitted; but this is not such that the two parties were mutually exclusive, but rather such that they supplemented each other. "We find variety coupled with agreement, and unity with difference, between Paul and the earlier apostles; we recognise the *one* spirit in the many gifts" (*Lechler*). The Judaistic antagonists against whom Paul had to contend were an extreme party with which the apostles themselves must not be identified. Further, the view is controverted that the struggle and the attempts at mediation and reconciliation were continued until the middle of the second century; on the contrary, it is contended that the destruction of Jerusalem severed the bond which had hitherto connected the converted Jews with their nation and its worship. With this ceased also the influence of Judaistic agitation upon the Gentile Christian Churches; and henceforth, in place of the Pauline-Judaistic controversies, we have the new struggle with the heathen political power and heathen heresy (Gnosticism), to which the Johannine Apocalypse already bears witness. Further, an attack is made on Baur's method of tracing in the New Testament writings products of a definite party movement, and of determining their place in the history of primitive Christianity by means of their supposed dogmatic or ecclesiastical "*Tendenz.*" These objections are generally urged, moreover (irrespective of just objections to exaggerations on the part of the Tübingen School), from an apologetic desire to save the traditional authorship of the Biblical writings, the most serious critical arguments being too little regarded. The Epistles of James and 1 Peter are asserted to be not only genuine, but pre-Pauline, and (by Ritschl and Weiss) to be nowise connected with Paul. Of the deutero-Pauline Epistles, *all*—even those to the Ephesians, Timothy, and Titus, regarded as spurious even by Credner and De Wette—are reclaimed as Pauline. Special ardour is shown in the contention for the genuineness of John's Gospel; the dilemma, admitted by Lücke, that either the Apocalypse or the Gospel, but not both, is genuine, is given up, and the development of the author of the Apocalypse into the evangelist is considered probable. But the more hotly the contention raged at first around this question, the greater is the significance of the fact that the former champions of the genuineness of John's Gospel could not altogether resist the adverse arguments, but were compelled to make greater or less concessions to criticism. Hase, Weizsäcker, and Reuss have recently attributed the Gospel not to the apostle himself, but to one of his disciples; and even Weiss limits the historical value of the speeches to a minimum of reminiscences, which have become confused in the mind of the author with his own reflections, and thereby transformed. With regard to other books also—*e.g.* the Pastoral Epistles or the Acts—we have to note concessions made by the above-named theologians to Tübingen criticism, so that a gradual agreement as to the main questions need not be regarded as impossible. It is a specially happy omen that, in the province of exegesis, a uniform method of philological objectivity and exactness has been more and more developed on all hands; the services of Meyer and Weiss to exegesis are everywhere acknowledged. A tribute should also be paid to Weiss's *Biblische Theologie des Neuen Testaments*, as a work of pre-eminent scientific soundness, containing copious matter arranged with exemplary clearness, and surpassing all others in practical utility as a textbook for students.

The Tübingen school was not behindhand in replying to these numerous and serious attacks. Besides Baur and Zeller, HILGENFELD, in numerous books and essays (in the *Zeitschrift für wissenschaftliche Theologie*), distinguished himself as the ready champion of the right of scientific criticism. Fond of emphasising his independence of Baur, he still, in all important points, followed in the footsteps of the master; his method, which he is wont to contrast as *Literarkritik* with Baur's *Tendenzkritik*, is nevertheless essentially the same as Baur's. In his view of the fourth Gospel, Hilgenfeld goes even further than Baur, making it altogether dependent upon Gnosticism. In the Synoptic question he leaves Baur's view essentially unchanged, only placing Mark between Matthew and Luke. He modifies somewhat the criticism of Paul's epistles, restoring Philippians and 1 Thessalonians to Paul. VOLKMAR differs decidedly from the other Tübingen critics only on the question of the Synoptists; he follows Wilke and Weisse in regarding Mark as the earliest Gospel, which was followed by Luke immediately, and only subsequently by Matthew, the last being dependent upon both the others, and a gospel harmony from the point of view of the Catholic Church, with its reconciliation of differences. This undoubtedly correct view Volkmar has exaggerated, after the fashion of Bruno Bauer, by making Mark the author of a "didactic epic," intended to illustrate the Pauline gospel. Though this seemed to do away with all historical foundations, Volkmar, in his *Religion Jesu*, and still more in his *Jesus Nazarenus und die erste christliche Zeit* (1882), tries to separate and establish a kernel of historical facts as the basis of the gospels. In his interpretation of the Apocalypse, he follows Tübingen principles, and refers the Apocalyptic imagery in the boldest manner to the party struggles of primitive Christianity. The book is now somewhat out of date, since Völter has shown that the Apocalypse is composed of elements belonging to different authors and times, and

Vischer has made a Jewish basis with Christian revisions very probable. With Hilgenfeld and Volkmar, we must mention HOLSTEN as a strict adherent of Baur in his line of criticism. In his commentary on Galatians, and in several works on Paul, he has discussed the Apostle's peculiar teaching with great acumen, though often with too great subtlety and exaggerated dialectic: his long-promised review of the entire Pauline theology has not yet appeared. The question of the Synoptists has also latterly engaged Holsten's attention: he tries very hard, but with doubtful success, to defend Hilgenfeld's view (Matthew–Mark–Luke). On this question, HOLTZMANN is the exponent of the view now most generally accepted. In his book on *die synoptischen Evangelien*, he maintains the priority of Mark; our Matthew he derives from Mark and Matthew's original "collection of sayings" (the λόγια of Papias), and finally Luke from our Matthew and Mark. Besides numerous essays, Holtzmann has furnished valuable contributions to New Testament exegesis and criticism in his works on the Epistles to the Colossians and Ephesians and the Pastoral Epistles; and his *Einleitung in das Neue Testament* gives an excellent summary of the present position of all the questions concerned. Whilst most critics were thus working at questions of detail, HAUSRATH was led by his natural love of artistic form, and his position as ecclesiastical historian, to combine details into a vivid account of the time as a whole. In particular his *neutestamentliche Zeitgeschichte* has the merit of showing the place of the development of primitive Christianity in the history of the world, and of describing the connexion, too much neglected, between the evolution of the Christian Church and the condition of the Græco-Roman world. As this work is further distinguished by a beauty of style rare in German theologians, it has attracted attention even among the laity, and contributed much to the diffusion of the results of modern research.

At the commencement of the sixth decade of the century, after Baur's death, the labours of Bible critics were so much confined to literary questions of detail that these purely learned controversies seemed to have put an end to the interest in the great fundamental questions. This interest was, however, revived in the same field in which a generation before the whole movement had originated. The appearance in quick succession of the works of RENAN[1] and STRAUSS on the life of Jesus, which were followed by several other books on the same subject, brought this question afresh to the front. The difference between Strauss's new book, *Leben Jesu für das deutsche Volk* (1864), and his earlier one, was that he intended it, not for theologians only, but for the nation at large, especially for the educated men of Germany. Accordingly, it is thrown into a different form; in the place of learned discussions of details we have a summary of the results of criticism with regard to the gospel history, popular in the best sense of the word. In this new work Strauss seeks to obviate the objections often brought against his earlier work, that it gave a critique of the gospel history without a critique of the authorities, and led merely to the negative result of the unhistorical character of what was previously regarded as historical, not to the ascertainment of a positive historical kernel. He now prefixes a tolerably thorough criticism of the authorities, though adhering too strictly to Baur's views on all questions, even with regard to Matthew and Mark,

---

[1] Renan's *Vie de Jésus* (1863) belongs, neither in its origin nor in its effects, to the history of German theology, but its international importance demands the following remarks. It is evident that a book which in a short time attained a world-wide celebrity must have had some special excellence. Not to do injustice to it, we must be careful not to judge it by a wrong standard. Such would be, in this instance, the standard of strictly scientific historical inquiry. If Renan's object had been to ascertain the actual ultimate foundation of the gospel narratives, he would, of course, have had to begin with a careful investigation of the sources—their composition, date, trustworthiness, and mutual relations, which would doubtless have led him to conclusions in particular with regard to the Fourth Gospel which would have made it impossible for him to make use of the contents of this Gospel unconditionally, and to co-ordinate it with the others. I doubt not that Renan's subtle historical insight would have enabled him without difficulty to arrive, by means of this criticism of the authorities, a calm comparison of the texts, and a careful weighing of the various probabilities, at a collection of data giving the most probable view we can form on these matters. A book of this kind would have possessed greater value as an historical treatise, but would have lacked all the merits and charm which make Renan's *Vie de Jésus* so unusually attractive. These merits are, in a word, not scientific, but poetical. With a faculty of poetical imagination, which paints characters, states of mind and feeling, and scenery with equal vividness, Renan has composed from the gospel stories a *religious epic*, which brings forth the Saviour from the unapproachable darkness of dogma into the midst of the life of his people, first as the idyllic national leader, then as the contending and erring hero, always aiming at the highest, but doomed to tragic failure from the resistance offered by the reality to his ideal. Even those who may disapprove of such a

without doing justice to the grounds of the opposite views. Strauss, as he himself remarks in the preface, is not interested in these questions. "What we really want to know is whether the gospel history is true as a whole and in its details or not, and such preliminary questions can only excite general interest in proportion as they are connected with this fundamental problem. In this respect the criticism of the Gospels has undeniably in the last twenty years somewhat run to seed. New hypotheses, particularly with regard to the first three Gospels, their sources, aims, composition, and mutual relations, crop up in such numbers, and are both maintained and attacked with as much zeal as if these were the only questions, while the resulting controversy is of such proportions that we have almost to despair of ever settling the principal question, if its solution has to wait for the conclusion of this controversy." We must indeed, Strauss says, have made up our minds as to the Fourth Gospel before we can enter into the discussion of these matters; but the mutual relation of the Synoptic Gospels is not of the same importance. Moreover,

---

poetical treatment of a subject sacred to Christendom, must admit that it has brought the human figure of Jesus nearer to countless men who had long lost all appreciative feeling and care for the Christ of dogma, and has made him the object of their sympathetic appreciation and reverent admiration. And if offence was given by Renan's bringing out shadows and weaknesses in his picture of Jesus, we might in general, without wishing at all to defend him in detail, reply by way of excuse, that shadows in a bright picture might appear expedient to make the human figure more life-like and his story more dramatic. Finally, it must be said for this religious epic, as for other historical romances, that, without teaching us history in detail, it enables us to realise an historical event or period as a whole by means of the poet's comprehensive and divining intuition better than the scanty accounts of the strict historian can ever do. The further volumes of Renan's great work on the genesis of Christianity, the scientific value of which cannot be denied, still leave something to be desired as regards critical rigour in the investigation and use of authorities. But this defect is counterbalanced by the merits of vivid description of the local and social environment of events and fine delineation of character. Renan always places before his readers real human beings of flesh and blood, with noble and base passions and motives, not mere ideal pictures upon a golden background. Of special interest is his description of the Apostle Paul. But he has too little sympathy with this Apostle of faith to be altogether just to him; he places him with Luther, as one of the historical men of power, but fails in the case of both men to appreciate the depth of their religious feeling and far-seeing speculation. The theological side of religion is indeed always neglected by Renan, while he has a true eye for its practical social side. He thus serves to supplement the German historians.

without deciding all those endless critical questions, we can at least arrive at the negative result, that in the person and work of Jesus there is nothing supernatural, nothing that need oppress mankind with the leaden weight of an infallible authority demanding blind belief. "And this negative result is for our purpose, which is not solely historical, but looks rather towards the future than the past, *an* important, if not *the most* important, point." Of the positive correlative to this negative result we can say nothing for certain; but a summing up of what in the present position of research must be considered probable is both permissible and desirable. "All those engaged in these researches are thus reminded of the real point at issue, and such reminding, such recall from the circumference to the centre, has always been profitable to science." It is in fact by such a balancing of the accounts that Strauss now, as in his former works, gave a useful impulse to the advance of science. The first of the two books into which this Life is divided gives the outline of the historical life of Jesus. This account has been called dry and meagre, and indeed is so in comparison with Renan's richly coloured poetry; but who can blame the historian, if his authorities are of such a nature that, on a critical examination, they fail to furnish him with sufficient material? Besides, it must be admitted that on the main questions as to the religious and Messianic consciousness of Jesus, and his relation to the Law, Strauss carefully weighs the various indications, and with subtle insight determines the most probable account. Like Schleiermacher and Renan, Strauss assumes that the religious consciousness of Jesus was the source of his consciousness of himself as the Messiah; but he expressly declines to accept the idea (with Renan) that in the latter Jesus made use of "accommodation" or "played a part"; since in the case of a personality of such immeasurable historical influence every inch must have been conviction; this conviction was the more natural in the case of Jesus, as the Messianic expectation had a religious and ethical as well as a political side, and the former side would appear to him of prime importance in proportion as the latter had always hitherto proved itself disastrous. The fundamental characteristic of the piety of Jesus, Strauss holds to be his transference of the indiscriminate kindness towards good and evil alike, which was the fundamental principle of his own nature, to God as the determining principle of his nature also. "By fully developing in himself this glad spirit, which was at one with God and embraced all men as brothers, Jesus had realised the prophetic ideal of a new covenant, with the law written in the heart; he had, to use Schiller's language, "*Die Gottheit in seinen Willen aufgenommen,*" identified his will with God's, and hence for him God, in Schiller's words, 'had descended from the throne of the universe, the abyss had been filled up, and the terror had fled,' in him man had passed from slavery to freedom. This gladness and integrity (*Ungebrochene*), this action from the delight and joy of a beautiful soul, we may call the Hellenic element in Jesus. But the fact that this impulse of his heart, and, in harmony therewith, his conception of God, were purely spiritual and ethical—this attainment, which the Greek could only attain to by philosophy, was in his case the dowry granted to him by his education according to the Mosaic law, and his instruction in the writings of the prophets." Jesus had not, like Paul, to pass through an agitating conflict and conversion, but was from the first a beautiful nature, his development went on in general uniformly, if not without great effort yet without violent crises; "this is the only living sense of the dogma of the sinlessness of Jesus, of which, in its rigid ecclesiastical form, as a purely negative idea, we can make absolutely nothing." After the first book has given a description of the conjectural historical kernel of the history of Jesus, the second book treats of his mythical history, which had formed the sole subject of the earlier work. But while it had there been treated analytically, it is here treated genetically. It is assumed as the result of the former work that the supernatural element in the gospel narratives is mythical; but the question now arises as to how we are to conceive the origin and development of this mythical history. As the first effect of the life and character of Jesus, we find the belief of his disciples in his resurrection; and thus we find their ideas of him transplanted into a temperature in which a luxuriant growth of unhistorical seedlings was bound to spring up, each more miraculous than the other. The inspired Son of David comes to be the Son of God without human father; the Son of God grows into the incarnate creative Word; the humane, thaumaturgic physician becomes the resuscitator from the dead, the absolute lord of nature and its laws; the wise popular teacher, the prophet reading the hearts of men, becomes omniscient, God's *alter ego*, his life on earth an episode in his eternal existence with God. This process, by which the various strata in the development of the conceptions of Christ were formed one after the other, as the expression of the Christian feeling prevalent in a given circle at a given time, is worked out in the second book. It thus both supplements and confirms the results of the previous work. For "if any one denies the historical validity of a story universally believed, we have a right to demand from him not only the grounds of his opinion, but also an explanation of the process by which the unhistorical narrative has come into existence." This explanation is here given with such thoroughness and perspicuity that the scientific value of the new work, in spite of its popular form, is decidedly superior to that of the earlier one. The fact that it, nevertheless, did not produce anything like the same sensation only proves that in the intervening generation the world had become accustomed to receive the results of scientific research even in religious matters much more calmly than had previously been the case.

The two works of Renan and Strauss were followed by a vast stream of literature on the life of Jesus, which, however, grew shallower as it increased in breadth. Most of the works of this class produced in the last twenty years have paid less and less serious attention to both literary and material criticism, and have almost retrograded to the position of pre-critical apologies and harmonies. Inasmuch as this branch of theology has thus completed its revolution, theologians ought without doubt to deduce the conclusion that a scientifically certain life of Jesus is impossible with the existing authorities. However painful it may be thus to resign ourselves, this might still be attended by the advantage of leading theology away from devotion to small details and the attempt to trace the steps of Jesus in Galilee and Judea, and to combine the mosaic of evangelical tradition, now in one way, now in another, to the study once more of history on a large scale, which would look for the sources of Christianity in the life of expiring antiquity as a whole, and see in the triumphant progress of Christ's spirit through the earth the proof of his divine mission, proof drawn from the wide history of the world, and independent of the ever problematical results of the detailed investigation of his earthly life. From the mass of this literature

I will call attention to three works as the most important, Schenkel's *Charakterbild Jesu*, Keim's *Geschichte Jesu von Nazara*, and Weizsäcker's *Evangelische Untersuchungen*.

SCHENKEL'S *Charakterbild Jesu*, which appeared almost simultaneously with Strauss's "Life of Jesus for the German People," provoked an outburst of opposition among German theologians, the reason of which it is hard to discover in the book assailed. This is so far from having an irreligious tendency, or being a frivolous treatment of sacred history, that on the contrary it is full of a passionate enthusiasm for the character of Jesus, such as satisfies the demands of the heart much more than those of strict scientific research. In its estimate of the value of the sources, Schenkel's book, it is true, excels all other works here mentioned; the priority of Mark is maintained with great decision, and all connection of the Fourth Gospel with the Apostle John, who did not live in Ephesus, denied with equal emphasis (so at least in the 4th ed., 1873). But in his use of the authorities, the author is far from deducing the necessary consequences from this correct conclusion. Instead of attending to the peculiarities of each Gospel, and seeing in them the influence of a later time and development of doctrine, all the Gospels are really used as if of equal value, and from their narratives and speeches (even the Johannine), by means of artificial harmonising and arbitrary interpretation, a life of Christ is constructed, which, with all its ideality, produces rather the impression of a modern reformer and champion of liberty and truth than of the real historical founder of the Church. Even those who are far from overestimating the historical value of Renan's life of Jesus, can scarcely avoid ranking it higher than Schenkel's representation of Jesus. Compare, for instance, Renan's keen insight into the social side of the work of Jesus with Schenkel's recasting of all the language of the passages of the Gospels in question, to bring them into conformity with modern ethics. Or let us hear Schenkel's description of the significance of the death of Jesus. "In order to kill the bondage to the letter of religion, Jesus, the inspired representative of the spirit of religion, had to die. The sanguinary law condemning freedom of belief was sentenced by his death; by his sacrificial blood he bought freedom of belief and through it liberation from the bondage of the letter and of sin. Thus his death became a victory of freedom and love, and thereby the source of a new religion, which overcame evil in the inmost core of personality, a ransom for the captives in Israel and the heathen world." Schenkel did not consider that "personal freedom of faith and of conscience" are ideals of very recent growth, which cannot without a serious anachronism be carried back to the rise of Christianity, and actually made the pivot of the whole work of Jesus. Indeed, Schenkel's own character was of such vigorous and yet one-sided subjectivity that he altogether lacked the impartiality of objective historical insight.

THEODOR KEIM became known about the year 1860 by his lectures on the human development and historical rank of Jesus (in the 2nd edition, together published under the title *Der geschichtliche Christus*, 1865) as an able writer on the life of Jesus, distinguished alike by his insight and religious feeling. When his extensive work *Geschichte Jesu von Nazara* (3 vols., 1867–1872) appeared, it was recognised even by antagonists as of first-rate scientific importance. In it there is collected and skilfully digested such a mass of learned material, that this alone suffices to render it a lasting storehouse of information for all students of the subject. The investigation of the authorities, too, is more thorough than in similar works (with the possible exception of Weizsäcker's). And yet it is here that the great error of the book lies. The discussion of the Fourth Gospel is indeed excellent, and Keim is as decided as Strauss with regard to its unhistorical character. But on the question of the Synoptists Keim has not got beyond the view of Griesbach and Baur, that Matthew is the original Gospel, and Mark a compilation from it and Luke. His advocacy of this totally erroneous view is feeble; the evident signs of the derivative character of Matthew are overlooked or attributed to later revision; his account of Mark is full of the strongest prejudices. This erroneous estimate of the authorities places the whole work from the beginning upon a false and unstable basis, the effects of which naturally disturb all that follows. The strangest thing is that Keim himself, in the course of his history, often deserts his critical canon and finds himself obliged to give Mark or Luke the preference over Matthew. To this uncertainty as to the relation of the Gospels to each other must be added Keim's failure sufficiently to appreciate the influence of apostolic and post-apostolic teaching on the gospel accounts, as well as of the personal influence of the writers themselves. When we further consider that Keim regards the Easter stories in the Gospels as historical accounts of actual Christophanies, and thus at the close of his book quits strictly historical ground altogether, we shall be justified in saying that his work, in spite of its great learning, fails to satisfy the rigorous demands of critical historical inquiry. Keim's style, too, lacks, according to my taste, the simplicity and sobriety appropriate to historical investigations. It is quite true that the lofty subject of this history demands a corresponding dignity of tone and language. But this does not cancel the difference between an historical inquiry and a sermon. When the emotional style of the pulpit is employed, as it is by Keim, in historical narrative, it is almost inevitable that emotion should substitute its language for that of the sober understanding, and the weight of high-sounding phrases take the place of material facts and arguments. Keim in this respect closely resembles Ewald.

Of all the writers on the life of Jesus, CARL WEIZSÄCKER has most carefully discussed the question of the authorities; this forms the first half of his book, *Untersuchungen über die evangelische Geschichte, ihre Quellen und den Gang ihrer Entwickelung* (1864). He comes to the conclusion that the three Synoptic gospels are based upon a common original, the *synoptische Grundschrift*, most closely followed by our Gospel of Mark, and that the speeches contained in the two other Gospels, and not in Mark, are derived from a second source, the "collection of sayings," incorporated in different ways by Matthew and Luke with the *Grundschrift*, Matthew giving the purer form of it. The Fourth Gospel he holds has a two-fold aspect, it has an ideal and also an historical side; it is not indeed composed of different elements capable of being externally distinguished, but its two-fold character pervades the whole work, which is on the one hand based upon great theological ideas, and on the other guided by quite definite historical motives. For the latter Weizsäcker appeals in particular to the small incidental remarks, such as definite notes of time or place, which in his opinion bear traces of personal recollection. Such traces he thinks he finds even in the Johannine speeches, his strongest argument, besides the hostility to the Jews, being the circumstance that the evangelist does not introduce his personal doctrinal view into the speeches of Jesus (an opinion which necessitates a very forced interpretation of many unambiguous utterances in the speeches of the Johannine Christ). Weizsäcker's explanation of this two-fold character of the Gospel is that it was founded upon personal recollections and communications of the aged Apostle John, and composed by one of his disciples towards the close of the first century. This intermediate position on the Johannine question, which Weizsäcker shares with Renan, Hase, and many more, is after all a great concession to Tübingen criticism; but it is allowable to ask whether this position is tenable, and not a halting-place merely on the retreat which must end in the complete surrender of all apostolic connexion with the Fourth Gospel. I hold Keim's view is the more correct one, and that these scholars have been influenced to some extent, if not by ordinary apologetical motives, yet by their dogmatic predilection for an ideal of Christ, which may be gathered from the Fourth Gospel, though only by a free interpretation of the speeches, and with which moderns have a good deal of emotional sympathy.

A valuable continuation of his book on the Gospels has lately been given by Weizsäcker in his work, *Das apostolische Zeitalter der christlichen Kirche* (1886). He first describes the formation of the primitive community by the appearances of Christ (which, like all critical theologians, he conceives as subjective experiences, or visions, of the Apostles), and its original condition before the activity of Paul, who forms the subject of the remainder of the first half of the book. Paul's conversion is first related and explained by its psychological conditions; then his first missionary journey, the form of his doctrine and theology are described; this is followed by the detailed consideration of the relations of the Apostle of the Gentiles to the Churches in Jerusalem and Antioch, and a comparison of the accounts of Galatians ii. and Acts xv. And it is most noteworthy that in all the chief questions here involved, in particular in his unfavourable view of the historical character of the Acts, Weizsäcker is in surprising agreement with the theory of Baur. Subsequently the Apostle Paul's missionary journeys, and the condition of the Churches founded by him, are described, under the guidance of the genuine Epistles, in a very thorough and instructive manner. A second part describes the further development of affairs from Paul's imprisonment down to the end of the first or beginning of the second century: (1) in Jerusalem, with an account of the Epistle of James and the origin of the Synoptic Gospels; (2) in Rome, with the discussion of the Epistles to the Romans and Philippians, the legend of Peter, and the Epistles of Clement and the Hebrews; (3) in Ephesus, with the consideration of the Johannine literature and the Epistles to the Ephesians and Colossians. The two questions as to the presence of Peter in Rome and John in Ephesus are both answered by Weizsäcker, like Renan, in the affirmative, the first with more assurance than the second; the chief evidence in the latter case being the Apocalypse, which he holds to have been composed not by the Apostle John himself, but by one of his disciples, who appealed to his authority. Weizsäcker's analysis of the Apocalypse is subtle and ingenious, but not sufficiently thorough; it is superseded by the researches of Völter and Vischer, who have shown the probability of a plurality of authors and a Jewish work as the basis of the Apocalypse. The final portion of the book treats of the Church of the first century, its assemblies and worship, its constitution and its life. The historian's skill is everywhere shown in discovering the most important and characteristic facts, and in producing, from minute and apparently unimportant indications, by skilful grouping and ingenious inferences, a vivid picture of the earliest state of the Christian Church and its natural evolution from small beginnings. Much is, of course, only conjecture of which the truth may be disputed; but even when it fails to produce complete conviction, Weizsäcker's account is so clearly conceived, and the reasons for it so carefully given, that it is in the highest degree attractive and suggestive. Since Baur's *Christenthum der drei ersten Jahrhunderte*, nothing has appeared on the earliest times of the Christian Church superior to the " Apostolic Age " by Weizsäcker, the worthy occupant of Baur's chair.

In conclusion, I may here refer to my own book, *Das Urchristenthum, seine Schriften und Lehren, in geschichtlichem Zusammenhang beschrieben* (1887). It is based on the Hibbert Lectures, delivered in England in 1885, on " The Influence of the Apostle Paul on the Development of Christianity," and forms an extension and continuation of my earlier work on *Paulinismus* (1873). In it I have tried to show that the development of primitive Christianity into the Catholic Church must not be conceived as a continued struggle and gradual reconciliation between Paulinism and Jewish Christianity, as Baur had thought; nor (with Ritschl) as a falling away from the apostolical religion and a degeneration of Paulinism; but as the natural evolution of the Christian Hellenism introduced by Paul, which soon cast off the Pharisaic elements in Paul's doctrines, and developed, on the one hand, in a speculative direction, into the Johannine theology of Asia Minor; on the other, in a practical direction, into the Church life of Rome (Epistle of James). But notwithstanding my difference from Baur, both in my general view and in my estimate of individual books (especially the Apocalypse, the Gospels of Matthew and Mark, the Acts and others), I shall never forget how much I, with all our generation, owe to the epoch-making achievements of the great Tübingen Master.

CHAPTER II.

OLD TESTAMENT CRITICISM AND EXEGESIS.

IN the same year with Strauss's *Life of Jesus*, which introduced the new era of New Testament research, appeared VATKE'S book, *Die Religion des Alten Testaments nach den kanonischen Büchern entwickelt*, which contained the beginning of a not less important revolution in the views held regarding the Old Testament. The book met with a strange fate. The able and original theories it contained were received with such universal disapprobation that it was scarcely considered worth while even to consider them with any thoroughness; for a generation they remained practically unnoticed, and it was only between 1865 and 1870 that the same critical views were again advanced in a different form, and evoked ever growing interest. To Vatke's book itself its unfortunate history was partly due. As a disciple of Hegel, Vatke had a keen eye for the laws of the mental development and religious consciousness of nations; approaching Old Testament research with his insight thus quickened by philosophy, he saw the impossibility of resting content with the traditional or even with the semi-critical views of the history of the religion of the Old Testament then in vogue. But this very philosophical training, which was Vatke's strength, constituted the weakness of his book in the eyes of the public. After the then prevailing fashion of his school, Vatke had prefaced his historical inquiry by philosophical prolegomena, enunciating in the most abstract form propositions concerning the idea and phenomenon of religion, which could only be understood by those initiated into the mysteries of Hegelian terminology; and even in the course of his history he employed this terminology much too freely. No wonder that this unfortunate form of the book had on many the deterrent effect described by Reuss[1] in his own case. "On the ap-

---

[1] *Gesch. der h. Schriften Alten Testaments.* Preface, p. ix.

pearance of the book, the table of contents, with its Hegelian formulæ, of itself terrified me to such an extent that I remained at the time unacquainted with it. A speculative treatment of history I trust no further than I can see. Since then indeed I have seen that theory and formula in this book were really only an addition which might be dispensed with, and that my inquiries might have been materially assisted if I had not let myself be deterred by them." Since it is one of the pleasantest duties of the historian to place misjudged merit in its proper light, I will here give a short account of Vatke's little known book, not of its philosophical superfluities, but of its valuable, historical, and critical essence.

Vatke starts from the indisputable fact that the sources for the earlier history of the Old Testament religion are derived from later legends, and are therefore incomplete and uncertain. Accordingly he not only passes over the whole history of the patriarchs as prehistoric legend, as others had done before him, but he also subjects the traditional account of Moses to a more searching criticism than any one had previously ventured to do. He finds that the notion of Moses having given the people its civil law and a pure belief in God is irreconcilable with later history. For he holds it to be impossible that a whole nation should suddenly sink from a high stage of religious development to a lower one, as is asserted to have been so often the case in the times of the judges and kings; and equally impossible for an individual to rise all at once from a lower to a higher stage, and raise a whole nation with him with the same rapidity. We must not separate individuals from the general life around them, and must therefore often supply connecting links omitted in the legend, or reduce our conception of the individuals in question to the standard of their age. "This is particularly the case with Moses, since on the assumption of the truth even of only the greater part of this tradition as to his work, both his own person and the whole course of Hebrew history become inexplicable; he would have come when the time was not fulfilled, and would thus be far more miraculous than Christ himself. The profound idea of the New Testament, that the law was introduced between the promises and their fulfilment, may after all be justified, since the Pentateuch in its completed form is in truth later than the promises of most of the prophets." From indications in later history, and from isolated statements of the prophets (Amos v. 25 *sq.*), Vatke infers that the Hebrews in the time of Moses shared the universal worship of the stars. With regard to the work of Moses, a critical examination of the tradition, in conjunction with the condition of the country under the judges, makes it certain in the first place that Moses did not found a state, since the main condition of this was wanting, viz. the establishment of a legislative and executive authority, which did not exist in Israel until the times of the kings. With the conception of actual sovereignty the Mosaic state lacked also all higher unity and all that belongs to the sphere of public justice. The legislation of the Pentateuch did not found a political constitution, and was not intended to do so; its object was the partial development of certain relations of the community, and it must therefore have originated within a state already constituted, and may be compared to canon law. With regard to the sacrificial and sacerdotal ordinances of the Pentateuch, the history of the times of the judges and earlier kings proves that the simple patriarchal method of worship was then in force,—a plurality of sacred places, the priesthood not confined to a single tribe, the forms of worship still very simple. Only in the later kingdom of Judah did the system of the Pentateuch become possible; it was then by degrees actually realised, and became the fixed ritual after the Babylonian exile. Composite ceremonies, such as those of the "Mosaic" ritual, are in general only comprehensible as the products of a lengthy development, and become, in their stereotyped permanence, the dead shells of a previous or a parallel spiritual growth; the rigid mechanism of form is never the original and direct product. That the laws concerning ritual in the Pentateuch are not derived from Moses, and do not belong to the early pre-prophetic period at all, is confirmed by the protests of the prophets against the ceremonial worship, which they regard as not a revelation from God, but an invention of godless and deceitful men; which would have been quite impossible if the Pentateuch had existed. But if Moses was thus neither a political nor ecclesiastical legislator, nor a sage speculating on the nature of God, he was still a true prophet, who came forward in consequence of direct inspiration as an ambassador from God, and hallowed the judicial and moral life of the nation by bringing it into relation with the divine will; he concluded a "covenant" between the people and Jehovah, and thus maintained the dependence of the historical and natural existence of the nation upon the sphere of justice and morality; this indicates that he beheld in Jehovah a *holy power*, and that he deduced the other attributes of the divine nature from this central idea. We must not however attribute to Moses all the consequences involved in this principle; for like the conception of the ideal unity of God, the attributes of his nature were realised in their fulness only in the course of time. The divine holiness was regarded partly as an exclusive principle on the side of natural existence and the service of nature, partly as the standard of a legal and moral life; in order therefore to separate the elements of the sensible and the higher order of things, and to arouse the moral sentiment from the dream of nature-life, this Power had to appear to men as severity, as a consuming fire and a jealous power; its instruments had to be full of a like holy zeal, while the abstract nature of their message only increased the necessity for sternness. For the question at issue was still the recognition of the Lord, of a holy Will, of law and morality in general; the first abstract stages of a great process of purification were still being passed through, which afterwards the earlier prophets, especially Elijah, similarly fought their way through. The principle of mercy and grace could scarcely be represented even in an infinitesimal degree in such a development. Although Moses received the idea of the holy national God, whose will was to guide the whole political and moral life of his people as an original intuition, *i.e.* as a revelation, we still must not disconnect his appearance and work from its historical conditions. For since natural religion produces some legal and moral institutions, we must not draw a hard and fast line between the two forms of religion; it only needed a distinguished personality, in whom were focussed the various rays of a better spirit, to find and announce the solution of the problem of the national mind, and thus give its development a new direction. But although part of the nation sided with the prophet of the higher spirit and carried on his work, still he was far from being able to lift the whole people up to his higher point of view. The mass of the nation still clung to the old Semitic worship of nature. Later tradition was therefore wrong in representing the people under and after Moses as repeatedly sinking to a lower stage from a higher one already attained; on the contrary, the development was a gradual one in an upward direction amid a constant struggle between the two parties. "Hence the later religion of the Hebrew nation had the Sabaic religion of nature, and particularly the worship of Saturn, as its empirical starting-point, and the revelation of the divine ideality and holiness as its higher principle."

This description of its Mosaic beginnings gives the key to Vatke's whole view of the history of the Hebrew religion. This view, as may be seen, is the outcome of an acute comparative examination of the traditions, and of general ideas on the philosophy of history. The latter indeed will not be a recommendation in the eyes of the public of to-day; but to me this appears an instructive example of the intuition of a philosophically trained mind showing empirical research the road to its most fruitful discoveries.

A curious contrast to Vatke's book is presented by EWALD's great work on the History of Israel (1st ed. 1843-52, 3 vols.; 3rd ed. 1864-68, 7 vols.). In the former the decisive points are noted with the penetrative glance of genius, and the outlines of an actual historical development are brought clearly before us, with the omission of unimportant particulars; while in the latter the reader's mind is confused amid an endless mass of details which prevent his ever arriving at a distinct idea of the history as a whole. His criticism of authorities exhibits Ewald's critical sagacity in its strength and weakness—keen-sighted in little things, shortsighted in great. Ewald distinguishes as the main sources of the Pentateuch, the Book of Covenants, the Book of Origins, three Prophetical Narrators, and lastly the Deuteronomist. But though he has much to say about the character of these sources and the determination of their date, he pays no attention to those serious objections which Vatke had already urged against the early pre-prophetic origin of the ritualistic and priestly legislation of Leviticus and Numbers; Ewald does not attribute this legislation to Moses himself, but he has no difficulty whatever in dating it (as the Book of Origins) from the time of Solomon. Ewald, moreover, has scarcely the faintest idea of the development of the religious consciousness, of which Vatke with so much insight gives a probably true description. He considers the revelation of the purely spiritual God, in whom love is superior to punitive justice, had been so completely given in Moses, that we can understand neither how such a phenomenon was possible at the time, nor what fresh and higher truth the subsequent prophetical, or even Christian, revelation could add. This is connected with one of Ewald's characteristic peculiarities. He lacked the primary qualification of an historian, the ability to sink his own personality and mode of thought and identify himself with other and alien modes of thought and feeling. When any historical figure impresses him (and all impress him which tradition in any respect represents as heroes), he is immediately carried away by his feelings, and ascribes to his heroes, forgetting the requirements of sober criticism, all the noble moral thoughts and feelings which he, the historian, entertains at the moment. We might call his history a didactic romance. His method of treating the Hebrew legends of miracles is more suitable to the edifying romance than to an historical inquiry. He does not actually believe the miracles, but does not openly deny them and explain the origin of the legends; he manipulates the individual traits of these Biblical narratives in so artificial a manner, and casts over the whole such a cloud of edifying phrases, that each reader may make what he likes out of them,—one a real miracle, another a natural and insignificant event, a third a moral allegory. But this was just what the public wanted in the middle of the century; the bright light of Tübingen criticism had given pain to weak eyes only just waking from the dreams of centuries; so it was comforting to have the Biblical history of the Old and New Testaments interpreted by so great a scholar and set in a dim, soft twilight, such as could not hurt the weakest eyes, while at the same time it flattered the cultivated mind with a considerable degree of *Aufklärung*. Thus this excellent philologian, but bad historian and worse theologian, was able to retard by his authority the healthy advance of Biblical criticism for a whole generation. The light of the two stars, Hengstenberg and Ewald, quite eclipsed that of Vatke; but at last Vatke's brilliant theory has been brought to the front by the labours of more recent inquirers, and made the centre of the Old Testament researches of the present day. Not for men only, but also for books, *die Weltgeschichte ist das Weltgericht!*

During the decades of Ewald's supremacy, when Vatke appeared to be forgotten, Reuss in his lecture room at Strassburg had given his auditors an account of the Old Testament literature and religion different from the prevalent one and very similar to that of Vatke. Two of his hearers, while the master himself cautiously deferred the publication of his views, made the theory, by their independent researches, the subject of a controversy which since then has never ceased. H. GRAF, in his book, *Die geschichtlichen Bücher des A. Testaments* (1866), by an investigation of the history of the Israelite ritual, as given in the more ancient sources (not in Chronicles, which is much later and is coloured by a marked *Tendenz*), arrived at the result that the priestly legislation in the middle books of the Pentateuch was later than Deuteronomy, and only after the Babylonian exile incorporated as a great interpolation with the earlier work of the Deuteronomist. He still, however, kept to the then usual view, that the Elohistic narratives, in spite of their close connection with the priestly legislation, were part of the "*Grundschrift*," and regarded them accordingly as the oldest part of the Pentateuch. He had thus divided this *Grundschrift* into two parts, which, although perfectly similar in language and thought, were supposed to differ in date by more than 500 years, the one being the oldest and the other the most recent portion of the whole Pentateuch. It was of course not a difficult task for criticism to prove the impossibility of such an hypothesis. But while the representatives of the older point of view believed themselves to have thus refuted the whole theory, and to have vindicated the antiquity of the whole *Grundschrift*, including the priestly code, keener critics considered Graf's error to consist in want of thoroughness in working out his own theory, and not extending it also to the narrative portions of the *Grundschrift*. Graf himself recognised this error, and in an essay published shortly before his death on "*die sogenannte Grundschrift des Pentateuchs*," drew the necessary inferences. Still, in spite of the great impression produced by his arguments, German theologians continued to reject the "*Graf'sche Hypothese*," through inability to get rid of the prejudice, supported by the authority of Ewald, that his theory was contradicted by the ascertained history of the literature of the Old Testament. In these circumstances it was again a former pupil and later colleague of Reuss, Professor KAYSER, of Strassburg, who by his book, *Das vorexilische Buch der Urgeschichte Israels und seine Erweiterungen* (1874), gave the death blow to this prejudice by proving, by an investigation of the literary interdependence of the books, that the Jahvistic book of history, with its naïve epic style, is the oldest, that then follows the Deuteronomist, and that lastly the Elohistic legislation was added, with its appropriate framework of narrative; the order of sequence inferred from the history of the ritual being thus confirmed by the literary evidence. Two years after Kayser's book, appeared WELL-HAUSEN'S essays on the composition of the Hexateuch (Joshua being taken with the Pentateuch), and then his *Geschichte Israels* (1878), in which the arguments for the new hypothesis, derived from the parallel development of law, ritual, and literature, were exhibited with such cogency that the impression produced on German theologians (especially of the younger generation) was almost irresistible; thenceforward "Graf's hypothesis," the resuscitation of the long-ignored theory of Vatke, was universally regarded as a question deserving most serious consideration, and by many as an ascertained fact. It was a special merit in Wellhausen's book to have excited interest in these questions outside the narrow circle of specialists by its skilful handling of the materials and its almost perfect combination of wide historical considerations with the careful investigation of details, and to have thus removed Old Testament criticism from the rank of a subordinate question to the centre of theological discussion. Personally I welcomed this book of Wellhausen's more than almost any other, for the pressing problem of the history of the religion of the Old Testament appeared to me to have been at last solved in a manner consonant with the principle of human evolution, which I am compelled to apply to the history of all religion. It is true, I was better prepared than the majority of German theologians to appreciate Wellhausen's book by my acquaintance with Kuenen's work, *Godsdienst van Israel*.

The Dutch scholar ABRAHAM KUENEN had even before Graf come to doubt the early date of the priestly *Grundschrift*, from observing that the impossibilities which Colenso had proved in his criticism of Old Testament history occurred with the greatest frequency in it. When Graf's book appeared, Kuenen saw at once that its separation of the *Grundschrift* into law and history was untenable; but in considering the further question, whether the historical portions should follow after the laws, or *vice versâ*, he decided unhesitatingly for the former alternative, perceiving that Graf's arguments for the post-deuteronomic origin of the priestly laws were valid, while his supposition of the early date of the corresponding historical narrative was neither proved nor to be proved. Hence he arrived at the conviction that "not only is the priestly legislation chronologically later than the preaching of the prophets, but the priestly historiography is later than the prophetic (Jahvistic)." From this point of view he composed his great work, masterly alike in form and matter, *Godsdienst van Israel* (1869-70), which in Holland met with deserved appreciation, but in Germany, on account of its foreign language, was less known beyond the narrowest circle of specialists than it deserved; it is all the more a matter for congratulation that an English translation has facilitated its circulation beyond the narrow limits of the Dutch tongue. The ability and originality of this history strike one at the outset. It had always hitherto been supposed that the history of a nation or a religion must follow the chronological sequence of events, and therefore begin with the earliest time; it was not remembered that the earliest history, since there exist no contemporary authorities for it, is the most uncertain and least adapted to form the secure starting-point of historical inquiry, constituting as it does at first only an obscure problem, the solution of which, so far as any solution is possible, can only be approached from other ascertained facts. If our conception of the earliest times is to be more than an arbitrary hypothesis, if it is to produce the impression of a well-considered conviction, we must first lay its grounds before the reader; but since from the nature of the case these can only consist of inferences from later well-attested facts, we must begin with an account of the latter. Hence it follows that the proper method is to start from some period that is historically clearly known (with the 8th century in Hebrew history, the time of the first prophets that left written records). The prophetic authorities for the history of this period directly supply only the conception of Israel's prehistoric life which was entertained in prophetic circles, they contain the national heroic legends as interpreted by the prophetic consciousness of the 8th century. Only by taking account of the alterations in the form of the legend made by this later time, either by addition or subtraction, can the historical kernel be approximately extracted from the legendary husk, its probability being greater in proportion to the extent to which it serves to explain the later development. This method combines the most careful analysis and criticism of the sources with a secure synthesis of the results, thus analytically obtained, in the positive construction of the historical process of evolution. This splendid method of historical research was, so far as I am aware, first applied to the religion of Israel by Kuenen; it is, however, exactly parallel to Baur's method of investigating the history of primitive Christianity. Baur started with the Apostle Paul, and used the indications as to the conditions of the apostolic age, as supplied by Paul, to explain the historical books produced in those conditions, and then only argued back to the state of Christianity before Paul; and in exactly the same way Kuenen starts with the first literary prophets, seeks from the conditions of their time to explain and estimate the historical books belonging to it, and thence draws inferences with regard to the previous period, which must be conceived in such a way as to account for the state of things in the prophetic age as the natural development from it. This exact similarity of method in different departments is the more interesting, as there is no doubt that Kuenen was uninfluenced by Baur's precedent, but worked out his method quite independently, led by his own sound historical instinct. Of the rareness of this fine historical instinct, and of the difficulty most people find in even following an inquiry into intricate questions in this way, we have evidence every day; I have myself been censured on all hands for beginning my account of Primitive Christianity with Paul and not with Jesus, who, everybody knows, preceded him! But Abraham and Moses preceded Amos and Isaiah, and yet Kuenen had good reason to begin with the latter instead of the former. Real historical insight seems as rare as philosophical, and perhaps they are one and the same—an eye for the reality behind phenomena.

It was not until after Kuenen and Wellhausen that the early teacher of Biblical criticism and originator of this new movement, EDUARD REUSS, gave publicity to the results of half a century's labours in two extensive works, the one in French (being the third part of his great undertaking, *La Bible*), *L'histoire sainte et la loi*, and the other in German, his *Geschichte der heiligen Schriften Alten Testaments* (1881). In the preface to the latter he states that the idea and plan of the work were determined on at the time of his first course of lectures on the subject in 1834, but only in the shape of an intuition, for which he could not at the time produce sufficient arguments. "Those who remember the literature of that period, not the conservative merely, but particularly the critical, will be able to understand my unwillingness at once to challenge the learned world to look upon the Prophets as older than the Law, and the Psalms as later than both. For these propositions, which were the main pillars of my conception of Hebrew history, were as yet rather a distant vision than a solid fabric." He tells us he hit upon this idea in his study of the legislation of Israel in hope of finding the thread of Ariadne, which might guide him out of the labyrinth of the current hypotheses into the daylight of a psychologically possible process of development of the people of Israel. While in his youth much effort was wasted in explaining miracles as natural occurrences, the most unnatural miracles were left unexplained, viz. the commencement of Israel's religious education with the developed Levitical ritual; the unacquaintance with it displayed by the greatest prophets, such as Samuel and Elijah; the censure pronounced by the Books of Kings on what those prophets approved by their example, and so on. Such difficulties as these, felt by Reuss when quite a young man, but which were overlooked by others, or explained away, led him to the bold solution which overthrew the whole mass of current hypotheses, and opened fresh channels for Old Testament criticism. On the other hand, he himself confesses that he was at first guilty of the same want of thoroughness as Graf (see above, p. 258), and that it was the works of others, especially of Kayser and Kuenen, which helped him logically to work out his present theory. The grounds of this theory are most fully given in the introduction to his book, *L'histoire sainte et la loi* (1879). He shows first negatively, by a thorough literary and historical examination, the impossibility of regarding the Mosaic traditions as historical truth; he then tries to find a secure starting-point for positive criticism, and discovers it in Deuteronomy. This book, discovered under Josiah, and no doubt composed not long before, is unacquainted with the most important regulations of the priestly (Sinaitic) legislation, and must therefore be earlier in date; on the other hand, it shows an acquaintance with the Decalogue and the Book of Covenants (Exod. xx.–xxiii.), as well as with the Jahvistic historical narrative. This "national epic of Israel" is therefore the earliest portion of the Pentateuch, dating from the ninth century B.C. With this was united, shortly before the Exile, the only book of laws then in existence, the so-called Deuteronomy, by the insertion of the introductory and closing chapters. It was not till after the Exile that the priestly legislation was produced, by following out the indications given by Ezekiel; it was codified by Ezra in Palestine, and at first promulgated as an independent book of laws. Finally, in Ezra's school, it was incorporated in the pre-exilic Jahvistic-Deuteronomic work, and now forms the larger portion of the middle books of the Pentateuch. On the basis of this criticism of the literature, Reuss has, in his *Geschichte des Alten Testaments*, described the evolution of the religious and political life of the people of Israel, from its historical commencement to the destruction of Jerusalem, in four sections, viz. the ages of the Heroes, the Prophets, the Priests, and the Scribes.

In order to give the reader a general idea of the history of Israel as it takes shape under these critical principles, it seems most suitable to take as my basis Wellhausen's short sketch, first contributed to the *Encyclopædia Britannica*, and then published by him in a somewhat enlarged German edition (1884) in the first number of his *Skizzen und Vorarbeiten*. It seems to me to contain a good summary of the conclusions as to which critics of the school of Reuss and Graf are agreed, and which may now perhaps be regarded as the certain result of the most recent critical labours; this of course does not exclude uncertainty on many questions of detail, and difference of opinion among critics even of this same school. This, however, rather affects unimportant questions, the solution of which may be interesting to specialists, but does not deeply concern the history of theology.

Long before the Hebrew tribes were united into one political community, Wellhausen tells us, they had a certain internal unity, going back to the time of Moses, and apparently due to Moses himself. The basis on which Israel's sense of national unity at all times rested was the belief that Jahve was the God of Israel, and Israel the people of Jahve. Moses did not invent this belief, but he succeeded in making it the foundation of the nation and its history. Necessity compelled a number of related families to quit their ordinary mode of life, and this gave him his opportunity. He undertook to lead them; he had faith in the result, and the result justified him. But the success of the undertaking, of which he was the moving spirit, was no merit of his. A tremendous occurrence, independent of him, and not even capable of being foreseen in the darkness of the future, concurred in a startling manner with his purpose; One whom wind and sea obey placed His power at his command. Behind him there stood a higher Power, whose spirit worked in him, and whose arm acted for him—not for his own good, but for that of the people. It was Jahve. Jahve was the moving, provident force in the history which the elements of the nation, collected by necessity, passed through together, and in which they gained the beginning of a real national consciousness. Moses was instrumental in producing this consciousness; he also succeeded further in keeping it alive and developing it. The extraordinary circumstances which had given the first impulse to the formation of the new nation still continued, and under their pressure the creation of Israel went on. The authority Moses had gained by his deeds naturally gave him the position of the judge of the people. By giving his judicial sentences in the name of Jahve, and connecting this function with his sanctuary, he established a fixed centre for traditions of justice, and began a *thora* in Israel, which imparted to the sense of nationality and to the idea of God a positive ideal content. Jahve was now not simply the God of Israel, but as such also the God of law and righteousness, the basis, motive, and unexpressed content of the national conscience. From that time forth Jahve continued to raise up men who were moved by the spirit to place themselves at the people's head; in them his own leadership took bodily shape. He marched among the warriors of the levy, and their enthusiasm marked his presence. Finally Jahve decided from heaven the struggle carried on on earth. He was always on the side of Israel; his interest was limited to Israel, although his power—being God—extended far beyond its borders. Thus Jahve was in truth a living God, but the tokens of his activity in the great crises of the history were separated by long pauses. His mode of working bore some resemblance to thunder; it was more suitable for extraordinary occasions than for daily domestic use. Still even in the intervals of quiet it did not altogether cease. As human leaders do not altogether lose in peace the influence gained in war, so was it with Jahve.

The ark of the covenant, an idol intended primarily for the life of soldiers in camps and on marches, continued also in peace, as the sign of Jahve's presence, to be the centre of his worship. And with the ritual was closely connected, both in the time of Moses and later, the sacred administration of justice, the *thora*. In all difficult cases inquiry was made of the mouth of Jahve, counsel being sought of the priests, who gave sentence in the name of Jahve,—either according to their own knowledge of his will, or according to a decision of the lot,—and possessed simply moral authority. The priestly *thora* was an institution wholly unconnected with and prior to political arrangements; it existed before the State, and constituted one of its invisible fundamental pillars. War and law were religion before they were changed into compulsion and civil order; this is the real meaning of the so-called theocracy. A regular state, with specific sanctity, was by no means built up by Moses on the principle, "Jahve the God of Israel;" and after him the old patriarchal constitution of families and clans, the elders of which were leaders in war and judges in peace, continued to exist. Only when the whole nation had some great special work to perform was an appeal made to Jahve as the last and extraordinary resource. The theocracy may be said to have arisen to supply the defects of anarchy. Out of the religious consciousness of nationality grew the State, the sanctity of which depended precisely on the fact that it arose as an ideal of religion, to be realized in conflict with indolence and selfishness. "Jahve the God of Israel" accordingly meant that national duties, both internal and external, were conceived as sacred. It did not mean at all that the almighty Creator of heaven and earth had first made a covenant only with this single people, that they might know and worship him. Jahve was not at first the God of the whole world, who then became the God of Israel; but he was originally simply the God of Israel, and then became much later the God of the world. In an enlightened idea of God, Moses would have given the Israelites a stone instead of bread; most probably he left them to think as their fathers had thought about the nature of Jahve in itself, irrespective of his relation to men. With speculative truths, for which there was then no demand whatever, he did not concern himself, but only with practical questions, definitely and necessarily brought before him by the time. The religious starting-point of the history of Israel is distinguished, not by its marked novelty, but by its normal character. In all ancient nations we find the gods brought into relation with national officers, and religion used as a motive power of law and custom ; but in none with such purity and force as in the case of the Israelites. Whatever Jahve's real nature may have been— the God of thunder, or whatever he was,—it retreated more and more into the background as something secret and transcendent, and no questions were asked concerning it. The whole emphasis was laid on his action in the world of men, whose aims he made his own. Religion did not call men to participate in the life of God, but, on the contrary, God in the life of men ; but in this it did not really fetter but free human life. The so-called particularism of the idea of God, the limitation of Jahve's interest to the affairs of Israel, was the real strength of this religion ; it liberated it from the fruitless play of mythology, and facilitated its application to moral duties, which are always first presented and fulfilled only in definite circles. As the God of the nation, Jahve became the God of law and righteousness, and as such grew to be the highest, and finally the sole power in heaven and earth.—After the settlement of the Hebrews in Canaan, the higher civilization of settled life was accompanied by a gradual weakening of their national and religious consciousness. In proportion as Israel coalesced with the conquered country, the gods of the two nations coalesced also, and then arose a syncretism of Jahve with Baal, which lasted on into the time of the prophet Hosea. But the course of national history fanned the smouldering coals into a blaze. The Philistines aroused Israel and Jahve from their slumber. In the struggle against them was founded Saul's kingdom ; and his more fortunate successor, David, became the founder of the united Israelite kingdom, whose military power remained always the proudest memory of the nation. Later Jewish tradition, however, was wrong in making him a Levitical saint and pious psalmist. Under Solomon the floodgates were opened to Oriental culture in the wider and higher sense ; closer intercourse with foreign lands widened the people's intellectual horizon, and at the same time deepened the sense of its peculiarity. His introduction of Phœnician and Egyptian institutions into the worship of Jahve might offend the true old Israelites of his time, but his temple became afterwards of great importance to the religion. The division of the kingdom under Rehoboam was caused both by the discontent at the innovations and strict discipline of Solomon's government, and also by the jealousy of the tribe of Joseph, which had always been the natural rival of the tribe of Judah favoured by David. Religion was at that time no obstacle to the separation, as the temple services in Jerusalem had not yet become exclusive, the worship instituted by Jeroboam at Bethel and Dan being equally legitimate; there were images in both places, and indeed wherever there was a sanctuary. There was in general no difference in the religious and spiritual life of the two kingdoms, save that religious movements generally first originated in Israel. A new stage in the history of religion began with the appearance of the prophet Elijah, the most striking heroic figure in the Bible, towering solitary above his time, and whose memory was preserved by legend and not by history. When Jahve had thus founded the nation and kingdom, primarily by its struggle with external foes, he commenced an attack, within the nation and in the spiritual sphere, upon the foreign elements which had been hitherto admitted without much opposition. Ahab's erection of a temple for the Tyrian Baal in Samaria was the occasion of Elijah's contention against the Baal cultus generally, and against the syncretism between Baal and Jahve, from which very few in Israel had kept free. For Elijah there were not several Powers with equal claims and equally worthy of worship, but everywhere only *one* holy and mighty Being, revealed, not like Baal in the life of nature, but like Jahve in the ethical demands of the spirit; the idea of God began in individual men to rise above national limitation.—In the flourishing period of the Northern kingdom, under Jeroboam II., Hebrew literature began. The religious lyrics, telling of the mighty deeds of God through and for Israel, which were originally handed down by word of mouth, were now committed to writing and collected; thus arose the "Book of the Wars of Jahve" and the "Book of the Upright," the oldest Hebrew histories. The next step was to write history in prose, making use of documents or family recollections. The books of Judges, Samuel, and Kings contain a considerable part of these ancient historical writings. At the same time certain collections of judicial maxims and decisions of the priests were written down, of which we have an example in the so-called "Book of the Covenants" (Exod. xxi., xxii.). A little later, perhaps, were recorded the legends of the Patriarchs and of the earliest times, which cannot have had a very early origin. When in this way a literary age had arisen, the prophets also began to write down their speeches.—With the growth of civilization and national prosperity, worship also became more stately than in the simple times of antiquity. This was also the channel by which heathenism could, and did again and again, make its way into the worship of Jahve; especially was this the case with the private sanctuaries, so that kings and prophets emphatically insisted on the publicity of worship, which provided a corrective for the worst excesses. The priests, moreover, did not merely offer sacrifices, but were also the advisers and instructors of the people, although these more important duties were neglected in comparison with the more lucrative ones connected with the sacrifices. The belief of the nation was the simplest possible : Jahve is the God of Israel, Israel's helper in need, the judge to secure him justice against his enemies. But Jahve's work was seen, not in the fate of individuals, but in that of clans and nations. Rarely has history so powerfully touched the chords of a nation's heart ; rarely has it been to this extent regarded as the effect of the divine action, to which human action can only inquiringly adapt itself, or prayerfully submit. Events were miracles and signs, chance the pointing finger of a higher hand. This way of looking at history was preserved from triviality because the history of a people, not of individuals, was the object of attention. The faith of men thus gained an emotional vividness, the conception of God a magnificent reality. Seers and prophets saw by second sight what Jahve did, but there was no theology which coolly speculated about him. Men did not seek to know his principles of action, but his immediate intention, in order to act accordingly. The living proof of actual experience was compatible with great freedom of expression ; the reality of experience did not fear even contradictions. Jahve had incalculable moods; he caused his face to shine, and he was wroth, it was not known why ; he created good and evil, punished sin and tempted to sin. Satan had not then robbed him of some of his attributes. In spite of all this, Israel did not doubt him. On the whole, times had hitherto been prosperous ; the disharmony between external experience and faith had not become so painful as to demand a reconciliation. The case was different when the great Assyrian power began to stretch out its arms towards Israel.—In anticipation of the coming troubles, the prophet Amos made his appearance, the first and purest representative of a new phase of prophecy. While all the minor nations trembled before the approach of the eastern conqueror, the Israelite prophets alone were neither surprised nor dismayed, but in advance solved the terrible problem history presented. They enlarged religion so as to embrace the conception of the world, which had proved fatal to other religions, before it had really become part of the profane consciousness of the people. Where others saw the ruin of what was most holy, they saw the triumph of Jahve over appearances and vain beliefs. Whatever might fall, what was valuable remained firm. The very time they lived in became for them the unfolding story of a divine drama, the course of which they watched with prophetic foresight and intelligence. Everywhere the same laws, everywhere the same goal of development. The nations are the actors, Israel the hero, and Jahve the poet of the tragedy. The prophets, of the line of whom Amos was the first, did not proclaim a new God, but they preached that the God of Israel was primarily and above all the God of righteousness, and Israel's God only in so far as Israel satisfied his righteous demands. They therefore reversed the traditional order of the two fundamental articles of faith. This delivered Jahve from the danger of coming into collision with the world, and suffering shipwreck; the sovereignty of right extended further than the might of the Assyrians. Thus an historical contingency enabled moral convictions to break through the limitations of the narrow faith in which they had grown to maturity, and so to bring about an advance in the knowledge of God. This is the so-called ethical monotheism of the prophets; they believed in the moral order of the world, in the unfailing validity of righteousness as the supreme law for the whole world. From this point of view Israel's prerogative seems to be annulled, and Amos, who states the new doctrine with the greatest abruptness and regardlessness of consequences, sometimes verges upon the denial of it; he calls Jahve the God of hosts, *i.e.* of the world, but not the God of Israel. Still, the special relation of Jahve to Israel was not doubted by the prophets; they only made its condition a moral instead of a physical one. They emphasised the idea—not as yet the name—of the Covenant and the corresponding idea of the Law, and made these the basis of religion. Nevertheless, their attention was directed, not as yet to the righteousness of the individual and the heart, but to national uprightness and social action. The negative result of their ethical monotheism was their attack on ritual, so far as it was regarded as a means of purchasing the favour of God without moral worth. Above all, the prophets attacked the sensuous rites connected with worship as a heathenish service of Baal. The prophets were taught by history to know the awful severity of the righteousness of Jahve; they are the founders of the religion of the Law. This is what constitutes their importance, not their being the forerunners of the gospel. Least of all are they the latter on account of their Messianic prophecies. In them they really fall back upon the patriotic but illusive hopes of the common people, and the "false prophets," whom they on other grounds assail. This was the proof of the insufficiency of their principle. In view of the facts and necessities of history, the position of the prophets inevitably led them to transcend the limits of their nation and the world. It was due to the prophets that the fall of Samaria did not injure but strengthened the religion of Jahve; they saved the faith by destroying the illusion; they also immortalised Israel by not involving Jahve in the ruin of the nation.—After the fall of Samaria, the kingdom of Judah, which had hitherto politically and religiously followed in the wake of the northern kingdom, succeeded to its position. The prophet Isaiah was the means of saving it from immediately sharing the fate of the northern kingdom, by being involved in the foreign politics of the time, and of securing for it a century of quiet and prosperous development. He despised politics, and yet understood them better than the short-sighted, practical politicians of his day; he took in at a glance the confusion of the time, for he stood outside and above it. A magnificent faith in the victorious, universal sovereignty of Jahve gave him courage and discretion amid the storms of the time. While the great military powers of the world threatened to stamp out Jerusalem, he beheld in spirit the time when the great nations should come to pay homage in the city of Jahve, and truth go forth from Zion. Truth never expressed its confidence in itself with greater assurance of victory. But this joyful confidence was mingled with tragic resignation. Isaiah recognised the inevitableness of heavy judgments, to which the greater part of the nation would succumb, and only a small remnant be spared as a sacred seed for the future. And to prepare this remnant to realise the ideal of a people of God, first on a small scale, he considered to be the most pressing duty of the age. The prophets thus entered on the path of practical reform, beginning with the purification of worship. Isaiah energetically resumed the attack on the worship of images, which Hosea had previously derided, and obtained its actual abolition under King Hezekiah. But the popular religion offered so stout a resistance to this reform that Hezekiah's son Manasseh had to comply with it in the restitution of ritualistic superstitions, and even permit its increase by the adoption of all kinds of heathen rites and forms. The counter-reformation aped in bloody fanaticism the sacred zeal of the prophets, children were sacrificed in honour of Jahve-Moloch in the valley of Gehenna. This period, in which the antithesis between ritualistic bigotry and pure morality reached its acutest form, witnessed the origin of the powerful warnings of the prophet Micah, and perhaps also the commands of the Decalogue, which concerned ritual only negatively by the command to abstain from idols, and constituted moral goodness the sole content of the divine Will, quite on the lines of Micah vi. 6–8.—A short but very fruitful triumph was obtained by the prophetic efforts at reform under King Josiah. One of their results was the Book of Deuteronomy, supplementing the Decalogue by an actual national code of laws, based chiefly on a modification of ancient legal maxims. It was the first book of Law and Covenant, the comprehensive programme of a reorganisation of the theocracy according to the ideals of the prophets. Here is shown more plainly than anywhere else that Prophets and Law are not opposed to each other, but are identical and related as cause and effect. Nowhere is the fundamental thought of the prophets expressed more clearly than in Deuteronomy, that Jahve demands nothing for himself, but regards and demands justice between man and man as the true religion, and that his Will is not hidden high above us or far off from us, but is to be found in the sphere of moral conduct known and understood by all. The most important regulation regarding ritual in this code was the centralisation of the worship of Jahve in Jerusalem, and the abolition of all other sanctuaries. The motive of this radical innovation was the consistent carrying out of the pure monotheistic religion, and opposition to the heathenish naturalism, which had taken such firm root in the idolatry of the high-places that it could only be exterminated by the abolition of the latter. The limitation of the worship of Jahve to Jerusalem was the popular and practical form of the prophetic monotheism; but the subsidiary consequence of this measure, and one not intended by the legislator, was to strengthen the hierarchy at Jerusalem. Thus the first practical consequence of the prophetic efforts at reform contained the germ of the subsequent degeneration of their work.—The theocratic zeal aroused in the people for Law and temple appeared to all to be a pledge of lasting prosperity. Only one man was not deceived by the external appearance, the prophet Jeremiah. In warning words he pointed those who thought themselves secure to the fate of Shiloh and the Ephraimites; he was rewarded with scorn and persecution. The patriotic fanaticism, which would not learn either from Jeremiah or the course of history itself, led to the destruction of Jerusalem, and the carrying away of the people into the Babylonian captivity. Jeremiah, who had foreseen this, did not despair, but turned his eyes towards a better future for religion and his people. In his hopeless struggle with popular infatuation and obstinacy he had come to see that the real want was a new heart, which could be created by no teaching and no form of worship, but could only be given by God to individual men. The endeavour to make religion individual and inward was the new tendency which sprang out of the decline of the nation, and was prefigured in the individualistic piety of the last and greatest of the prophets, Jeremiah. In place of the nation he was himself the subject of religion; he only, not Israel, had fellowship with Jahve. He knew that the future and eternity depended upon him, for the nation was not eternal, but the truth which the nation despised, and of which he was certain.—The small Jewish colony that returned from the exile was no longer a State, but only a religious community. The means for its organisation could only be supplied by the temple service and the priesthood of Jerusalem. The hierocracy, for which even at the beginning of the Exile Ezekiel had begun to prepare, was now inevitably realised. The high-priest, with the nobility of the priests, beside whom the common Levites sank to mere temple servants, became the centre and rulers of the community. But in the confusion of the next decades the religious spirit threatened to die out, and the Jewish colony to perish by its mixture with the semi-heathenism of the inhabitants of the country. Then came, under Ezra, a new reinforcement of Jews from Babylon, who aroused afresh in the colony in Palestine the spirit of strict loyalty and the exclusiveness of the Jewish nature towards everything not Jewish, which had been more fully developed in a foreign land. The introduction of Ezra's priestly code laid the foundation of the Judaism of later times. This post-Deuteronomic legislation deals, not with a nation, but with a community, and regulates chiefly the worship. Political matters are left out, as they concern the foreign government. The constitution of the community is assumed to be the hierocracy. The head of the worship is the head of the whole community; the high-priest takes the place also of the king. The other priests are officially his subordinates, as the bishops are subordinate to the pope. They are distinguished from the Levites, the lowest rank of the clergy, not only by their office, but also by their noble birth. In this clerical organisation the government of holiness is outwardly realised. Inwardly the ideal of holiness governs life by a net of ceremonies and observances which separate the Jew from the man. The renovated ritual of the Temple, augmented by fresh sacrificial rites, had essentially the same object; it provided a fixed and united centre for the new theocracy, and formed a protecting shell around the faith and customs of the Fathers for the preservation of ethical monotheism until it could become the common property of the world.—Underneath this husk of ceremonial precepts the kernel of prophetic religion did not altogether die. On the contrary, the individualisation of piety made further progress. Men began to reflect upon religion. The so-called "Wisdom" was evolved, of which we have literary remains in the Book of Job, in the Proverbs of Solomon and of the son of Sirach, and in Ecclesiastes. And that reflection was not injurious to depth of feeling, but that, on the contrary, individualism tended to make religion a matter of the heart, is shown by the Psalms, which all belong to this period. It was an immense advance that the devout Hebrew became assured of his communion with God, as he does in many Psalms, by inward experience, and thus dared to trust to himself in his religious relations. This was a subsidiary product of prophetism, but of equal importance with its chief product, the Law ; it was the universalisation of the personal experience which the prophets, while outwardly unsuccessful, had had in themselves of the inward saving power of truth. While Judaism in the following centuries was petrified under the influence of the externality of ceremonial law, the germ of a nobler future lived on in the depths of inward feeling such as occasionally finds its expression in the "Wisdom" books and the Psalms. The gospel developed these hidden impulses of the Old Testament, while it protested against the dominant tendency of Judaism. And the religious individualism of the gospel remains the salt of the earth.

I hope I have not wearied the reader with this excerpt from Wellhausen's sketch of the history of Israel. Its insertion was necessary, inasmuch as it is possible to properly estimate the great importance of the Old Testament criticism of to-day only by a comparison of this new conception of Israelite history with the earlier traditional one. There we had from beginning to end a series of riddles, of psychological and historical puzzles ; here everything is comprehensible, we have a clear development, analogous to the rest of history, the external history of the nation and the internal history of its religious consciousness in constant accord and fruitful interaction ; and though not an unbroken advance in a straight line of the whole people, still a laborious struggle of the representatives of the higher truth with the stolid masses, a struggle in which success and defeat succeed each other in dramatic alternation, and even failure only serves to aid the evolution of the idea itself in ever greater purity from its original integuments. This is human history, full of marvels and of Divine revelation, but nowhere interrupted by miracle or by sudden, unaccountable transitions.

So bold an innovation necessarily provoked considerable opposition. This was often expressly, and perhaps still oftener silently, directed against what seems to us precisely the advantage of this new theory, viz. the substitution of a humanly comprehensible development for mysterious miracles and revelations. Since this opposition rests on dogmatic assumptions lying outside history, it cannot determine the course of the historian. Serious consideration, on the other hand, is due to such objections as have been raised by learned, dogmatically unbiassed, Old Testament scholars, and are based on scientific research. Specially important, in this connection, are Ewald's eminent scholars: Dillmann, Schrader, and Nöldeke; further, Riehm, Delitzsch, Strack, Bredenkamp, Ryssel, Curtiss, Finsler, König, Kittel, and others. I cannot here enter on the various, often conflicting, views of these scholars as to the composition of the Pentateuch. Their chief objections to the theory of Reuss and Graf may be summarised as follows: From the fact that in a given historical period we find no traces of the observance of a law, we cannot forthwith infer the non-existence of the law at that time, since it is possible for laws to be in existence long before they come to be observed in practice. Further, the difference between the prophets and Deuteronomy on the one hand, and the priestly code on the other, is exaggerated by the critics; some variations may be explained by the difference in the points of view and objects aimed at. The view that the prophets and the Deuteronomist had no acquaintance with the priestly code must be qualified, for both the prophets and Deuteronomy presuppose the existence of a *thora* relating to the ritual.[1] The distinction between priests and Levites was not first introduced by Ezekiel, but was presupposed by him as already long in existence. Finally, the chief objection is, that the priestly code itself contains several directions which cannot be explained from the time of Ezra, but point to a very early, certainly pre-Deuteronomic date. Also the linguistic peculiarities of the priestly code present indications of an early period, not that after the exile, and in part even point to the earliest period of Hebrew literature.

The advocates of the Reuss-Graf theory have not been slow to answer these objections. Kayser, in his essays on the present position of the question of the Pentateuch,[2] has subjected them to an examination, the conclusion of which is that the three lines of attack made by Old Testament scholars on Graf's theory have been repelled. "The theory has maintained all its positions without giving way an inch. When the history of ritual has shown that the laws of the Elohistic book were first promulgated in the time of Ezra; when the history of literature makes it plain that the book was unknown

---

[1] This is also maintained by Vatke in his posthumous Introduction to the Old Testament (1887), though without renouncing the main principle of his early book—*The Prophets before the Law.*
[2] *Jahrb. für prot. Theol.,* vii. 2–4 Heft.

to all previous writers, and can only be properly understood by a reference to Ezekiel's mode of thought; when, finally, the history of language is compelled against its will to show that the book bears all the characteristics of this time,—then what further proof can we possibly expect of its really belonging to it? Until further evidence is forthcoming, we shall be justified in regarding Graf's theory as the best substantiated and alone satisfactory explanation of the Pentateuch." Still even the adherents of this theory admit that various questions of detail have still to be answered. It is acknowledged that the pre-Deuteronomic historical book, even after the removal of the priestly code, is derived from two sources, a Jahvistic and an Elohistic one; as to the mutual relation of which opinions are still quite divided. In Deuteronomy it is doubtful whether the introductory and concluding chapters come from the author of the book himself, or whether they were added by a later hand, for the purpose of connecting it with the earlier historical work. Of still greater importance is the question whether the law promulgated by Ezra was the whole of the Pentateuch, or only the main contents of the priestly code, which was afterwards incorporated by the disciples of Ezra in the earlier work, perhaps enlarged by the legal additions and historical narratives.

The most recent thorough investigation of all these questions, including a consideration of antagonistic views, is given by Kuenen in his *Historisch-kritische Einleitung in die Bücher des alten Testaments hinsichtlich ihrer Entstehung und Sammlung* (1885, German trans. by Weber, 1887; English by Wicksteed, 1887). He comes to the conclusion that in the year of the reforms of Ezra and Nehemiah (444 B.C.), the Deuteronomic-prophetic sacred history and the priestly legislative historical book were still separate, and that the two were first combined to form the Hexateuch in the course of the fifth century by the Sopherim of the school of Ezra; that the text of the Hexateuch even then underwent numerous revisions during a considerable period, of which traces remain in the discrepancies between the three recensions (textus receptus, Samaritan Pentateuch and the Alexandrine translation). Of further advocates of this theory, we may here mention Stade (*Geschichte Israels*, incomplete), Budde (*Die biblische Urgeschichte*, 1883), Smend (*Commentar zu Ezechiel*), Duhm (*Theologie der Propheten*, 1875), Schultz (*Alttestamentliche Theologie*, 2nd ed., 1878).

CHAPTER III.

ECCLESIASTICAL HISTORY AND THE HISTORY OF DOGMA.

THE way in which ecclesiastical history is written is always largely determined by dogmatic or philosophical theology. The extent and character of his own comprehension of Christianity guides the ecclesiastical historian in his view of the Church's past and in his judgment of the action of the historical personages and the growth of the institutions, customs, and doctrines of the Church. Again, on the other hand, a comprehension of the history of the Church is a factor in the formation of a dogmatical view of the nature of Christianity, and of the significance of its traditions in the doctrine and customs of the Church. Hence an account of the development of theology in our century is bound to include works on ecclesiastical history, so far at least as the most important of them are typical of a definite tendency or stage of theological knowledge.

During the flourishing period of Rationalistic theology, at the end of the last and beginning of this century, church history was written on the pragmatic method, of which the best known exponents were SPITTLER and PLANCK, both Swabians by birth, and invited from Tübingen to Göttingen, where they entered on long and successful careers both as teachers and authors. Spittler's *Grundriss der Geschichte der christl. Kirche* (1782), is written from the point of view of the Aufklärung, in order to show how the human mind had risen through the revolutions of eighteen centuries to its present freedom in religious matters. The book is mainly descriptive of the secular-political side of the Church; its religious and theological side being cast into the background. Like Gottfried Arnold, Spittler sympathised with the heretics in their opposition to the orthodox Church; but this sympathy was not due in Spittler, as in Arnold, to religious mysticism, but to the dogmatic indifferentism of the Aufklärung, to which the nature of Christianity as religion had become problematic and incomprehensible. Since Christian history is thus from the beginning deprived of any guiding principle, it is impossible to discover any theological coherence in it, and it comes to be "one long lamentation over the weakness and corruption of the human mind," which, however, is still gradually improved by the happy dispensations of Providence, which from time to time, by the sending of wise men, brings about a change for the better. The persons and phenomena of history are not explained and judged according to the principles and motives of their own time, but all alike are estimated by the standard of the modes of thought of the Aufklärung, and anything not agreeing with it is forthwith condemned as stupidity, phantasy, and error.

More moderate in tone, but written essentially on the same pragmatic method, are Planck's works, *Geschichte der Entstellung, der Veränderungen und der Bildung unseres protestantischen Lehrbegriffs von Anfang der Reformation bis zur Einführung der Concordienformel* (6 vols., 1781–1800), and *Geschichte der christlich-kirchlichen Gesellschaftsverfassung* (5 vols. 1803–1809). The excellence of these works consists in the exactness of the examination of authorities, the careful regard of the various concurring circumstances, external relations, and inward inclinations conditioning actions, and the sagacity in the discovery and combination of motives, thus producing a lifelike and vivid picture of historical events. But the weak side of this "psychological pragmatism" is also specially evident in Planck: he tries to explain everything that happens by the accidental subjective motives of individual persons, and fails to understand the deeper causes lying in the general ideas and prevailing tendencies of an age. The subjectivism of the Aufklärung, which isolates and lays stress on the individual, with his peculiar nature and arbitrary will, is reflected in this treatment of history, which substitutes for the great objective forces of human society the trivial play of accident and the caprice of individuals. And since the psychological motives of men, especially of those living in the past, can never be known with certainty, but at most only conjectured, this pragmatism, which aims at explaining all events by men's subjective motives, leads unavoidably to the ascription of motives really quite foreign to the actors. We often get the impression that the astute aims and plans described by the historian are rather an invention of his own than a part of the history itself. With this principle of the Aufklärung is further connected the incapacity to enter, impartially and sympathetically, into the modes of thought and the religious interests and wants of the past. Such phenomena as the papacy, scholasticism, and mysticism, find as little favour in the eyes of Planck as of Spittler. That these things were in their time the necessary and therefore legitimate expressions of the spirit of religious society, is a fact the subjective understanding of the Aufklärung cannot comprehend, but it regards them categorically as lamentable errors, fanaticisms, or even frauds. From this point of view the historian fails to perceive the objective rationality of history, the development of mind through various stages, and the functions of individuals foreign to himself, in whom the common spirit of their time found a peculiar and forcible expression.

Among Planck's auditors from 1808–10 was AUGUST NEANDER, who had shortly before given up Judaism for Christianity, and under the influence of Schleiermacher's *Reden* had resolved to study theology, in order, as he confessed to a friend, to "make war for ever on the common understanding, which gets further and further away from the eternal centre of all being, the Divine." This confession sufficiently shows how different was the spirit of the scholar from that of his master; nevertheless Neander was first led by Planck to study the sources of ecclesiastical history, though with very different results in his case. When, in 1813, Neander was called to a chair in the newly founded University of Berlin, he became, after Schleiermacher, the most important representative of the new theology, which by its profounder appreciation of the religious life gave him new insight into early Church history. In quick succession he published a series of monographs, on Julian and his Age, on St. Bernhard, Chrysostom, Tertullian, the Gnostic Systems, and Memorials from the history of Christianity, and the Christian life; then his *Allgemeine Geschichte der christlichen Religion u. Kirche* (10 vols., 1826–45). During its publication appeared, as an independent supplement, *Die Geschichte der Pflanzung und Leitung der christlichen Kirche durch die Apostel* (2 vols., 1832), and *Das Leben Jesu* (1837). His departure from the earlier method of writing Church history was described by Neander himself in the preface to the 2nd ed. of his St. Bernard as follows: "A new life of faith had arisen, which began to revivify theological science also. This gave us the impulse to trace the stream of Christian life in former centuries, and lovingly to include everything Christian. A shallow Aufklärung, without mind or heart, had, in its conceit and boastful poverty, taught us to despise what was greatest and noblest in former centuries; but now this had been condemned alike by life and science. An unhistorical age had given way to new insight into history and to a new desire sympathetically to understand it, and thoroughly comprehend the characteristic individuality of historical phenomena." Neander's chief aim was everywhere to understand what was individual in history. In the principal figures of ecclesiastical history he tried to depict the representative tendencies of each age, and also the types of the essential tendencies of human nature generally. His guiding principle in treating both of the history and of the present condition of the Church was—that Christianity has room for the various tendencies of human nature, and aims at permeating and glorifying them all; that according to the divine plan these various tendencies are to occur successively and simultaneously and to counterbalance each other, so that the freedom and variety of the development of the spiritual life ought not to be forced into a single dogmatic form. This was the source of his sympathetic appreciation of the most different historical characters, of gnostics and mystics, of saints and heretics, not even excepting the apostate Julian, in whom he admired the pathos of phantastic religious enthusiasm even in its heathen garb. Hence also his generous tolerance of tendencies in his own time with which he could not sympathise (*e.g.* that of his teacher Planck), his championship of the freedom of scientific teaching, even on behalf of Rationalistic opponents, such as the Halle professors, Gesenius and Wegscheider, when denounced to the government by Hengstenberg. In one direction only Neander failed to exercise his usual tolerance, viz. towards the Hegelian school and the Tübingen criticism. This was so distasteful to him that in his judgment of it he became unjust and bitter—a sign of the consciousness of having before him a scientific movement, not only opposed, but superior to his own. Doubtless that too was incomplete, and needed to be supplemented by Neander; but it is equally certain that it was strong just where Neander was weak. Neander divided history into a series of separate pictures, drawn with the loving hand of a master as edifying and instructive examples; but he failed to grasp the connection between phenomena, or the general ideas which dominate each age and give to it its special character, or the regularity of the general development of the religious spirit in the Church. His was too much an emotional nature, and his theology was too much governed by the subjective point of view of Romanticism for him to be able to do justice to the importance of ideas in religion and to the mental conflict in the different movements of thought in the Church. The great dramatic forces of history were hidden from him by the lyrical emotions of single individuals. The same preponderance of emotion in his nature prevented him from fully appreciating historic characters of marked individuality. His own generous heart enabled him indeed sympathetically to study the character of historical persons, but he always saw in them mainly those features which were in accordance with his own feelings; the corners and angularities, in which the peculiarities of character find their most significant expression, he smoothed down, and idealised his heroes into copies, more or less, of his own individuality. This was the opposite error to that of the Rationalistic method; in the latter a want of sympathetic appreciation had led to the misrepresentation and caricature of the figures of history, but in Neander these figures become dim ideal forms, like stars hard to distinguish in the surrounding mist. Finally, Neander's pectoral theology involved a serious lack of historical criticism. This failing was indeed shared by almost all Romanticists; as they had grown tired of the sole sovereignty of the understanding, the understanding was henceforth to have no authority at all, and clear rational investigation be doomed to silence, even in its proper province—historical criticism. Too much influenced by the modern historical spirit consistently to exclude criticism on principle, and yet too much of an emotional theologian to make thorough-going use of it where it assailed treasured and beautiful traditions, Neander never freed himself from that hesitation and want of thoroughness which strikes us so painfully in his *Life of Jesus*.[1] Neander, moreover, regarded miracles, in the proper sense, as possible, not only in Biblical times, but down to the third century. If so late, why should they not be accepted much later, or throughout all history? Because on that supposition

---

[1] Comp. *ante*, p. 219.

the scientific weakness of a supernaturalistic treatment of history of such a kind would be much more strange and intolerable than it actually is in Neander.

Closely allied to Neander, but of a more independent and versatile mind, is the ecclesiastical historian, CARL HASE. His strength likewise lies mainly in the loving study and delicate, subtle description of individual phenomena in history. His pictures of mediæval saints (*Franz von Assisi, Katerina von Siena*), and of *neue Propheten* (*Die Jungfrau von Orleans, Savonarola, Thomas Münzer*) are both in form and matter model monographs, and evince a power of sympathetically entering into peculiar phases of religious life such as was possessed in an equal degree only by Neander. But Hase's attitude towards the figures of history is more independent than Neander's; he does not emphasise merely those sides of a character which appeal to himself, but contrives, in a few brief, pregnant lines, to sketch a clear and complete objective picture of it. He does not, like Neander, seek for what is edifying in the religious life of men and nations, but for what is characteristic; so that some details may be far from edifying, for the simple reason that the actors in history are men, and often caricature what is sublime. In his *Lehrbuch der Kirchengeschichte* (1 ed., 1834, now 11th ed.), Hase has succeeded in compressing an unusually large amount of material into the smallest possible space without anywhere creating the impression of a dry skeleton, but he makes "the wealth of life meeting us in the original monuments of each age reveal itself even in the most compressed outline." This was possible only to an historian who combined a mastery of style, formed on classic models, such as is possessed by few scholars, with a happy instinct in separating the essential from the unessential. "Only what has at some time truly lived and thereby become immortal, by representing a ray of the Christian spirit, forms part of history, which is a history of the living and not of the dead." This excellent principle, enunciated in his preface, is adhered to by Hase throughout his work. By throwing overboard much of the worthless cargo usually carried by the pedantry of scholars, he found room, in the small compass of a single volume, for matter hitherto omitted or insufficiently treated in Church histories, such as the religions of the heathen nations with which Christianity came into contact, or the history of ecclesiastical art. Although the strongest point of

Hase's Church History is its artistic presentation of a wealth of material, he gives us also from the stores of his wide historical knowledge, general reflections, birds-eye views, and main points of observation, as well as his personal verdicts on men and things. With the kindly tolerance which can be just to other points of view, he combines a courageous honesty which shows the dark as well as the bright side of his own Church, and even of the period of the Reformation, which to other Protestant historians is generally too sacred to be freely criticised. This incorruptible impartiality in judgment is a merit of Hase's history all the more valuable from its rareness among our theologians. In the year 1885, the aged historian published the first volume of a Church History, to be completed in three volumes, in which the brief outlines and indications of his text-book are further expanded for educated readers generally. A glance at this volume shows how thoroughly Hase, usually regarded rather as the historian of the middle ages and recent times, is acquainted also with ecclesiastical antiquity. He has, he himself acknowledges, learnt much from Tübingen criticism; his refusal to follow it in every thing, we can only regard with approval. For my own part, at all events, I have, in following my own line of study, become more and more convinced of the truth of the verdict pronounced by Hase (p. 175): "The Tübingen school has perceived a part of the truth,—the profound division in the Apostolic Church (formerly lightly passed over), two forms taken by primitive Christianity. But, as often happens, the discoverer of a new truth overrates its importance. A definite Jewish Christianity existed towards the close of the century in Palestine only, although there may have been a few individual Churches in Syria also. On the other hand, Paul's victory must not be understood to mean that the converted Gentiles at once grasped his profound ideas in opposition to the necessity of the law; they in their strict consistency are not for the popular mind; the Churches composed of Gentiles would be likely to feel themselves morally strengthened and quickened religiously by the spirit proceeding from Christ, without troubling themselves about the Jewish law." If it is granted to the venerable author to complete this admirable work, it will remain a lasting and valuable monument of the life-work of a German theologian and scholar.[1]

---

[1] Since the text was written the venerable historian has died.

GIESELER's Church History (3 vols., down to the Peace of Westphalia, published by himself, 1824-1853, the subsequent vols., 4-6, edited by Redepenning from his remains), is an excellent aid to the study of ecclesiastical history, giving as it does more fully than any other handbook the original authorities for the views taken. Gieseler wished that each age should speak for itself, since only by this means can the peculiarity of its ideas be fully appreciated. The author's own account is so completely subordinated to his quotations that the meagre text is often little more than a heading to the notes. We get little more than the bare materials of the history; what he is to think of them, is left by the learned historian to the reader himself. This objectivity is related to that of a Hase or a Baur as a skilfully arranged photograph to the picture of an artist.

NIEDNER's Ecclesiastical History is praised for its independence and individuality of thought, but is also censured for its heaviness and obscurity. At any rate its success has not been great. HAGENBACH's work is distinguished by the qualities of an agreeable and edifying narrative, and is popular in lay circles. The Ecclesiastical History of KURTZ, written from the point of view of the Lutheran orthodoxy, has appeared in two or three editions of varying length; it contains a collection of materials conveniently arranged for the purposes of students.

The most important work of this century on Church History is that of C. F. BAUR, his last great work, and the ripest fruit of his far-reaching scientific researches, of which the works on New Testament criticism above discussed [1] are only a fragment, although the most important one. In order to review his achievements in this department, we must first go back to his earlier works on the history of religion and dogmas, which preceded his epoch-making critical labours. The first of these, *Symbolik und Mythologie oder die Naturreligion des Alterthums* (1824), is written from the position of Schleiermacher's theology, and also shows the influence of Schelling and Creuzer. Religion is traced back to the spiritual nature of man, and its realisation discovered in the history of religion at large, which as a divine education of the human race is a continual revelation of God; mythology is also to be regarded as a portion of this revelation, and hence the antithesis of

---

[1] p. 227, sqq.

supernatural and natural revelation is reducible to a mere difference in the degree of truth contained in each particular religion. Even in this, Baur's earliest work, is noticeable his effort to discover the rational content of the creations of the religious imagination (Vorstellung), combined with the disposition to thrust into myths philosophical ideas foreign to them, and to overlook their natural psychological sources. The first literary fruits of his theological professorship in Tübingen were the works lying on the borderland between mythology and the history of dogma, *Das manichäische Religionssystem* (1831), *Apollonius von Tyana* (1832), *Die christliche Gnosis* (1835), and *Ueber das Christliche im Platonismus oder Sokrates und Christus* (1837). The choice not less than the treatment of these subjects is indicative of the large breadth of view and the insight of the historian into the comparative history of religions; he seeks for the points where Christianity came into contact—now as a friend, then as a foe—with other religions, and in conflict with them proved itself the higher, the "absolute religion." His investigation of Gnosticism has admittedly thrown light upon this obscure subject, though we must likewise acknowledge that he interpreted and idealised this mixture of Oriental mythology and Greek philosophy too much from the point of view of modern philosophy.

Baur first entered on theology in the stricter sense by his book, *Gegensatz des Katholicismus und Protestantismus nach den Prinzipien und Hauptdogmen der beiden Lehrbegriffe* (1834, and 2nd ed. enlarged, 1836). This is a defence of Protestantism, evoked by Möhler's *Symbolik*, not indeed of the empirical Protestantism expounded in the confessions of the Churches, but of an ideal Protestantism on the lines of Schleiermacher's *Glaubenslehre* and Hegel's Philosophy of Religion, with the speculative doctrines of which the dogmas of the Protestant communions are identified with a certain naïve ingenuousness. This disregard of the profound difference between his own views and those of the Churches is characteristic of Baur; it is partly the result of his conscientious conviction that he was faithful to the Protestant principle and its normal doctrinal development; partly also of his tendency to convert dogmatic conceptions (*Vorstellungen*) too directly into philosophical ideas, overlooking their actual origin in the religious spirit. This defect is most apparent in the larger histories of dogma published next, *Die christliche Lehre von der Versöhnung in ihrer geschichtlichen Entwicklung bis auf die neueste Zeit* (1838), and *Die christliche Lehre von der Dreieinigkeit und Menschwerdung Gottes in ihrer geschichtlichen Entwicklung* (3 vols. 1841–43), followed by the *Lehrbuch der christlichen Dogmengeschichte* (1847), which contains a concise survey of the whole history of dogma. His method of treating these subjects is characterised by Baur himself in his prefaces as follows: The object of history is to give an account of the nature of mind itself, its inner movement and development, its consciousness of itself, advancing from point to point. This can only be done by a speculative treatment of the materials. For whenever there is inner connection there is reason, and whatever is by means of reason must also be for reason, for the contemplation of mind. Without speculation historical research fails to get below the surface and outside of the matter, and in proportion as the subject is comprehensive and important, and belongs directly to the sphere of thought, it is necessary not merely to reproduce in oneself what individuals have thought and done, but also to follow in thought the thoughts of the eternal Mind of which history is the work.—This is indeed a magnificent conception of the historian's task, to trace the divine thoughts in history and comprehend the ideal or teleological necessity in the development of mind. But when Baur thought with Hegel that the development of the living religious spirit was identical with the dialectical development of logical categories, and that the rise and growth of dogmas in the Christian Church can be adequately rendered in the formulæ of Hegelian terminology, this was a decided error by which the value of his learned works was sensibly diminished. We are not told exactly what the real meaning of the Fathers was—for their opinions are always translated into the language of Hegel; nor do we get a clear account of the various factors, religious and secular, individual and social, universal and temporal, contributing to the formation of dogma—for instead of all these real factors appears always the imaginary cause in the "self-movement of the idea." We may in fact affirm that Baur's slavery to the formulæ of the Hegelian philosophy was a weak point in his treatment of the history of dogma, which only served to obscure the truth and profundity of his conception of history as a true development of the human mind, and to give the opponents of his principles many apparent advantages.

It is all the more important to notice that Baur in his later years freed himself to an observable degree from this defect, (which is specially characteristic of the monographs written when in middle life on the history of dogma), and advanced to a more independent conception of religious and historical life ; of religious life, by subsequently more definitely distinguishing between religion and philosophy, and making the former primarily ethical instead of intellectual ; and of historical life, by recognising the importance of the personalities, before almost concealed under the generality of the idea, as representatives of the idea, and as the concrete motive-forces of history. This advance is seen in his last work, his *Kirchengeschichte*, which is therefore the maturest and most substantial fruit of his labours, while its superiority to all his former writings in point of clearness and ease of language is no doubt connected with this improvement in matter. Baur had thoroughly prepared himself for this work, in which he intended to exhibit in connection the results of the labours of his life, by a critical account of the *Epochen der kirchlichen Geschichtsschreibung* (1852), in which he showed the deficiencies of previous methods, and demanded that ecclesiastical history, like the secular history of our time (above all that of Ranke), should abandon its trivial discussion of proximate and accidental causes, and rather describe the great connexion and general causes of the phenomena in the ruling ideas of each age. This essay was followed by *Das Christenthum und die christliche Kirche der drei ersten Jahrhunderte* (1853); next came, in Baur's lifetime, *Die christliche Kirche von Anfang des vierten bis zum Ende des sechsten Jahrhunderts* (1859). The three subsequent volumes, containing the history of the mediæval age, of the modern age, and of the nineteenth century, were published from his remains in the years immediately following his death (1860). In the preface to the first volume, Baur announces his intention of giving a more connected account of the early history of Christianity than had previously been done ; in particular the basis provided in history itself for Christianity in the form of a Church must be more accurately and thoroughly investigated, the connexion and unity of the whole must be made plain, the differences and mutual relations of the various co-operating forces and principles explained ; in short, as harmonious a picture as possible formed of all the individual traits which distinguish this rich period. This conception of the object and method of Church history will remain a model for all time. In the execution, advancing knowledge will, of course, discover and correct errors in detail, but taken as a whole, it is the first thorough and satisfactory attempt to explain the rise of Christianity and the Church on *strictly historical* lines, *i.e.* as a natural development of the religious spirit of our race under the combined operation of various human causes. This is what makes Baur's Church History, and especially its first volume, a classic for all time. It may perhaps be of some interest to those who do not read German, and have not direct access to this work, if I here give a short sketch of Baur's account of primitive Christianity, thus carrying on the above (p. 263 sqq.) outline of Wellhausen's history of Israel, which will assist in the formation of an approximately true idea of the results of modern criticism in respect to Biblical and early ecclesiastical history.

Baur begins with the preparation for Christianity in the Gentile and Jewish world. This includes, besides the political universalism of the Roman Empire, the Græco-Roman philosophy; the Socratic and Platonic idealism and the Stoic and Epicuræan search for the *summum bonum* contain the closest parallels to the religious questions of Christianity, and in the later eclecticism of a Cicero and Seneca we have the outlines of a natural theology, which was subsequently further developed on Christian soil. We may therefore say that in Christianity the various movements of the time converge towards the same goal, and find in it their ultimate idea and most complete expression. Simultaneously, Judaism had assumed in Alexandrine Hellenism a more subtle and spiritual form, new ideas were borrowed from the Greeks, and in particular the Old Testament conception of God was lifted out of the narrow sphere of the Jewish theocracy. Even the dread of contact with the world and the religious self-contemplation of the Essenes was one of the points of spiritual affinity between Judaism and Christianity. Thus the whole previous history of mankind was a preparation for Christianity; it contained nothing which had not already in some form or other been recognised as a result of rational thought, or as a want of the human heart, or as a demand of the ethical consciousness. In order to ascertain the original character of Christianity, Baur starts from the Sermon on the Mount, Matthew v. In the Beatitudes we get a glance into the centre of the principle of thought and feeling of which it was the product, viz. "an infinitely sublime religious consciousness, which, though pervaded by the deepest feeling of the pressure of the finite and all the contradictions of the present, rises far above everything finite and limited. It is the pure feeling of the need of salvation, still undeveloped but containing within it the antithesis of sin and grace, and as such necessarily involving the reality of salvation." The emphasis laid by Jesus on the heart and character, as that in which alone man's absolute moral worth consists, is an essentially new step, a departure in principle from Mosaism, and is the fundamental principle of Christianity. And just as the idea of righteousness is deepened into a perfect surrender of man's own will to God's, so the Old Testament idea of the theocracy is so much spiritualised that everything relating to man's connexion with the kingdom of God is made dependent solely upon ethical conditions. "Christianity, thus viewed, is in its most essential and primitive elements a purely ethical religion, and its highest and peculiar excellence is its wholly ethical character as rooted in the ethical consciousness of mankind." But this spiritual substance of Christianity took concrete form in the Messianic idea, and by its aid entered on its historical development, the consciousness of Jesus widening to universality by means of the national consciousness. By the name "Son of man" Jesus expressed his truly universal Messianic vocation; in Peter's confession this became an acknowledged fact for himself and for his disciples; in Jerusalem he put the nation to the test, whether they adhered to their traditional, material and particularist Messianic belief, or would recognise a Messiah such as he was and had shown himself by his whole life and work. The answer could only be the one of which he had long himself been assured. But his apparent overthrow was really the most decisive victory and entrance upon life. His death was the complete rupture between him and Judaism. What the Resurrection really was lies outside the province of historical inquiry, which has only to maintain that in the belief of the disciples the resurrection of Jesus was the most certain and incontrovertible of facts. So far as history is concerned, the necessary pre-supposition for everything that follows is not so much the fact of the resurrection of Jesus itself as the belief in it; but no psychological analysis can penetrate the *inward spiritual process* by which this belief was generated in the mind of the disciples. In their view the return of Jesus at the end of the world was so closely connected with his departure, that by this expectation the old Messianic hopes might easily be renewed and strengthened in them, whereby the difference between the disciples and the other Jews would sink into insignificance. What was it that raised the belief in the risen Jesus to a new principle of universal importance? It was, Baur answers, the work of the Apostle Paul, prepared for by the Hellenist Stephen. His conversion, even though we cannot get to the bottom of it by any psychological analysis, may be conceived as brought about by the help of the great impression made on him by the death of Jesus, which from the very fact of its contradicting all Jewish national assumptions, necessarily gained in Paul's view an importance extending far beyond Jewish particularism, so that he first fully grasped the universalism of Christianity. The two points of view which had been united in the person of Jesus—the universal or ethical and the national Jewish or Messianic,—were respectively divided amongst his disciples, the elder apostles, generally laying emphasis on the national character of Jesus, while Paul gave energetic expression to his ethical universality. He did not indeed appeal to the details of the life or teaching of Jesus, since the whole of Christianity was for his mind concentrated in the person of Jesus and the great facts of his death and resurrection. After Paul had for a considerable time been working among the mixed Churches in Syria, he and the Jewish Christians, including the Apostles, became involved in a dispute, which ended with the resolution that each of the two parties should pursue its own independent course separate from the other. How deep the disunion really was, in spite of the brotherly shake of the hand, was soon seen at Antioch, in the personal quarrel between Paul and Peter, which left a lasting impression on both sides. In none of Paul's epistles have we the slightest sign of the two apostles having afterwards been in any way reconciled; the Acts passes over the scene in Antioch in such deliberate silence that we can plainly enough infer how little the recollection of it accorded with the conciliatory *Tendenz* of the writer; and in the pseudo-Clementine Homilies (of the latter half of the second century) we can still see that even then the Jewish Christians could not forgive Paul his harsh words about their chief apostle. Soon after we meet with the systematic opposition of the Jewish Christians to the Apostle Paul in Galatia, where they wished to convert the Pauline Church to Jewish legalism; and then in Corinth, where they tried to destroy Paul's authority by all the resources of intrigue and under the pretext of the authority of the original apostles. And even in Rome, Baur holds, Paul had to contend with Jewish Christians; in order to defend his mission to the Gentiles against their prejudices he wrote his Epistle to the Romans, the last, in Baur's view, which we have of his. During the Apostle's last stay in Jerusalem also, the Jewish Christians took part in the tumult which led to his imprisonment, and thus proved the implacability of their hatred of the Apostle of the Gentiles, whom they regarded as an apostate from the Law of their fathers, by which they continued to feel themselves bound.—The reconciliation, so far as possible, of these two parties, hitherto sharply opposed to each other, by the adjustment of their differences and the softening of their antagonism, was, according to Baur, the chief object aimed at in the sub-apostolic age; the whole literature of this period appears from this point of view as a series of monuments of this opposition, and its gradual reduction by the advances of both sides. Of the Gospels, Luke is the purest and most important record of Paulinism, while Matthew represents Jewish Christianity. The latter found its strongest anti-Pauline expression in the Apocalypse, which Baur regarded as a work of the Apostle John, and interpreted thoughout from the point of view of the primitive Christian party struggle; so that even in the censure of the Balaamites and Nicolaitans (*i.e.* libertine Gnostics), he only saw an attack on Paul. As further chief witnesses for the continued power and even supremacy of Jewish Christianity, Baur appeals to Hegesippus and the pseudo-Clementine writings, from the middle of the second century, but he is too hasty when he makes use of the " Tendenzroman " of the latter as a sign of the Judaistic tendencies of the Church at that time. But in spite of this bitter enmity to Paul, he holds that Jewish Christianity had an infinite capacity for development, and was so prudent in everywhere meeting the needs of the Church by the sacrifice of its former legalism, that it came to exercise an influence on the formation of the Christian Church which cannot be exaggerated, as is specially proved by the development of the hierarchy, altogether an outcome of Jewish Christianity. At the head of the canonical writings, which were at once the expression and the agents of this process of conciliation, he places the Epistle to the Hebrews, which by the emphasis it lays on the priesthood is shown to be a product of Jewish Christianity, although of a higher and more spiritual form of it, already influenced by Paulinism. (This opinion receives a remarkable correction in a note which describes the characteristics of the Epistle to the Hebrews as "Alexandrinism," which is neither Judaism nor Paulinism, but intermediate between them, and by its limitation of them superior to both —an excellent remark, which only needs to be consistently worked out to lead to a different conception of the development of post-Pauline Christianity.) The same effort at reconciliation, represented in the Epistle to the Hebrews on the Jewish Christian side, is represented on the Pauline side by the Epistles to the Ephesians and Colossians; they emphatically insist on the unity of the Church, as the essential result of Christ's death as healing all division, and of Christ's central all-inclusive position in the universe. In the Pastoral Epistles, and in those of the pseudo-Ignatius, the Pauline party displays an eirenical readiness, for the sake of an effective opposition to the heretics, to meet the efforts of the Jewish Christians in the direction of a hierarchical organisation of the Church. In return, the Jewish Christians, in the Epistle of James, so far made concession to the followers of Paul that in spite of its rejection of Paul's doctrine of justification, it still speaks of a "law of liberty" and a "royal law of love," and by its practical morals makes a contribution to the formation of Catholic Christianity. In particular the First Epistle of Peter proves that the Jewish Christians were even able to accommodate themselves to the dogmatic ideas of Paulinism by direct quotation of Pauline Epistles; and the Second Epistle of Peter even gives "brother Paul" a certificate of orthodoxy, and only laments that some things in his epistles are hard to be understood, and had been misinterpreted. Finally, in order to remove all disturbing recollection of the Apostolic struggles out of the way of the union of parties desired by both sides, the Acts of the Apostles gave an ideal picture of the Apostolic age, in which the two party leaders, Paul and Peter, were designedly made so much alike that they really seem to have changed places. Since this deviation from history must be intentional, the Acts must be regarded as "an effort at conciliation and a proposal of terms of peace on the part of a Paulinist, who wished to procure the recognition by the Jewish Christians of Gentile Christianity, by concessions from his own party to Judaism, and sought to influence both parties in this manner (on this view, compare the remarks above, p. 229). A similar position is taken by Baur with regard to the writings of the Apostolic Fathers and of Justin Martyr, and he explains the legend of the death of both Paul and Peter in Rome as the expression of the finally consummated reconciliation of the primitive Christian parties. The same process of development, of which this was the practical side in the Roman Church, is seen on its ideal side in the Gospel of John; while in the former case the object was the realisation of the idea of the Church, it was here the evolution of an ideal theology. As there Peter and Paul were fraternally united as patrons of the Roman Church, so here in this Johannine theology faith and works disappear in love as their higher unity. The opposition through which Paulinism had been compelled to fight its way, is in John removed into the far distance. The particularism of Judaism, with all the contradictions it included, is lost in the general contradiction of the two principles of light and darkness, which forms the background of John's theology and also dominates the sphere of ethics. This is a point of affinity between the Johannine Gospel and Gnosticism, that great movement of the second century, which both directly and indirectly greatly contributed to the formation of catholic and ecclesiastical Christianity. Here fresh questions present themselves, the horizon is widened, but new dangers threaten. God and world, spirit and matter, origin, development, and consummation of the world, are the conceptions here involved, and in their development the antitheses of the religions take a share. The questions of salvation and of the ethico-religious consciousness are generalised into questions of metaphysical speculation. But the Catholic Church, everywhere careful to preserve the proper mean, had to avoid this extreme equally with that of Jewish particularism. For it was here threatened by an equally serious peril from ideas by which the Christian consciousness would altogether lose its historical character. The tendency of Gnosticism is to regard Christianity not primarily as the principle of salvation but as the principle of the development of the world generally; it does not rest so much on a religious as on a philosophical basis, and conducts again to philosophy as the highest product of the heathen world; it is the extension and development of the Alexandrine religious philosophy which had sprung from the philosophy of Greece. But in so far as it clothes philosophical ideas less in the form of abstract conceptions than of myths and allegories, it is in this respect more akin to religion than to philosophy; it is therefore neither pure philosophy nor pure religion, but both together, a combination of the two elements which Baur (perhaps not very happily) calls "*Religionsphilosophie.*" He further distinguishes three main forms of Gnosis, in one of which Christianity is mixed with heathenism, in another with Judaism, and in the third is opposed to both. With Gnosticism Baur contrasts Montanism as the opposite heresy. While in the former the idea supplants the historical reality, the latter is a reaction of the realism of the Jewish Christian hope of the future against its idealistic evaporation and ecclesiastical secularisation. In an age in which the belief in the nearness of the parousia failed, prophetic ecstasy grew rare or ceased, and when, with this enthusiasm of the early Churches, their ascetic zeal and love of holiness grew faint, there sprang up in the Montanists a new form of ecstatic prophecy, a burning chiliastic belief and a rigorous penitential zeal. These movements of the second century, so different in character, and crossing each other in all directions, all led to the development and consolidation of the Church's doctrine and constitution as the indispensable breakwater against the billows of the time. Not only had the practical religious side of Christianity to be maintained against the transcendental speculations of the Gnostics, but also the very ground to be conquered against the chiliastic fanaticism of the Montanists, which cut off all possibility of the historical development and progress of Christianity in the world. It was therefore by means of its antagonism to the Gnostics and Montanists that the definite consciousness and growing solidity of the Catholic Church were developed out of the reconciliation of Jewish and Gentile Christians. In the struggle with the Gnostics was evolved the principle of ecclesiastical tradition as the final court of appeal in all disputes, the appeal to the Apostolic writings having proved insufficient, owing to the possibility of various and especially allegorical interpretations. That only on which the Apostolic Churches agree can be received as true, for that must have been taught by the Apostles; what is inconsistent with it is heresy, *i.e.* an arbitrary and new individual opinion. But who was to decide what was Apostolical tradition and the common faith of the Church? The bishops alone could do this, it being assumed that they were appointed by the Apostles as their successors. It is true this assumption did not correspond to the fact, since all indications go to prove that the Churches were originally autonomous and chose their own presidents, who were bishops and presbyters in one, while the function of teaching was not confined to this office. It was not until the struggle with the heretics showed the need of a stricter centralisation of the Churches, that there was instituted, at first in the individual Churches, the monarchical episcopate superior to the presbyters. This episcopate provided a fixed rallying point against the separatist tendencies of the heretics, and applied the Christian conception of a supernatural world to the practical needs of the present, thus initiating the further historical development of Christianity on the basis of a universal Church. But the same effort at unity which had first raised the bishop of the individual Church above the presbyters, went on to elevate the Bishop of Rome above the others who were originally his equals. That the Roman bishop was Peter's successor in Rome, is an historical fiction, Peter never having been in Rome. The unhistorical legend about Peter took its rise at first merely in Rome's political importance, and since the papacy itself depends on this legend, we must seek for the origin of the papacy in the simple fact that the importance enjoyed by Rome, as the capital of the world, was transferred to the bishop of the Roman Church. The most striking feature of the hierarchical system thus established is the simplicity of the forms on which it depends. The fundamental form is the relation of the bishop to the Church of which he is the head. This form continues unchanged, however much the system may be developed, enlarged, or modified. The bishop of the smallest Church is essentially the same as the pope at the summit of the papacy. At all stages of this hierarchical system the same fundamental form repeats itself, its greatest peculiarity being its capacity of indefinite extension. And this hierarchical system is at the same time essentially theocratic; everything rests on divine authority; the relation of the bishop to his community is a repetition of the relation of Christ to the Church. "The whole system is conditioned by a stage of religious development in which men require to see a visible representation of the relation in which Christ as the Lord of the Church stands to it." The form assumed by the Church in its episcopal constitution demanded also a corresponding fixed and systematic expression in dogma. The close connexion between the evolution of the constitutional form and of dogma as its expression, is made very manifest at the close of the first period of ecclesiastical development: the œcumenical synod at Nicæa saw the completest representation of the episcopate and also the enunciation of the highest content of the Christian consciousness in the dogma of the Homoousia. In this period the whole development of dogma is concentrated in the doctrine of Christ's person. This is the reflection and concrete expression of the current view of Christian salvation as a whole. The Christ of the Synoptists was still a human Messiah, miraculously born, it is true, and anointed with the Spirit, and raised by his resurrection and ascension to divine honours, but still essentially man. In Paul's view also Christ is man, not, however, an earthly and phenomenal man, but a heavenly and spiritual one, the eternal type of the spiritual sons of God, appearing in time in the flesh, the second Adam. This higher phase of Christology in Paul was connected with his higher view of Christianity as the universal revelation of salvation for all the world. The Christ of the Apocalypse also has divine attributes predicated of him which seem to leave no essential difference between him and God, but they are only externally connected with the person of the Messiah, who is essentially the instrument for the execution of the divine judgment. The Christology of the Epistle to the Hebrews and the smaller Pauline Epistles, on the other hand, rises to a higher stage of development, and marks the transition to the Johannine Christology, in which the idea of the Logos, borrowed from the Alexandrine religious philosophy, and widely current in the philosophy of the time, is transferred to Christ, the doctrine of the Church corresponding to the Gnostic doctrine of the æons. As in philosophy, the Logos in the Fourth

Gospel is the intermediate being connecting the transcendental God with the world. This being becomes by the incarnation the person of Jesus, who is accordingly regarded by the Fourth Gospel as the self-revelation of a divine principle, the historical view of the Synoptists being thus left far behind. In the latter half of the second century the Johannine conception of the Logos came to be the dominant one, superseding the earlier less definite ideas. This imposed on the theological thought of the Church the duty to define the relation of this divine Logos or Son to God the Father. This was first done in the sense form of a gradual emanation, corresponding to the materialistic realism of Tertullian's conception of God; while in the abstract, transcendental idea of God of the Alexandrians (Clement), almost all personal distinction vanishes between the Father and the Son. This view lived on in the "Monarchians" of the third century, of whom Sabellius particularly is ably interpreted by Baur. In the Christology of Origen the two views, hitherto running parallel, the one emphasising the distinction between God and the Son, and the other their unity, balance each other in such a way that his Christology became the turning point in the history of the dogma, and the point of separation of the two views, which were henceforward opposed to each other as Arianism and Athanasianism. At Nicæa, with the victory of the Athanasian formula of Christ's equality with God (*homoousia*), the hierarchical aristocracy of the episcopate also triumphed over the democratic presbyters. When Christianity had, under Constantine, overcome the Roman world, its consciousness of being the sole true and valid, or the "absolute," religion found expression in the dogmatic enunciation of the orthodox doctrine of the absolute equality of its founder with God. Thus the inner history of the consciousness of the Church, simultaneously with the external history of the relation of the Church to the world and State, came under Constantine to a climax which marked the close of an era.

Here I must end this extract from Baur's *Christianity in the First Three Centuries*, space forbidding me to give more. But I hope that enough has been given to show the magnificently historical spirit of this work, and to prove that the traditional accusations of an "*à priori* construction of history," "twisting of facts," etc., are baseless conventional fables, by which smaller men try to protect themselves in view of the superiority of Baur.

Since Baur's, no important work has appeared embracing the whole of Church history (of Hase's unfinished work we have spoken above, p. 283). Much labour has, however, been devoted to the more accurate investigation of particular questions, both of the ancient Church, and especially of the period of the Reformation, and valuable material for the illumination of the past has been accumulated in monographs and biographies. An enumeration of these works does not, however, fall within the scope of this book. We can here mention only the most recent work on the history of dogma, as it represents, with pre-eminent ability as well as partiality, a new school of historical theology; it is ADOLF HARNACK's *Lehrbuch der Dogmengeschichte*, vol. i., *die Entstehung des kirchlichen Dogmas* (1886), and vol. ii., part i., *die Entwickelung des kirchl. Dogmas* (1887). On the publication of the first volume, the work at once attracted general attention, and gained for its author the well-deserved reputation of an eminent historian. It is based on a thorough independent investigation of the authorities, and the vast mass of material is arranged with rare skill and clearness; the writer's style is lucid and vigorous, and he is always pleasing and suggestive, even when not convincing. But the book owes its special importance to its fundamental view of the history of dogma, by which it gives typical expression to a prevalent mode of thought and feeling of our time. Perhaps we can most simply describe its character by saying that to Baur's optimistic evolutionary theory of history it opposes a pessimistic view of Church history, which makes this history to consist, not in a progressive teleological and rational development and ever richer unfolding of the Christian spirit, but in a progressive obscuration of the truth, in the progress of disease in the Church, produced by the sudden irruption of Hellenic philosophy and other secularising influences. We can understand that such a view is acceptable to a realistic and practical age which has long lost all touch with the ancient dogmas; we cannot deny that it contains relative truth, and might, in fact, serve as a salutary complement to Baur's optimism; but is it adapted to form the supreme guiding principle of ecclesiastical history, or can it justly claim to be the only scientific view, or the right to condemn as unscientific scholasticism the teleological theory of evolution, which, in the manifold play of individual causes, recognises the governance of a higher Reason? These are questions to be seriously asked. Moreover, this pessimistic verdict on Church history is by no means a new one; it is found, in a certain sense, in the Magdeburg Centuriators, in a different form in the mystic Gottfried Arnold, and in yet another in the Rationalists. All these historians, however, in their condemnation of the development of the Church had a definite standard in what they assumed to be the original truth of Biblical Christianity. But if we ask wherein, according to Harnack, uncorrupted Christianity consists, we nowhere get a clear answer. He cannot regard it as consisting in the whole teaching of the New Testament, or he would not with such surprising indifference hurry over the Pauline and Johannine theology. Are we therefore to go back to Jesus? But Harnack leaves us in complete uncertainty whether we are to take as the genuine, permanent constituents of Christianity all that is reported in the Gospels as the preaching of Jesus, including the declarations regarding the permanent validity of the Jewish law, the limitation of the preaching of the gospel to Israel, Christ's visible return to establish an earthly kingdom, and similar matters. But where a definite conception, based on history, of the nature of Christianity is so wholly wanting, the question as to whether individual phenomena are truly Christian or a degeneration, corruption, and secularisation of true Christianity, can only be answered according to personal taste. In so far this method of writing Church history is at least as subjective as the Rationalistic method of the last century. Harnack's keen-sighted realism is undoubtedly of great value, but it needs to be combined with the profound idealism of a Baur to form the true combination which can yield a completely satisfactory treatment of Church history.

BOOK IV.

THE PROGRESS OF THEOLOGY IN GREAT BRITAIN SINCE 1825.

CHAPTER I.

THE SCHOOLS OF PHILOSOPHY IN THEIR RELATION TO THEOLOGY.

AT the opening of the present century the state of religious life in England was substantially the same as in Germany. On the one hand, a rational supernaturalism prevailed, which sought to combine faith in revealed religion with the empirical philosophy of Locke. This was attempted by showing the possibility on rational grounds of revelation, and by basing the fact of revelation on the external evidence supplied in the miracles and prophecies of the Bible. At the same time it conceived the God of revelation under Deistical forms, and repudiated all vivid religious feeling as mystical "enthusiasm." Utilitarian considerations, which formed the practical side of the empirical philosophy of the period, also played a prominent part in orthodox belief; either on the ground of the tangible use of the doctrines of the Church in promoting social order, or with a view to the transcendental benefits implied in the divine reward of virtue. In contrast with this unemotional and rational faith of the upper classes, satisfaction for the religious needs of the lower classes was sought for in a quickening of the consciousness of sin and grace after the manner of Methodism. But in this "Evangelical party" quickened religious feeling and zealous philanthropic effort were so much cut off from any living relation to the thought of the age and to theological inquiry, that any influence from this quarter upon the theology of the Church was not more, in fact still less, possible than was the case with the older German Pietism. To bring new life and movement into theology, a complete revolution in the minds of men was needed. This followed in England from causes similar to those which had produced a like result in Germany; and in part the revolution was due to the direct influence of idealism as it had sprung from German Romanticism.

The ultimate and profoundest source of this mental revolution, which, at the beginning of the century, spread through all cultured nations, must be sought in the nature of man. After the cold understanding had in the eighteenth century exercised despotic sway, starving the emotions and fettering the phantasy, these wronged sides of our nature once more claimed their rights, and rebelled against the despotism of the understanding with an imperious violence which was as tyrannical and exclusive as that of the understanding had been. "A return to nature and natural emotions," was now everywhere the watchword, and Rousseau became the prophet of the new age. The cry found its echo in the "storm and stress" spirits of *belles lettres:* Herder and Goethe were its heralds in Germany, Wordsworth and Shelley in English poetry. Emotion, entering into loving sympathy with *Nature*, could no longer behold in her the dead mechanism to which sensualistic philosophy had degraded her; the machine, which had been robbed of its divinity, was once again transformed into the living garment of God. But Nature owed her reanimation to the soul of man, which had taken possession of her. It was therefore impossible that men should go no further than external Nature: they turned their gaze upon their own nature, and sought in the depths of the feeling heart, in its unconscious surmisings and unutterable sighs, the presence of a divine spirit, the witness of our kinship to God. Thus from the Gospel of Nature of Rousseau sprang the philosophical idealism of Kant and of Fichte, and the religious pantheism of Herder and Novalis. In like manner, in the case of Wordsworth, the poetic love of Nature became a devoted self-surrender to the God whose rule we recognise *within* not less than *around* us. If the standpoint which was thus reached was still only the subjectivism of the eighteenth century, the events of *history* were, at the same time, bringing about an important advance.

Rousseau's Gospel of Nature had been marked by an anti-social and anti-historical tendency; its aim had been the emancipation of the self-sufficient individual from the limitations of an outlived order of society. At first it was everywhere taken up in this sense. In Germany the "schöne Seelen" greeted with enthusiasm the French Revolution, and in his *Robbers*, Schiller depicted the Titanic endeavour of the individual, in the fresh consciousness of its strength, to break up the old order of the world and to construct a new one to its own mind. In the same spirit the youthful Coleridge wrote poems breathing sympathy with revolutionary democracy, and, with Southey, planned a "grand scheme of Pantisocracy," a Utopian commonwealth of liberty and equality, to be established in America. Out of this intoxication of individualism the idealists of Europe were rudely awakened by the thunder of the cannon of Bonaparte. As the social system of Europe collapsed like a house of cards under the hand of the new Cæsar, it was made clear whither the principle of selfish individualism, which breaks up society into helpless atoms, inevitably conducts. When it appeared that the separate nations were to be broken up and converted into the one empire of the Cæsar, the national spirit everywhere rose up against the foreign tyranny, patriotic feeling, which distinguishes in such a marked manner the nineteenth from the eighteenth century, was aroused from its slumbers. And as the nations became conscious of their own peculiar characteristics and rights, they once more called to remembrance their own past history. With admiring love they recurred to the period of their youth and early manhood, and discovered, precisely in those epochs which Rationalism in its ingratitude and want of insight had despised, stores of national strength, virtue, and honour, forming a humiliating contrast to the weakness and disgrace of their own time. Thus the enthusiasts of individual freedom were transformed into the patriotic champions of national liberty in the anti-Napoleonic wars, and out of poetic Romanticism sprang the *Tugendbund* of young Germany, based upon an earnest sense of duty and patriotic devotion. The Kantian imperative of the subjective reason was enlarged and deepened, in the philosophy of Hegel, into the consciousness of the dependence of the individual on the rationality of history as realised in the State. The true freedom, which is alone worthy of man, was now seen to consist, not in opposition to the commonwealth, but in unselfish devotion to it; not in defiance of the State, but in subordination to it as loyal citizens, and in securing individual, by labouring for universal ends. Precisely the same transformation was effected in England. Whilst young men hailed enthusiastically the French Revolution, when it seemed that "temple and tower were to fall to the ground" before its trumpet-blast of "natural rights," Burke raised his voice, as "one crying in the wilderness," against the delusion of the individualistic idea of freedom, and pointed out the unreasonableness of the endeavour to separate the individual from the nation, to which he owes his existence, or from society and its historical arrangements, to which really all human culture is due. What Burke's eloquence failed to effect, the course of history brought about. Under the pressure of a "Continental System" and the wars of Napoleon, English national feeling was aroused, the poets of Nature and Freedom became the heralds of patriotic love, of an admiring piety towards the history of the past, which Sir Walter Scott's genius restored to new life in the hearts of his contemporaries by poetic idealisation.

But in the history of Christian nations, the Church, with her institutions, customs, and doctrines, plays such an essential part, that their inner and outer life could not be at all understood without the consideration of this factor. It was natural, therefore, that the newly awakened interest in the history of the past generally should quicken also the appreciation of the history of the Church, and therewith of the positive and traditional elements in the faith and customs of the nations. In those things which had been an offence to the critical understanding of the eighteenth century, there was now discovered, by the new historical sense, suggestive symbolism, fine human feeling, natural poetry, and prophetic truth; in short, so much nourishment for the famishing soul and the thirsty fancy, that the sons began to revere deeply what the fathers had thrown aside as worthless superstition. Thus, from the same Romanticism which had begun with Rousseau's Gospel of Nature, sprang at last the revival of religious and ecclesiastical taste and feeling. Rousseau was followed by Chateaubriand and the Italian Manzoni; by Schleiermacher and Neander, and the Catholic convert Schlegel, in Germany; and by Coleridge, and John Henry Newman and Pusey, in England.

In order to last, and to influence the life of a nation from various sides, a new mode of feeling always requires a new mode of thought as its accompaniment, with new ideas and associations of ideas as its vehicle and support. In Germany this want was met in the idealistic philosophy founded by Kant, which in all its various developments had this in common, that it connected man with the higher world of spirit, and set before him conscious devotion to it as the object of his own perfection. In England, however, no such philosophy as this existed. For the philosophy of Locke was, in reality, in its popular form, the formal expression of that barren view of things which binds man to the world of the senses as the sole reality, makes the individual complete in himself, and prescribes as his highest end the pursuit of his own advantage; which was therefore precisely that view of things which the new and more profound poetry and religious and historical Romanticism indignantly repudiated. Under these circumstances it was very natural that the originators of this new mode of feeling in England should seek their weapons of defence and attack in German philosophy. We shall see as we proceed in what various ways this philosophy affected the most thoughtful minds in England. Yet it remained, after all, but a foreign growth on English soil. So true is it that a philosophy is able to exercise a determining influence upon the ecclesiastical and theological thought of a nation only when it has penetrated it so profoundly as to determine the popular philosophy of the educated classes concerned. As regards the idealistic philosophy of Germany, no such reception of it was possible in England. On the other hand, the English philosophy of the past could no longer satisfy the requirements of the new poetic and religious feeling. The revived religious consciousness accordingly failed to find the indispensable intellectual basis and regulative principles, without which it could not develop into definite theological teaching, or guide the development of the mind of the Churches in harmony with the general thought of the nation and the age. It seems to me that we have here the explanation of the remarkable fact that the Church life of England, until within the last decade, has remained almost completely untouched by the vast progress of the scientific thought of the educated classes, and that wherever the two come into contact, such a violent collision is the consequence that popular feeling is shocked, and not a few despair of the possibility of any mutual understanding. It is true that latterly this tension has been somewhat relaxed, and just now signs are not wanting of the rise of a new philosophical view of the world suited to the British genius, under the auspices of which a reconciliation of the Church and the world, of theology and science, may be hoped for.

I propose, in the first instance, to offer a review of the various philosophical schools in their relation to religion and theology. This review must commence with the idealism of Coleridge and Carlyle, which was so greatly influenced by German philosophy. This idealism is met by the reaction of the empirical philosophy of Mill and the critical philosophy of Hamilton, connected with which is an agnosticism in various forms. There follows then an evolutionary philosophy, with more of systematic completeness, and in two forms: first, realistic, with an agnostic basis, represented by Herbert Spencer; second, idealistic, represented by the Neo-Hegelians, Caird and Green, with whom are connected, finally, the living representatives of speculative theism.

SAMUEL TAYLOR COLERIDGE was a true representative of Romanticism with all its bright and dark sides. He was a man of wide culture, of fine sensibility, of vivid imagination, of ready intellect; but as a thinker his efforts were spasmodic and fragmentary, lacking steadiness, consistency, and thoroughness; and he displayed a surprising want of moral strength. As a young man he was an enthusiastic worshipper of Nature and Freedom; afterwards, when sobered down under the influence of personal and historical experiences, he sought in German philosophy consolation for the shipwreck of the ideals of his youth. He studied Lessing and Kant, Jacobi and Schelling; and by the aid of philosophical idealism he reconciled himself to the faith of the Church, from which he had been totally estranged. Yet the reconciliation was in such a form that he no longer based his faith upon supernatural authority, but upon the ideal constitution of the human mind itself, regarding Christianity as the perfection of human reason. With Herder and Schleiermacher, Coleridge maintained that Christianity is not a theory or speculation, but a life and a living process, that the proof of it therefore must consist in the inner personal experience of that life. While he thus related himself to the supernaturalism of the orthodox party of that time by going over to the side of the Evangelicals (the Pietists of England), on the other hand he departed from the latter in that he regarded Christianity not as something absolutely supernatural in antithesis to the human, as the germs of it lie in the nature of man himself and are brought to their perfection by Christianity; for which reason the truth of Christianity can never contradict reason when properly understood. Coleridge expounded these views in his *Aids to Reflection* (1825), not, it is true, in a systematic form, but in suggestive aphorisms and explanatory examples, which should serve to arouse independent reflection in the direction indicated.

Coleridge attached the greatest importance to the distinction, taken from Kant's Critique, between the "understanding," as "the faculty judging according to sense," and the "reason," as the faculty of "universal and necessary truths." He further distinguishes the speculative from the practical reason, the former as applied to formal or abstract truth, the latter as applied to actual or moral truth, as the fountain of ideas and the light of the conscience. While he is thus far apparently quite in agreement with Kant, Coleridge ascribes nevertheless to the practical reason a meaning which passes beyond the moral sphere : like Jacobi he describes it as the feeling or instinct of supersensible truths, or, with Schelling, as an intellectual intuition of spiritual objects. Whilst the understanding is confined to the world of the senses, and can accordingly pronounce only conditional judgments, the reason is the source of unconditional and necessary judgments, the intelligible spiritual nature of man, which is one with the Divine Spirit. From overlooking this distinction and from the illegitimate application of the understanding to supersensible objects, arises "unbelief or misbelief." "Wherever the forms of reasoning appropriate only to the *natural* world are applied to *spiritual* realities, the more strictly logical the reasoning is in all its *parts*, the more irrational it is as a *whole*."—Propositions such as these, to which the parallels may be found here and there in German Romanticism and speculative philosophy, have a certain meaning as a protest against a shallow and negative Rationalism, but they betray none the less a questionable inclination to suppress intelligent criticism in religious questions. Nor did Coleridge altogether escape this danger, although he had the good sense to acknowledge the logical understanding as a negative canon in religious questions, since absolutely inconceivable propositions cannot be true. It is only the positive proof of the truths of religious faith which must not be derived from theoretical argumentation, but from the moral and spiritual nature of man. It is, as Coleridge well observes, the peculiarity of Christianity that, unlike philosophy, it does not seek by workings upon the intellect to elevate the character, but its first step is to cleanse the *heart* and afterwards to restore the intellect likewise to its natural clearness. If the effects were not proportionate to the Divine wisdom of the method, it was because " the doctors of the Church forgot that the heart, the moral nature, was the beginning and the end." " This was the true and first apostasy, when in council and synod the Divine Humanities of the Gospel gave way to speculative systems, and religion became a science of shadows under the name of theology, or at best a bare skeleton of truth, without life or interest, alike inaccessible and unintelligible to the majority of Christians."

Coleridge illustrated his view of Christianity in its application to selected doctrines—original sin, redemption, baptism, inspiration. In doing this he everywhere seeks so far to rationalise the dogma as to surrender its scholastic husk while preserving its religious and moral kernel. The affinity of his theology with Schleiermacher's, especially as represented by the conservative wing of Schleiermacher's school, strikes the student at once. The dogma of "original sin" is made to mean that sin as spiritual evil is a condition of the will, which is the ground and cause of all sins, that it was not inherited from without, but is the act of the will itself, and so "self-originated." This is certainly much more a Kantian than Biblical or ecclesiastical doctrine. In complete agreement with Kant, Coleridge says "that in respect of original sin, every man is the adequate representative of *all* men," and that the first man in time, the Adam of Genesis, is only the type of the race. Hence all statements as to the perfection of man in Paradise must be cast aside as phantastic and valueless. With regard to the doctrine of redemption, according to Coleridge, the cause of redemption is not so much the death of Christ as the incarnation of the Creative Word in the person of Christ. This manifestation of the Divine in the human life, labours, and death of the Saviour produces, as its effect, our transformation from fleshly to spiritual men, and, as further consequences, our progressive sanctification by the Word and the Spirit. But the various forms of expression which are used by the apostles to set forth the actual consequences of the act of redemption show by their diversity that they ought to be taken as metaphors only, borrowed in part from Jewish theology and in part from the opinions prevalent amongst the readers and opponents of the apostles.

Specially interesting and instructive is Coleridge's essay, entitled, *Confessions of an Inquiring Spirit*, published after his death (1840), in which he assails the dogmatic theory of the inspiration of the Scriptures with very rational arguments, while adhering tenaciously to his conviction of their incomparable religious and moral value. He shows admirably that the Biblical writers themselves lay no claim to the verbal inspiration of their writings, and that this doctrine, really borrowed from the Jewish Rabbis, must therefore be regarded as an unscriptural superstition. He goes further, and asks, "How can infallible truth be infallibly conveyed in defective and fallible expressions," such as all human words and sentences must be? Moreover, we should gain nothing by such an unnatural supposition, but on the contrary be simply losers. For if all the heart-awakening utterances of human hearts, such as we find in the Bible, were nothing more than "a Divina Commedia of a superhuman ventriloquist"; if the sweet Psalmist of Israel were himself as mere an instrument of the inspiring Spirit as his harp, an automaton poet, all sympathy and all example would be gone, and we could listen to his words only in fear and perplexity. The Bible is undeniably "the appointed conservatory, an indispensable criterion, and a continual source and support of true belief; but we must not confound this with the statements—that the Bible is the sole source, and that it not only contains but constitutes the Christian religion, that it is in short a creed consisting wholly of articles of faith; and that consequently we need no rule, help, or guide, spiritual or historical, to teach us what parts are and what are not articles of faith." As the Church herself has admitted it as a canon—that each part of Scripture must be interpreted by the spirit of the whole, it has thereby practically granted "that it is the *spirit* of the Bible, and not the detached words and sentences, that is infallible and absolute." We see that it is the view of the Bible—at once free and reverent—of Lessing, Herder, and Schleiermacher, which Coleridge commends to his countrymen. We shall find in the next chapter, in the case of the representatives of the Broad Church party, that though this view has met with opposition in the English Church, it has gradually made its way there to a considerable extent.

THOMAS CARLYLE spent his early youth in the midst of the simplest conditions of country life, as the eldest son of a

Scotch mason, in a family in which a plain and serious Puritanical piety held sway. These impressions of his childhood engraved themselves so deeply on his heart that they continued powerfully to influence him after he had given up the dogmas of the Church. From the bright inquisitive intellect of the youth, who sought for truth at any price, the defects of the traditional arguments in support of orthodox dogmas could not long remain concealed, and an eager study of the works of Gibbon and Hume, to which he devoted himself during his university course in Edinburgh, added all that was needed to make him a decided sceptic. But he could not rest satisfied in mere negation. He was profoundly unhappy when, under the influence of Hume's philosophy, the God of the orthodox faith could no longer be believed in, or had become the unconcerned absentee spectator of a mechanically rotating universe, and when the idea of duty had also seemed to change from a Divine messenger and guide to a false earthly phantasm, made up of desire and fear. But his profound love of truth and sense of duty formed the rock on which the waves of doubt broke. Whilst his intellect, beclouded with sceptical and pessimistic horrors, pictured to him the world as the sport of chance and the work of the devil, his moral consciousness attained to the certainty of the indestructible freedom of the soul as the lord of the world. With this the "Everlasting Yea" obtained the conquest over the "Everlasting No." It was the repetition in an individual of the same process as had been passed through in German philosophy a generation earlier; when the world of orthodox belief, destroyed by the criticism of the understanding, was reconstructed from the subjective resources of man as a moral and rational being; when the moral self-consciousness expanded into the ideal world of the great German thinkers and poets.

And it was not in Carlyle's case merely a similar process of development, but it took place in direct dependence on German thought. In the critical period of his life he occupied himself closely with the writings of Goethe and Schiller, Jean Paul and Novalis; translations from their works were his earliest literary efforts. To Goethe especially he felt himself under great obligations. From the many fine things which he has written upon Goethe, the following passage, as especially characteristic of Carlyle himself, may be quoted here: "He who would learn to reconcile reverence with clearness; to deny and defy what is false, yet believe and worship what is true; amid raging factions, bent on what is either altogether empty or has substance in it only for a day, which stormfully convulse and tear hither and thither a distracted expiring system of society, to adjust himself aright; and working for the world and in the world, keep himself unspotted from the world—let him look here. This man (Goethe), we may say, became morally great, by being in his own age, what in some other ages many might have been, a genuine man."[1]

"To reconcile reverence with clearness, to deny and defy what is false, and yet to believe and worship what is true"—this is in fact an admirable summary of Carlyle's own character and labours. A believer, in the sense of orthodox theology, he never became, but always expressed most unreservedly his poor opinion of it, at times indeed with a vehemence which might surprise one in the case of an historian who showed on other occasions such loving sympathy with antiquity, did we not remember that the orthodox system does not yet belong to ancient history, but is still a power in the world, often making itself felt as a retarding fetter to minds that are striving after truth and clearness for themselves and others. It is not any want of religion, not frivolous scepticism, but rather a good piece of old Scotch Puritanism, combined with modern ethical idealism, which makes him ruthlessly indignant at every form of religious cant, at all ecclesiasticism that has become external form and convention. Yet what is almost more repulsive and hateful to him than the latter are the empty and windy negations of frivolous scepticism, atheism, and materialism. In one of his masterly characterisations of the present age[2] (to be compared with Fichte's discourses on the *Grundzüge des gegenwärtigen Zeitalters*) he says: "The fever of scepticism must needs burn itself out, and burn out thereby the impurities that caused it; then again will there be clearness, health. The principle of life which now struggles painfully in the outer, thin and barren domain of the Conscious or Mechanical, may then withdraw into its inner sanctuaries, its abysses of mystery and miracle;

---

[1] *Miscellanies*, vol. iv. p. 49 (Popular Edition, 1872).
[2] *Ibid.*, vol. iv. p. 35.

withdraw deeper than ever into that domain of the Unconscious, by nature infinite and inexhaustible; and creatively work there. From that mystic region, and from that alone, all wonders, all poesies, and religions and social systems have proceeded; the like wonders, and greater and higher, lie slumbering there; and, brooded on by the spirit of the waters, will evolve themselves, and rise like exhalations from the deep."

In his essay on Diderot,[1] Carlyle shows that his mechanical materialism was the natural outcome of his barren logical intellect, but that two consequences of some value have followed from it: First, that all speculations of the sort we call Natural Theology are unproductive, since of final causes nothing can be proved, they being known only by the higher light of intuition; secondly, that the hypothesis of the universe being a machine, and of "an Architect who constructed it, sitting as it were apart, and guiding it, and seeing it go, may turn out an inanity and nonentity"; that "that 'faint possible Theism,' which now forms our common English creed," which seeks a God *here* and *there*, and not there where alone He is to be found—inwardly, in our own soul,—that this Theism cannot be too soon swept out of the world. To the individual who with hysterical violence theoretically asserts a God who is a mere distant simulacrum, Carlyle exclaims, "Fool! God is not only *there*, but *here*, or nowhere, in that life-breath of thine, in that act and thought of thine,—and thou wert wise to look to it."[2] "Whosoever, in one way or another, recognises not that 'Divine Idea of the World,' which lies at the bottom of appearances,' can rightly interpret no appearance; and whatsoever spiritual thing he does, must do it partially, do it falsely."[3] With the theoretical perversities of the mere logical understanding, which makes of the universe a dead mechanism, go hand in hand the moral and spiritual perversities of selfish utilitarianism. This blind pursuit of pleasure, which will have God's infinite Universe altogether to itself, and therefore necessarily remains for ever deceived and dissatisfied, is the root of all evil. For this reason sorrow is so good and needful to man, that it teaches him that happiness is not his highest end and good, but rather, as Goethe maintains, life really begins with self-renunciation. "Love not pleasure, but love God!

---

[1] *Miscellanies*, vol. v. p. 49 *sq.*   [2] *Ibid.*, p. 51.   [3] *Ibid.*, p. 52.

This is the 'Everlasting Yea,' wherein all contradiction is solved : wherein whoso walks and works, it is well with him."[1]

This is in brief the *Weltanschauung* of Carlyle, an ethical idealism after the manner of Fichte, Herder, and Goethe. It is undoubtedly not "Theism" as commonly understood, but it is as little an abstract and systematic "Pantheism." Carlyle hated all such formulæ, and the endless controversies about them. With him the essential thing was to feel God in one's own soul as a living reality, to behold reverently his rule in the world of nature and history, and from this feeling and vision to labour for the good and true in unselfish devotion. For himself he did not require a more definite formulation of his philosophic view of things, and declined it as an impediment. But he was too good an historian not to know that the clothing of tangible symbols is necessary to make ideal truth the faith of an historical community. The forms of ecclesiastical creeds and life are, like institutions of the State, the "clothes" of the idea ; without such clothes and historical vestures, Carlyle expressly maintains, society has never existed, and never can exist.[2] But, he forcibly remarks, that it is with these spiritual as with our bodily clothes—we always need them, but cannot always have the same. Time, which adds much to the sacredness of symbols, at length desecrates them again. Symbols also wax old, as everything in the world has its rise, its culmination, and its decline. As in the past new prophets have always arisen at the right moment, who as God-inspired poets created new symbols, so will it be in the future also. " Meanwhile, we account him Legislator and wise who can so much as tell when a symbol has grown old, and gently remove it."[3]

Carlyle has nowhere expounded connectedly his view of the nature and development of religion (and we must remember that he was really not a philosopher, but an historian), but his ideas thereon may be gathered from various passages of his writings, forming an inwardly connected whole. Religion— we may thus summarise his opinion—is to be found in every man as part of his spiritual constitution, as a God-given faculty, enabling him to apprehend intuitively the Divine in the world and in human life, and to worship it in reverent obedience. But the constitutional endowment becomes an actual living

---

[1] *Sartor Resartus*, p. 133. [2] *Ibid.*, p. 149. [3] *Ibid.*, p. 155.

power in historical society only; and there only by the instrumentality of those leading minds which as seers and prophets apprehend in clear thought, and reveal in intelligible speech what slumbers unconsciously in the souls of all. Their word brings to consciousness the truth which was previously unperceived, although longed for and dimly surmised, which lay in the depths of the soul, and which is then incorporated in the symbols of religious societies. These symbols are the indispensable means of presenting to men's minds in an intelligible and realisable form the Divine and Eternal, which is itself a nameless and unutterable mystery. For this reason they are the sacred bond binding souls together, tokens, signs, standards, and garments of the Eternal and Divine, acknowledged by multitudes in common. Yet they are not themselves the Eternal and Divine, and, as having arisen in time, they have only limited duration. Waxing old with the progress of time, they lose the intelligible meaning which they had at the beginning, and then become empty masks, delusive simulacra, and hindrances of the truth and religion. It is then time to remove them cautiously, and to supply their place with new symbols from the perennial source of truth—the depths of the unconscious, intuitive spirit. But the time of transition, when the old is no more understood and received, and the new has not yet been generally recognised and acknowledged, is a time of difficulty and trouble. Doubt and denial then prevail; the cold understanding thrusts its barren logic into the place of creative genius; science, history, the universe are made mechanical; and only a few profounder minds perceive beneath the surface of chaos the signs of a new world of order, in which reverence shall be combined with clearness. Such a prophet of a nobler future Carlyle saw in Goethe, in the midst of this desert age of the barren understanding. And we may add that Carlyle was himself such a seer, who beheld prophetically, in the light of eternal ideas, not the past only, but also the future courses and destinations of human history, and illuminated them with his inspiration.

It is well known and intelligible enough that Carlyle stood very much alone with such views amongst his fellow-countrymen,—the Conservatives regarding him as a dangerous Radical, and the Liberals as a reactionary. It is, therefore, the more noteworthy that in the middle of the century a few more men are found, who, like Carlyle, and to some extent influenced by him, sought to combine the severest criticism of the traditional belief of the Churches with genuine and profound piety and moral earnestness.[1] Chief amongst these was FRANCIS WILLIAM NEWMAN, younger brother of John Henry Newman, who will come under our notice in the next chapter, to whom he was in no degree inferior in point of delicacy and religious feeling, and far superior in depth and clearness of thought and in moral courage, although English society has persistently placed the daring heretic, whose free thought was inconvenient, below the socially distinguished and dignified ecclesiastic with his polished style. In the book, *Phases of Faith* (1850), Francis Newman, following his own religious development,—really a typical case for our age,—describes the process by which a truth-loving mind is compelled by the logic of facts to resign one position after another in the authoritative creeds. It is not *à priori* presuppositions, not considerations of the undevout understanding, not speculative theories, that shake the foundations of his inherited belief; it is simply the application of the intellect to the examination of the received authorities, resulting in the conviction of their insufficiency, and human and historical conditionality, and accordingly of their want of divine authority, and of their unfitness to serve as the firm ultimate bases of belief. Thus, in the first instance, the orthodox creed is examined by the test to which it itself appeals—the Scriptures, and is found not to accord with them, and to be therefore unsatisfactory. The examination is then carried further; the Bible itself is submitted to it; the parallel narratives are compared (*e.g.* in the Gospels and the historical books of the Old Testament), and are found not to agree; then one doctrine is compared with another (*e.g.*, predestination and eternal torments with the goodness and mercy of God), and here, again, irreconcilable contradictions are presented; finally, notions of the Bible are compared with undoubted facts of science (*e.g.* of astronomy, geology, human history), and once again the fallibility of Scripture has to be acknowledged. If, with the Unitarians of that generation, the attempt was made to fall back from the teaching of the Bible as a whole upon the teaching of Jesus, as the final and sure authority, it could not be made out his-

---

[1] One of these was William Rathbone Greg, the author of *The Creed of Christendom*, 1851.

torically, from the traditions, what the teaching of Jesus certainly was; all such attempts show ever afresh that it is a self-destructive contradiction to seek to base an authoritative system upon free critical inquiry. When the great primary questions of religion are proposed, there are only two solutions possible: either we follow the inward law of the reason and conscience and disregard the external law of authority, or *vice versâ*. The middle course of orthodox Protestantism, which requires on the one hand the submission of the proud reason to the infallible authority of the "Word of God," and on the other hand appeals from the authority of the Church to the right of the individual "conscience" (which must mean the reason), is illogical and contradictory; and the sense of this sends many to Rome.

This position of Newman's is undoubtedly logically impregnable, but in his statement of it he has overlooked an essential point. The education of reason and conscience, by which the individual is fitted to form true judgments, is the result of the historical development of humanity, and cannot therefore be separated therefrom, but must always seek from thence instruction and guidance. From this point of view the antithesis of inward and outward authority becomes less absolute than Newman makes it, being the constant interaction of historical universality and individual spontaneity.—The closing remarks of Newman's are excellent: Religion was created by the inward instinct of the soul, its longing for the sympathy of God with it and for fellowship with him. But it had afterwards to be purified and chastened by the sceptical understanding; the co-operation of these two powers is essential for its perfection. While religious persons dread critical and searching thought, and critics despise instinctive religion, each side of man remains imperfect and curtailed. Surely the age is ripe for a religion which shall combine the tenderness, humility, and disinterestedness that are the glory of the purest Christianity, with that activity of intellect, untiring pursuit of truth, and strict adherence to impartial principle which the schools of modern science embody.

Newman has sketched an ideal picture of a Christianity thus chastened and combined with the knowledge of the present day, in the two short but valuable essays, *The Soul, its Sorrows and its Aspirations: an Essay towards the Natural History of the Soul as the true Basis of Theology* (1849, 3rd ed., 1852), and *Theism, Doctrinal and Practical* (1858). A profound and genuine piety breathes through both of these books, combined with clear and sound thought, which places in a bright light the fundamental religious problems, and seeks their solution in the depths of personal consciousness, and also in the wider region of the consciousness of humanity as reflected in history. As confessions of a devout thinker (akin to St. Augustine's Confessions), they form a true book of devotion for thoughtful religious readers. The comparison with Schleiermacher's *Reden* is also obvious; but it cannot be denied that Newman's idea of the nature of religion has this superiority over that of the *Reden*, that it is based upon a truer psychology, and the mysticism involved in it is less æsthetical than ethical, and consequently the conception of God in Newman's essays is more Christian than Spinozistic.

The empirical philosophy of the 18th century was handed on and attained to new significance in the two Mills, father and son. Following Hume and Hartley, JAMES MILL, in his *Analysis of the Phenomena of the Human Mind* (1829), had traced all our intellectual and moral judgments to the association of ideas, which in consequence of frequent occurrence together become constantly connected. This doctrine of the association of ideas forms also the basis of the philosophy of JOHN STUART MILL, though it does not there retain the logical thoroughness which it has in the father's system. In re-editing his father's book, the son added notes in explanation and correction which amount to an abandonment of the fundamental principle of this philosophy. But as he sought nevertheless tenaciously to cling to it, remarkable inconsistencies and uncertainties found their way into his doctrine, both on its theoretical and its practical side.

According to J. S. Mill we have knowledge of our sensations and ideas only, but neither of an object external to us nor of a subject as the basis of those feelings. Things are only the permanent possibilities of sensation, and mind is only a series of feelings with a background of the possibility of feeling. Having had his attention called by Hamilton to the fact that an association of ideas is possible only by a comparison of similar sensations, that comparison involves remembrance, and remembrance is possible only by virtue of the identity of the ego as existing throughout the series of different feelings, Mill extended his definition of mind by the addition, that it is "a series of feelings which is aware of itself as past and future." That this is a paradox, an inexplicable puzzle, he himself admitted, without on that account, however, amending the erroneous idea of the mind with which he had set out, and to which alone the puzzle is to be ascribed. He likewise admitted that the phenomenon of memory is a puzzle which his psychology is unable to solve, as no explanation of it can be assigned which does not involve belief in the identity of the ego, which is the thing to be accounted for. Under the pressure of this difficulty he wavers between such indefinite descriptions as an inexplicable "link of sensations" or "thread of consciousness" and the supposition of a real permanent element which is different from everything else, and can only be spoken of as the ego. But he is far from making any actual use of this as an original active principle.—Nor do our sensations reveal any more the reality of external objects than of the ego. Things, bodies, are simply groups of sensations, which arise according to the law of causality, which, however, is the law of subjective association. The theory gives no explanation of the source whence these groups come, or of how they can affect each other, of how it comes about that we associate with the perception of certain moving bodies the idea of persons external to ourselves.—Cause is the name simply of the regular recurring connexion in experience of certain sensations; when we speak of the "law of causality," we mean only the uniformity, observed in experience, of a series of occurrences—an abstraction which, according to Mill himself, is not reached until an advanced stage of observation has been attained, whilst really thought is subject to the category of causality from the beginning. Of course, with this explanation of causality from the association of ideas, the element of necessity is put out of court, and Mill accordingly regards it as by no means inconceivable, that in other worlds than this the connexion between cause and effect may not exist. Mathematical truths, in like manner, possess nothing beyond the probability of inferences from uniform experience, and by no means unconditional certainty. The contrary opinion would lead to the metaphysics of innate principles, with which the doors would be opened to the unscientific method of intuition and all kinds of mysticism. In order, therefore, to protect science, empiricism is carried through to its extreme sceptical consequences, by which the ground is cut from under the feet of all science!

The final outcome of the philosophy of Mill is no better on its ethical side. From the school of his father and of Bentham, he adopts the principle that happiness is the one desirable object, though it is not merely one's own happiness, but that also of others, yet the latter only for the sake of the former. No other reason can be assigned why the general happiness is desirable, except that each person desires his own happiness. In his autobiography,[1] Mill speaks, however, of an important crisis in his life, when he learnt that "the end of happiness was only to be attained by not making it the direct end. Those only are happy (I thought) who have their minds fixed on some object other than their own happiness; on the happiness of others, on the improvement of mankind, even on some art or pursuit, followed not as a means, but as itself an ideal end. Aiming thus at something else, they find happiness by the way. Once make the enjoyments of life a principal object, and they are immediately felt to be insufficient." Beyond doubt, noble utterances, to which an almost verbal parallel is to be found in the idealist Carlyle[2]; but Mill has not shown how we are to harmonise with them the fundamental principle of his ethical philosophy, according to which the idea of happiness, and in the last instance one's own happiness, is the highest motive of action. Here also, as in the theoretical section of his philosophy, he has failed to carry through his psychological analysis to the final decisive point; he has not made it clear to himself that the question *why* we feel ourselves under moral obligation at all, is quite distinct from the question as to the content, the *what*, of right moral conduct. It is undoubtedly true that in relation to the latter question the consequences of an action to society and to the individual must be taken into consideration as an essential criterion. But if this criterion of the specific action is confounded with the motive of the moral will, if the desire for happiness is made the chief motive, and put in the place of the sense of duty, the actual facts of the true moral consciousness are rendered as inexplicable as theoretical knowledge is when the association of ideas, which is only a means of logical thought, is put in its place. The utilitarian principle of the empirical philosophy has its proper place as an heuristic principle in

---

[1] Page 142. [2] See *ante*, p. 314.

practical sociology, when the existence of the sense of duty is assumed as a matter of course; but when it claims to be an explanation of the moral consciousness generally, and when the sense of duty is accordingly derived from calculations of utility, the true science of ethics is not served, but rendered impossible.[1]

It is intelligible that with such premises the religious views of Mill could not rise far above sceptical negations. His father, who had lost all belief in a good God in consequence of his education in the creed of Scotch Presbyterianism and of his reflections on the evils of the world, brought up his son without any religious belief. As compared with the purely negative position of his early days, it marks, therefore, a certain advance when, in his essay on *The Utility of Religion* (written between 1850 and 1858), he allows that in early times religious belief in the Divine sanctions of moral laws was an excellent means of introducing and establishing them, and that even now religion, like poetry, answers to a craving in men for higher and nobler ideas than actual life supplies. But it is doubtful whether "the idealism of our earthly life, the cultivation of a high conception of what *it* may be made, is not capable of supplying a poetry, and, in the best sense of the word, a religion, equally fitted to exalt the feelings and still better calculated to ennoble the conduct, than any belief respecting the unseen powers." "The essence of religion is the strong and earnest direction of the emotions and desires towards an ideal object, recognised as of the highest excellence, and as rightfully paramount over all selfish objects of desire. This condition is fulfilled by the Religion of Humanity in as eminent a degree, and in as high a sense, as by the supernatural religions even in their best manifestations, and far more so than in any of the others," which, by their threats and promises, strengthen the selfish element of our nature instead of weakening it. Besides, these religions suffer under so many contradictions and irrationalities that the simple and innocent faith which their acceptance involves can co-exist only with a torpid and inactive state of the speculative faculties, whilst persons of exercised intellect are able to

---

[1] The folly of such a mode of procedure in ethical science, Carlyle has admirably satirised by setting the problem, "Given a world of knaves, to produce an honesty from their united action?" (*Misc.*, iv. p. 36.)

believe only by the sophistication and perversion either of the understanding or of the conscience. Finally, the Religion of Humanity leaves open an ample domain in the region of the imagination, which may be planted with possibilities and hypotheses, of which neither the falsehood nor the truth can be ascertained.

In the later essay on *Theism*, written between 1868 and 1870 (which had not received the final revisions which it was his habit to make), likewise published after the author's death, Mill appears to have advanced beyond this purely critical standpoint. The inquiry is not now merely with regard to the utility of religion, but as to the truth of religious ideas, and the result of it leads to the acceptance of the preponderating probability of certain suppositions, although undoubtedly they are still far enough removed from orthodox belief. From the adaptations in nature, Mill now considers, there is evidence which points, not to the creation of the universe, but of the present order of it by an Intelligent Mind; though the imperfections in nature necessitate the supposition that its Author has but limited power over it; and that he has some regard to the happiness of his creatures probably, though we are not justified in supposing this is his sole or chief motive of action. It is also possible that a Being thus limited in power may interfere occasionally in the imperfect machinery of the universe, though in none of the cases in which such interposition is believed to have occurred is the evidence such as could possibly prove it. In the same way the possibility of life after death must be admitted, though it cannot be converted into a certainty. "To me it seems that human life, small and confined as it is, and as, considered merely in the present, it is likely to remain, even when the progress of material and moral improvement may have freed it from the greater part of its present calamities, stands greatly in need of any wider range and greater height of aspiration, for itself and its destination, which the exercise of imagination can yield to it without running counter to the evidence of fact." . . . "The indulgence of hope with regard to the government of the universe, and the destiny of man after death, is legitimate, and philosophically defensible. The beneficial effect of such hope is far from trifling. It makes life and human nature a far greater thing to the feelings, and gives greater strength as well as solemnity to all the sentiments which are awakened in us by our fellow-creatures and mankind at large." Religious belief in the reality of the divine ideal, notwithstanding all the perversions and corruptions of it, has proved its force through past ages, a force beyond what a merely ideal conception could exert. And this belief can only increase in value when the critical thinker resigns the idea of an *omnipotent* ruler of the world, as then the evils of the world no longer cast a shadow upon his moral perfection. The Divine ideal is still more valuable as it is to be beheld incorporated in the human personality of Jesus. However much of the accretions of legend and speculation may be taken away from us by rational criticism, Christ will remain a unique figure; on his words and deeds "there is a stamp of personal originality, combined with profundity and insight, which must place the Prophet of Nazareth in the very first rank of the men of sublime genius of whom our species can boast. A better translation of the rule of virtue from the abstract into the concrete cannot be found, than to endeavour so to live that Christ would approve our life." In the continual battle between the powers of good and of evil, it is to the good man an elevating feeling to know that he is helping God by a co-operation of which God, not being omnipotent, really stands in need, and by which a somewhat nearer approach may be made to the fulfilment of his purposes.

The religious idealism which speaks through these words of Mill's is the more gratifying that it could not be looked for from the principles of his philosophy. After individual happiness had been made in morals the main principle, it is surprising to find unselfish devotion to the requirements of goodness or the purposes of God constituted the ideal in religion. These are, surely, two standpoints far removed from each other, the reconciliation of which Mill has not supplied. And after he had in logic referred causality to the association of subjective ideas, and the objectivity of knowledge had been denied, we are taken by surprise when finally an intelligent Designer and Ruler of the world is inferred by means of the law of causation. Evidently Mill's personal feeling and thinking were better than his philosophical prejudices strictly allowed.

The principal representative of the intuitive philosophy, which, Mill supposed, was inclined to consider cherished dogmas as intuitive truths, and intuition as the voice of God and Nature, having a higher authority than the voice of reason, was the Scotch philosopher, Sir WILLIAM HAMILTON. Against his system Mill wrote his book, *Examination of Sir William Hamilton's Philosophy*, which he subjected to a searching criticism from his own empirical standpoint. But he seems to have ignored the fact that the "intuitive," or critico-speculative philosophy has other and more important representatives than Hamilton; and his knowledge of the history of philosophy, particularly of German philosophy, was defective.[1]

Hamilton was indebted to both Reid and Kant: he endeavoured to combine the realism of the former with the subjective criticism of the latter, but without any great success. He himself published an edition of the works of Reid with notes, and after his death his pupils, Mansel and Veitch, edited his *Lectures on Logic and Metaphysics* (1860, 4 vols.). But he had previously plainly indicated his philosophical position in his *Review of the Philosophy of Cousin*, which appeared first in the *Edinburgh Review* (1829), and finally in the volume of *Discussions on Philosophy and Literature*, in 1852. There are, he considers, four views with regard to the Unconditioned: according to Cousin it is cognisable and conceivable by means of reflection; according to Schelling, though it is not comprehensible by reflection, it is knowable by intellectual intuition; according to Kant, though not theoretically knowable, it is knowable as a regulative principle, and its notion is more than a mere negation of the Conditioned; finally, according to Hamilton himself, it is neither conceivable nor in any way knowable, because it is simply the negation of the Conditioned, which alone can be positively conceived. With regard to Kant, Hamilton admits that to him belongs the merit of having first examined the extent of our knowledge, and of having limited it to the conditional phenomena of our consciousness, but maintains that Kant's deduction of the categories and ideas was the result of great but perverse ingenuity, and his distinction between the understanding and the reason surreptitious. As Kant admits that the "ideas" involve

---

[1] As critics of Mill, may be mentioned, McCosh, Green, Bradley (*Principles of Logic*), Martineau.

self-contradiction, and yet makes them legitimate products of intelligence, the speculative reason becomes in his system an organ of simple delusion, and this must lead to absolute scepticism. For if our intellectual nature be perfidious in one revelation, it must be regarded as misleading in all. When the falseness of the speculative reason has been once proved, it is impossible to establish the existence of God, Freedom, and Immortality on the ground of the supposed veracity of the practical reason. Because Kant did not completely exorcise the spectre of the Absolute, it has ever since continued to haunt the German school of philosophy. Though Schelling perceived the impossibility of getting a philosophy of the Unconditioned by means of conceptual reflection, his "intellectual intuition" of the Absolute was the product of arbitrary abstraction and a self-delusive imagination; for when the antithesis of subject and object, which constitute consciousness, has been annihilated, all that remains is *nothing*, which is baptized with the name of "Absolute."

According to Hamilton, the Infinite and Absolute is simply an abstraction of the conditions under which thought is possible, and accordingly a negation of the conceivable. For to think is to condition, and conditioned limitation is the fundamental law of thought. Thought cannot get beyond consciousness, and consciousness is possible only under the antithesis of subject and object, which are conceivable only in correlation and mutual limitation. Whence it follows that a philosophy which claims to be more than a knowledge of the conditional is impossible. Our knowledge of mind and matter cannot be more than a knowledge of the relative manifestation of an existence, the essence *per se* of which the highest wisdom must acknowledge as unknowable, as Augustine had confessed, *ignorando cognosci*. But as the power of our thought cannot be made the measure of existence, so neither may we limit the horizon of our faith to the realm of our knowledge. By miraculous revelation we have received our faith in the existence of something unconditioned beyond the sphere of all conceivable reality. The saying of Jacobi is therefore true: an understood God would be no God at all, and to imagine that God is what we think would be blasphemy. The ultimate and highest consecration of all true religion must be an altar to the unknown and unknowable God. In this Nature and Revelation, Heathenism and Christianity agree.

These ideas of Sir W. Hamilton's were further expanded and made the basis of a system of dogmatic supernaturalism by his disciple MANSEL, in his Bampton Lectures, *The Limits of Religious Thought* (1852, 5th ed. 1870). The position taken is, that if philosophy undertakes to subject the contents of revealed religion to criticism, it must first show its right to attempt this by the proof of its power to conceive the nature of God. But this proof has hitherto never been forthcoming, and from the very nature of the mind can never be given. For the "Absolute," the "Infinite," the "First Cause" of philosophy involve irreconcilable contradictions. The Absolute is one and simple; how then can we distinguish in it a plurality of attributes? The Infinite is that which is free from all possible limitation; how then can it co-exist with its contradictory—the Finite? And how can the Infinite be at the same time the First Cause, since there is involved in the very idea of cause the antithesis of effect, and accordingly limitation? From the nature of human consciousness, too, the proof is given that these ideas involve hopeless contradiction. Consciousness is the relation of an object to a subject and to other objects, but the idea of the Absolute precludes all such relation. Further, our consciousness is subject to the laws of space and time, and cannot therefore think the thought of a Being not likewise subject to them. But, Mansel holds, we must not thence infer that the Infinite cannot exist, but only that *what* the Infinite is and his relation to the Finite is for us incognisable. From this our duty is plain—to accept without addition or subtraction whatever revelation, that is, the Bible, teaches as to God, on its authority. This will be the more easy when we remember that the greatest difficulties of belief have their parallels in philosophy; for instance, the doctrine of the Trinity, in the relation of one Absolute to a plurality of attributes; the Divine sonship of Christ, in the relation of the eternal cause to effects in time; the two natures in Christ, in the relation between the Infinite and the Finite; miracles, in the conception of government by law at all, and in the relation of the law of causality to freedom generally. If the reason is incapable of solving these philosophical problems, it is not justified in rejecting the doctrines of revelation because they are also, but not more, inconceivable. As little may the reason on moral grounds criticise revelation. For neither are moral principles by any means the eternal truth of reason, but are laws which God has revealed with reference to our human nature, without being himself bound by them. When therefore the inspired word of God records commands of God which seem to involve apparent immorality, we may not argue therefrom that God cannot have revealed such commands, but only that God's nature is not less incomprehensible to our moral than to our speculative reason. Such instances must be treated as "moral miracles," which prove that God has the right to occasionally suspend the moral laws not less than natural laws, without cancelling their validity in ordinary practical life.

To the obvious question, how with such incapacity of reason we can be in a position to recognise a Divine revelation as such, and to distinguish the revelation of the Bible as the only true one from the alleged revelations of other religions, Mansel replies at the end of his book only, and there but briefly. He warns us not to lay the main stress of the proof on the internal evidence, which would involve an appeal to the incompetent reason. "The crying evil of the present day in religious controversy is the neglect or contempt of the external evidences of Christianity; the first step towards the establishment of a sound religious philosophy must consist in the restoration of those evidences to their true place in the theological system." Though unconditional certainty does not belong to any one of them taken singly, in conjunction they constitute a sure foundation of faith in the revelation of the Bible, and the revelation thus established must be accepted from beginning to end, without criticism on the part of the incompetent reason. If the teaching of Christ is in any one thing not the teaching of God, it is in all things the teaching of man, and Christ was an impostor or an enthusiast; but if Christ is in truth the Incarnate Son of God, every attempt to improve his teaching is more impious than to reject it altogether, for this is to acknowledge a doctrine as the revelation of God, and at the same time to proclaim it inferior to the wisdom of man.

It is significant as to the condition of theology in England at that time, that this unqualified dogmatism of Mansel's should have met with a large amount of approbation, and that the author was considered a true *Defensor Fidei*. It is all the more to the honour of F. D. MAURICE that he at once discerned not merely the irrationality of Mansel's theory, but also the danger to which it laid open Christian faith, and that he boldly and energetically opposed it. He very properly considers that the fundamental mistake of Mansel is, that he starts from ideas which he has himself set up, and then argues from the contradictions, which he has himself put into them, that the ideas themselves involve contradictions. He falls at once upon the question of the Infinite, and overwhelms his readers with a discussion of metaphysical problems, without so much as touching the fundamental problem of consciousness, without having asked, " How does our consciousness get at reality at all?" Mansel holds the question as to the nature of reality, of personality, as insoluble, because we cannot know anything beyond the phenomena of our own consciousness, but does not consider that while phenomena constitute the immediate content of our consciousness, it is the very function of philosophical science to deal not with them, but with what is, *das Ding-an-sich*. It is precisely this—to distinguish what *is* from what merely *appears* to be, which is the province of reason, without which man would sink to the level of the animal. The same distinction which is necessary in daily life, must also be applied in the highest relations of knowledge. When Mansel denies this, he casts aside the Bible as well as reason. If he pronounces Kant's Practical Reason, with its faculty of ideas, as merely a faculty of lies, then conscience and the faith of the simple Christian are faculties of lies without any support in reality. In order to deliver English theology from the influence of German philosophy, Mansel falls back upon the scepticism of Hume, with whom he shares also the indifference of Positivism, which in the absence of personal conviction advocates the re-assurement of men's minds by means of the established religion of the State. Mansel's endeavour to base faith upon sceptical agnosticism can only serve to strengthen thoughtless indifference and traditionalism, which is the greatest danger for England.

What a dangerous two-edged sword this agnosticism of the apologists is was very soon made evident. In the course of the next decade, upon this agnosticism Matthew Arnold based his ethical idealism, Seeley his æsthetical idealism, and Herbert Spencer his evolutionism, three theories which, with all their dissimilarities, have this in common, that they all regard the impossibility of a Divine revelation and revealed religion to be the necessary consequence of the incognisability of God.

In his works, *Literature and Dogma* (1873), and *God and the Bible* (1875), MATTHEW ARNOLD has advocated, as a substitute for supernatural religion, an ethical idealism very much of the same nature as that of Fichte. He had convinced himself that in an age like this, which will take nothing for granted, but must verify everything, Christianity in the old form of authoritative belief in supernatural beings and miraculous deeds, is no longer tenable, and that the only method of defending the Faith which has any promise of success, is that which confines itself to such ethical truths of Christianity as can be verified by experience, and rejects everything beyond them, or admits it only as their merely poetic garb. According to Matthew Arnold, religion has no more to do with supernatural dogma than with metaphysical philosophy: it is ethical, it has to do with "conduct," but as distinguished from ethics, it is "ethics heightened, enkindled, lit up by feeling," in a word it "is morality *touched* by emotion." The mistaken notion that religion is something more than and different from this, and in some way supernatural, arose from a misunderstanding of the poetic and rhetorical form of speaking natural to it; what was meant as a poetic and imaginative representation of ethical experience and emotion, was taken for strictly scientific truth. This holds very specially of belief in God. It would be folly to make religion depend on the conviction of the existence of "the moral and intelligent Governor of the universe" of theology,—a belief which cannot possibly be verified by experience. The God of religion is a poetical personification of that which alone constitutes the object of religious faith in its moral sense. For this object Arnold has coined the phrase, "the Eternal, not ourselves, which makes for righteousness." All that we can say of this power, on the evidence of experience, is that it is not ourselves, but is ever revealing itself in the universe as the Power making everywhere and always for righteousness, in consequence of which also all things have and tend to fulfil the law of their being. That this Power should be converted by the religious imagination into a personal God, who thinks and loves and rules the world, does no harm so long as we treat the personification simply as representing in a poetic form the unknowable Not-ourselves, of which we can become aware only as working for the production of righteousness. But as soon as ever we try to treat the personal God of religion as a really existing being and object of scientific thought, we enter the region of fanciful anthropomorphism or abstract metaphysics, where the possibility of verification by experience, and therefore of sure conviction, ceases. The traditional philosophical arguments for the existence of an intelligent First Cause are equally baseless with the popular proofs from miracles, and have, indeed, less value, as the latter belong to a great and splendid whole—a beautiful and powerful fairy tale, while the former are only the hollow talk of philosophical sophism. Of a personal Governor of the world we can form no clear conception, and can have no certain conviction based upon experience, but we can form an idea and have experiential certainty of a Power making for righteousness. That idea of a personal God had its origin in metaphysics, and must be banished, with metaphysics, from religion, that in the future religion may occupy the only solid ground supplied by the moral experience of mankind.

It need create no surprise that this theory met with a considerable amount of favour in England, for it falls in with the agnostic tendencies of our age, and at the same time endeavours to be just to the moral consciousness, and to retain reverence for the Bible. In Holland, too, it is known and extensively held under the name of "ethical idealism." To us Germans it presents little that is new, but is simply another form of the *sittliche Weltordnung*, which Fichte at the end of the last century pronounced the essence of the idea of God. Arnold also shares Fichte's moral earnestness, and his enjoyment of an onslaught on other opinions, without always observing due moderation in his attack. And as regards the tenability of the theory, the development of Fichte's philosophy seems to offer an instructive anticipation. It is at all events certain that the idea of an "Eternal Power not ourselves, which makes for righteousness," is far from being a clear idea derived from experience, as Matthew Arnold maintains; but is, on the contrary, an abstract philosophical conception, behind the vagueness of which the possibility of very various interpretations is hidden. At one time this "Not-ourselves" is described as a real, efficient power, to which we feel we are subject, and for which we feel reverence. In that case, the inference can scarcely be withheld, that the effects which we experience presuppose an active, effective, and therefore actual subject, who intends to produce these effects, and who must accordingly be conceived as a being capable of having spiritual, moral purposes, which would bring us to a position very much like theism. On the other hand, other passages point to an entirely different interpretation. The "Not-ourselves" is also spoken of as a law of nature after the manner of the law of gravitation, or the law of spiritual beauty; as the latter was personified by the Greeks in Apollo, so the law of moral conduct was personified by the Hebrews in Jehovah, which is not at all inconsistent with the supposition that they might have reached the law by the Darwinian method of adaptation and heredity. Now, since a "law" is not itself an operative, effective force, but only the manner of the operation of actual beings, the interpretation of Arnold's theory just given conducts necessarily to the Positivist view, according to which the divine consists simply in the morally good feelings and actions of man himself, not in any power outside and above man. But, in that case, where is the *Not*-ourselves upon which Arnold lays so much stress? To a more thoroughly logical agnostic will it not seem to be a remnant of mystical speculation, which is not verifiable by experience, but must be got rid of, and the Positivist idea of humanity put in its place? But then we get the atheistic religion of humanity of Feuerbach and Comte. To bring that, however, into harmony with Biblical theism would be more than Arnold could accomplish, even with his very bold and free exegesis.

It must be doubted whether Arnold's idea of a "Power not ourselves, which makes for righteousness," which admits of such various and in fact contradictory interpretations, is superior in point of clearness and credibility to the conception of God which has hitherto been generally held. Arnold would not have deceived himself so far as he did on this head if he had tried more seriously to think out his ideas. But he often declares, with characteristic mocking irony, that for philosophical thinking he has no faculty. In this he was undoubtedly perfectly right. For a fuller discussion of Arnold's position, I refer the reader to Martineau's essay on *Ideal Substitutes for God* (3rd ed., 1881), to his work, *A Study of Religion, its Sources and Contents* (1888); further, to Tulloch's essay on *The Modern Religion of Experience*. Tulloch remarks that Arnold's "Power not ourselves, which makes for righteousness," can as little be verified by experience in the sense of natural science as any ancient dogma. All that can be proved by the method of this science is the recurrence of certain external conditions, to which Arnold gives the name of "righteousness," and behind which he supposes a Power causing them. But this is beyond question as much his belief as the creed of any one else is his. The idea of righteousness is as certainly a product of the conscience, or of what Arnold calls metaphysics, as the idea of personality; both arise from within, and are not brought from without. In fact, the two are twin ideas, inseparably connected in the Hebrew and the universal conscience—a law of conduct and a lawgiver, or personal authority, from whom it issues. This is undoubtedly the voice of experience, though not in Arnold's, but in a higher and truer sense of the word. Accordingly, Arnold's notion of dogma as an excrescence or a disease of religion is superficial. Of course religion and dogma are not identical. But the latter is the product of religious thought, or of the thought of the Church upon the facts of religious experience. The creeds of the Church are the fruit of the best possible efforts of theological thinkers of every age, accordingly living expressions of the Christian consciousness, deserving as such more respect than they meet with from the representatives of the modern spirit. So far the judgment of Tulloch. His remarks in the same essay on the personal and literary characteristics of Matthew Arnold I will not repeat here, incontrovertible as they appear to me to be.

The author of the anonymous book, *Natural Religion* (1882), who is, we are told, Professor SEELEY, of Cambridge, is Arnold's equal in the lucidity and beauty of his style, and superior to him in breadth of view and acuteness of thought. He also proceeds from the conviction that the supernatural elements of traditional religion are rapidly losing their hold upon the mind of the men of this age, while religion itself is to-day as needful and indispensable as ever it was. He, too, seeks to ascertain how much of traditional religion will be left when the supernatural has been abandoned. But the answer returned by Arnold, that the essential element of religion is morality, does not satisfy Seeley, inasmuch as religion makes itself felt in other and equally important departments of man's "Higher Life." It is not so much a manner of acting as of feeling, namely, the habitual feeling of admiration and reverence, combined with love and devotion. It is not merely the God of wonders who can be the object of such a religious worship, but whatever is *beautiful, good,* and *true* in nature and man. Seeley accordingly distinguishes three kinds of religion, each of which has its own peculiar value, and can be harmoniously combined with the others. First, the religion of the beautiful in nature, the æsthetic religion of the Greeks; second, the worship of the morally good in man, the religion of ideal humanity, the very essence of Christianity, which though propagated at first under the supernatural form of the Christology of the Church, has since the middle of the last century, freed from that husk, developed into the religion of Humanity. Third, to these must be added now the worship of the Unity and Eternity of the universe, which, under the name of "God," is conceived as the Supreme Power, comprehending nature and man; a religion which will remain though all belief in the supernatural is abandoned. Reverence for the supreme unity and the law of all being is so natural to men, that it will continue to be felt, however they conceive the relation of the One to the various elements of the universe, or of God to the world. We do not find the difference of theories as to man and the relation of his physical and mental powers to one another hinders the practical reverence we feel for human nature; and as little is our practical worship of the Unity and Regularity of the universe affected by the theological question as to the relation of the *one* Principle to the multiplicity of phenomena. The name "Nature" does not adequately represent this Unity, inasmuch as often in the usage of scientific men it leaves out of view the moral and human side of the universe, which is to us the more important side. But the word "God" combines the greatness and glory of nature with "whatever more awful forces stir within the human heart, whatever binds men in families and orders them in states." God "is the Inspirer of kings, the Revealer of laws, the Reconciler of nations, the Redeemer of labour, the Queller of tyrants, the Reformer of Churches, the Guide of the human race toward an unknown goal." The worship of this God, who reveals himself in Nature and in History, is not merely possible in an antisupernaturalistic age of art and science, but it is very necessary. For nothing else than the worship of the Divine and Eternal in phenomena is able to confer upon art and science the virtue of ideality, and to raise them above commonplace and triviality. The State and Society rest, too, upon the basis of religion, reverence for the eternal laws of human life, free from all the supernatural wrappings of the past, which render religion stationary and cut it off from the living stream of modern life. Natural religion, on the other hand, occupies a place in the centre of the movements of the present and is the uniting and elevating force of all manifestations of human life. It is the attainment of the ideal which the Reformation proposed, which was, in fact, the ideal of the Hebrew prophets, for their religion was social, political, historical, and supernaturalism was not its mainspring. But Seeley does not wish to exclude everything supernatural from religion: he desires that faith may hold that a higher world than that known to us exists, only this transcendental world must not be made the chief thing.

Interesting as this æsthetic agnosticism beyond doubt is as a transitional phase in an age of scepticism, it is not possible to entirely withhold assent to the criticisms of those who maintain that thus to widen religion till it becomes simply the admiration of everything beautiful and great in Nature and history, is to water it down and empty it of significance, till the wants of the devout soul are not met. Religion, as Tulloch urges, undoubtedly does not ignore Nature, but discovers therein the rule of God; but the distinctive mark of religion is an ideal transcending both Nature and man. The Holy One of the Prophets and the Heavenly Father of Christ are not merely higher conceptions, but also truer ones, than any ideas of Nature of previous religions. The real problem is, Is there a spirit above nature and Man, a universal Consciousness, with which our higher life can have communion? To make religion the admiration of the laws of Nature and the ideals of art and science, is to introduce confusion into language, and to throw back moral ideas, which Christianity had grafted upon our thought, to the outlived stage of heathen thinkers. Perhaps we may add that thought itself is unable to rest finally in such a vague, problematic relation of the world to the *one* principle as Seeley expounds; and this must be felt the more in proportion as the effort is made to comprehend the totality of the universe in the unity of thought, which is the tendency of evolutionism in its various forms.

HERBERT SPENCER is regarded as at present the chief representative of agnosticism. But the agnosticism which Spencer adopted from Hamilton and Mansel forms but the one aspect of his philosophy, to a certain extent the convenient background into which all metaphysical problems can be relegated, so as to construct with fewer hindrances a system of natural evolution from the results of modern science. The significance of his philosophy lies in the boldness with which it makes the idea of evolution, which has controlled natural science since Darwin, the dominant point of view in the formation of a connected and systematic theory of the world. In order to save his doctrine of natural development from collision with the presuppositions of existing belief, he has placed the doctrine of the incognisability of the Absolute as a wall of separation between philosophy and religion, that an eternal peace may be concluded between them; but, in reality, with the result that he has deprived religion of its contents and his philosophical system of its prime principles. But, as in Spencer's system the idea of a harmonious and orderly world, or of a systematic unity among phenomena is so prominent, and this idea requires, or presupposes necessarily, a connecting principle, or a basis of unity, he has not been able to consistently carry out his agnostic theory, but has surreptitiously converted the bare negative, which Hamilton's Absolute amounted to, into a reality, which bears the relation of a positive cause to phenomena, only that nothing definite can be known as to its nature and its further relation to phenomena.

In his *First Principles* (1862), the ultimate principles of his philosophy, Spencer starts from the position, that as religion has always been of great importance in the history of mankind, and has been able to hold its ground in defiance of the attacks of science, it must contain an element of truth. But as there are various religions which claim to be true, and as science also can make the same claim, while yet truth is but *one*, the latter, Spencer holds, must be looked for in what the various religions have in common with each other and with science. This common element cannot be a definite conception of the Absolute or the First Cause of the world, for it is precisely on this point that opinions diverge, and in every one of the three main theories—Atheism, Pantheism, and Theism—is shown the impossibility of a satisfactory solution that is not self-contradictory. It follows that God, the Absolute, the Unconditioned, is not for us cognisable, but a great mystery, as all religions to some extent acknowledge, and the higher their rank, so much the more fully, only that the philosopher regards this mystery as not merely relative, as the religions regard it, but as absolute. Science and religion agree in this, for science knows nothing about the most universal ideas—force and matter, space and time; it can know things only by comparing them with others that resemble them, and on that very account is unable to know the Absolute, which cannot be compared with anything.

But although it is involved in the very nature of our consciousness that it can know only what is finite and limited, Spencer declines to go with Hamilton in maintaining that the Absolute is a purely negative concept. On the contrary, he holds that the reality of the Absolute is the necessary correlative of the Relative. This is both a necessity of thought and of the analysis of things. For if every definite state of consciousness has a limited content, the latter presupposes an unlimited and general content as the raw material of limiting thought. Our self-consciousness, as it is the consciousness of the conditioned ego and non-ego, presupposes an Unconditioned which is neither the ego nor the non-ego: this is the Absolute, which is accordingly the necessary correlative of our self-consciousness. And this *à priori* proof from consciousness is confirmed by an *à posteriori* proof from the analysis of external things. The results of modern physics and chemistry reveal as the constant element in all phenomena *Force*, which manifests itself in various forms that change places with each other, while amid all their changes it remains unaltered. If, accordingly, every specific force is only a relative changeable phenomenal form of one universal unchangeable force, this must be regarded as the absolute reality which must necessarily be presupposed as the background and basis of all that is relative and phenomenal. The entire universe is to be explained from the movement of this absolute Force, which takes place rhythmically as attraction and repulsion, integration and disintegration, evolution and dissolution; the phenomena of nature and of mental life come under the same general laws of matter, motion, and force, which are however only symbols of the absolute Reality or Force which is in itself unknowable.

It is obvious that Spencer has thus very seriously modified the doctrine of Hamilton and Mansel as to the incognisability of the Absolute. The Absolute of Spencer, of which substantiality, causality, eternity and immutability are predicated, is no longer the simple Unknown, which would be beyond all our conceptions. The only question which arises is whether Spencer's doctrine of the Absolute is adequate to account for the world of mental life, and whether it is adapted to serve as the basis of the reconciliation of science and religion. An affirmative answer can hardly be given to this question. For there is surely much force in the contention of Spencer's opponents, that his agnostic evolutionism is really only a disguised materialistic (hylozoistic) Pantheism; for if the supreme principle is nothing but force manifesting itself in various motions, it does not land us beyond materialism. On the other hand, it must be allowed that Spencer's real intention is directed to something higher, the attainment of which has been frustrated by his entanglement in the principle of empiricism and the psychology of association, though in many of his statements he approaches very nearly a higher position. If the Absolute must be conceived as the necessary correlative of our self-consciousness, can it be conceived simply as physical force, and not rather as universal self-consciousness, as a spiritual self? And if we get the idea of force from the experience of our own power of volition, its action and its resistance, is it not natural to think of mind-force as prior to physical, and accordingly of the absolute Force at the basis of all specific forces as Mind? The doctrine of evolution would harmonise perfectly well with these inferences, only it would have to become idealistic instead of materialistic, and only after this transformation had been made would a practicable basis be supplied for the reconciliation of religion and science which Spencer has done well to attempt.

Spencer would probably himself have taken this further step, if he had been able, on the decisive question as to the fundamental act of knowledge, to set himself free from the superficiality and confusions of the association-psychology. This he has failed to do, and defines consciousness as a succession of sensations or changes, which implies a relation of different states, and is brought about by different impressions of force. The question here arises, as in Mill's system, Can a succession of feelings or changes be consciously felt without a subject to recognise the change, without an active synthetic principle to combine the changing states of feeling into the unity of consciousness? But Spencer has no place in his system for such a subject, as he holds that the ego consists simply of a "faint" and the object of a "vivid" series of sensations. He acknowledges therefore really nothing more than passive sensations, or impressions of force, and supposes he can explain consciousness from their changes alone, while undoubtedly it is wholly inexplicable without the active synthesis of the ego. Spencer can have ignored this prime factor only because, like all empiricists, he "confuses the succession of feelings with cognition of succession, changes of consciousness with consciousness of change." When he speaks of change of states of consciousness as the result of changing impressions of force, he seeks to find the origin of consciousness in effects produced from without, which cannot, however, surely, be perceived as in succession and changed save by reference to previously existing consciousness; he really, therefore, presupposes consciousness as already inwardly present, while he seeks to explain it from external action. In fact, we must concur in the searching criticism of Green,[1] that Spencer has not grasped the fundamental problem of the source and nature of knowledge, as it was proposed by Hume and solved by Kant in the synthetic function of the ego. Spencer supposes that Kant has been refuted by the new discovery of the doctrine of natural evolution, namely, that the supposed *à priori* or innate ideas which are considered to precede experience, are in reality only the result of the experience of the race which the individual inherits.[2] But Spencer here fails to perceive the real nature of the problem, which is, How is experience in any form possible? A problem which remains unaltered whether the experience is that of the individual or the race, and to the solution of which no historical "psychogenesis" of nature can contribute in the smallest degree. And while his evolutionary psychology contributes nothing whatever towards a solution of the problem as to the nature of knowledge, Spencer really makes

---

[1] *Works of Thomas Hill Green*, vol. i. pp. 383 sqq.
[2] See Martineau's critique of this doctrine, *Types of Ethical Theory*, vol. ii. pp. 357 sqq.

a solution of it impossible by degrading the relation of subject and object, the ego and the non-ego, to a mere difference of degree in the strength or vividness of a series of sensations. An error so fundamental at the crucial point can do no other than produce a fatal effect upon the whole system built upon it. If a man fails to perceive in himself the active subject, the self-conscious mind, it cannot be expected of him that he should find it in the Absolute.

With reference to the religious import of the Spencerian doctrine of the Unknowable, the forcible criticisms of MARTINEAU and J. CAIRD may here find a place. The former[1] says that "Spencer's testimony against the purely phenomenal doctrine is of high value"; for "it betrays his appreciation of that outlook beyond the region of phenomena for the conditions of religion which cannot eventually be content to gaze into an abyss without reply." But his position, that we can know only *that* the absolute power is, but not *what* it is, is untenable, because it is self-contradictory. We can know the first fact by thought only, and " how can there be a thought with nothing thinkable?" "By calling this existence a '*Power*,' Mr. Herbert Spencer surely removes it by one mark from the unknown; but, besides this, 'we are obliged,' he says, 'to regard that Power as omniscient,' as eternal, as one, as cause manifested in all phenomena; a list of predicates, scanty indeed when measured by the requisites of religion, but too copious for the plea of Nescience." When we distinguish this Absolute from all that is related to it, we know it, for to distinguish is to know. "This negative ontology which identifies 'the supreme reality' with total vacuity, and makes the infinite in Being the zero in thought, cannot permanently poise itself in its precarious position; it must either repent of its concessions to realism and lapse into the scientific commonplace, 'all we know is phenomena'; or else advance, with what caution and reserve it pleases, into ulterior conceptions of the invisible cause, sufficient to soften the total eclipse into the penumbra of a sacred mystery." Martineau makes further the pertinent remark, that "it is but natural that the pretensions of men to more knowledge than they can substantiate should lead to this reaction into

---

[1] *A Study of Religion*, vol. i. pp. 131 sqq.

imaginary ignorance." "The Gnosticism of theologians is responsible for much of the Agnosticism of this century."

John Caird, in his *Introduction to the Philosophy of Religion* (1880),[1] has given a searching criticism of Spencer's agnosticism, the chief points of which are as follows. The two propositions that our intelligence is confined to the finite and relative, and that we have cognisance of an existence beyond the finite, are contradictory and cancel each other. Whoever maintains that human knowledge is limited shows thereby that it is not limited *merely* by the relative, because in that case it could have no knowledge of its own limits. The true conclusion from the principles of Spencer's theory of knowledge is not the incognisability of the Absolute, but its non-existence; his "unknowable Absolute" is simply the negation of thought; and therewith of being, in every sense in which we can use the expression. In reality, the assertion of the unknowableness of the Absolute is based upon an abstraction; a fictitious logical entity is first created, and then consciousness is charged with imbecility because of its inability to think that fiction. Nothing can possess any reality for us save as it is capable of forming a part of our thought, or is in itself a thinkable reality. All science proceeds on the tacit assumption that nature and the world of man are intelligible, of the presence of reason, thought in things, and of rational relations in the events of history. This general presupposition cannot leave us when we rise beyond nature and humanity to the ultimate basis of all phenomena. If reason is irresistibly impelled (even according to Spencer) to seek, above and beyond the manifold and changeful phenomena, a permanent unity, an infinite and absolute reality, it can at this stage, as little as at any previous one, fall into the suicidal contradiction of seeking by thought an object which has no relation to thought, and of seeking the ultimate explanation of all rational relations in the irrational. The presupposition and the final goal of thought cannot be an Absolute which is simply the negation of thought, but rather that which comprehends all finite things and thoughts only because it is itself the Unity of Thought and Being, and in which therefore our human thought finds its fullest revelation. Lastly, Caird observes,

---

[1] Pages 10-38.

that Spencer's demand of religious worship of the Unknowable is an impossible one for the human heart to meet. It is true all religion contains an element of mystery, inasmuch as finite intelligence cannot be the measure of the infinite; but a religion *all* mystery is an absurd and impossible notion, and would be nothing else than the apotheosis of ignorance. The homage which we render to the Being in whom are hid all the treasures of wisdom and knowledge, all the inexhaustible wealth of that boundless realm of truth in which thought finds ever increasing stimulus to aspiration, to wonder and delight, is totally different from the dumb wonder of ignorance or the grovelling awe of the supernatural, as it is exhibited in the fetish-worshipper, whose religion is the nearest approach to the religion of the Unknowable. True religion is not the blind fear of an unknown Being, but trust, sympathy, and love toward the " God who is light, and in whom is no darkness at all," and to know whom is eternal life for the human spirit.

As is evident from this critique of Spencer's position, and as he himself intimates in his "prefatory note," John Caird takes essentially the standpoint of Hegel's Philosophy of Religion. He founds his proof of the existence of God on the fundamental principle of Hegelian speculation, in which he finds the essence of the *ontological argument*, namely, that the correlation of thought and being in our consciousness involves as its necessary presupposition the absolute unity of both in the divine consciousness. After the example of Hegel, he describes the forms of the religious consciousness as the representative, figurative form of knowledge, as the abstract, disintegrating logical understanding, and as synthetic, reintegrating speculation, which discovers in the contradictions, to the understanding insoluble, of finite and infinite, freedom and necessity, etc., the inseparable moments or members of a concrete unity. Caird's idea of religion is also formed after Hegel's, though with a stronger accentuation of the ethical side, and in that respect related to Fichte's ethical mysticism. Religion is the realisation of the ideal, which in morality is never more than approximately reached; for religion is the surrender of the finite to the infinite will, the abnegation of all private individual volition, and complete identification of the personal will with God's. Hence entrance upon the religious life is the termination of the struggle between "the false self and that higher self which is at once mine and infinitely more than mine," the realisation of the divine self in the human. The last chapter in the book, which deals with the relation of the philosophy to the history of religion, offers excellent observations on false and correct applications of the idea of development to the history of religion. This idea is according to Caird in no way inconsistent with the claim of Christianity to a divine origin, if the latter is not understood in such a sense as to sever Christianity from human history, which it is not the interest of the apologist to do. There is reason to resist the application of the idea of evolution to Christianity in a sense which would assert that there was nothing new and original in it, but only a combination in new forms of pre-existing elements. The connection of Christianity with the past must be conceived as the transmuting of the past by a new creative spiritual force. Thus, based upon Hegel, we have here an idealistic form of evolutionism in opposition to that of Herbert Spencer.

The Scottish philosophers, Edward Caird and Hutchison Stirling, and the Oxford Professor, Thomas Hill Green, have successfully endeavoured to introduce their countrymen to the philosophy of Hegel; the two former by excellent monographs on Kant and Hegel, in which, while differing on many points, they concur in representing the Kantian philosophy as the fundamental basis of the speculation which reaches its climax in Hegel. This conception of the relation of the two great German philosophers appears to prevail pretty generally in England and Scotland, and it is without doubt much more correct than the view which prevails in Germany, in consequence of the interpretation of Kant brought into vogue by the Neo-Kantians during the last decades. According to this interpretation, in order to remove him as far as possible from the tabooed Hegel, Kant is to be explained in the sense of Hume and Locke, whereby the epoch-making element of his philosophy is totally ignored. It is really a remarkable phenomenon in national psychology, that in the same years in which in Germany the younger generation discovers the progress of philosophy in a backward movement from Hegel to Kant, and from Kant to Hume and Locke, the younger generation in Great Britain has gone in the exactly opposite direction. In his elaborate *Introductions* to Hume's works (1874), by which he first obtained a name as a philosophical thinker, THOMAS HILL GREEN sought to show that the English philosophy of the last hundred years has remained stationary, because it has continued to build upon the foundation of the empiricism of Locke, although Hume had shown its untenability, and that therefore the first condition of an advance is a serious reconsideration of the problem proposed by Hume, a problem the solution of which Green considers possible only in the direction of the speculative philosophy begun by Kant and carried further by Hegel. He had given expression to this conviction a few years earlier (1868), in the suggestive essay on *Popular Philosophy in its Relation to Life*, at the close of which he says:[1] "A peculiar characteristic of our times is the scepticism of the best men. Art, religion, and political life have outgrown the nominalistic logic and the psychology of individual introspection; yet the only recognised formulæ by which the speculative man can account for them to himself, are derived from that logic and psychology. Thus the more fully he has appropriated the results of the spiritual activity of his time, the more he is baffled in his theory, and to him this means weakness, and the misery of weakness. Meanwhile, pure motive and high aspiration are going for nothing, or issuing only in those wild and fruitless outbursts into action with which speculative misery sometimes seeks to relieve itself. The prevalence of such a state of mind might be expected at least to excite an interest in a philosophy like that of Hegel, of which it was the professed object to find formulæ adequate to the action of reason as exhibited in nature and human society, in art and religion."

As a tutor in Oxford, Green exercised, by the force of his strong and sterling personality, directed always, both speculatively and practically, to the highest ideals, a powerful influence, which continues to work, upon the young minds that gathered around him. His importance as a philosophical thinker became known to wider circles only after his death by his posthumous writings. For our purpose it is his *Prolegomena to Ethics*, and his theological essays and addresses (in the third volume of his collected works), that are of special importance. On these and the references of his editor, in the memoir prefixed to the third volume of his

---

[1] Works, vol. iii. p. 124.

works, the following sketch of his religious philosophy is based.

In a review of J. Caird's *Introduction to the Philosophy of Religion*, Green complains that Caird does not "sit looser to the dialectical method" of Hegel, and identifies thought and reality without sufficient explanation; that the vital truth which Hegel had to teach must be presented in a form which will be more acceptable to serious and scientific men generally. Green thus summarises this "vital truth" of Hegelianism: "that there is one spiritual self-conscious being, of which all that is real is the activity or expression; that we are related to this spiritual being, not merely as parts of the world which is its expression, but as partakers in some inchoate measure of the self-consciousness through which it at once constitutes and distinguishes itself from the world; that this participation is the source of morality and religion." The exposition of these propositions constitutes the subject matter of Green's philosophy of religion. He finds the foundation of faith in God in the intellectual and moral nature of man. Our knowledge of the world, being the mind's active combination of various appearances into the unity of consciousness, becomes the ground of the knowledge of a self-conscious Mind in the universe, which is the necessary condition of the existence of a like activity in ourselves, and the source and bond of the ever growing synthesis called knowledge. But as the source of all knowledge God is not knowable by us in the same sense as any other object, and can only be thought of under metaphors and practically experienced as the power by which our minds think and love. As our thought presupposes as the ground of its possibility an eternal thinking Mind, so our moral action presupposes an eternal Will employing man as the instrument of the realisation of its ends. For all moral action is self-realisation, the development of our true nature, the endeavour to perfect our actual nature in the direction of a highest ideal. This effort after self-improvement is the practical proof of an absolute perfection. For the possibilities of our nature which wait for realisation presuppose a superhuman self from which, in which, and for which they are actual; there must be an eternal subject which is all that the imperfect subject is destined to become by the unfolding of its powers. It is in this sense that Green uses the somewhat bold expression, "God is our possible or ideal self." But he does not mean by this that this self is an empty, merely imaginary ideal; on the contrary, it is the only realising principle, or cause, of our personal self, which is never more than a relative reality. As little may this be understood in the sense of a pantheistic identification of God with man, because our imperfect, perpetually developing being distinguishes us essentially from the eternally perfect being of God. But what the expression does mean is that the human mind is in principle one with the Divine, relatively participates in God, is a reproduction of the Divine under the conditions of the finite. According to Green, the inner essence of Christianity lies in its sense of this fact, that God is not an alien, far-off outward Power, but the Father, whose "word is nigh unto us," of whom we may say that we are reason of his reason, whose spirit lives in us, and for whom we live in living for the brethren; and thereby we live freely, because in obedience to a spirit which is our self; and in communion with whom we have assurance of eternal life. A self which can think and will eternal ideas, can seek to realise eternal ends, is itself above time, shares in the nature of the eternal; the perfect development of its capacities cannot be its annihilation, although we can form no conception of the positive state of the realised ideal, because it lies beyond our experience.

The philosopher is accordingly conscious of being in essential accord with Christian faith when this is conceived in its religious sense, that is, as a disposition of mind or character, consisting in the consciousness of potential unity with God, and issuing in the effort to realise this unity in life, in self-denial, and in confiding love. This faith is independent of historical proofs in every form, and carries the evidence of its own certainty along with it. As a religious faith it cannot come into conflict with knowledge, as both alike have their source in reason or self-consciousness, which is itself again a revelation of the Divine reason. But religious faith in its empirical ecclesiastical form has another side, by which it necessarily comes into conflict with knowledge. The one spiritual truth is clothed in the forms of the imagination, which can never adequately represent the idea. The progressive revelation of God in the spirit of man and in the whole course of human history is narrowed to an event of the past, occurring but once or occasionally, and of an exceptiona and absolutely miraculous nature. Events of this kind are then made to constitute the immediate object of faith, and this faith in miracle the indispensable condition of Christian piety and morality. But in this view it is forgotten that assent to historical traditions, be they well or ill attested, true or untrue, can never be more than an act of the intellect, which would make no difference to the moral value of a man, to his religious and moral character. From this faith, still required in the churches, in the miraculous as the specific form of divine revelation, the moral feeling and the intellectual culture of our day have revolted. For when once the idea of "nature" is conceived as a continuous, uniform system of laws, "a supernatural event" would be a breach of the continuity of the order of which it was supposed to be an element, that is, it would contradict the conditions under which alone a thing can be an event. "As long as the truth of religion is supposed to depend on supernatural events, science is right in pronouncing it a fiction and in identifying faith with unreason." The business of apologetics can be no other than to distinguish faith in its spiritual and religious essence from the inadequate forms of the imagination, and to learn to understand historically the rise and growth of the latter.

It was not within the scope of Green's vocation as a philosopher to deal with the critical history of Christian faith, but he everywhere shows a close acquaintance with the results of recent historical criticism, as far as they could serve to confirm his philosophical speculations. "The glory of Christianity," he says,[1] "is not that it excludes, but that it comprehends; not that it came of a sudden into the world, or that it is given complete in a particular institution, or can be stated complete in a particular form of words; but that it is the expression of a common spirit which is gathering together all things in one. We cannot say of it, Lo, here it is, or Lo, there; it is now, but was not then. We go backward, but we cannot reach its source; we look forward, but we cannot foresee its final power. We do it wrong in making it depend on a past event, and in identifying it with the creed of a certain age, or with a visible society established at a particular time. What we thus seem to gain in definiteness, we lose in permanence of conviction; for importunate inquiry will show us that the event can only be approached through a series of fluctuating

---

[1] *The Witness of God*, Works, iii. pp. 240 sqq.

interpretations of it, behind which its original nature cannot be clearly ascertained; that the 'visible Church' of one age is never essentially the same as that of the next; that it is only in word, or to the intellectually dead, that the creed of the present is the same as the creed of the past." But if it is doubtless true that the roots of the system of practical ideas which we call Christianity are as old as mankind, the ideas would never have been developed save through definite historical events and personal influences, among which some outweigh all others in importance. The Son of Man came, who was conscious, in the meanness of human life and death, of the communication of God to himself, and through him to mankind. Then came Paul, who found his idea of the "heavenly man," borrowed from the philosophy of his day, realised in Jesus, and made the death and resurrection of Jesus the symbol of the fundamental principle, that man comes to his true self only by the passing out of his old narrow self into the true divine self. But while Paul had placed this moral and spiritual element above the miraculous, subsequently the relation was reversed: the miraculous overpowered the moral and the spiritual. Yet two generations after Paul followed the author of the Fourth Gospel, "who gave that final spiritual interpretation to the person of Christ which has for ever taken it out of the region of history and of the doubts that surround all past events, to fix it in the purified conscience as the immanent God." By combining in faith the spiritual with the moral, God with man, "this Gospel has filled the special function of presenting the highest thought about God in language of the imagination, and has thus become the source of the highest religion."[1] But while according to Paul and John Christ dwells and works as spirit in believers, in the Church he has been step by step "externalised and mystified." Thus arose dogma with its mysteries, from which knowledge and the purest moral culture are estranged. But trustful, child-like love, set before us by the Biblical presentation of Christ, and made an inward part of our life and character, is sufficient to meet and overcome all the blows of criticism and the problems as to historical events. And if, as must be allowed, it is no longer possible for the modern thinking Christian to retain the communion

---

[1] Works, iii. p. 219.

and fellowship of the confessions and creeds of the ancient Church, he must, nevertheless, continue to feel bound to his fellow-Christians by the ties of practical love. Green's own life was an example of this, and he combined in an uncommon degree practical social labours with philosophical pursuits.

There are not wanting various indications that, as in Germany the original Hegelianism, so in England Neo-Hegelianism, is so far from being the final end of philosophy, that even those thinkers who are intimately conversant with the latter, and ungrudgingly acknowledge its noble and massive idealism, have nevertheless not been able to convince themselves of the tenability of the system, and so find themselves compelled to advance in the direction of speculative theism (which also predominates in the post-Hegelian speculation of Germany). We must mention, as written on these lines, the able book of ANDREW SETH, *Hegelianism and Personality* (1887), which appears to have been occasioned by the writings of Green; for it begins with critical observations on the crucial doctrine of Green's system, that a universal or divine self is present in every individual as the efficient principle of its theoretical and practical knowledge. In order to understand and fairly judge this doctrine, Seth holds it is necessary to go back to its genesis in the philosophy of Kant and his successors, especially of Hegel. An acute analysis and critique of these systems leads to the result that the fundamental error of Hegelianism and the allied English doctrine is the identification of the human and the divine self-consciousness, and that this identification depends throughout on the tendency to take a mere form of consciousness, which is the same in all individuals, and so universal, as a real being, to hypostatise and call it the self common to God and men. This is contrary, Seth maintains, to the characteristic nature of the self, which, although in knowledge a principle of unity, is in existence, or metaphysically, a principle of isolation (?). For the most certain testimony of consciousness is, that I have a centre of my own—a will of my own. Nor does the religious consciousness lend any countenance to the representation of the human soul as a mere mode or efflux of the divine. On the contrary, religious self-surrender of the will to the divine will presupposes the active self of the man. What Hegel calls "spirit," "absolute spirit," is at bottom nothing more than the abstract scheme of intelligence, which Fichte constructs in his *Wissenschaftslehre*. But this abstract form has neither reality nor real value. The attempt of the Hegelian schools to unify the divine and the human subject is ultimately destructive of both. We cannot rightly conceive either the divine or the human self in this impossible union; nor is this wonderful, seeing they are merely two inseparable aspects of our own conscious life isolated and hypostatised. If we are to ascribe real existence to God, Seth declares with truth, there must be a divine centre of thought, activity, and enjoyment, which can no more be lost in its manifestations in the universe than human personality in its life for others. The admission of a real self-consciousness in God is, moreover, demanded by the fundamental principle of the theory of knowledge—interpretation by means of the highest category within our reach: if the self-conscious life is the highest in us, we cannot deny it to God; he may, indeed must, be infinitely more than we know ourselves to be, but he cannot be less. The Hegelian system, continues Seth, is as ambiguous on the question of man's immortality as on that of the personality of God, and for precisely the same reason—that the self of which assertions are made is not a real but a logical self. The two positions are two complementary sides of the same view of existence. If we can believe, with the Hegelians of the Left, that there is no permanent Intelligence and Will at the heart of things, then the self-conscious life is degraded from its central position, and becomes merely an accident in the universe; but, on the other hand, to a philosophy founded upon self-consciousness, and especially upon the moral consciousness, it must seem incredible that the successive generations should be used up and cast aside—as if character were not the only lasting product and the only valuable result of time. Seth summarises his critique of Hegel and Neo-Hegelianism in the sentences, "Hegel is the protagonist of idealism, and champions the best interests of humanity; but in its execution the system breaks down, and ultimately sacrifices these very interests to a logical abstraction styled the Idea, in which both God and man disappear."

The speculative theism towards which Seth seeks to bring Hegelian speculation is represented also in the writings of ROBERT FLINT, Professor of Divinity in the University of Edinburgh, *Antitheistic Theories* (1877) and *Theism* (1876), and in his brief but very instructive article on Theism in the ninth edition of the *Encyclopædia Britannica*. In the first-named book Flint has passed under review the naturalistic, positivist, pessimistic, and pantheistic theories, and shown their untenability; he does not in this work deal with agnosticism, but has reserved it for a separate work, which has not yet appeared. This will be looked for with the greater interest, as the article on Theism in the Encyclopædia offers some excellent observations upon the agnostic position. Flint maintains that agnosticism is so far from being the necessary corollary of Kantian criticism, that, on the contrary, it contradicts its true principles. For if it is the categories which make experience possible, their validity cannot be restricted to sense experience, but extends as truly to the realm of moral and religious experience. And if the objective validity of the categories, or the necessary forms of thought, is generally called in question, it is not merely theology which is thereby deprived of all foundation, but equally all other sciences, which are then all resolved into castles in the air. But against such scepticism human consciousness testifies, for it cannot think the mere subjectivity of a true category. As against Hamilton and Mansel, Flint observes that the idea of the Absolute so far from being, as they alleged, an empty negation, abstraction, and fiction, because out of all relation to the knowable, contains the foundation of all relations, the basis not less of existence than of thought, and therefore far from being unknowable, is the richest and highest idea, to which all other knowledge conducts as its necessary completion. In it all the metaphysical categories are included, for God is the absolute Being; all the physical categories, for he is absolute Force and Life; all the mental categories, for he is absolute Spirit; all the moral categories, for he is the absolutely Good. Thus the idea of God brings all ideas which are the conditions of human reason and the basis of a knowledge of things into an organic system; the whole truth of the world, unfolded in the various sciences, as well as the truth of the mind, is included in the idea of God. A philosophy of the Absolute, such as Hegel's, may in its controversy with Agnosticism fall into some extravagances of Gnosticism; but a theist may nevertheless sympathise with its general aim and appropriate many of its results. Undoubtedly this philosophy needs correction, so far as it fails to do justice to the personality and transcendence of the Divine. And this error is due to its having obtained the idea of God too exclusively by the method of formal logical thought, and to its neglect of the other sides of the mind, the moral and religious experience particularly. The idea of God cannot be laid hold of solely by the scientific organising intellect, but only by the combined theoretical and practical powers of the mind. It is a truth ever more clearly perceived, that the divine glory has its centre in moral perfection, in holy love. On the other hand, the general movement of theism tends to a mediation between the extremes of pantheism and deism, to a harmonious combination of the personal self-equality and the universal agency of God. Positive science has powerfully co-operated with speculative philosophy in promoting this movement. The modern scientific view of the world has not as its result pantheism, but it gives sanction to the relative claims of pantheism, and demands a theism which acknowledges God's immanence in the world while holding fast to his personality. The theory of evolution as applied to nature and history does not lead to Agnosticism, but to a more vivid knowledge of God, from whom and through whom and to whom are all things, who is the eternal source of all forces in nature, and also the power in history working for truth and righteousness. These excellent views of Professor Flint seem to me to contain, in fact, the quintessence of the best thoughts of modern speculative philosophy and the programme of its further development.

Lastly, as tending in a similar direction, must be mentioned the works on the philosophy of religion of JAMES MARTINEAU, the revered and venerable theologian who has spent his life outside the Established Church as a preacher and theological tutor amongst the Unitarians. By his *Essays Philosophical and Theological* (2 vols., 1869), which appeared originally chiefly in the *National Review*, and his college addresses, he was known as one of the ablest antagonists of agnostic and materialistic philosophy; and his two larger works, *Types of Ethical Theory* (2 vols., 1885), and *A Study of Religion* (2 vols., 1888) have more than sustained his reputation. In his "Introductory chapter on recent developments," prefixed to the re-issue of the second edition of John James Tayler's *Retrospect of the Religious Life of England* (1876), Martineau could speak of the emendation of the idea of God which had been effected since the days of the older Natural Theology, "an emendation which had taken place long ago among the Unitarians," that "God is no longer conceived as the First Cause prefixed to the scheme of things, but as the Indwelling Cause pervading it: not excluded by Second Causes, but coinciding with them while transcending them; as the One everliving Objective Agency, the modes of which must be classified and interpreted by science in the outer field, by conscience in the inner." And he considers that "this change of conception is due to the lessened prominence of mechanical ideas and the advance of physiology to a dominant position, substituting the thought of life working from within for that of transitive impulse starting from without." Modern science, with its doctrine of evolution, leaves theism, he maintains, undisturbed and unharmed, as no physical knowledge can prevent it from conceiving the unity of the Causal Power, which evolution presupposes, as *mind*, a thesis implied in the very idea of causality. This thought Martineau has worked out in his *Study of Religion*. After a valuable introductory book on the limits of human intelligence, from which we quoted above,[1] the idea of causality is reduced to that of operative power, and this again to that of voluntary activity; whence the conclusion is drawn, that all that takes place in nature has one kind of cause, which we can only conceive as a will analogous to our own; that therefore the universe of originated things is the product of a supreme Mind. To the charge of anthropomorphism, Martineau replies, that whatever idea we form of the ultimate principle of the universe, it must be taken from the analogies of human experience, and the one thing that makes the difference is, whether it be drawn from the lower or the higher aspects of our human nature. The notion, too, that God as a designer must be separated from the world and left outside of it, is unfounded, for "theism is at liberty to regard all the cosmical forces as varieties of method assumed by God's conscious causality, and the whole of Nature as the evolution of his thought." Yet the immanency of God must not be so conceived as to leave no room for the personality of created minds, or to make the actual cosmos the boundary of the possibilities of the divine activity. To get the more definite contents of the idea of

---

[1] *Ante*, p. 340.

God, the inference from our own moral nature to God as the perfect Ideal is made, since that Ideal cannot be merely subjective fancy, but the objective authority, in whose legislation our conscience finds its origin and its explanation. Martineau had previously maintained in his essay on *Ideal Substitutes for God*, in opposition to the ethical idealism without God, of such writers as Matthew Arnold and F. A. Lange, that the truth of our religious and moral consciousness stands or falls with the reality of the divine ideal.

Martineau's *Study of Religion* is a most instructive and suggestive work; what it seems to lack is a closer analysis of the psychological nature of religion, and particularly a more thorough examination of the historical development of the religious consciousness of mankind. But it is not only this work, but the English philosophy of religion generally which seems to me to require supplementing and developing in this direction. It would thereby exert greater influence upon the theology of the Church, which appears to have remained hitherto too much out of touch with the progress of philosophical thought.[1]

---

[1] During the translation of the manuscript of this book has appeared Martineau's work, *The Seat of Authority in Religion* (London, 1890), which supplements his *Study of Religion* in a desirable way. For it follows up the philosophical examination of the ultimate ground of religious certainty, and of the relation of the divine and the human factor in all revelation with an historical analysis of the traditional authorities (the Church, the Bible), and with a review of the historical process by which the religion of Jesus was transformed into a religion about him, and the kernel of moral and religious truth was covered by a husk of "Christian mythology." Even those who may think Martineau's critique of the early Christian traditions here and there too radical, must be compelled to admit that it is the result of a thorough examination of the facts, and of a penetrating and discerning judgment. And every unprejudiced reader can convince himself by a careful study of the fine concluding chapter, that this bold critique is quite consistent with a fervent reverence for the religious personality of Jesus, and accordingly does not detract from the essence of Christian faith. The work with which Dr. Martineau has crowned the labours of his long life will be a lasting monument of a mind not less free than devout. May it find many grateful readers at home and abroad!—O. P.

CHAPTER II.

PARTIES AND MOVEMENTS IN THE THEOLOGY OF GREAT BRITAIN.

IT was remarked at the beginning of the previous chapter that that general revolution of thought and feeling, commonly known as "Romanticism," which took place at the commencement of this century, produced good fruit in the revival and reanimation of the religion of the Church. The first and most influential representative of this new tendency in England was Coleridge, in whose *Aids to Reflection* (1825), German idealistic philosophy was transplanted to English soil, and employed in the revivification of theological thought. We have seen that in Coleridge, as in Schleiermacher, his German predecessor, intellect and feeling, faith and knowledge, entered into such a close alliance with each other, that he appeared on the one hand as the apologist of the faith of the Church, in opposition to anti-religious rationalism; and, on the other, as at the same time the champion of a more liberal view of traditional doctrines, in opposition to a literal orthodoxy. These two aspects of Coleridge's thought, while combined in his own person, separated into two distinct parties or tendencies in the Church, their common origin, in the set of feeling in Romanticism, betraying itself outwardly in the fact that both parties proceeded from the same circle of Oxford students, and were represented by men who were personal friends in their university days, far as their courses subsequently diverged. In this also we meet with a striking similarity to the early days of modern German theology. The relation of J. H. Newman, the originator and early leader of the Anglo-Catholic movement, to his liberal teacher and mentor, Whately, may be compared with Neander's relation to his teacher Planck; and the parallel between the friendship of Thomas Arnold with Keble, the friend of Hurrell Froude and Newman, and the friendship of the youthful Schleiermacher with Novalis and Friedrich Schlegel, is still more obvious. We must begin with the movement of the High Church, or Tractarian, or Puseyite party, and then take up that of the Broad Church, led by Thomas Arnold and F. D. Maurice, which, from the first, existed by the side of the Tractarian movement, but did not obtain general influence until the latter had passed the zenith of its power. This movement of the Broad Church party has been more recently followed by a liberalism of a more decided type, which has been represented during this generation in the rise of Biblical criticism in Great Britain.

The Tractarian movement dates from the summer of 1833, though its roots extend a few years further back. In the year 1827 appeared Keble's *Christian Year*, a collection of religious lyrics on the principal festivals of the ecclesiastical year; the poems clothe a tender and deep piety in the symbolic garb suggested by the seasons of the natural and Christian year, and are the production of a true poet. We might call Keble the English Novalis, the poet of religious idealism, to whose vision "two worlds" lie always open, the visible being but a type of the invisible, which always lay nearest his heart. Only Keble did not possess the philosophical culture and learning of Novalis, and lacked consequently his largeness of view: in Keble's mind, profound personal piety was so exclusively associated with the forms of Anglican doctrines and ceremonies, that he could not conceive Christianity or religion at all, apart from the Anglican system; his religious intolerance went so far, that when the Queen selected a Lutheran prince to be godfather to one of her sons, he set on foot a protest against it from English clergymen. The religious poems of the *Christian Year* gave such perfect and admirable expression to a wide-spread state of feeling amongst English people, that the little volume found everywhere the warmest reception, and probably obtained more friends than all the subsequent theological tracts and learned books for the new movement in the Church. It produced a still deeper effect on the convictions and the subsequent life of John Henry Newman, who had hitherto passed amongst Oxford men as a disciple of Whately's, though as early as 1826 his mind began to take another turn, chiefly through intercourse with his friend Hurrell Froude. This young man seems to have played a similar part amongst the allies of English Romanticism to that played by Friedrich Schlegel in the same movement in Germany. From Froude's *Remains*, which were published (1836-9) after his death by Newman and Keble, one gets the impression of a man not of great natural capacity, but of loose and neglected mind, which was greatly lacking both in moral strength and solid learning; a man who loved to indulge in paradoxes, which aimed at being clear and profound, but were often meaningless, and who, from his limited aristocratic Anglican standpoint, passed sentence upon everything outside and beyond it with the greater arrogance in proportion to his ignorance. He hated the Reformation and the Reformers, especially " Luther, Melanchthon and Co.," because they denied the *jus divinum* of the Catholic Church, preferred preaching to the sacraments, and put an end to ecclesiastical discipline. He demanded the restoration of monasticism, celibacy, fasting, ancient ritual and art, but especially the emancipation of the Church from the supremacy of the State. The fanatical thoroughness with which Froude advocated his views made a deep impression on John Henry Newman, to whose nature submission to a stronger personal authority was a necessity, and who was just then passing through a mental crisis. When then at length, soon after the appearance of the *Christian Year*, a friendship between Keble and Newman was brought about by Froude, the triumvirate was constituted, the object of which was nothing less than a second Reformation, or counter-Reformation, of the English Church.

The movement thus prepared for in this circle of Oxford friends was brought to a head through the political and ecclesiastico-political agitations at the beginning of the thirties. In order to allay the agitation in Ireland, Sir Robert Peel had carried his Bill for Catholic Emancipation, to the great alarm of the Oxford orthodox party. The French Revolution of July, 1830, and the accession of William IV., brought the Whigs into power, who, after a violent conflict with the Tory lords and prelates of the Upper House, passed in 1832 the Reform Bill, a measure which had been long and loudly called for by the majority of the nation. The next year followed a Bill to remedy abuses in the Irish Church, by which the income of the Anglican Church in Ireland was greatly reduced, and one-half of its (superfluous) sees were abolished. The unyielding opposition on the part of the nobility and clergy to all these absolutely necessary reforms had so much excited liberal feeling amongst the people generally, that the bishops were on several occasions insulted and attacked; and the premier, Lord Grey, advised the bishops "to set their house in order." In High Church circles the feeling prevailed, that the very existence of the Church was imperilled, and that what was required was to create a powerful counter-movement to the liberal tendencies of the day. The Assize Sermon of Keble's in the University pulpit at Oxford, on the "National Apostasy," formed the signal for its friends; and in July, 1833, at a conference at Hadleigh, it was resolved to take immediate action. Under the conviction that "living movements do not come of committees," but depend on personal influence, Newman placed himself at the head of this, and began in 1833 the issue of the *Tracts for the Times*, as their editor and principal author; this being the origin of the name "Tractarian." In the space of eight years (1833-41), ninety tracts were published, which are collected in six volumes. Contemporaneously there appeared also, by various writers, extracts from the Church Fathers, under the title of *Records of the Church*. When in 1835, Pusey, Professor and Canon of Christ Church, joined the movement, an English translation of the whole of the Fathers was projected, which began to appear in 1838, under the title of *A Library of the Fathers of the Holy Catholic Church*.

The design of this movement was certainly not purely religious by any means, but ecclesiastico-political, not to say political; it was a general war against the Liberal tendencies of the age, and in defence of custom and tradition in the Church and society. As a means to this end, the revival and confirmation of the doctrines and usages of the Anglican Church was to be taken in hand. But while to all appearance the object was only to restore historical Anglicanism in its original purity, in reality the tendency to Catholicism was so decided that Anglicanism was from the very first left a long way behind, and the end of the movement, it could be foreseen, must be Romanism. This could be perceived in the first declarations of the Tractarians, the principal of which were the following: that salvation is based upon the objective efficacy of the sacraments, which again depends on their administration by apostolically appointed priests, that is, on the apostolic succession of the bishops, who, as successors of the apostles, are the inheritors of the gifts of the Holy Ghost, and are thereby the highest authority, in complete independence of the State, in matters of life and doctrine. The writings of the Tractarians were devoted to the exposition and the dogmatico-historical (rather than the Biblical) proof of these positions. A few special points may be here mentioned. A tract of Pusey's, which appeared in 1835, on Baptism, attacked the evangelical doctrine of regeneration through faith, and its separation of the baptism of the spirit from the baptism of water; Pusey taught that the real regeneration is effected by the act of baptism, that the only condition presupposed is that no bar be placed in the way by unbelief; that since this cannot be the case with infants, the baptized child is regenerated. The Catholic doctrine of *opus operatum* is adopted as correct; but as the grace of baptism may be lost again, for sins committed after baptism satisfaction must be made by earnest penance, which has to be shown also in the old ecclesiastical form of ascetic observances. Hence the necessity of Church discipline as a means of grace. The mere preaching of the cross of Christ can lead to carnal security. It is not preaching, but ecclesiastical discipline that forms moral character.—In the sacrament of the Lord's Supper, such is the doctrine, the body and blood of Christ is present, without transubstantiation, in reality in a mystical manner, and the sacrament is a sacrifice (*sacrificium*, not merely *sacramentum*), that is, the mystical application of the sacrifice of Christ on the cross, in which Christ and the Church are together the subject and the object of the sacrifice. R. J. Wilberforce connected this theory with the doctrine of the Incarnation of Christ, holding that the Incarnation is perpetuated in the consecration and the sacrifice of the eucharist in a spiritual but real manner. To confession also, sacramental significance is ascribed; frequent private confession, in accordance with prescribed rules, is advocated. But as the sacraments owe all their saving efficacy to their administration at the hands of the Church, the whole stress falls ultimately, as in the Catholic doctrine, upon the true doctrine of the Church. It is the actual visible saving institution founded by Christ through the agency of the apostles; by the bishops, as the successors of the apostles, the Holy Spirit descends through it, the means of grace are efficaciously administered and the truth infallibly taught. The invisible Church is composed solely of the living and perfected members of the visible Church, so that to the latter salvation is unconditionally confined. The "notes" of the true Church are apostolicity, catholicity, and autonomy. The most important condition is the apostolical succession of the bishops, which includes the other essential signs. The most perfect Church is the Anglican. The other episcopal Churches are branches of the one Catholic Church, but diseased branches (especially the Romish Church), on account of their errors; on the other hand, all communities of Dissenters, as well as the Protestant Churches of the Continent that have no bishops, are severed branches, sects, which do not possess the means of salvation. For it is only through the apostolic succession of the bishops that the gift of the Holy Spirit, and therewith the saving efficacy of the sacraments, has been preserved to the Church. As Christ is the supreme Mediator, the bishop is his representative on earth, the mediator between the Church and Christ, the highest authority for the laity. The Scriptures cannot be taken as the final and sufficient *norma fidei* on account of their ambiguity; they must be interpreted according to the rule of tradition, especially of the earlier centuries. Thus we have in the Nicene Creed the witness of the whole Church, affirming that the doctrine of the Trinity is the teaching of Scripture when properly understood. In the Preface to the translation of the Fathers, it is maintained that the New Testament is the source of doctrine, but that the Catholic Fathers are the channels through which it comes down to us, and that an earnest study of Catholic antiquity conducts those who are tired of modern questionings into the haven of security.

This love of ecclesiastical antiquity sprang out of the historical impulse of Romanticism as much as Sir Walter Scott's poetical revival of Scottish and English antiquity, or again, the sympathetic learned study of German antiquity by the brothers Grimm and the poet Uhland. But the mystical realism of the above doctrine of the sacraments sprang likewise from the inclination of Romanticism towards a certain *Helldunkel*, something neither light nor darkness, neither sensible nor supersensible, a love of mysteries behind experience; Novalis, for instance, liked to call himself a *magischer Idealist*. So, again, the emphasis laid on the supernatural authority of the bishops by virtue of their supposed succession from the apostles was equally acceptable to an age that had grown tired of disputation; and it was at the same time adapted to confirm afresh the position of the bishops, which had been shaken by political events. It is, therefore, not surprising that Tractarian doctrines were received at first with great favour in the English Church, especially amongst the clergy. It is true that there was at the beginning no lack of opposition, particularly on the part of the Evangelicals, who at once perceived, and passed sentence on, the weak place in the new movement—its drift towards Rome. Newman, indeed, endeavoured to defend his Anglo-Catholic position as the true "Via Media" between Romanism and Protestantism. This he did by undertaking to show the complete agreement of the doctrines of the Church of England with apostolic, that is, ancient patristic teaching, making use of a very free and sometimes sophistic method of interpreting the language of the Thirty-Nine Articles (in Tract 90). But it was precisely this daring attempt to set aside the distinctive points of the Anglican creed in relation to Roman doctrine by the aid of forced and spurious interpretation, which brought about the revulsion of public opinion. Tract 90 was censured by the University (1841) and the Bishop of Oxford, and Newman felt called upon to discontinue the series. Newman resigned the leadership of the movement, which passed into the hands of the more learned and cautious Pusey, who had previously cast round it an academical nimbus, and at length gave to it his name also. Many who had been so far its friends now withdrew, or went over to the opposite party. But this, again, produced the effect on the more faithful ones of causing them to abandon all reserve in following out their principles in their full consequences. In the course of his studies in Church History, which he carried on in the retirement of his country parish, Newman himself arrived at the conviction by degrees that his *Via Media* was untenable: more and more the catholicity of the Romish Church outweighed in his estimation the apostolicity of the Anglican; and the more he felt the defects of the latter, the dark spots in the disk of the former tended to vanish. When at last the Church of England committed what was in the eyes of himself and his friends the unpardonable crime of associating itself with the Lutheran and Calvinistic sects of the Union-

Church of Prussia, with the view of founding a new bishopric in Jerusalem, it appeared to Newman, as it had appeared still earlier to some more zealous friends, that to continue in such a Church was no longer possible. In October, 1845, he was received into the communion of the Romish Church, and in the course of a year he was followed by 150 clergymen and laymen of position belonging to his party. The party itself survived the heavy blow, but has subsequently shunned cautiously the slippery region of dogmatics, and devoted itself with the greater zeal to the elaboration of a ritual as nearly like that of the Catholics as possible. This Ritualism, however, has very little in common with theology.[1]

After his conversion Newman published several books, which are of interest as giving an insight into his own religious character, and as throwing indirectly light upon the movement of which he was the author and at first the chief leader. This is especially the case with his *Apologia pro Vita Sua: being a History of his Religious Opinions* (1865, 1st ed.). This autobiography owes its attractiveness, not only to the universally acknowledged beauty of its style, but also to the honest openness with which the author describes the various phases of his religious opinions. A sincerely religious character is unveiled, as it struggles to reach the certainty of conviction with deepest earnestness; and if the appearance of ambiguity and want of sincerity sometimes arises, it is not from the slightest wish to conceal anything from others from external considerations, but because the writer is not clear in his own mind, and because he is trying to hold perforce what is untenable and to conceal from himself consequences that are inevitable. But honourable as such a character may be, its weak side cannot be overlooked. The weakness consists rather in a moral than an intellectual inability to distinguish between religion and a particular form of its transmission in doctrine and ritual;[2] because the firm centre of religious and

---

[1] In one of his letters to Emerson, Carlyle criticises this ritualistic Puseyism in his somewhat pessimistic strain, as a symbol of the speedy dissolution of the superannuated English Church. In *Past and Present*, and elsewhere in his writings, he gives vent to similar vaticinations.

[2] Comp. *Apologia*, p. 49. "From the age of fifteen, dogma has been the fundamental principle of my religion: I know no other religion; I cannot enter into the idea of any other sort of religion; religion as a mere sentiment, is to me a dream and a mockery."

moral certainty cannot be found in the man himself, he clings to external authorities, maintains vehemently their inviolability, and all the time is driven further and further by the inevitable feeling of their insufficiency, until, weary of searching and inquiring, the secure haven of Romish infallibility is at last resorted to. What a different picture is presented in the religious history of Francis Newman, the younger brother of John Henry, as it is described in his *Phases of Faith*![1] In both brothers we have the same deep religious nature and the same restless desire for real conviction; but in the case of the younger brother there is also the moral courage to abandon traditional opinions about the truth and to search for the truth itself, to let the outward props of authority fall one after the other, to gain in the soul itself true certainty of the revelation of God. John Henry Newman has also formulated a theory of religious certainty, with a view to justifying his dogmatism, and has expounded it in the two books, *An Essay on the Development of Christian Doctrine* (1845), and *An Essay in Aid of a Grammar of Assent* (1870). In the latter he works out a principle which he had learnt from Keble,[2] namely, that religious conviction does not rest on intellectual but emotional grounds, which cannot be theoretically proved, probability being converted into certainty by a voluntary assent and believing reception. Although this principle is not wholly devoid of truth, there is reason to object to it,[3] that a rule of certainty which is based neither on the reason nor on proofs from fact, but on the simple power of the will to hold something to be true, possesses no value, and may easily become as fruitful a source of superstition as of faith. In fact, the subjective character of this purely emotional certainty is acknowledged by Newman himself in the very remarkable words: "The argument from probability, in the matter of religion, became an argument from personality, which, in fact, is one form of the argument from authority." It will be difficult to avoid this conclusion, if it is once granted that religious certainty rests merely upon emotional motives without rational grounds; in that case it is, of course, only a subjective cer-

---

[1] See *ante*, p. 317.
[2] *Apologia*, p. 19.
[3] See Tulloch, in the *Edinburgh Review*, Oct., 1870, and his *Movements of Religious Thought*, p. 103.

tainty that cannot rest upon itself, but to render it secure stands in need of the support of the greatest possible number of other subjects, that is, of external authority.

Newman's work on the *Development of Christian Doctrine* takes as its starting-point the incontestable principle, that Christianity, like every historical institution, has passed through a process of development, of growth, in doctrine and custom, and was not given to the world at the beginning in a perfect form. He offers a number of instances going to show that orthodox Protestantism is under a delusion, when it supposes that all its doctrines and practices are taught in Scripture and are prescribed therein, or are to be directly deduced therefrom. It is impossible to remain in the mere letter of Scripture, because the necessities of interpretation, for instance, of such a phrase as "the Word became flesh," lead at once to a series of further questions. Other questions, such as the Canon of Scripture, its inspiration and authority, cannot be answered from Scripture itself, because the Apostles had not then given any decision on them. As within the Biblical religion itself there is a development through the Prophets to Jesus, so, again, in "the apostolic teaching no historical point can be fixed at which the growth of doctrine ceased, and the rule of faith was once for all settled." Finally, in Scripture itself the necessity of such a progressive development is distinctly indicated, for instance, in the parables of the Leaven and the Mustard Seed. If in all this the author displays undoubtedly a degree of sound historical sense, the reader is immediately surprised by a very unhistorical and genuinely dogmatic application of the true principle! In order to guide the process of the development of Christianity, to distinguish correct developments from false, and to sanction them, there is required an infallible authority outside the development—namely, the Church. If Christianity is, as a whole, a revelation, the results of its development must share the guarantee of its credentials. Revealed religion is distinguished from Natural by the very fact that it substitutes the voice of a Law-giver—an objective authority, Apostle, Pope, or Church—for the voice of conscience. In Protestantism this authority is the Bible; but as it can be proved that this authority is insufficient, we must conclude that this required living and present source of revelation can only be the infallible arbiter of all true doctrines—the Church. Nor is personal judgment precluded by this infallible authority, but is only limited to its proper range and preserved from error.—We must allow that this defence (following in the footsteps of the German Catholic Theologian Möhler) of the principle of Catholic tradition and authority is conducted very cleverly. It rests, all the same, upon a great fallacy. The fact is overlooked that the alleged infallible authority is itself a product of the general development, and that it participates in its changes, and is therefore subject, like every historical phenomenon, to the law of relativity. Moreover, the false traditional idea of development is throughout taken for granted—namely, that development consists solely in positive growth, in an extension and more complete definition of older truth; we hear nothing of the great fact, that development has also a negative aspect, that new truth does not come merely as an addition to the old, but often abrogates the old, so that in reality there is accomplished in it the continuous criticism of mind in the process of its development. We readily grant that this process does not go on without obedience to an inner law of rationality; but precisely because reason is realised in the process of historic development, it does not require a special infallible institution to guide it, which can only become an impediment to the living spirit.

In the same year in which Newman set on foot the reactionary High Church movement, THOMAS ARNOLD, the Head Master at Rugby, published his pamphlet on *The Principles of Church Reform*, which, though it provoked at first a storm of indignation on all sides, presented in its fundamental thoughts the ferment of a new progressive movement in the English Church in the next decades. Arnold had, like Newman, been a pupil of Whately's at Oxford, and a friend of Keble's. But while in the case of Newman the influence of the devout friend soon overcame the cool intellectual acuteness of the tutor, with Arnold it was the reverse. Throughout his life Arnold continued to combine a profoundly earnest piety with clearness of intellect, a manly love of truth, and a restless desire for practical work; indeed, it is not easy to say which of these aspects of the noble man's character was most marked. Arnold was at the beginning of the thirties not less alarmed than Newman and his Oxford friends at the political troubles and threatening tempest which appeared to be gathering thick over the Church; but while they sought salvation by the abandonment of the Reformation in a reform of dogma and the constitution and ritual of the Church, by which its boundaries would be narrowed and more sharply separated from the pulsating life of the nation, he demanded a reform in the opposite direction. In order to preserve to the nation the blessings of the State Church, he advocated the opening of its doors to the Dissenters, and the widening of its boundaries, so that all Englishmen who were, and wished to be Christians, should find a place in it. As the condition of membership, nothing more than an acceptance of the essential doctrines of the Christian faith, common to all parties both within and outside the Established Church, was to be required, differences in doctrine, constitution, and ritual being considered minor matters and permissible. The essential thing in Christianity is practical godliness, based on the revelation of God in Scripture, and especially in the person of Jesus, and manifesting itself in the moral purification and sanctification of personal and social life. It is the function of Church and State equally, though from a different point of view, to be instruments and organs of this ideal. There may not, therefore, be any separation between them, or jealousy and quarrel; the State needs for its moral ends the religion of the Gospel, as the Church can exercise its educating influence over the nation only within the constituted forms and regulations of the Christian State.—These are the main principles of Arnold's pamphlet on Church Reform, principles which have as their basis, not only an ideal view of the nature and ends of the State, but also a broad view of the nature of Christianity; a standpoint exactly the same as that represented by Rothe in his *Anfänge der Kirche* and his *Ethik*.[1] But this combination of Christian idealism and large-hearted humanity was then so new in England, that Arnold's proposed reforms were obnoxious to all parties alike: to the High-churchmen they breathed heresy and revolution, and the Liberals considered them too conservative and narrow.

The storm of opposition from all sides did not shake Arnold's conviction of the truth and wisdom of his ideas. The force of his personal character; the success of his work

---

[1] Though Arnold differed from Rothe as to the source of the corruption of the true idea of the Church. See Arnold's Letter to Bunsen, Jan. 27, 1838.

in the school at Rugby, by which he initiated a reformation in the entire system of public schools in England ; his powerful sermons, in which he proclaimed the eternal truths of the Gospel with profound earnestness in simple undogmatic language, and with constant reference to the various departments of moral life ; lastly, his work as a scholar in the field of classical literature and Roman history—all this combined in compelling his opponents even to respect the assailed and censured man, so that his sudden death (1842) was lamented on all sides as a national calamity.

It is Thomas Arnold, if any one, who must be regarded as the pioneer of free theology in England. It is true he wrote no considerable theological work—his vocation led him into the field of scholarship and history : and his views with regard to the interpretation of the Bible were neither quite new, nor do they meet completely the present requirements of historical criticism. But Arnold was the first to show to his countrymen the possibility and to make the demand, that the Bible should be read with honest human eyes without the spectacles of orthodox dogmatic presuppositions, and that it can at the same time be revered with Christian piety and made truly productive in moral life. He was the first who dared to leave on one side the traditional phraseology of the High-Churchmen and the Evangelicals, and to look upon Christianity, not as a sacred treasure of the Churches and sects, but as a Divine beneficent power for every believer ; not as a dead heritage from the past, but as a living spiritual power for the moral advancement of individuals and nations in the present. If the universality of his interests and occupations was a hindrance to strictly scientific theological inquiry, it was really very favourable to his true mission : he showed how classical and general historical studies may be pursued in the light of the moral ideas of Christianity, and how, on the other hand, a free and clear way of looking at things may be obtained by means of wide historical knowledge, and then applied to the interpretation of the Bible and the solution of current ecclesiastical questions. Thus he began to pull down the wall of separation which had cut off the religious life of his fellow-countrymen, with their sects and churches and rigid theological formulas and usages, from the general life and pursuits of the nation. It is also clear as day, that if longer life had been granted to him, the result of the further prosecution of his historical studies, which had been made, in his last year, part of his vocation by his appointment to the chair of Modern History at Oxford, would have been further insight and courage to apply his historical and critical principles to the Bible. At all events, his work was subsequently further prosecuted in this direction by his friends and pupils.

Arnold was pre-eminently an independent character, both in his scientific and his political principles. For this reason he was prepared to learn from men of different schools. Samuel Taylor Coleridge exercised great influence upon him, and he confesses that he found in him what he had never been able to find in any other English theologian: "His mind is at once rich and vigorous, and comprehensive and critical; while the ἦθος is so pure and so lively all the while."[1] From Coleridge Arnold adopted the distinction between the reason and the understanding, and the determination of the relation of reason to faith as of two modes of perceiving religious truth, which are not antagonistic but supplementary. Of Coleridge's *Letters on Inspiration*,[2] which he saw in manuscript, he expressed the opinion,[3] that they were "well fitted to break ground in the approaches to that momentous question which involves in it so great a shock to existing notions, . . . but which will end, in spite of the fears and clamours of the weak and bigoted, in the higher exalting and more sure establishing of Christian truth." His friendship with Bunsen, too, whose acquaintance he made in Rome in 1827, had an important influence on Arnold's mind; it was through this scholar particularly that he kept himself in close relations with German literature, though principally only with its historical and Biblical exegetical works, but not with German philosophy or systematic theology; of Schleiermacher he read only his critical essay on 1 Timothy, the results of which appeared to him too bold.

The most direct and lasting influence on the mental development of Arnold was that of WHATELY, who had been in Oxford his tutor and adviser, and with whom, as Archbishop of Dublin, he kept up a close friendship and constant

---

[1] Letter No. 209, to Mr. Justice Coleridge, Sept. 25, 1839.
[2] See *ante*, p. 311.
[3] Letter No. 94, to Mr. Justice Coleridge, Jan. 24, 1835.

intercourse. Whately was a man of clear intellect, happy humour, and benevolent heart, but not a learned theologian. His best known book is his *Logic*, constructed upon Aristotelian principles, which was once largely used in English colleges and universities. He carried his sound common sense into theological questions also, and found that not a few orthodox dogmas have no foundation in the Scriptures. Thus the orthodox doctrine of election is not in harmony with Paul's teaching, for in the latter what is dealt with is not the unconditional predestination of individuals to salvation or destruction, but only the appointment of the whole Church to salvation in Christ, which is elected from the rest of the Heathen, as previously the people of Israel had been elected from the other nations. The final destiny of individuals depends solely on whether they personally do or do not make use of the advantages offered to them, by participation in the revelation of the Church. The doctrine of justification by faith, too, must not be understood of an imputation of the merits of Christ, but of the forgiveness of sins on the fulfilment of the moral conditions. The death of Christ as a sacrifice must be received on the authority of Scripture, but it cannot be shown to be necessary. It is the same with the Deity of Christ: it must be believed on the ground of Christ's own declarations in the Gospels, but interpreted essentially in the sense of Christ being the perfect moral example. The object of Christ's coming was the foundation of the kingdom of God as a moral commonwealth. The claim of an apostolical episcopal succession, with power to impart the Holy Spirit, cannot be proved from Scripture, and is wrecked on the historical improbability of a chain of tradition being kept unbroken through eighteen centuries; the true succession is holding fast to apostolic principles, that is, the moral character of Christianity. This is violated by the Tractarian doctrine of the sacraments, which substitutes the *opus operatum* for the heart. The rigorous observance of the Sabbath, too, is not in harmony with the New Testament, the law of the Sabbath having been abrogated for Christians with the rest of the Mosaic legislation; Sunday is a voluntary institution of the Church for the good of men. Generally, the Bible does not claim to be a lawbook for the regulation of faith and practice, but it contains a system of practical truths, motives, and principles in a popular form.[1] The unwearied diligence with which Whately devoted himself to his ecclesiastical duties, to promoting the education of the lower classes, and unostentatiously assisting the poor, both Protestant and Catholic, of his diocese in Ireland, reflects favourably on his practical and rational theology, which was not either in philosophy or in history and criticism profound. In the latter respect there is much affinity between it and the Rationalistic (Kantian) supernaturalism, as it was represented in Germany in the first decades of the century by not a few theologians deserving of all respect.

As contemporaries and men of a kindred spirit with Arnold and Whately, we may mention the Oxford theologians HAMPDEN and MILMAN, and the Cambridge theologians THIRLWALL and JULIUS HARE. The name of Hampden is associated with an episode of considerable moment in the Tractarian movement. When he was nominated in 1836 to the Regius Professorship of Divinity at Oxford, the dominant party there, with Newman and Pusey at its head, got up a protest against his appointment, and charged the learned theologian with heresy on the ground of his Bampton Lectures of the year 1832, on *The Scholastic Philosophy in its relation to Christian Theology*, which had till then remained unimpugned. In his lectures he had shown how orthodox theology, as having risen in its Patristic and Scholastic form under the influence of the philosophy in vogue at the time, is not identical with the doctrine of the Scriptures, but is in many respects an adulterated reflex of the simple Christian belief. This indisputably correct account of the origin of orthodox dogmas gave naturally great offence to Highchurchmen, whose fundamental principle was the identification of Christianity with Scholastic theology. Pusey[2] maintained that this distinction between uncertain Scholastic doctrines and certain facts of Scripture was but the beginning of scepticism and rationalism, as the example of Semler had shown. The defence of Christianity then in vogue, which threw the stress entirely upon the practical side of our religion, he declared tended directly to unbelief, since every-

---

[1] These are the leading principles of Whately's theological works, *Essays on the Difficulties in the Writings of St. Paul* (1828), *The Kingdom of Christ* (1841).

[2] *Hampden's Past and Present Statements*.

thing that could not be brought under the rubric of practical applicability, would be forgotten, and in the end denied. Hampden himself, in his inaugural lecture, professed his full belief in all the doctrines of the orthodox faith in a way not easy, it must be confessed, to reconcile with the expositions of his Bampton Lectures. Consistency seems rather to have been on the side of his assailants. But the manner of their attack upon him, their denunciation of detached propositions torn from their context, in order to convict him of heresy, aroused the fierce indignation not only of Whately and Arnold, but of wider circles, in which the reaction against the principles of the Oxford party began from this time to make itself felt. A pamphlet published at that time gives the following not complimentary picture of higher education at Oxford. In all higher branches of knowledge the aim is to put down free opinions. The endeavour is to give a safe direction to young minds, and to confine their movements within the narrowest limits possible. No inquiry which might possibly lead to other results than those of the established formularies is permitted. It is not easy to form any idea of the extent of moral terrorism with which this intellectual tyranny is practised, with what jealousy the words, behaviour, reading of those is watched, who are under the suspicion of having diverged from the majority. This system is commended in and outside of Oxford as a thoroughly practical and wholesome method of training devoted servants of the Church, who shall be free from all doubt. But the evil fruits of it are a terrible distortion of sound intellect, widespread ignorance and hypocrisy. The student who comes at every step upon the warning, "Not too deep!" is discouraged and takes refuge in deliberate ignorance. He persuades himself that knowledge at best is a dangerous acquirement in his career. In the consciousness of his own inability to defend rationally a position he has taken, he regards all speculations that are foreign to his mode of thought with vague fear. The consequence is that theology is studied in Oxford to no purpose, however much is said about it, because it is studied apart from the simple object of discovering the truth, and merely with the object of finding proofs in support of dogmas which dispense with all further inquiry. Such was the view taken by an Englishman of the Oxford of those years. The less reason we have to doubt the truth of the picture, the more cheering is it to observe how great progress has been made there in the course of the last half century.

Even in those years bright exceptions were not wanting. Milman was connected with Whately, Arnold, and Hampden, belonging like them to the pre-Puseyite generation. His *History of the Jews*, which appeared in 1829 (2nd ed. rewritten 1863), treated the narratives of the Old Testament in the same way as the historical traditions of any other ancient people, took up a critical attitude towards the chronological data of the Bible, explained not a few narratives as oriental poetry and allegory, and sought generally by its graphic style, catching the national and antique character of early Hebrew times, to deliver Biblical history from the bonds of traditional sanctity, and bring it nearer to the mind and heart of the present day. It is the same freer attitude towards the Bible which is seen in Arnold's method of interpretation, but Milman was as far as Arnold from holding the principles of scientific criticism now followed by Wellhausen or Robertson Smith. He was rather an imaginative narrator than an acute investigator of history. Nevertheless, by his *History of the Jews*, and his later *History of Latin Christianity*, Milman contributed his share towards making in the bulwarks of traditionalism breaches through which a freer spirit might enter when the time arrived.

The same is true of the Cambridge theologians Thirlwall and Julius Hare, who by their joint translation of Niebuhr's *History of Rome*, and by theological works, did good service in spreading the knowledge of German historical science amongst their countrymen. Thirlwall published in 1825 a translation of Schleiermacher's book on the Gospel of Luke, with an introduction of some length, in which he accepted and defended the principles of Schleiermacher's Biblical criticism—a bold thing to do in those days, when the strict doctrine of inspiration was still in full force, and German theology was but little known in England, and on that very account was the more summarily condemned as heretical! Next to Coleridge, whose way of thinking on philosophy he adopted, Julius Hare was above all his English contemporaries the student best acquainted with German theological science. As a youth he had felt on the Wartburg the breath of Luther's spirit, and subsequently wrote a thoroughly learned

Vindication of the German Reformer, in reply to the charges of the historian Hallam and the Scottish philosopher Sir William Hamilton, and the Puseyites. Against the latter he wrote the important polemical essay, *The Contest with Rome*, 1842, which had the greater influence as Hare's Christian devotedness had been placed beyond doubt by his earnest and thoughtful sermons. Speaking generally, it appears that Hare made a deeper impression on his contemporaries by his noble and amiable character than by his writings, which were comparatively few, and of which the best known is his volume of sermons, *The Mission of the Comforter*, dedicated to the memory of Coleridge, 1846, in which he maintained the principle of development of Christian doctrine. Amongst his closest friends were Thomas Arnold and Frederick Maurice. Maurice was Hare's pupil at Cambridge, and later his brother-in-law, and to this intimate relation owed the most powerful stimulus in his mental development.

FREDERICK DENISON MAURICE was one of the most important English theologians of this century, with great individuality of mind. To describe his mode of thought in theology in a brief sketch, such as this necessarily is, is not easy, for his theology is more complicated than that of any other theologian, and is on many points extremely vague. In his biography, published by his son in two large volumes, there is presented the picture of a man of deep religious feeling and of decided speculative and dialectical power, but at the same time of a man who failed to reduce his convictions into a consistent logical whole such as could fully satisfy himself, or make a dominating and prevailing impression upon his contemporaries, because his own thought lacked clearness and steadiness, and his knowledge concentration and thoroughness. In reading his biography, the comparison of F. D. Maurice with the German theologian Dorner has again and again forced itself upon me. In both the same high moral and religious character compelling profound respect, the same multiformity of learned and moral interests, the same combination of speculative theological thought with a vivid concern for practical Church life, the same restless endeavour to mediate both practically and theoretically between opposing parties and modes of thought; but in both also the same incapacity for taking a clear and logically consistent position on questions of principle, the same indefiniteness in dogmatic speculation, the same dislike of rational historical criticism, the same shrinking from the consequences of their own ideal principles, the same hesitancy in estimating the real factors of life; finally, as a result of all this, the same fatality of giving offence on all sides and the same waste of power on the endless frictions of the actual world.

Maurice's father was a Unitarian minister, but his mother and three sisters abandoned the faith of the father and joined various other religious communions. This division in the household made a profound impression upon the loving heart and thoughtful mind of the boy, and early led him to the conviction that every one's faith is true in what is positively asserted by it, and untrue in what it denies, in its negations, in charges against the opinions of others when they are not sufficiently understood. But this charitable view of religious differences did not prevent his own secession to the Established Church, nor even his re-baptism, by which he accordingly declared the Unitarian faith of his father un-Christian. At Oxford he became acquainted with the leaders of the Tractarian movement, which had just commenced; and appeared as a zealous convert in his pamphlet, *Subscription no Bondage*, in which he sought to prove that subscription to the Thirty-Nine Articles (though a few years previously he had left Cambridge without taking his degree rather than sign them) is no infringement of liberty, but rather a help in the pursuit of the studies of a University. The Tractarians believed that they had found in him a hopeful ally for their cause, but they were soon disappointed, for he quickly turned his back upon them on account of Dr. Pusey's tract on Baptism, which he considered most dangerous, although, as he thought, it contained a very important doctrine which was denied by the Dissenters, and was adapted to unite all Churches. Soon after this he published his first book, *The Kingdom of Christ* (1838), in which he seeks to show that the English Church is the true incorporation of the spiritual universal fellowship of the kingdom of Christ, because it alone teaches the *full* truth as to baptism, the eucharist, apostolical succession, Scripture and tradition, and establishment, whilst Quakers, Lutherans, Calvinists, Philosophers, and Roman Catholics respectively hold but a part of it. But the optimistic champion of Anglicanism was later on compelled to find by bitter experience that it is for the dogmatist but a short step from the position of the *defensor fidei* to that of the condemned heretic. When Maurice taught in his *Theological Essays* (1853) that the Biblical phrases "eternal life" and "eternal death" do not signify states of time of indefinitely long duration in the future, but spiritual states of communion and oneness with or separation from God, that divine punishments are instruments of God's love employed for our salvation, and that the Gospel of God's love for all men, and not the fear of eternal torments in hell, constitutes the object of faith,—it was found that these doctrines are not by any means in harmony with the Creeds of the Anglican Church, and Maurice was removed from his theological professorship at King's College, London. But though thus deprived, he continued to assert his attachment to the Thirty-Nine Articles, when properly understood, that is, according to *his* interpretation of them. And when Bishop Colenso, who had been on terms of intimate friendship with Maurice, and had defended him at the time of his removal from King's College, gave offence to the orthodox by his criticism of the Pentateuch, our unaccountable theologian put himself on the side of the same denunciators against whom Colenso had been his advocate a few years before; in fact, he declared to his former friend that he expected from him the resignation of his bishopric, to which he had no claim as an unbeliever, receiving from Colenso the cutting reply that there were many who were similarly of opinion, that the author of the "Theological Essays" had no right to retain his chaplaincy at Lincoln's Inn.

It is plain from all Maurice's letters to his friends and connexions that through all these paradoxes he was absolutely sincere and in earnest; that the various changes through which he passed were not owing to outward considerations; that his want of consistency was due to the indefiniteness of the fundamental principles of his thinking, to the disharmony existing between his heart and his intellect, between the need he felt of adhering to an authoritative ecclesiastical communion and his strong theological individualism. To his father (Feb. 12, 1832) he explains his secession to Anglicanism from the necessity of his heart to have God, the Invisible and Unsearchable, revealed in a human form as a man such as can be understood, "a man conversing with us, living amongst us," who, in order thus completely to reveal God, cannot be less than God. The greater simplicity of the Unitarian faith he considers is of no value if it does not satisfy wants which we feel, if it does not account for facts which we know. As regards the Athanasian Creed, his explanation to a friend of the supposed difficulties in the way of its acceptation is simply this: To know God is eternal life; God is perfect Love, the Father dwelling with the Son in *one* Spirit is this perfect and eternal Love, which is the basis of all things, whereupon we base our hopes for ourselves and the world. (Certainly a very wide and free interpretation of this Creed, an interpretation which may be made to include both Arianism and Sabellianism as well as Athanasianism.) Particularly characteristic of Maurice's theological thought is a letter to his mother (Dec. 9, 1833), in which he endeavours to comfort her in her doubts as to the evidences of her being in Christ. The truth is that every man is in Christ, created in him, who is the Head of *every* man; the difference between the believer and the unbeliever is that the latter does not perceive or acknowledge the truth, that except he were joined to Christ he could not think, breathe, live a single hour. It is the devil's lie to imagine that we are something apart from Christ, and have a separate, independent existence. To believe that we are in Christ does not require any special religious experience. We have the warrant for this faith in that we cannot do one living act, or obey one of God's commandments, or pray, or hope, or love, without him; and yet God bids us do all these things. The state of independence, the fleshly Adam state, is no state at all, it is a life of our own vain imagination. The one thing therefore is to believe in the Lord Jesus Christ as the Lord of our own spirit, that our spirit belongs to him and not to the flesh, that Christ is in us, and that we must let him do his will in us and through us. This is a Christology which is a long way removed from orthodoxy, and is to a certain extent speculative and philosophical; very much like Dorner's. Christ is the ideal man, or the Divine idea of Humanity, which is as a principle in the whole race, but exists also, *realiter*, in one eternal Person, who by the Incarnation became the historical Saviour Jesus. If humanity is thus from the first essentially associated with Christ, a saving revelation pervades human history from the beginning; there is no need for the reconciliation of a world alienated from God, but the work of the historical Saviour can be no other than by his word and example to reveal and bring home to the consciousness of men what had always been the fact— their being in the eternal Christ, and thereby in God. Consequently Maurice reconstructed in this sense the orthodox doctrine of the atonement. In his book, *The Doctrine of Sacrifice* (1854), he teaches that Christ so far partook of sin as to identify himself in sympathy with sinners. He did not bear as a substitute the punishment of sin, but by his loving participation in the miseries of sin he delivered men from their sins, by teaching them to believe in the love of the Father towards them, for with this faith in the loving God the separation from God is ended, which constitutes the essence of sin. It is a heathenish view of God to suppose that the punishment of sin had to be removed by a sacrifice presented to him. The Christian view is that God by the perfect self-sacrifice of his Son, who was in his sympathy one with sinners, made known his eternal love to the sinful world, and that on that ground peace has been offered which men could not of themselves have found. By this act of love on the part of Christ the one possible method of peace and harmony in the world generally is revealed. The principle of self-sacrifice is revealed as the truth in which God displays his inmost character and which all creatures must obey by appropriating the mind of the loving Christ. Thus Christ, the eternal Head of mankind, becomes the Head of a new moral world, in which no longer selfish discord reigns, but lasting and self-sacrificing love.

These ideas tend obviously in the direction of that idealistic philosophy of Christianity which is represented in the speculative theology of Germany and in the writings of such men as Caird and Green in Great Britain. But Maurice even more than the kindred German theologian Dorner failed to work them out consistently and thoroughly. The cardinal contradiction of making the eternal idea of humanity at the same time an historical individual of an absolutely supernatural nature necessarily involved everywhere the diversion of all ideal speculative effort of thought into traditional supernaturalism. And in the case of Maurice this supernaturalism was the more pronouncedly narrow, inasmuch as he found the spiritual community of humanity, founded by the revelation of Christ, embodied not in the universal kingdom of God, or the invisible community of the children of God, but in the Church of England.¹ Accordingly, while he teaches on the one hand that the entire human race is created and has its essential nature in Christ as its ideal Head, he seems to maintain on the other hand that it is only in the Church of England that the Kingdom of Christ has attained actual existence! This is a contradiction that a German intellect finds it hard to comprehend, or can only explain by supposing that the strong national feeling of the Englishman had got the better of the intellect of the theologian.

The sources of the characteristic points of Maurice's teaching are to be found in the idealistic philosophy of Coleridge (whose metaphysical ideas, however, acquire in Maurice's system a Platonic modification), and in the doctrines of the Scottish theologians, THOMAS ERSKINE, of Linlathen, and John McLeod Campbell, at whom we must take a brief glance. The first of these men, an advocate by profession, had, by his own independent study of the Bible, arrived at the conviction that the orthodox representation of the Gospel did not properly represent its real and scriptural nature.² For the Gospel announces the forgiveness of sins not as a reward of faith any more than as a reward of works, but as the free unconditional gift of God, which was bestowed on mankind once for all in their representative Head, Christ, so that every man may appropriate it. Yet forgiveness is not itself salvation, but only the means of it; and salvation itself is not a future good, but is spiritual fellowship with God in the sanctification of the character by means of his holy love. The very purpose for which God offers his free unmerited love, as forgiving mercy to sinners, is that they may thereby be encouraged and impelled to love him in return, and to grow themselves into the image of his holy love. Glad devotion to God, a loving dependence on the Creator, is the perfect condition of the creature, in which all the faculties

---

¹ This, the fundamental thought of his book, *The Kingdom of Christ*, is stated in strong and emphatic language in a letter of July 12, 1834 (*Life*, i. p. 166).

² The most interesting of Erskine's writings, which has been followed in the above account of his system, is *The Unconditional Freeness of the Gospel* (1828); to it must be added *The Brazen Serpent, or Life coming through Death* (1831); *The Doctrine of Election, and its Connection with the General Theory of Christianity* (1837); his first work, *Remarks on the Internal Evidence for the Truth of Revealed Religion* (1820), is of less importance.

of the soul are kept in their proper order by that ruling principle. The Fall of man consisted in the rise of the spirit of independence, in that "each man became an independent individual, loving and desiring and approving things according as they affected himself, without regard to the will of God or the sympathies of the universal family." And this sin of man was also his misery, his hell. The punishment of sin did not consist in external evils, which might be removed by arbitrary acts, but it consisted in the very fact that the man himself had revolted from saving fellowship with God, and had exchanged the love of him for the love of self and the world. "Restoration to a condition of salvation cannot therefore be effected otherwise than by the restoration of the love of God to its place as the paramount principle in the heart, resulting in the due subordination of self and the creature under it. Any remedy which falls below this restoration falls below man's need. No pardon which leaves this undone is of any value to him. He needs no infliction from without to make him miserable; and it is not the removal of any outward infliction that can give him happiness. He must know that God is better than happiness, and that sin is worse than sorrow. The love of God, not the desire of happiness, is the true keystone of the arch." The means which God has provided for the attainment of this blessing is the Gospel. It shows us, in the appearance of Christ, the gracious character of God in relation to his rebellious creatures, in order thereby to draw back our hearts to him, which had been estranged through hatred, fear, or indifference, and thus to restore love to God and to the whole divine human family to its true place in the heart. It is particularly the sufferings of Christ in which the holy love of God has been revealed; but not in the sense that God had to be reconciled, that his love had to be purchased, by the sacrifice of his Son; on the contrary, his holy love itself was the source of the mission and the self-sacrifice of Christ. Christ, by his patient endurance of all the misery that had sprung from the sin of the world, overcame sin itself by love and glorified God by his obedience. His glorifying of the Father, by obediently enduring suffering from love of his sinful brethren, was both the expiation and the putting away of sin; and because it was the Head of mankind who accomplished this as representing all men, the sin of the entire race is once for all forgiven in Christ; the resurrection of Christ was the seal of this forgiveness. The message of this forgiveness is proclaimed to all the world as the free gift of God offered for its acceptance, but only those who actually accept it are really justified and made part of the Church of Christ. The fear lest the Gospel of free, unconditional mercy should produce a false peace in a world dead in sins, and expose the moral interests of Christianity to the dangers of antinomianism, rests, as Erskine is continually reiterating, upon a misconception. For the pardon, which is the free gift of God in Christ, is of advantage to men only as they receive it, and with it Christ himself, the revelation of the holy, loving character of God, into their hearts; and thereby the principle of holy, self-sacrificing love is made the dominant power and the root of personal holiness and salvation. Pardon is, therefore, really received only when it evinces itself as the effective means of sanctification and accordingly of salvation. It is not itself salvation, for salvation cannot be given to men gratuitously without conditions; it consists in the fellowship of the Holy Spirit; heaven is holiness, and the forgiveness of sins is a blessing only in so far as it produces holiness. Holiness is the ultimate object God has in view with us, and the Gospel message serves only as a means to this end.

These ideas of Erskine's were further worked out and established by his friend, the theologian, J. McLeod Campbell, in his very suggestive book, *The Nature of the Atonement, and its Relation to Remission of Sins and Eternal Life* (1856, 5th ed., 1878). As a believing Biblical theologian, Campbell does not deny that Christ presented an expiatory sacrifice for us, but he maintains that when this sacrifice is not interpreted in accordance with preconceived opinions, but is looked at as it is, and as it is represented in the Scriptures, it cannot be regarded as the suffering of the punishment due to man's sin in his stead, but a moral and spiritual meaning must be put upon it. Christ effected our salvation by becoming the mediator between God and man, and representing both—God with man and man with God. This twofold relation of the atonement is worked out with reference to its retrospective and its prospective action. In the first respect, Christ's work was to reveal the Father in humanity and for humanity, to be the witness of God's holy love, a love which hates sin and seeks to save the sinner by converting him. Christ felt the pain on account of sin that filled the holy heart of God, and in a perfect, vicarious contrition acknowledged the righteousness of the divine condemnation of sin, as the representative of mankind before God. When he identified himself with his brethren in the flesh by his compassionate sympathy, he endured the deepest pangs, such as only the Holy One could feel, on account of the sins of men, both as guilt before God and as the source of human misery. This pain on account of sin, and this perfect repentance of it, offered to God in the name of mankind, constituted the true atonement for the sins of mankind, a sacrifice well-pleasing to God, such as no execution of punishment could have supplied. With this complete condemnation of the sinful past of mankind by its representative Head, full satisfaction was offered to the holy will of God. But this moral atonement of Christ had at the same time *prospective* significance. It must be conceived as effecting salvation, or eternal life, not merely as the indirect result of Christ's work, but as inwardly connected with it, as, in fact, already included in that work. This would not be the case on the supposition of an imputation of vicarious punitive suffering to sinners, which leaves their moral condition in relation to God unchanged, and makes salvation only a future state of happiness. The atonement must therefore be conceived thus: Christ in his person represents humanity as holy, well-pleasing to God, and animated solely by love to Him, and by means of his identification with his brethren Christ communicated his righteousness as a new life to them. He thereby not only revealed the Divine Fatherhood to men, but he also discovered the treasure of the Divine image in man, which had until then been veiled under their sin. The righteousness of Christ was the revelation of the latent capacity in man for righteousness, which he possessed by virtue of the indwelling Son of God. Christ must not be conceived as so standing apart from humanity that his righteousness could not avail for it otherwise than by imputation. He is, as the second Adam, the Head of humanity, so truly one with it that his righteousness counts in the sight of God as the righteousness of mankind generally, and that it can pass from Christ to all men. Christ himself had in his human consciousness the witness to the ability of mankind to be filled with the love of God. In his love to his brethren lay the prophetic hope that they also would open their hearts to the love of God, from which they had for a time been estranged. Accordingly, the atoning work of Christ did not consist in the deliverance of men from future punishment and the obtaining of future happiness; but in communicating to them his knowledge and love of the Father, and making them thereby children of God, in the possession of eternal life and a righteousness well-pleasing to God. Everything that the Son accomplished, and that the Father accepted, had the prospective intention of being reproduced in us; both his pain on account of sin, and his confiding and obedient love to the Father, were intended to be appropriated by us. Nothing of a mere external nature that God could do with us or could give to us, which is not involved in the relation of our souls to God and in the relation of our own hearts answering to his heart, can possibly be our salvation.

This is manifestly the same reconstruction of the Christian doctrine of salvation which was effected by Kant and Schleiermacher in Germany, whereby it is converted from forensic externality into ethical inwardness and a truth of direct religious experience. Erskine and Campbell appear, however, to have reached their convictions in entire independence of German theology, by their own absorbing study of the Bible; and I regard their ideas as the best contribution to dogmatics which British theology has produced in the present century. That the Scottish Church rejected and thrust out from its midst, in the person of Campbell, this line of theological thought, was the heaviest blow that it could inflict upon itself; thereby it arrested its healthy development for more than half a century. For it is only just now that Scotch theologians begin to start once more from Campbell, though, it must be confessed, with great timidity, as may be seen from the book of the Glasgow theologian, Alexander Bruce, *The Humiliation of Christ in its Physical, Ethical, and Soteriological Aspects* (1876). It is here taught (following rather Hofmann, of Erlangen, than Campbell) that the Son of God entered into the condition of humanity, as it lay under the wrath of God, in such a way that he felt in himself the effects of that wrath, though he was not himself in his personal relation to God the object of it. The value of the sacrifice of Christ, Bruce holds, was equal to his Divine dignity multiplied by his perfect obedience, multiplied by his boundless love, multiplied by his sufferings, which reached the utmost limits of what a sinless body could endure. As God took all this into account, and was thereby satisfied, we also must take it all into consideration, in order to say "Amen" to the Divine view of the sacrifice of Christ. This is an attempt to mediate between the old and the new, which does not approach in clearness of principle the thought of Erskine and Campbell, although we must acknowledge that it is in the same direction which they took.

Though condemned in the land of their birth, the ideas of Erskine and Campbell were received in the soil of the Liberal theology of England. The religious profundity of the Scotchmen admirably supplemented the thought of the Englishmen, which is characterised more by a practical breadth than religious and speculative depth. It is to them that Maurice's theology owes its best features. And from Maurice again CHARLES KINGSLEY received the dominant direction of his theology, which gave fitting expression to the feelings of his heart in its warm sympathy for everything truly human, and supplied the theoretical rallying-point for his philanthropic aims. In the history of the Christian-socialist movements of the century, the names of Maurice and Kingsley occupy a foremost place. They showed by their deeds what was the fundamental thought of their theology—that Christianity is the leaven which is destined to regenerate and to hallow the life of human society. Side by side with them stands the great preacher FREDERICK W. ROBERTSON, whom death too soon removed, who was equal to them in nobility of character and their superior in the wealth and depth of his mind. The biography of this man, so admirably executed by Stopford A. Brooke, reads like the life of a saint, but of a Protestant and modern saint, who does not escape out of the world, but, as a soldier of God, fights the great fight with all ungodliness, with the sins of the upper and the lower classes, with the unreality and falsehood of even religious parties, who at the same time keeps his own soul unspotted from the world, and who is compelled often and deeply to drain the bitter cup of suffering, which no soldier of God can escape in this world of wickedness and folly. There is little in homiletical literature to compare with the four series of Robertson's sermons, in respect of wealth and depth of thought, strength of moral pathos, warmth of religious emotion, clearness and vividness of style, and elevation and beauty of language. As his biographer says, Robertson "felt that Christianity was too much preached as theology, too little as the religion of daily life; too much as a religion of feeling, too little as a religion of principles; too much as a religion only for individuals, too little as a religion for nations and for the world. He determined to make it bear upon the social state of all classes, upon the questions which agitated society, upon the great movements of the world." After painful inward conflicts, which arose not merely out of theological difficulties, but from a perception of the falsehood and unrighteousness of the various political and ecclesiastical parties, he found rest in the Gospel of Christianity, the truths of which seemed to embrace the truth of Conservatism and the progressive tendencies of Liberalism, and to offer the solution of the questions of the day, not by setting up laws or external limitations, but by the spread of a spirit of love, of duty, and of mutual respect. Those salutary truths he beheld embodied in Jesus, the perfect type of man as the child of God. He held that Christ was humanity, and in Him alone is our humanity intelligible. It is only in the feeling of fellowship and union with this life, in the acknowledgment of like feelings and conflicts, in a similar estimate of the world and its maxims, that our own life becomes bearable and desirable. Judging humanity in the light of this ideal, Robertson had, on the one hand, the keenest eye for its sins and weaknesses in their endless forms and disguises, and yet, on the other, he never lost sight of the Divine heart and root of human nature. The greatest truth which Christ revealed, as Robertson is always urging, is that all men are as men children of God, and each other's brothers; they do not become children of God by baptism or by faith and regeneration, but are already such by virtue of the divine image in which they were created; baptism is the messenger to each one in particular, declaring that he is a child of God *de jure*. But in order to be this *de facto*, it is needful for him to receive this message in faith, and to realise it in life, *i.e.* that he should be regenerated. Faith does not *create* the fact of Divine sonship, but *receives* it and converts it from an unconscious reality, which would avail nothing, into a conscious and voluntary life after the likeness of Christ. Christ is our Saviour not by the vicarious suffering of the penalty due to our sins, but by being actually the typical realisation of that which every man is potentially, as a child of God, and ought to be actually. The death of Christ was an atoning sacrifice, in so far as, having been endured in sympathy with human misery, it established the eternal principle, that salvation for man must always come from the sacrifice of self in ministering and patient love, a principle that is so universally asserted in nature and history that it must be regarded as a law of the universe. Faith is the life of Christ begun in us, which God counts as righteousness, because, as the Divine life in the soul, it is the root and spring of righteousness. As the inward principle of a morally good will, it sets us free from external laws, which can only incite to transgression or produce conventional legality. This thought Robertson applied energetically in relation to the Sabbath question; he openly declared the legal observance of the Sabbath a relapse from the spirit of the Gospel into Judaism and Pharisaism. On account of this genuinely Lutheran view of the question, he claims almost more than any other English theologian the sympathy of Germans[1]; and not less on account of his views as to the authority of Scripture and the dogmas of the Church. Deeply as Robertson revered the Bible as the inexhaustible spring of profoundest truth, he pronounced " bibliolatry " as superstitious, as false, and almost as dangerous as Romanism. The Bible is inspired, he says, but not dictated; it is the word of God, but in the words of man; as the former, perfect; as the latter, imperfect. Indeed, the Divine wisdom is shown in the fact, that it has given a spiritual revelation, that is, a revelation concerning the truths of the soul and its relation to God, in popular and incorrect language; for how otherwise could it have been understood by unscientific men and ages? The highest truths, he maintained, rest ultimately, not upon the authority of the Bible, or of the Church, but upon the witness of the Spirit of God in the human heart,

---

[1] He claims this sympathy also for the reason that he did not share the national prejudices of his countrymen, but, on the contrary, spoke with fitting contempt of their contempt for everything German (see his remarks on " German Neology," in his letter of 1849, *Life and Letters*, p. 97 of People's ed.). In this respect how far he stands above Maurice!

a witness which is to be reached not by the cultivation of the understanding, but by the loving obedience of the heart. Accordingly, in interpreting the dogmas of the Church, he never troubled himself about their intellectual husks, but only about their kernel, the religious truths and moral principles which are to be found under the various dogmatic opinions as their real meaning. He was consequently, with all his strictness in the condemnation of what is morally wrong, extremely charitable and catholic in the views he took of dogmatic differences of opinion. There was one principle which probably Maurice recognised in the dim distance, but which in his case remained confused eclecticism, but Robertson's deeper and clearer mind endeavoured to work out distinctly, and applied with unerring tact in various regions of controversy: it was the principle, that the *one* truth which underlies the various partial views of opposing parties, and by this very partiality and onesidedness becomes falsehood, must be brought out into clear light as the essential thing common to both parties. An acute dialectical intellect and a rare power of sympathy in entering into the thoughts and feelings of others qualified him to perform, as few men could, the work of a peacemaker amid contending religious parties. If a longer life had been granted him (he died 1853, at the age of thirty-seven), and if he had had leisure to write the theological works which he had proposed to himself (that on Inspiration, *e.g.*), what a beneficial influence he might have exerted on the development of theological thought, both in his own country and abroad! But as it is, his Sermons and Letters are a rich source of truth and light, from which no one can draw without feeling their purifying, strengthening, and elevating power; they are the monument of a genuine religious genius, in whom for some time to come later generations will reverently recognise a prophet of the higher development of Christian thought and feeling.

We have still to take a glance at the course of Biblical criticism in Great Britain, and the review may be the more rapid as the labours in this department of theology practically commenced but a generation ago, and have hitherto produced little of independent value. The credit of having done the work of pioneer in these studies in England must be accorded to the learned classical scholar and theologian, JOWETT, who published in 1855 his exegetical work *The Epistles of St. Paul to the Thessalonians, Galatians, and Romans, with Critical Notes and Dissertations* (2 vols.), in which he introduced to his countrymen the results of Baur's critical labours. His own views hold a place midway between those of Baur and the traditional ones as to the relation of Paul to the earlier Apostles: there was not complete harmony, but neither was there absolute antagonism; the difference was not so much of a dogmatic as of a practical nature, and on the part of the Twelve was due more to want of consistency than to antagonism of principles; though in accord with Paul on fundamental principles, they were attracted to Jewish practices by their national sympathies and habits. Some points of Pauline theology are discussed in the appended Dissertations with characteristic acumen and without dogmatic prejudice (*e.g.* the doctrine of election). Of special value is the careful criticism of the text, and the amended authorised English version. The principles of interpretation which Jowett applied in his Epistles of Paul he has expounded in the extremely interesting essay, *On the Interpretation of Scripture* (in the *Essays and Reviews*, 1860), in which he demands, quite in the spirit of Arnold, that the method of the classical scholar shall be applied in Biblical exegesis, in short, that "the Bible must be interpreted like any other book," and thus the study of the Scriptures be raised to the rank of the most valuable portion of the study of history and antiquity; the best book for the heart ought to be made the best for the intellect, so that its moral judgment of history might seem to complete and correct the æsthetic standard of the classics. "Before we can make the Old and New Testaments a real part of education, we must read them not by the help of custom and tradition, in the spirit of apology or controversy, but in accordance with the ordinary laws of human knowledge."

The year 1860, in which the *Essays and Reviews* appeared, may be regarded as an epoch in the history of English theology, corresponding to the year 1835 in the history of German theology. The storm which this collection of theological essays by various authors called up in England had great similarity with the commotion produced in Germany by Strauss's *Leben Jesu*. It is quite true that the causes of the commotion in the two countries were by no means of equal importance. For the *Essays and Reviews* contain nothing that had not already been thought and said from the days of Whately and Arnold by not a few writers belonging even to the Anglican Church. The first essay, by Temple, Arnold's successor at Rugby, deals with the gradual and progressive education of the world, a thought which had from the time of Lessing formed part of the ordinary consciousness of the educated world, and which is to be found indicated in the Church Fathers, and in fact in the New Testament. The second essay, by Rowland Williams, gave an account, expressing substantial agreement, of Bunsen's Biblical Researches. This was one of the essays which the opponents, High-churchmen and Evangelicals combined, selected as the basis of a prosecution for heresy. The charge was laid, that the general scope, tendency, or design of the essay as a whole was to disseminate unbelief in the Divine inspiration and authority of Holy Scripture, to degrade it to the level of mere human writings, to deny prophetic predictions and miracles, or to interpret them in an unorthodox way, and to explain away articles of the creeds. The trial, which took place in the Court of Arches, before Dr. Lushington, and in which Mr. James Stephen defended the accused essayists in a masterly manner, ended in a complete triumph for Liberal theology. Mr. Stephen remarked in the course of his defence that a poor compliment would be paid to the English people if they were deemed incompetent to bring into open discussion the views of Baron Bunsen. The design of the accusation was really nothing else than to put asunder reason and faith, which God had joined together. But the questions which learning and criticism had raised would have to be settled; the decisive question was whether the clergy should be allowed to co-operate freely in the settlement. The authorities might perhaps close the mouth of the clergyman, but not of the layman, or of literature and history. Is it allowable to make a compact between Christ and darkness; reason and Satan? It is of greatest moment to Christianity itself that theologians should be free to study the Bible. The decision of the Court, which was in accordance with these principles, sanctioned the rights of free theology in the English Church.

A leading representative of this new party, which may be described as the left and progressive wing of the Broad Church, was ARTHUR P. STANLEY, the pupil and biographer of Arnold. The fact that his high ecclesiastical position as Dean of Westminster did not prevent his sustaining friendly relations with Dissenters and heretics largely helped, no doubt, to modify the dogmatic exclusiveness of the Established Church. His theological writings were valuable contributions in aid of a free and unfettered study of Biblical and ecclesiastical history. Simultaneously with Jowett's commentary on St. Paul, he published his kindred work, *The Epistles of St. Paul to the Corinthians, with Critical Notes and Dissertations* (1855), which had been preceded by his *Sermons and Essays on the Apostolic Age* (1847), in which the realistic historic method of Arnold was applied to the history of the New Testament period in a way that departed far from the lines of customary dogmatic exegesis. To the same category belong his *Lectures on the Jewish Church* (1862), in which the history of Israel is treated in a manner midway between poetry and criticism, following very much the lines of Ewald. In an essay on the *Theology of the Nineteenth Century*, published in *Fraser's Magazine*, Feb., 1865, Stanley characterised the method which he had followed. The theory of *development*, he maintains, has taken the first place in every field of religious and philosophical thought. It has had an important effect on the proper understanding of the Bible itself. The gradual growth, the imperfect forms, the varied degrees of Revelation itself are now understood, and thus the greatest difficulties in the way of understanding the Bible are removed. We no longer expect to find in the Jews of the Old Testament premature Christians, or premature astronomers or geologists. Together with this historical spirit, a characteristic of modern theology is the importance it attaches to the moral and spiritual aspect of religion. The value of internal evidence has now been recognised in theory as well as in practice, in theology as well as in philosophy, and its superiority to the proof from miracles. The spirit is placed above the letter, and practice above dogma. The first and clearest statement of this new principle is found in Arnold's *Essay on the Interpretation of Scripture*, the man to whose memory Stanley has dedicated such a noble monument in his biography.

That the problems of Biblical criticism can no longer be suppressed, that they are as it were in the air of our time, so that theology could not escape them, even if it took the wings of the morning and dwelt in the uttermost parts of the sea, was strikingly shown at the beginning of the sixties by the remarkable case of Bishop Colenso. He had gone as Bishop to Natal with the orthodox belief in the inspiration of the Bible, with the object of converting the Zulus, and returned home as a critic to call in question the integrity and historical character of the Books of Moses. In the course of his instruction of the heathen, their doubts led him to make a more careful examination of the Biblical text, and in the process it grew arithmetically certain to the keen and mathematical intellect of the Bishop, that it was impossible to maintain the correctness of the Mosaic records. The historical inquiries thus started led him step by step to further results; he perceived the composite character of the Pentateuch as consisting of component parts of various ages and sources (the Elohistic and Jahvistic sections), he perceived the gradual growth of the Levitical Law, of which some portions originated before Deuteronomy, that is, before the time of Jeremiah, other portions not until after Ezra, being inserted into the earlier portions of the Pentateuch. In a word, Colenso arrived, by his originally quite independent path of inquiry, at results which are in substantial agreement with the views of the Biblical science of our day. But the Bishops of the Anglican Church, instead of calmly examining the honest studies of their brother, felt called upon to break a lance for Moses and the infallibility of the letter of the Bible, and demanded the deprivation of the Bishop of Natal. Once more the Secular Court, the Queen's Privy Council, was wiser than the Churchmen, and pronounced the Bishop the legitimate occupant of his see (1865).

Amongst the opponents of Colenso was to be found not only Maurice, who had himself suffered as a persecuted heretic, but even Matthew Arnold, who substitutes the moral order of the world for the God of the Bible, and with this object in view takes great liberties in the interpretation of the Bible. In an essay in *Macmillan's Magazine* (Jan. and Feb., 1863), he demanded that the Biblical historian should show great consideration for the edification of his readers. In order not to do violence to their devout feelings, and not to endanger the interest of the practical religious life, he ought, Arnold thinks, to attenuate the difficulties which might be a stumbling-block to faith in the Bible, to go out of the way of what is doubtful, such as the miraculous stories, by using nice generalities, a method of which Stanley had given a perfect model in his *Jewish Church*. Without doubt Matthew Arnold expressed the views of the great majority of Englishmen on this matter, and perhaps the views of the men of his age. It may also be granted that there are practical interests at the bottom of such advice which have some justification. On the other hand, it ought to be perceived, as Matthew Arnold seems to have subsequently perceived, that the claims of the purely scientific spirit to present the simple historical truth are equally well founded, and that both those practical religious, and these absolute scientific interests will be better promoted by the separation of the two kinds of Biblical interpretation— the practical and the learned,—than by a confused amalgamation of both. These hybrid forms, with their indefiniteness, half-truths and compromises, have little value in the promotion of an exact knowledge of the historical facts; the only use they serve is to check, in a time of transition, such as ours is, the too rapid advance of some and to prepare others gradually to receive what is new; in that way facilitating and securing an orderly and steady development of general opinion, and avoiding sudden leaps and catastrophes of a dangerous kind. This is without doubt the duty which the modified orthodoxy of the English Broad Church party has to perform at present, and perhaps for some time to come. The acknowledgment of the legitimacy of this purpose, and respect for those men who endeavour to realise it, is quite consistent with a decided assertion of the rights of strictly scientific historical research in theology, uncontrolled by any secondary considerations whatsoever. The representatives of this purely scientific research are, however, so much in the minority, not only in Great Britain, but everywhere, that there is no reason to fear lest the development of the general religious consciousness should go on at too rapid a rate.

Whilst the Colenso controversy was still engaging public attention in England, R. W. MACKAY, (who had previously by his *Progress of the Intellect, as exemplified in the Religious Development of the Greeks and the Romans* (1850),—a learned work, but burdened with too great weight of material—made himself known as a free inquirer in the department of religion) published the very instructive book, *The Tübingen School and its Antecedents* (1863). An introductory review of the relation of religion to theology, of the origin and development of dogma, of the influence of modern philosophy on the doctrine of the belief in miracles and inspiration, and of the history of Biblical criticism from the Socinians to Strauss, is followed by an excellent account of the critical labours of F. C. Baur and his disciples, of their method and its new results, the author professing himself an adherent of the school. In an appendix polemical notes against the opponents of the criticism of Baur, amongst others Ewald, Ritschl, and Lechler, which show accurate knowledge, are added. To this book the merit is to be ascribed of having promoted an acquaintance with the stricter form of German criticism in wider circles in England. Nor are there wanting signs of the ferment produced by this criticism. Oxford itself could not escape its influence, where T. H. Green introduced, together with German speculative philosophy, the critical results of the Tübingen school to his circle of friends.

A pendant to the various Lives of Jesus which appeared on the Continent during the sixth decade originated in Cambridge, *Ecce Homo: A Survey of the Life and Work of Jesus Christ* (1866). This anonymous book (said to be by Professor Seeley, the author of *Natural Religion*), produced a deep impression, and greatly promoted the cause of more unfettered religious thought in Great Britain, although, or perhaps because, it was not directly critical, but, upon the basis of the narratives of the four Gospels, drew a picture of the moral personality of Jesus with great delicacy of feeling and a profound perception of his peculiar greatness and originality. The nature of Christian morality, as distinguished from Jewish and Heathen legality or philosophy, is derived from the character of Jesus and the personal impression he made upon his disciples. If, therefore, the personality of Jesus as delineated by Seeley produces to some extent rather the impression of an artificial composition than that of real historical truth, this is the unavoidable consequence of the author's neglect of any critical examination of the sources; the personal claims of Jesus in the Fourth Gospel, and the Synoptics' discourses of the Messianic Judge being ascribed to Jesus himself straightway. By this means the portrait of the *man*, which is really the object aimed at, acquires an unintelligible, problematic aspect. Still, *Ecce Homo* takes a foremost place amongst the books of this class.

At this point the learned work of the late Dr. EDERSHEIM, *The Life and Times of Jesus the Messiah* (2 vols., 1883), may be mentioned. It is a harmonistic combination of the narratives of the Gospels, with a decided apologetic purpose, and without any concession to the most important objections of historical criticism. But the scientific value of the book consists in its rich collection of materials as to the condition of Jewish life and beliefs at the time of Jesus. It meets thereby a real and urgent want of Biblical research in our day. For it is very true, as the author observes in his preface, that a light is cast by these contemporary circumstances and analogies upon many parts of the gospel history itself, by which our knowledge of the origin of our religion under the forms of Judaism, and yet in opposition to its spirit, is essentially furthered. It is probable that strictly critical research may make often another use than the author himself would wish of the learned materials which his book supplies; where he finds confirmation of the historical character of a narrative in the New Testament, or of a discourse in the Fourth Gospel, others may discern rather the source of the literary origin of the narrative or the discourse in question. But in any case, the good service the author has rendered should be thankfully acknowledged; by laborious studies, pursued through many years, in out-of-the-way Jewish literature, he has collected an extremely rich and useful mass of materials bearing upon primitive Christian history.

SAMUEL DAVIDSON'S *Introduction to the Study of the New Testament* (2 vols., 1868), presents noteworthy evidence of the progress of historical criticism in England since the beginning of the sixth decade. In the first edition (1848-51) the author had maintained the genuineness of the whole of the New Testament writings, not excepting even 2 Peter, against all the objections of criticism. He then published an *Introduction* to the Old Testament (1862-3), in which the standpoint of the apologist was abandoned, and the intermediate position of Ewald was taken (*e.g.* the Pentateuch not by Moses, but not completed until the reign of Josiah, the Priestly Legislation preceding the Prophets). Six years later, the author having in the meantime resigned his position as theological professor in the Lancashire Independent College, and acquired full freedom to prosecute his critical studies, appeared the second edition of his Introduction to the New

Testament, entirely rewritten, in which the standpoint of the Tübingen school was taken with almost too little reservation. The counterwork to it is the strictly apologetic Introduction of Salmon, which appears to enjoy well-nigh the rank of an authority in orthodox circles.

The latter is the case with the *Introduction to the Study of the Gospels*, by WESTCOTT, now Bishop of Durham, the English Tischendorf. This work, which appeared in six editions between 1851 and 1881, belongs to that class of apologies which, by their learning, an air of superiority towards the main arguments of the critics, and occasional minor concessions on secondary points, are accustomed to make a great impression, and really perform the service above referred to, of retarding the progressive theological spirit of an age. The best part of the book is the introductory chapters on the Jewish religion, and particularly the Messianic faith of the century immediately preceding our era. But with regard to the Gospels, the author holds that their contents are in complete harmony, or that only unessential differences in the form of narrative are to be met with. These are to be explained by the varied individuality of the writers, in whom the Divine image of the Saviour was reflected in diverse but mutually complementary forms. For the Gospels are all Divine in the highest sense, because they are in the highest sense human. The spirit in the Evangelists searched into the deep things of God, and led them to realise the mysteries of the Faith, as finite ideas, and not in their infinite essence. This is such language as we have long been accustomed to hear from Neander; instead of getting intelligible answers to definite questions, we have to listen to the mystical phrases of devotional literature, which appeal to the emotions and presentiment (*Ahnung*), where, from the nature of the case, the intellect alone is qualified to speak. Westcott's lectures, entitled *The Historic Faith* (1882), have the same apologetic purpose, being an historical and dogmatic exposition of the Apostles' Creed.

But influential as these and similar apologetic works (they are essentially so much alike that it does not seem necessary to give a list of their titles) may be for the present moment, they cannot arrest the stream of time.[1] This we may, finally,

---

[1] The papers on the results of recent criticism of the Old Testament, read

assure ourselves of by a glance at three important works of the last three *lustra*, with which our survey of English theology may conclude.

The anonymous work, *Supernatural Religion. An Inquiry into the Reality of Divine Revelation* (3 vols., 1874-1879, in seven editions) seeks, with the aid of an acute and scientifically trained intellect and extensive historical learning, to overthrow the popular view of Christianity as a religion transcending the human reason and based upon supernatural institutions and miracles. With a view to this, the belief in miracles is first examined in general, its untenability being shown less from metaphysical than epistemological considerations and analogies from experience, and the origin of the belief is explained from psychological and temporal conditions. When the proof from miracles has been thus in general deprived of its force, positively by the immutability of the order of nature, and negatively by the unreliability of human observation and testimony, the Christian legend of miracles is next submitted to trial by a detailed examination of the evidential value of the Biblical documents—the Gospels and the Acts. From an examination of the testimony of the Fathers the author finds that not one of the canonical Gospels is connected by direct testimony with the men to whom they are traditionally ascribed, and that the later, in itself valueless, tradition is divided by a long interval of profound silence from the period of its alleged authorship; the canonical Gospels continue to be anonymous documents until the end of the second century, without evidential value with regard to the miracles which they record. The internal evidence confirms this result of the external; to say nothing of minor discrepancies which run through the first three Gospels, it is impossible to bring the accounts of the Synoptists into harmony with the Fourth Gospel; they annul mutually the force of their testimony. Like the Gospels, the Acts is a legendary composition of a late date, and cannot be regarded as a sober historical narrative, which renders the reality of the numerous miracles it reports

---

at the Church Congress, at Manchester, in 1888, by Dr. Perowne, the Dean of Peterborough, Professor Cheyne, of Oxford, and Mr. J. M. Wilson, the Head-master of Clifton College, supply one of many proofs of this. Mrs. Ward, the author of *Robert Elsmere*, very justly regards the debate on these papers as "The glorification of criticism." See her striking article on "The New Reformation" in the *Nineteenth Century* for March, 1889.

incredible. The testimony of the Apostle Paul as to the resurrection of Christ remains then to be considered. A close examination of his evidence shows that, so far as it concerns the earlier events, it rests upon indefinite hearsay and does not agree with the accounts of the Gospels, whilst the Apostle's own experience, in view of his peculiar and highly nervous temperament, must be looked upon as a subjective vision, as are also most probably the appearances to the excited disciples of Jesus. Accordingly the proof of the resurrection and ascension must be pronounced as absolutely and hopelessly insufficient. The examination of the historical sources has therefore confirmed the view of the improbability of miracles formed upon general grounds.

So far the author of this interesting book stands upon firm historical ground, and it will be difficult to upset his main position. But when he proceeds to draw the inference that the claim of Christianity to Divine revelation has no better foundation than the like claim made by other religions, he is advancing no longer an historical but a philosophical opinion, which is not by any means the necessary consequence of his critical results, but is based upon an inadequate estimate of the distinctive properties of Christianity as an ethical religion, and upon a superficial, external, dualistic idea of revelation. The defect of the work *Supernatural Religion*, as of Strauss's *Leben Jesu*, is that it employs destructive criticism exclusively, and neglects to make clear, or even so much as to indicate, what is the lasting moral and spiritual truth that lies at the basis of the supernatural legends and dogmas. But while this is beyond doubt a very serious defect, it is equally certain, on the other hand, that the work of negative or destructive criticism must everywhere be first done as the *conditio sine quâ non* of the positive or constructive task of a better understanding of the historical religion. And as the author himself describes his labours as but the negative preparation for positive construction,[1] we are not justified in judging them by any other standard; and within the limits which he proposed to himself, the value of his contribution to the end in view cannot be called in question.

Naturally, a work of this kind attracted great attention

---

[1] Preface, p. lxxvii, "Under such circumstances, destructive must precede constructive criticism."

wherever the English language is spoken. Never before had such a systematic attack, based upon solid learning, been made in English upon the external evidences of the Christian religion, which still continue to hold a foremost place, not merely in the popular, but also in the theological apologetics of England (Mansel, Newman, Mozley). It may, undoubtedly, be taken as a sign of the times that this book, in the first year of its publication, passed through six editions, and that the periodical press of all parties gave long extracts from it, and reviews of it, which were for the most part, as appears from Lightfoot's complaint, of a favourable and even laudatory nature. The answer which Lightfoot, the late Bishop of Durham, offered in the name of orthodoxy in a series of articles in the *Contemporary Review*, subsequently published as a book, is extraordinarily weak. Instead of calmly surrendering the outworks and establishing the claim of the Christian religion to be a revelation (which was called in question) by an appeal to its spiritual nature and its position in the whole course of history, by which means the solely negative standpoint of the author of *Supernatural Religion* would have been successfully impugned, the short-sighted scholar found nothing better to do than to submit the author's examination of references in the Fathers to the Gospels to petty criticism; while, even if all the Bishop's deductions were correct, the general result of the author's inquiries would not be in any way altered. It is not surprising that in his reply to Bishop Lightfoot, which has recently appeared, the author not only adheres to his historical positions as not upset, but that he also repeats his general conclusions in a form of more pronounced antagonism. For his refutation, it needed really other means than Bishop Lightfoot had at his command; it required a free, profound, and far-seeing philosophical and historical defence of Christianity, as the growingly perfect stage of the religious development of humanity.

And to such a defence the last decade has made in the highest degree valuable contributions in the works of Robertson Smith and Edwin Hatch, which, though they belong to very different departments, are closely allied by a common, genuinely scientific method, an unprejudiced and acute criticism of authorities, and a fine insight into the conditions and causes of historical development. In 1881 and 1882 Robertson Smith published two series of lectures, the one on *The Old*

Testament in the Jewish Church, and the other on *The Prophets of Israel and their Place in History*, which, together with the author's articles in the ninth edition of the *Encyclopædia Britannica*, hold a place amongst the best things that have been written on the religion of the Old Testament. He considers that the historical documents of our religion must be treated according to the same principles as are applied with such valuable results to the other sources of ancient history. "The timidity which shrinks from this frankness, lest the untrained student may make a wrong use of the knowledge put into his hands," is, as Robertson Smith truly remarks, "wholly out of place in Protestant Churches," which ought to regard it as "a religious as well as an historical gain to learn to read every part of the Bible in its original and natural sense. Much unnecessary exacerbation of dogmatic controversy would be avoided if theologians were always alive to the fact that the supreme truths of religion were first promulgated and first became a living power in forms that are far simpler than the simplest system of modern dogma." The revelation recorded in the Bible had a history which was "subject to the laws of human nature, and limited by the universal rule that every permanent spiritual and moral relation must grow up by slow degrees and obey a principle of internal development." This application of the idea of development to the history of the religion of the Bible is so far from detracting from its character as a revelation that, as Robertson Smith admirably shows, the best way of proving it is to show historically the unity and the consistent progress through centuries of the development of the religion of the Bible. "If the religion of Israel and Christ answers these tests, the miraculous circumstances of its promulgation need not be used as the first proof of its truth, but must rather be regarded as the inseparable accompaniments of a revelation which bears the historical stamp of reality." Without endangering, therefore, religious faith in the truth of the religion of the Bible, free discussion of the details of historical criticism may be fearlessly conceded. Of this freedom, Robertson Smith himself makes use without any reservation. He confesses in the preface to his lectures on the Prophets his adoption of the main positions of the newer school of criticism, represented by Wellhausen, that the priestly legislation did not precede but follow the prophets, that the latter were therefore not the interpreters of a religion which had been previously fixed in the Law, but were the original representatives of the ethical idea of God which was developed along with and out of the national history of Israel. To show this in detail, is the noble design of his excellent lectures on the Prophets.

Simultaneously with Robertson Smith's lectures on the history of the religion of the Old Testament appeared the Bampton Lectures of the late Dr. Edwin Hatch, on *The Organisation of the Early Christian Churches* (1881). In the opening lecture the author gives a very instructive account of the historical method which ought to be followed in the inquiry before him. The first thing is, to test the documents as to their origin, their temporal and local surroundings, and the value of what they say. When the facts have thus been ascertained, the inquiry must proceed to the consideration of the probable causes of the facts. Here careful attention must be paid to the difficulty arising from the fact that the same words do not always bear the same meaning, but alter it with the development of the institution designated ($e.g.$ ἐπίσκοπος). The history of the past can never be properly understood when a series of historical facts is interpreted by its modern form and meaning; we have to begin at the beginning, and trace the new elements step by step through succeeding centuries. To understand this process of development, it is needful also to consider the resemblances which exist between Christian and non-Christian institutions, in order that similar phenomena may be referred to the same causes. Nor may the historian be deterred from such an inference by the supposition of the supernatural character of the Church. For the formation of the Church has been effected by God according to the same laws by which the life of human society generally is produced. The divinity which clings to the Holy Catholic Church is the divinity of order. "It is not outside the universe of Law, but within it. It is Divine as the solar system is Divine, because both the one and the other are expressions and results of those vast laws of the Divine economy by which the physical and the moral world alike move their movement and live their life." It is then shown in detail how the Christian communities were organised at first after the analogy of the Jewish synedrion and the Gentile associations, borrowing from them both the presbytery, or council of "old men," and the executive organs of self-government—the bishop and the deacons. The bishop, at first only the president of the administrative body, gradually became of greater importance, in proportion as the need of an authoritative organ for preserving the unity of doctrine and of discipline arose. But all the time the right to teach and administer the sacraments still belonged to all members of the Churches in common; the right of the priority of the clergy was as yet not exclusive. When the bishops laid claim to the exclusive possession of this right, the claim was energetically disputed by the Montanists, who maintained the superiority of individual gifts of the Spirit to official rule. Nor was ordination at first anything more than appointment to an ecclesiastical office, of the same kind as any appointment to a civil office, without implying the idea of the communication of exclusive spiritual powers. The clergy did not become a separate class before the fourth century, and then partly in consequence of the grant of special privileges from the State to ecclesiastical dignitaries, partly also from the growth of the influence of the analogy between the Christian and Mosaic dispensations, whereby Christian ministers became priests. The connexion between the individual Churches was also at first loose and voluntary; it was under the influence and after the pattern of the State, again, that the organisation of the confederation of the Churches was brought about.

Hatch then raises the question, whether the organisation, thus effected, of the Christian communities into one general Church can be justly identified with the ideal Church of the New Testament, the "body of Christ." He denies this, and establishes his position with great acuteness. The unity of the Church, he shows, was in the earliest period only "a common relation to a common ideal and a common hope." In the second period, the age of conflict with heretics, "the idea of definite belief as a basis of union dominated over that of a holy life"; Christians were to be held together by their possession of the only true tradition of Christian teaching. In the third period was added insistence on Catholic order, without which dogma seemed to have no guarantee of permanence. "It was held not to be enough for a man to be living a good life, and to hold the Catholic faith, and to belong to a Christian association; that association must be part of a larger confederation, and the sum of such confederations constituted the Catholic Church."

This is the permanent form of the idea of Catholic unity since the fourth century. It is true, it was not universally accepted; the Donatists were not to be convinced of the value of an outward unity which lacked inward purity and sanctity. They were put down with the aid of the State; but the question they raised was not thereby solved, but still retains its full significance: the question whether external organisation constitutes the Church? And Hatch answers the question in a truly Protestant spirit: "Subtler, deeper, diviner, than anything of which external things can be either the symbol or the bond is that inner reality or essence of union—that interpenetrating community of thought and character—which St. Paul speaks of as the 'unity of the Spirit'!"

Hatch's book belongs, as is widely acknowledged, to the best that have been written on the origins of our Church. If he had been spared to write the history of Church doctrine, after the same method as he has followed in his account of the organisation of the Church, what an instructive work that would have been! The unexpected and sudden death of this fine scholar must be regarded as a heavy loss not to Oxford only, but to Protestant theology generally; yet we may hope that the seed sown by him will bear fruit far and wide. The place where Green and Hatch laboured and cast the light of philosophical and historical knowledge cannot fall back again into the night of the Middle Ages. The days of a Newman and a Pusey are for ever past for Oxford and for England.

INDEX.

Ammon 89.
Arnold, M., 330 sq., 390.
Arnold, T., 365 sq.

Bauer, Bruno, 226.
Baur, F. C., 224 sq., 284 sq.
Biedermann 137 sq.
Bleek 237.
Bredenkamp 275.
Bretschneider 89.
Bruce, Alexander, 382.
Budde 276.

Caird, John, 340 sq.
Campbell 380 sq.
Carlyle 311 sq.
Colenso 390.
Coleridge 308 sq., 355.
Curtiss 275.

Daub 132.
Davidson, S., 393.
Delitzsch 275.
De Wette 97 sq., 227.
Dillmann 275.
Dorner 156, 373.
Duhm 276.

Edersheim, 393.
Eichhorn 209, 227.
Erskine (of Linlathen) 378 sq.
Ewald 237, 256.

Feuerbach 135.
Fichte, J. G., 57 sq.
Finsler 275.
Flint 350 sq.
Froude, Hurrell, 356.

Gieseler 209, 284,
Graf, H., 258.
Green, T. H., 344 sq.

Hagenbach 284.
Hamilton, Sir W., 325.
Hampden 370.
Hare, Julius, 370, 372.
Harnack 298.
Hase 205, 237, 282.
Hatch 399 sq.
Hausrath 240.
Hegel 68 sq.
Herder 21 sq., 210.
Hilgenfeld 239.
Hofmann, C. von, 173 sq
Holsten 240.
Holtzmann 240.
Hume 6 sq.

Jowett 386.

Kant 3 sq., 32 sq.
Kayser 258.
Keble 356.
Keim 247.
Kingsley, C., 383 sq.
Kittel 275.
König 275.
Köstlin 234.
Kuenen 259, 276.
Kurtz 284.

Lange, J. P., 170 sq.
Lechler 237.
Lightfoot (Bp.) 397.
Lipsius 195 sq.

Mackay 391.
Mansel 327.
Marheincke 131.
Martensen 164 sq.
Martineau 340, 352 sq.
Maurice, F. D., 328, 373 sq.
Meyer 237.
Mill, James, 319.

Mill, J. S., 319 sq.
Milman 370, 372.
Müller, Julius, 124.

Neander 219, 279 sq.
Newman, F. W., 317 sq.
Newman, J. H., 358, 361 sq.
Niedner 284.
Nitzsch 123.
Nöldeke 275.

Paulus 211.
Pfleiderer 250.
Planck 233, 277 sq.
Pusey 358.

Renan 241.
Reuss 237, 261.
Riehm 275.
Ritschl, Alb., 183 sq., 235.
Robertson, F. W., 383, sq.
Röhr 89.
Rothe 148 sq.
Ryssel 275.

Schelling 62 sq.
Schenkel 177 sq., 246.
Schleiermacher 44 sq., 103 sq., 209, 228.
Schrader 275.
Schultz 275.
Schwegler 233.
Schweizer 125 sq.
Seeley 333 sq., 392.
Seth 349.

Smend 276.
Smith, Robertson, 397.
Spencer, Herbert, 336 sq.
Spittler 277.
Stade 276.
Stanley, A. P., 389.
Stirner, Max, 136.
Storr 86.
Strack 275.
Strauss 132, 213 sq., 241 sq.
Supernatural Religion, 395 sq.

Temple 388.
Thirlwall 370, 372.
Tieftrunk 87.
Tulloch 332.
Twesten 124.

Ullmann 123, 220.

Vatke 252 sq.
Volkmar 239.

Wegscheider 89.
Weiss 237.
Weisse, C. H., 145 sq., 222, 226.
Weizsäcker, 238, 248 sq.
Wellhausen 259, 263 sq.
Westcott 394.
Whately 368 sq.
Wilberforce, R. J., 359.
Wilke 222, 226.
Williams, Rowland, 388.

Zeller, Ed., 229 n., 232.

www.ingramcontent.com/pod-product-compliance
Lightning Source LLC
Chambersburg PA
CBHW050851300426
44111CB00010B/1211